CONTENTS

PREFACE

This book, as much as the institutions which are its subject, comes out of a particular history, a certain intellectual climate, and specific funding possibilities. It consists of papers selected and revised from a considerably larger number presented to a series of three workshops held between December 1993 and October 1994 at Emory University, the University of Michigan, and the University of California at Berkeley. The idea behind these workshops first came under discussion in 1987 when its two editors were members of the Joint Committee on African Studies of the American Council of Learned Societies and the Social Science Research Council. As Africanists, we were concerned that a powerful apparatus of social scientific inquiry was being turned toward Africans—their histories, their cultures, their literatures, their politics—without a comparable examination of the investigatory apparatus itself, or indeed of those institutions of the western world which impinged directly and indirectly on Africans' lives. Our concerns were certainly shared by other scholars, particularly in anthropology and literature; Valentin Mudimbe's book *The Invention of Africa* (1988) was notable around this time as much for its probing examination by an African philosopher of the ways in which Europeans created their own Africas as for its assertions that Africans might have their own Africas. But it was far from clear that this concern was a general one in the social sciences, least of all in those parts of the field most concerned with change.

The development concept, our own historical studies were suggesting, was at the heart of the conceptual apparatus with which American and European social scientists and policymakers since the 1940s had come to grips with Africa's place in the world and their own concerns with changing that place. What was most striking about these concepts—as distinct from those which governed Europe's relation to Africa in the previous century or more—was the appeal they had to many Africans, most notably those struggling to find an alternative vision of the future to that set out by colonial rulers. Equally striking was the extent to which development constructs started with an imagined future and a repudiated past rather than a carefully spelled out analysis of the present. We felt that the concepts themselves—and the historical and political context which shaped them—deserved further examination.

From the start, we were concerned that such an examination should not be limited to Africa. In some ways, Africa represents the quintessential object of a very particular approach to development, one focused on the project, on the target population, whereas regions that had decolonized earlier in Latin America and Asia had a different conception of change and their own role in it. Yet by the 1960s, which the United Nations proclaimed the Development Decade, the idea of being a developing country or a part of the third world was being seized by a quite varied array of national leaders and radical dissidents to assert leadership and make claims on the rest of the world. Our efforts to make this project more inclusive soon ran up against the limits of our own knowledge and connections, but the Social Science Research Council and numerous colleagues were extremely helpful in bringing in people with a variety of regional specialties, different disciplinary affiliations, and different points of view.

There ensued a series of planning sessions interspersed with discussions within the Joint Committee about how to define the project; there was far from a uniformity of viewpoints. In the end, the present editors—with a great deal of help—put together a proposal for an internal Social Science Research Council funding competition that was successful and allowed a more extensive meeting (cross-disciplinary and cross-area) held at Berkeley in 1992. We are particularly grateful to Michael Watts for his role in hosting this session. Besides some enlightening discussions of the basic issues, there emerged proposals for organizing a coherent set of workshops and considerable discussion of what kind of work was being done, and—a point that emerged throughout the process—how little actually was known about development institutions. This plan called for six workshops divided into two sections, one—whose result is the present volume—focused on Development Knowledge and the Social Sciences, and the second on Development Encounters. The idea was to move from an historical, sociological, intellectual, and political analysis of the institutions that constituted the development apparatus toward a closer examination of the dynamics of interaction that occurred on the sites of development activities. A successful application was made to the National Endowment for the Humanities for the first series, and we are very grateful to the

Endowment for its generous support, as well as to the staff of the Social Science Research Council, which administered the grant and provided the logistic support for the three workshops. The staffs of Emory University, especially the Institute for African Studies; the University of Michigan, notably its International Institute; and the University of California, Berkeley, particularly its International Center; generously provided time, material, and logistic assistance, as well as supplemental funding. The second series of workshops—shortened to two and put together by Frederick Cooper and Pauline Peters of Harvard University—was funded by the Rockefeller Foundation and hosted by the Harvard Institute of International Development. The first of these workshops took place in October 1995, the second in May 1996.

A special word of thanks to Tom Lodge and Priscilla Stone, the staff associates for the Africa Committee during the period of gestation and birth of this project; to Michael Watts who hosted the October 1994 workshop as well as the earlier planning meeting and who came to all three workshops; and to Priscilla Stone, James Ferguson, and Thomas Biersteker, who (along with the editors) gave the series continuity by participating in all three workshops and in planning decisions. At each of the three host universities, faculty commentators were enlisted to add a variety of perspectives to the workshops, and we learned much from these efforts to frame issues and point to problems that needed to be pondered.

The editors would like to thank not only the authors of the papers in this volume for their efforts, but all participants in the workshops, paper givers, and commentators, whose intellectual contribution to the endeavor was considerable. We have tried at some points in the introduction to indicate the range of material covered in the workshop papers and some of the points emphasized in discussion. For careful criticism of earlier drafts of the introduction, we would like to thank Sara Berry, Sugata Bose, James Ferguson, Martha Finnemore, Akhil Gupta, and Michael Watts. This has been a collective endeavor, characterized by much constructive criticism and contributions of different perspectives, and it is our hope that the present book will encourage others to push the inquiry well beyond where we have gone.

CONTRIBUTORS

Sugata Bose is Professor of History and Diplomacy at Tufts University. He has published widely on the economic and social history of modern South Asia and is currently studying culture and political economy on the Indian Ocean rim from 1850 to the present. His books include *The New Cambridge History of India: Peasant Labour and Colonial Capital* (1993).

Michael R. Carter is Professor of Agricultural and Applied Economics at the University of Wisconsin, Madison. His research focuses on the nature of agrarian growth and transformation in low-income economies, giving particular attention to how the distribution of land and other assets shapes and is shaped by economic growth. He recently completed a multicountry study on the impact of agro-export booms on the rural poor in Latin America, results of which are summarized in "Level Playing Fields and Laissez Faire: Post-Liberal Development Strategies in Inegalitarian Economies", *World Development* (1996).

Frederick Cooper is Charles Gibson Collegiate Professor of African History at the University of Michigan. He has been studying the period of decolonization, especially its relationship to social movements, economic and social policy, and the categories through which Africa is perceived and described. His most recent book is *Decolonization and African Society: The Labor Question in French and British Africa* (1996).

Mamadou Diouf is Associate Professor of History at the Université Cheikh Anta Diop in Dakar, Senegal, as well as Director of Research and Documentation at the Council for the Development of Social Science Research in Africa (CODESRIA). His publications include *Kajoor au XIXe siècle: Pouvoir Ceddo et conquête coloniale* (1990) and *Le Sénégal sous Abdou Diouf* (1990, with M. C. Diop), and he is editor, with Mahmood Mamdani, of *Academic Freedom in Africa and the Social Responsibility of African Intellectuals* (1994). His current research is on urban and popular culture in Senegal since the nineteenth century.

James Ferguson is Associate Professor in the Department of Anthropology at the University of California, Irvine. He is the author of *The Anti-Politics Machine: "Development," Depoliticization, and Bureaucratic Power in Lesotho* (1990), and coeditor with Akhil Gupta of *Anthropological Locations: Boundaries and Grounds of a Field Science* (1997). He is currently completing a manuscript on urban-rural relations and conceptions of modernity on the Zambian Copperbelt.

Martha Finnemore is Assistant Professor of Political Science and International Affairs at the George Washington University in Washington, D.C. She is interested in the ways in which global norms, meanings, and culture are created and affect various arenas in world politics. Her book *National Interests in International Society* (1996) investigates the role of international organizations in these processes.

Akhil Gupta is Assistant Professor of Anthropology at Stanford University. He has been studying the relationship between agriculture, states, and forms of knowledge in north India. He is the author of *Postcolonial Developments: Agriculture in the Making of Modern India* (forthcoming), and is currently working on a manuscript on the ethnography of the state.

Randall Packard is the Asa Griggs Candler Professor of African History at Emory University. He holds a joint appointment in the Rollins School of Public Health and directs Emory's Center for the Study of Health, Culture, and Society. His research focuses on the social history of health and healing in southern Africa and on the history of international health and development. His most recent book is *White Plague, Black Labor: Tuberculosis and the Political Economy of Health and Healing in South Africa* (1989).

Stacy Leigh Pigg is Assistant Professor of Anthropology at Simon Fraser University. Her work in Nepal addresses the cultural impact of national ideologies of development, with a focus on constructions of "modernity" and "tradition" through ideas about medicine. A portion of this work appears in "The Credible and the Credulous: The Question of 'Villagers' Beliefs' in Nepal," *Cultural Anthropology* (1996).

John Sharpless is Professor of History and Demography at the University of Wisconsin, Madison. He was Scholar-in-Residence at the Rockefeller Archive (1992–93) researching the role of nonprofit foundations in the development of U.S. population policy since 1945. He is currently completing a book on that subject.

Kathryn Sikkink is Associate Professor of Political Science at the University of Minnesota. She studies how new ideas emerge and influence international and domestic politics. Her book *Ideas and Institutions: Developmentalism in Brazil and Argentina* (1991) examines these questions in the context of development debates in Latin America in the 1950s and 1960s. Her current work explores similar theoretical issues in regard to transnational social movements around human rights and women's rights.

Introduction

Frederick Cooper and Randall Packard

The last fifty years have witnessed the transformation of the political geography of the globe, as vast areas that were once known as "colonies"
became "less developed countries" or "the third world." People in the
declining empires, in the rival superpowers that now dominated international affairs, in the countries born of earlier decolonizations, and in the
new nations of Africa and Asia had to rethink how the world was constituted. The idea of development—and the relationship it implied between
industrialized, affluent nations and poor, emerging nations—became the
key to a new conceptual framework. Unlike the earlier claims of Europe
to inherent superiority or a "civilizing mission," the notion of development appealed as much to leaders of "underdeveloped" societies as to
the people of developed countries, and it gave citizens in both categories
a share in the intellectual universe and in the moral community that grew
up around the world-wide development initiative of the post–World War
II era. This community shared a conviction that the alleviation of poverty
would not occur simply by self-regulating processes of economic growth
or social change. It required a concerted intervention by the national
governments of both poor and wealthy countries in cooperation with an
emerging body of international aid and development organizations.

The problem of development gave rise to a veritable industry in the
academic social sciences, with a complex and often ambiguous relationship to governmental, international, and private agencies actively engaged
in promoting economic growth, alleviating poverty, and fostering beneficial social change in "developing" regions of the world. From Oxfam to
the United States Agency for International Development to the World
Bank to rice research institutes in India to the World Health Organization,
a diverse and complex set of institutions—funded with billions of dollars—

has focused on research and action directed toward development. Meanwhile, people from developing countries have studied economics or public health in European or American universities, done stints in international organizations, attended international conferences, and staffed government and nongovernmental organizations in their home countries. Missions go out from agencies in the United States or Europe to investigate problems and set up projects and work with experts, bureaucrats, and politicians in "host" countries.

Such processes have created overlapping networks of communication within which ideas and theories of development have emerged, circulated, and been appropriated within a wide variety of institutional settings—from Washington to Dakar and back again. The goal of this book and the three workshops out of which it emerged is to locate the production, transmission, and implementation of this development knowledge within its historical, political, and intellectual contexts.

THINKING CRITICALLY ABOUT DEVELOPMENT

The development process has from its inception been self-critical and subject to critiques. Most projects include an element of "evaluation." Development specialists have found old ideas to be wanting and have moved on to others.[1] For all the shifting fashions, it is possible to discern a wide—but far from universal—set of operating assumptions emerging since the 1940s, often considered to constitute a "development orthodoxy": that foreign aid and investment on favorable terms, the transfer of knowledge of production techniques, measures to promote health and education, and economic planning would lead impoverished countries to be able to become "normal" market economies.

More radical alternatives came from Latin American theorists of "underdevelopment" who argued that international exchange itself widens the gap between rich and poor. Such arguments actually reinforced development as a category, by insisting that there is a normal pattern of economic development which Latin American, African, or Asian countries fell "under." Marxist theorists (for example, Amin 1974, 1993; Mandel 1975) came from a different direction—moving from an analysis of production in capitalist societies to a consideration of capital accumulation on a global scale—but ended up in a similar place: while claiming that capitalism was making poor societies poorer, they insisted that another kind of directed social change could bring about prosperity and justice.[2]

Particularly since the 1980s, two quite distinct sets of critics have rejected the entire developmentalist framework. One set might be called ultramodernist.[3] It consists of economic theorists who insist that the laws of economics have been proven valid, that the invisible hand of the market allocates resources optimally. Therefore, there is only economics, not development economics. When governments or outside agencies try to make the market work better, they introduce distortions which make it work worse. The free market does not guarantee equality of outcome, they say, but it produces as optimal an allocation of resources as is possible.[4]

A second set is postmodernist. This group sees development discourse as nothing more than an apparatus of control and surveillance. Development is but one of a series of controlling discourses and controlling practices—a "knowledge-power regime"—that has emerged since the Enlightenment, the extension of a universalizing European project into all corners of the globe. That most development projects fail—a point postmodernists and ultramodernists agree on—actually reinforces developmentalism, they say, for the failure defines a "target population" bounded from the rest of humankind by its aboriginal poverty, ignorance, and passivity, and hence by its need for the intervention of knowledgeable outsiders (Escobar 1995; Apffel Marglin and Marglin 1990; Sachs 1992; Nandy 1988; Crush 1995).

The ultramodernist and the postmodernist critiques actually have a lot in common, especially their abstraction from the institutions and structures in which economic action takes place and which shape a power-knowledge regime. The ultramodernists see power only as a removable distortion to an otherwise self-regulating market. The postmodernists locate the power-knowledge regime in a vaguely defined "West" or in the alleged claims of European social science to have found universal categories for understanding and manipulating social life everywhere.

James Ferguson (1990) points to a way of analyzing development as a controlling discourse while locating it in a specific set of international and national apparatuses. The state in "less developed countries" and international agencies such as the World Bank each find a role by accepting each other's: the national government allocates development resources and portrays itself as the agent of modernity, while outside agencies legitimately intervene in sovereign states by defining their services as benevolent, technical, and politically neutral. Both are content with development as a process which depoliticizes and disempowers local populations; both portray poverty as "aboriginal," disconnected from the history which gave rise to unequal access to resources; both are content with an expertise-driven structure of development; both are reinforced by failure as much as success. Ferguson's study opens the possibility of an ethnographically and historically situated analysis of development institutions, where the ability to deny or provide funds intersects with the ability to define what kinds of knowledge are or are not acceptable.

Locating power does not show that it is determinant or that a particular discourse is not appropriable for other purposes. That development interventions are both technical and moral renders them subject to critique through research findings and theoretical revision and to debate within the framework of universal rights and global citizenship upon which the development regime draws. Within poor countries, states' attempts to portray themselves as development agents do not immunize them from having their populist rhetoric thrust back upon them or prevent a debate on what is and what is not development. The marvelous ambiguity of the word development—eliding in a single concept notions of increased output and improved welfare—does not in itself prevent debates over its meanings, within and across national boundaries. What at one level appears like a discourse of control is at another a discourse of entitlement, a way of capturing the imagination of a cross-national public around demands for decency and equity.

The strange convergence of free market universalists and anti-universalist critics thus leaves a great deal to be discussed: of all the ways to conceptualize political and moral issues in international relations, how do some emerge while others are marginalized? to what extent are the terms of development discourses susceptible to becoming the basis of popular mobilization or of claims on national elites or international institutions?

Those were some of the questions the workshops sought to address. Our goal was neither to bury development nor to praise it.[5] We witnessed—albeit to a limited extent—some of the passionate confrontations development has engendered over the past fifteen years: postmodernists accuse developers of imposing an undesired modernity, while free marketeers denounce the nihilism of the postmodernists and the statism of the more orthodox; people working in the trenches of development projects insist that they do practical work, that they need coherent and reasonable frameworks through which to make day-to-day decisions, and that the problems of sickness and poverty which they address are not going to be helped by sweeping evocations of "community values" or "getting prices right." No side in these tussles has a monopoly of virtue, and all have something to gain by a more introspective, contingent view of the terrain upon which these battles have taken place.

Development, over the last half century, has been a framework for debate. But those debates have not taken place on level ground: some ideas have had the backing of powerful institutions and others have not. At times, conditions in the world economy have widened the possibilities of policies that could be tried, at others times alternatives have been narrowed. Social science theorizing and projects in Africa, Asia, and Latin America; funding priorities; and projects in the field have had ambiguous relations: the extent to which academic social science responds to the kinds of knowledge that political institutions demand of it and the degree to which social science helps to define what kinds of problems are recognized and deemed to be solvable are important and quite open questions. Learning does take place within institutions, but it is far from clear that ideas about eradicating poverty or disease have been influential merely because they were good.

Social scientists and development practitioners—and their ambivalent relationship to one another—should be as much the subject of investigation as the cultures and histories of African, Asian, or Latin American peoples. They are all part of a complex encounter. Our hope is that the studies in this volume will inspire more research, for perhaps the clearest conclusion of our three workshops is that we do not know the answers to the most interesting questions we have posed. Studying "up," as anthropologists call it, is difficult: any study of the powerful focuses on people and institutions with power to exclude themselves from the realm of the discussible. Yet it is far from clear that such power is absolute or that the people involved consider that they have something to hide. The following papers, with their variety of emphases, suggest a wide range of possibilities for the future.

In part, these papers approach problems in the sociology of knowledge; they tell a historical story about the end of empire and the rise of a new regime of unequal international relations; they look at the intellectual history of academic disciplines and political thinking; they analyze institutions; they explore how ideas are deployed and contested within "developing" societies. The authors, using a variety of tools, try to understand better the ways in which ideas and categories of social science knowledge have become enmeshed in the theory and practice of development.

How different fields of inquiry claim authority, police the boundaries of professionalism, and position themselves in relation to governments and foundations has been the subject of a rich and growing body of literature.[6] Of all the social sciences, anthropology has probably worried the most over how it constitutes the object of its analysis, debating what constitutes "ethnographic authority" and how that authority is related to the structure of power in colonial and postcolonial societies (Clifford and Marcus 1986). Economics—the most self-consciously "hard" of the social sciences and the one which has tended the most to claim "development" as its territory—seems the least likely territory for such explorations. Yet Donald McCloskey, in *The Rhetoric of Economics* (1985), opens up such a possibility. This conservative, Chicago-school economist shows elegantly that an economic argument is fundamentally an exercise in persuasion. He presents his argument as an attack on "modernism," on the claim to present a singular and scientific truth. Instead, he insists, economists—like anyone trying to make a case—use a series of tropes which convey authority within their professional milieu. Economists don't prove; they convince; and his central metaphor for how a social science proceeds is that of the "conversation."[7]

The "conversation" about development is an extraordinarily extensive one, taking place all over the world, involving people from numerous cultural origins. Development experts are a very cosmopolitan community, a kind of "new tribe" (Hannerz 1990) involving the diverse staffs of institutions like the World Bank and giving rise to linkages—cemented by the languages of expertise—between developed and developing countries.[8] Development language is simultaneously universalistic and pliable. Yet this phenomenon gives rise to a series of questions not fully developed by McCloskey and his colleagues: who is excluded from a conversation, and on what grounds? How are rhetorics defined historically and what are the processes within communities of experts that determine which rhetorics are deemed convincing and which are not? We need to take equally seriously the institutional and discursive mechanisms which made the transnational conversation possible and those which reproduced inequality within it. This calls for the kind of careful examination that puts institutions and ideas in the same frame, that looks not only at rhetoric but at historical and social processes (as for example in Sikkink 1991).

This perspective leads to questions of how discourses and practices are bounded: is there a clearly definable "mainstream" of meanings and representations and an established repertoire of actions—from the report of the visiting mission to "strategic planning" to technical assistance—that developers consistently draw on? How does the professionalization of a discipline and the creation of institutions engaged with development distinguish the persons and ideas included within acceptable practice from those labeled as marginal, as pedants, or as quacks?

This volume thus presents a view of development as a contingent, contextualized, and changing phenomenon. There is great theoretical uncertainty in the development field and even less awareness of how policymakers and development practitioners define the economic and social problems on which they work. And yet the world has fifty years of experience with development initiatives in Asia, Africa, and Latin America.[9] The lessons of this experience have not been fully assimilated. Pressing human problems are at issue, and the question remains whether we can appreciate the complexity of social processes and the elusiveness of our categories for analyzing them without becoming paralyzed.

DEVELOPMENT IN HISTORY

Many of the activities that now fall under the rubric of development—as well as the ethos of directed progress—have a long history. Catherine Coquery-Vidrovitch referred in the first workshop to "predevelopmentalist development" before the 1930s, and David Anderson detailed the phases of British action in the areas of forestry, agriculture, and health. In mid-nineteenth-century Europe, theorists—Friedrich List most notable among them—and political leaders in "late industrializing nations" debated the need for national policies to catch up. The creole elites of Latin America since at least the early nineteenth century have wondered whether they should model their economic and cultural aspirations on European bourgeoisies or emphasize their distinctiveness; follow ideas of laissez-faire or pursue specifically national approaches to economic growth; join the "progressive" causes of their era, such as abolishing slavery, or defend their own way of doing things against outside pressure.[10] For intellectuals and social scientists in Europe—and those defining themselves in relation to Europe—the idea of development provided a way of narrating world history, but not necessarily a rationale for acting upon that history.[11]

The form of the development idea that captured the imagination of many people across the world from the 1940s onward had quite specific origins—in the crisis of colonial empires. That colonial states were supposed to facilitate exports had long been a given, but only through investments expected to bring a rapid return. France and Britain both had firm doctrines of colonial financial self-sufficiency—each colony was supposed to pay its own way—in the name of which long-term initiatives to improve colonial infrastructure were repeatedly rejected. What was new in the colonial world of the late 1930s and 1940s was that the concept of development became a framing device bringing together a range of interventionist policies and metropolitan finance with the explicit goal of raising colonial standards of living.[12]

From Colonial Empires to Less Developed Countries

Great Britain, in 1940, and France, in 1946, moved decisively to embrace the development framework in an effort to reinvigorate and relegitimize empire as it was being challenged by nationalist movements, labor militance, and increased questioning of colonial rule (Cooper, this volume; Coquery-Vidrovitch et al. 1988). In fact, the intrusiveness of development initiatives caused more conflict than they resolved, and African political and labor leaders seized the vocabulary of state-directed change to escalate demands for wages like those of European workers, for social services on a higher standard, and for the power to direct change themselves. In the end, the colonial development effort had quite a different effect: it provided a means by which imperial powers could reconcile themselves to their loss of power, while maintaining a connection with their ex-colonies and a continued sense of their mission in shaping their future. Declining imperial powers were caught in an ambivalence that has attached itself to development ideas ever since: were they a description of ongoing, self-propelled models of social change, or blueprints for action?

The movement between 1945 and the 1960s toward a world of nation-states, as opposed to a world of diverse sorts of political entities, brought former colonies into relationship with the United States, the Union of Soviet Socialist Republics, and international organizations—a world of sovereign equivalency but enormous de facto inequalities. In a sense, the colonizer's conceit that "other" people needed to adopt new ways of living was internationalized, making development simultaneously a global issue and a concern of states. The standard of living of a poor Bengali became an issue debatable at Geneva as well as Dacca, while the terms of such a discussion (per capita income or other national statistics) reinforced the centrality of the national unit's economic role even as it opened up its performance to international examination. The development concept was crucial to all participants to rethink unequal relationships in the era of decolonization. Yet the historical trajectory that brought the different nations of the world to this point framed development in a particular way: former colonial officials were holding before themselves a future in which their conception of economic behavior could be a model for the world, while African and Asian leaders were eager to look away from their colonial past. Neither side was looking very clearly at the present, where complex yet dynamic forms of production and exchange presented opportunities and constraints.

New actors recognized the importance of the development framework in coming to grips with the opportunities and dangers of the postwar world. For the United States, the opportunity lay in an assertion of the mutual benefits coming from expanded world commerce, as the opening of markets once dominated by European colonial governments would stimulate European recovery and enhance colonial well-being. The Marshall Plan was both a precedent for American aid and a flexing of economic muscles. By the late 1940s, however, American economic leaders became increasingly skeptical that they could wait for the benefits of opening more areas to the market. The shift away from market-driven development was encouraged by the expanding threat of communism, with its supposed appeal to the world's poor. It was in this context that Harry Truman announced in 1949 that the United States would undertake an effort to mobilize "our store of technical knowledge in order to help [the people of underdeveloped nations] realize their aspirations for a better life." In doing so he took development out of the colonial realm and made it a basic part of international politics.[13]

The growing convergence of U.S. and European interests around the need to generate development through technical assistance programs played an important role in fostering the creation of a series of international organizations during the late 1940s and early 1950s. Founded in the context of European reconstruction and the Bretton Wood agreements in the late 1940s, the World Bank and International Monetary Fund expanded their field of action from financing European recovery and financial stability in the 1940s to fostering international development in the 1950s. Equally important was the United Nations system of development organizations—the Food and Agricultural Organization, the World Health Organization, UNICEF, UNESCO, and the UN's Expanded Programme of Technical Assistance. The creation of these multilateral agencies contributed to the internationalization of development. Although the administration of these organizations was initially dominated by Europeans and Americans and debates within the organizations reflected specific national interests, the organizations served to de-emphasize such interests and make the case that a prosperous, stable world was a shared goal (Lumsdaine 1993). And the increasing presence of "developing" nations in the United Nations organization made it easier for their leaders to insert their conceptions of development into debates, even as western-controlled institutions funded projects and multinational corporations exercised great power over capital flows.

Different Developments?

One cannot appreciate the power of the development idea without realizing that the possibility that modern life and improved living standards could be open to all, regardless of race or history of colonial subjugation, was in the 1950s a liberating possibility, eagerly seized by many people in the colonies. Development gave African and Asian leadership a sense of mission, for they were positioned to assimilate the best that Europe had to offer while rejecting its history of oppression and cultural arrogance. These elites positioned themselves to broker relationships among diverse societies, world markets, and international organizations.

As Stacy Pigg (1992) writes in regard to Nepal, intellectuals and political elites—through education and ties to the development apparatus itself—became part of a world-wide community intent on classifying, analyzing, and reforming indigenous social institutions, which increasingly settled into the generic category of "backward," "village," or "bush." As she puts it (1992: 512),

> By virtue of their participation in this language of categorization, cosmopolitan Nepalis stake out their place in a global society and legitimate their political authority over villagers who do not understand their villageness. This is why the ideology of modernization in Nepal is not simply a matter

of western influence, but a matter of simultaneous Nepalization and globalization.

We thus need to see the engagement of people in former colonies with
the development concept in dynamic terms. They had already turned the
post-1930s version of colonial development into claims for material welfare and political power, so that the development framework turned into
something quite different from what it originally was supposed to be.
From the Bandung conference of 1955 onward, a "third worldist" conception of social justice emerged, built around claims for a larger share
of the world's resources to be devoted to the poorest countries without
compromising the latter's sovereignty (Diouf, this volume).

In different countries, there emerged important variations on the development theme which did not necessarily accept the idea of North-
South interaction as naturally beneficial to both parties or of development
as an act of generosity of the rich to the poor. It is thus too simple to
assert the emergence of a singular development discourse, a single knowledge-power regime. The appropriations, deflections, and challenges
emerging within the overall construct of development—and the limits to
them—deserve careful attention.

It is a mark of the power and the limits of the development framework
that emerged out of the crisis of colonial empires that it was both embraced and reshaped by policymakers and social scientists from Latin
America, a century beyond its own decolonization. For Latin American
elites, the development framework offered new terms for articulating
grievances in regard to the trade, investment, and financial policies of
domineering economic partners and opened a new arena in which they
could assert leadership, both abroad and at home. Most interesting were
the contributions to development theory and policy. In the late 1940s,
when economists in the United States and Europe were just beginning to
work through what interventionist policies in the world's poorest economies implied for their discipline, the Argentinean banker Raúl Prebisch
and some of his colleagues presented a "structuralist" approach to international economics that reversed the notion of mutually beneficial interaction that was crucial to the appeal of development to leaders on both
sides of the colonial divide. They distinguished between a "center" of the
world economy producing manufactured goods and a "periphery" producing primary products, and they argued that the operations of the
world market tended over time to go against the latter.[14] Such arguments
had an ambiguous relationship to the pragmatic, coalition politics that
led to Brazilian and Argentinean "developmentalism" in the 1950s (Sikkink 1991), and some of their features—such as the call for import substitution industrialization—resonated strongly with the more pro-trade

theories that were just becoming the orthodoxy in the United States and Great Britain. A more radical set of deductions from the structuralist analysis of Prebisch appeared in Latin America in the 1960s in the form of dependency theory, with its insistence that first world development was in fact the *cause* of third world underdevelopment and that delinkage was necessary for a true course of development to be pursued in the periphery. The influence of Latin American structuralism spread to Africa as well (Rodney 1972).

Meanwhile, newly independent India experimented with combinations of Soviet planning models and capitalist production in ways that reveal points of convergence as well as the clear contradictions of the opposed visions of societal transformation and economic growth. India's experience revealed as well the possibilities—and the tensions—of combining an explicitly progressive, western-influenced notion of development (associated particularly with Nehru) with a conception of Indian history (symbolized by Gandhi) which stressed the virtues of tradition and simplicity (Bose and Gupta, this volume). Yet as Bose makes clear, this dichotomy oversimplifies the complex political debates that took place from the 1930s onward: critics of the "modern" nation-state could become enthused about the possibilities of "science" or economic planning, while the most vigorous developmentalists often saw themselves as doing what was necessary to preserve the distinctiveness of Indian culture.

What was striking about the 1940s was how much was open for debate: the usefulness of specific colonial institutions or social structures, the specific aspects of what was "western" or "Indian" that were to preserved, emulated, rejected, or changed. The Indian National Congress attached itself to development as a national project even before the British government had made up its mind about the colonial variant, and after 1947 India set itself the task not only of building a nation, but also an economy relatively insulated from foreign investment and control. As Bose points out below, once independence came about, this identification of development with nation made it harder for a newly independent country to debate exactly what either concept should mean. Development had come to bear the weight of a new leadership's quest for legitimacy, just as in Great Britain by 1947 the political and economic burden development had come to bear made it difficult to probe the meanings of the concept too deeply (Cooper, this volume). National development had its achievements, not least of which was the creation of a knowledge-building apparatus, so that India not only was capable of managing its economy but contributed some of the most important figures to the economics profession worldwide. India has also produced a strong attack on the very idea of development and fora, like *Economic and Political Weekly*, where different viewpoints clash at a high level of sophistication. As Gupta's chapter reveals, debates are not simply an elite phenomenon; social movements among the poor also articulate and press demands for reforms, while other movements oppose projects like large dams perceived to be harmful to communities (see also Fisher 1995). Both Bose and Gupta show that struggles do not line up neatly between the friends and foes of development, between "modernity" and "community," but engage differences in a more nuanced manner and involve people who have been immersed as deeply in international organizations and communication as in local social movements.

Africa was the latest of the late developers, the least able to generate its own academic knowledge. Yet African political leaders and intellectuals also pushed a distinct view of economic development, one less oriented than the conventional view toward a generic "developed economy" and more focused on the communitarian roots of African economies. As Mamadou Diouf shows (this volume), Senegalese planners drew on relevant foreign knowledge—notably from French social Catholic theory—and began with a detailed investigation of social and economic structures in different parts of Senegal. They tried for a time in the late 1950s to establish a distinct kind of political-knowledge regime, eventually frustrated by the ability of certain Senegalese to appropriate the fruits to themselves and by the continued power of French firms and the French government. There were other variants of these approaches—some self-serving attempts by elites at self-aggrandizement and at covering up inequalities within their own states, some more far-reaching attempts to find distinct paths (Young 1982).

The heterodoxy of development theory in the last half century implies neither randomness nor equality: certain sets of ideas and theories have gained prominence at particular periods of time, while others have been excluded from international debates. As is already clear, some of our authors have shown how within particular domains the development construct has become a framework that rationalizes and naturalizes the power of advanced capitalism in progressivist terms—as the engine bringing those on the bottom "up" toward those who are already there. Packard's discussion of health, for example, shows a "hegemonic" discourse at work; Pigg finds the appeal of development to the Nepalese intermediaries of development efforts precisely in its lying outside the norms of village life. Bose, Cooper, Gupta, and Diouf put more stress on the ways in which this very framework became a basis for claims and mobilization, clashing with often powerful forces intent on containing or suppressing such initiatives. Carter, Ferguson, Sharpless, Finnemore, and Sikkink show how the contents of such a discourse shifted within institutions and gave rise, in various situations, to orthodoxy, heterodoxy, and ambivalence in social science disciplines. Disciplinary knowledge could variously give coherence and depth to elites' world views, bring out the complications of development prescriptions, or point to fundamental flaws in policy frameworks and underlying biases in public discourse. At the workshops there was considerable debate over how to think through arguments about the power of certain discursive frameworks and the importance of agency in transforming them. The point is not to decide whether or not development discourse is truly hegemonic, but to examine projects of building and fracturing hegemonies: how financial, political, and discursive power was deployed, how such projects were contested within their own terms and through efforts to redefine the terrain of debate, and how one can find where room for maneuver remains in international institutions and in the numerous sites where development initiatives encounter the complexity of particular social struggles.[15]

Demarcating a New Terrain for Academic Inquiry

The break toward a new conception of change in colonial societies came from colonial states—and the challenge of their subjects—not from the academy. But these changes influenced western academia in two ways. First, the world-historic trend toward decolonization, the creation of new nation-states, and the uncertainties of how such states would fit into international relations set out a terrain for inquiry.[16] Second, the colonial initiative—followed by the initiatives of new states and international organizations—created a sudden, very large demand for new kinds of knowledge. The Colonial Office in the 1940s created a whole range of advisory committees which included academic expertise (Anderson, workshop paper) and the huge expansion of the technical side of bureaucracy—a redirection from the district administrator who "knew his natives" to the specialist who knew his science—created a demand for training more relevant to the conditions of poor societies in the tropics.[17]

Intellectual and practical priorities affected academia: universities were offering training courses for colonial servants even before they had much knowledge to offer. Eventually universities did develop new subjects or new emphases within old ones.[18] The most striking innovations occurred in economics, itself still experiencing the Keynesian revolution (Hall 1989). The key texts of what became a new subdiscipline of development economics appeared in the mid-1940s, in studies of how states and international organizations could promote industrialization and how a "big push" could get poor economies into a position where self-generating growth could begin—studies focused as much on southeastern Europe as on former colonies (Rosenstein-Rodan 1943). By the mid-1950s, Arthur Lewis—himself from the British colony of St. Lucia and in his graduate student days a sharp critic of the stifling effects of colonial rule and landlord power—was among the pioneers of an attempt to develop a systematic theory of development, one which addressed the specific conditions of extreme backwardness and proposed ways in which economic analysis combined with planning could lead to strategies to push such economies into a terrain where "normal" economic rules applied.[19] Some of the pioneers of the field in the 1950s—Albert Hirschman comes most directly to mind—did not see themselves as recipe writers for a "how to" approach to development, but as intellectuals thinking about and acting on social change in a far broader sense. Whether such perspectives could survive the routinization of practice and the abstractions of theorizing was another question (see Carter's contribution to this volume).[20] In any case, the creation of graduate programs in development economics, the founding of journals, the holding of conferences—and the recruitment of economists into national bureaucracies and international organizations—helped to shape an international community of expertise, with members from almost every country in the world.

Where academic initiatives were to be located was very much in question. Nationalist elites wanted education to have a strong national dimension; the providers of development assistance recognized education as a key component of any program. But who would control the contents of that education? However influential the initiatives of the British or French governments or of the Rockefeller Foundation in shaping higher education in former colonies, academic structures—research institutes as well as universities—could become the focus of challenge and argument, where alternative conceptions of development itself might be nurtured or contested. But would they, or would academic institutions become mechanisms for extending orthodoxies? Equally important—and depressingly relevant to the crisis of African education in the 1980s and 1990s—would institutions remain strong enough to be agents of anything, from challenge to conformacy? Contrasting instances are India—where a strong institutional base has supplied the ranks of development economists throughout the world and served to attack the development establishment head-on, as with the Development Studies Institute in Delhi or the journal *Alternatives*—and Latin America, where the Economic Commission for Latin America (ECLA) provided an articulate and influential site for critical studies (Sikkink, this volume). Looked at globally, "academic" knowledge of development cannot be seen as singular, yet the institutional resources behind different approaches can hardly be seen as equal.

Three papers in this volume allow us to examine how different academic disciplines in the West—economics, anthropology, and demography—confronted their own quests for generalizable knowledge with the specificity of situations in developing societies. Dudley Seers (in Martin and Knapp 1967) called development the problem of the "special case."

Within economics, this created ambiguous reactions: here was a new set of problems for economic analysis, yet the profession valued universalistic theories and powerful models above all else, and was not well equipped to deal with the messy particulars of markets that did not clear or of nonoptimizing institutions. Bardhan (1993) believes that development economists contributed to the mainstream of the discipline in ways not fully recognized. Michael Carter (this volume) argues that it is precisely through engagement with the complexities of "real markets," information asymmetries, and the nonoptimal outcomes of rational economic behavior that the cutting edge of economic theory emerged, both drawing upon and contributing to analysis of inequality, exploitation, and poverty, as much as growth.

Anthropology, as James Ferguson shows here, has been skeptical of the idea of development and deeply caught up in it. Its place in the division of labor among mid-twentieth century social sciences was based both on a theoretical stance that stressed the integrity of individual societies and a methodological one that stressed fieldwork and hence the complexity of particular instances. Yet anthropology had never quite got over its older evolutionist perspective on societies, and by the 1930s many of its practitioners were drawn to models of progressive change that could liberate Africans from the racial oppression they observed around them. Hence anthropology's deep ambivalence about development: welcoming yet distrusting social and economic progress, worrying about the damage change might inflict on diverse cultures yet acknowledging the misery of the present. When development institutions asked anthropologists to contribute their culturally specific knowledge to projects, anthropologists found at the same time job opportunities, a chance to insert their sensitivities into projects and to validate the usefulness of their discipline, and a danger of becoming immersed in a system of deploying knowledge within which they would have a secondary role (see also Escobar 1995 for a biting critique of anthropology's encounter with development). Anthropology—as several contributions to the workshops made clear—has at least complicated the social sciences' picture of development, showing its unpredictable effects, raising fundamental questions about the clash of cultures, and pointing to the possibility of ethnographic analysis of the development apparatus itself.[21]

Demography, John Sharpless points out, is a postwar discipline. Sharpless shows that its breakthrough into public policy required a conjuncture of intellectual and political processes: a fear among policymakers of a population crisis that would undermine economic growth and lead to political subversion, academic work that seemingly pinpointed where the problem lay and where intervention could take place, the new availability of technical solutions (birth control pills) to the problem, well-endowed foundations seeking their own role in the process, and a government willing to treat population as a policy problem. Yet there is a major ambiguity in the relationship of this discipline and policy: demographic transition theory implied that fertility changed with complex transformations in society, yet intervention implied change at a single point.

The authors of this volume both exemplify and scrutinize the varied disciplines in which their own training, expertise, and affiliations lie. Finnemore and Sikkink participate in political science's efforts to fashion a causal grid to explain change, but they insist that their field needs to take ideas more seriously than to see them as the direct product of interests.[22] By doing so, they end up with a picture of change in institutional frameworks that gives considerable attention to specific conjunctures and stresses process—notably "learning"—in how change comes about. Historians—such as Bose, Cooper, Diouf, Packard, and Sharpless—follow narrative threads, illuminating how various processes come together in certain moments, the contingent ways in which conflicts get resolved, and the way such resolutions shape the options that exist down the road, but they do not necessarily try to specify causality in a generalizable way. Carter's perspective on his discipline of economics is a critical one, but he sees more possibilities within economic analysis than many outsiders' perception of a neoclassical orthodoxy would allow; the problem is both that the highest prestige in the profession is allocated to people who produce elegant general theory rather than sort through particularities and that when it comes to influencing policy, it is the complexities of recent theory that drop out. The anthropologists represented here—Ferguson, Gupta, and Pigg—expand their profession's basic concern with close, detailed observation toward a wider range of objects of study and interrogate the process by which categories are created—in Ferguson's paper toward an introspective reflection on the discipline not so much for its own sake, but to open space for a deeper engagement with poverty, power, and directed change in a global context.

One can see the tension between the contextualizing fields (history, anthropology) and the universalizing fields (economics), as well as the more profound tension inherent in the relationship of social science and policy and the fact that abstract theory and empirical research both arise in concrete situations, in relation to funding possibilities and distinct knowledge communities with their own prestige systems. Carl Pletsch (1981) argues that the Cold War strongly shaped the way in which the kinds of knowledge asserted by the colonial "experts" gave way to different disciplinary domains: the realm in which universalistic social sciences actually had relevance, mainly the West (where sociology, political science, and economics reigned supreme) versus the nonwestern exceptions (given over to anthropology, history, and new area studies centers focusing on Africa, Asia, or Latin America) versus the exceptions who had nuclear weapons (demanding the special expertise of Kremlinologists and Sinologists).

From the side of organizations doing practical work, tensions over knowledge are equally profound. Such institutions may assert power through their command of technical expertise and insist on academic qualifications for their personnel yet complain that the economists coming out of universities are taught "ingenious models" that give "a hopelessly oversimplified view of how economies really work" (Coats 1986: 127). Ambitious economists from western countries may find the developing world too confusing, too unpredictable to be a place to build a career, while economists from India or Pakistan find the international development apparatus attractive (Rosen 1985: 230–33). Global development efforts seem to require replicability, yet taking an integrated approach to social and economic change demands deep local knowledge (J. Lewis 1988: 7). Project design demands prediction; investigation frequently points to uncertainty.

Development brings out such tensions in a particularly vivid way: it makes distinctions among human beings; it raises questions of when suffering is to be observed and when it is to be remedied; and it cannot escape questions of when the intervention of knowledge-bearing people brings about constructive change or when it merely demeans those who cannot claim such knowledge.

If different disciplines have tried to take pieces of social change and give them analytic precision, it is not clear that a kind of evolutionism—a desire to make "traditional" people into something else—has gone away despite all the criticism such perspectives have received within different social sciences. The 1950s and 1960s were the heyday of modernization theory, a social science approach that purported to demonstrate that change in one domain of life implied comprehensive reconfiguration, leading virtually to the creation of a new sort of person—rational instead of superstitious, oriented toward achievement rather than status. Modernization theory has been effectively discredited, but the ethos behind it lies behind less comprehensive approaches to development.[23] As Ivan Karp pointed out during the workshops, the idea of creating a new person is much older than development policies; it goes back to missionaries, in a sense the first NGOs to work in colonized regions. The idea of making a new person was downplayed in Africa as colonial governments came to realize how little control they had over such a process: in the 1920s colonial governments claimed to favor change within existing cultural traditions while the anthropology of the 1930s tended toward cultural conservationism. But the development drive of the 1940s brought to the fore once again the possibility of reconstructing Africans or Asians in all aspects of their beings, this time in a way that was as attractive to leaders of newly independent countries as it was to social scientists eager to chart the movement from tradition to modernity.

The flip side of the new person being created was the categorization of the person who had not made the transition: the "indigenous person," the "traditional" person, the "community," the "village," the "local"— generic categories that collapsed the variety and complexity of life in particular locations into a single word (Pigg, this volume). The very importance in development programs of defining a "target population" has tended to bring evolutionism back in, whether explicitly or inexplicitly (Ferguson, this volume). And as Pigg points out, the "local" intermediaries working with international development projects were particularly likely to want to see themselves as new people, distinguished from the constraints and backwardness of village life, even when overseas development personnel were trying to stress their own cultural sensitivity.

Critics of development interventions are as likely as proponents to reify the categories of traditional and modern, of "community" and "West," giving the category of community positive value instead of negative. Historically, however, the two sides are more deeply imbricated in each other than such a dichotomous suggestion implies.[24] Development initiatives came about as much through the initiatives of impoverished workers in Jamaica as those of visionaries in London. The most powerful organizations in the world have seen their initiatives fail because they did not resonate in a local context. As development policies oscillate from basic needs to participation to getting prices right to sustainability—and perhaps back again—it is not clear that the determinants of these policies are as independent of what goes on at the grassroots as they appear to their authors or their critics to be. Nor are villages homogeneous or harmonious entities: some people within them may find in initiatives from outside a way to get ahead, a way to get away from an oppressive local landlord or patriarchal authority.

Development in the 1940 was a framing device through which colonial regimes tried to respond to challenges and reassert control and legitimacy, but it was a device that could itself be challenged and seized, used for different ends by a Nehru or by an ambitious young man in a remote village. The dialectic of control and contestation is an ongoing one, and after fifty years of development initiatives, the objectives and strategies— as well as the ethical implications and material effects—of development are still being debated (Dasgupta 1993).

IDEAS, INSTITUTIONS, AND CONTEXTS:
STICKY THINKING AND SHIFTING PARADIGMS

Much development knowledge is down to earth—agricultural technologies, methods of keeping government accounts—and institutions are often eager to portray development knowledge in such terms. Yet development is fundamentally about changing how people conduct their lives, and the very claim to technical knowledge is itself a political act.

While the frame of development has opened up intense struggles over means and ends, not all ideas or positions have held the same valence or power. At certain moments and in certain places there has been a broad convergence of thinking about development around certain models or theories. Some of these convergences have had long lives, while others have been more fleeting, emerging at one moment as orthodoxy and then losing support to a new paradigm. In some cases—as with current interest in sustainable agriculture or market-led development—earlier paradigms reemerge.

The chapters in this volume explore a number of these paradigm shifts: from growth models to poverty alleviation in the World Bank in the 1970s (Finnemore), toward military-style programs of disease eradication in international health organizations after World War II (Packard), from structuralism to neoliberalism in ECLA in the 1980s (Sikkink).[25] But development ideas have shown considerable staying power too: even the ECLA shift to neoliberalism followed thirty years in which structuralism reigned supreme, and the image of the backward African farmer survived much evidence of innovation and the arrival of Africans in power (Cooper). Allen Hoben argued that influential environmental paradigms have been based on a vision of a harmonious past and a fall from the Garden of Eden that has persisted for decades despite much contradictory evidence. Even self-consciously empirical social sciences, like economics, are notably resistant to taking into account contrary evidence, a point stressed in papers and discussion by Sara Berry and Ali Khan. The longest history of all, as Ivan Karp made clear, belongs to the assumption that certain kinds of societies can be defined as "backward" and means devised for transforming an "underdeveloped person" into a "developed" one.

The tough problem is how to explain both the shifts and the stickiness. Conventional explanations in political science based on analysis of interests and rational actor theories evoked skepticism among political scientists at the workshops: it is not clear that an interest can be perceived and acted upon without a perceptual scheme, which itself requires analysis. While there was wide consensus on the importance of trends in the global economy, simple Marxist explanations based on the logic of global capitalism or the power of dominant classes run into the problem that development interventions appear precisely where the logic of capitalism fails to produce results that political elites desire. Whether one emphasizes the concrete aims of development projects (to open markets, foster agricultural productivity, or expand industry) or the ideological work the concept does (to assert the mutual benefits of participation in global economic institutions) complex questions arise about the ways in which economic problems are conceptualized at the interface of social science and policy and the responsiveness of leaders of states or international institutions to counterhegemonic claims. The rise and decline of theories within development-oriented social sciences, the convergence and divergence of strategies within development organizations, and the persistence of certain images of backwardness and styles of intervention across long periods of time thus raise questions shared with the history of scientific paradigms and with the study of institutions, as well as issues of political conflict and economic change.

The paper givers did not think it possible or necessarily desirable to have a unified theory of paradigm shifts and stickiness. Instead, they focused on isolating the key variables in question and stressed the importance of conjunctural analysis: the interaction of shifts in global economic trends, the openings and closures of social science paradigms, and the dynamics of key institutions. Paradigm shifts, they show, occur through complex, historically specific interactions.

Institutions and the Production of Development Knowledge

Within the world of development, power is distributed in a highly uneven manner. Acceptance by key institutions, like the World Bank, gives power to ideas and imposes consensus. Yet as Finnemore suggests, the acceptance of new ideas within an institution like the Bank calls for explanation. Without denying that institutions respond to political and economic interests, Finnemore calls for a more specific examination of how and why institutions learn and why an institution adopts new sets of policies at particular moments in time. Trends in the economics profession—particularly criticisms of growth models and the rise of human capital theory—opened up disciplinary space but could do no more than give professional legitimacy to arguments with a more complex institutional appeal. The arrival of Robert McNamara clearly played a key role in the Bank's shift in policy. The workshop discussion raised the possibility that McNamara's policies may have been shaped by his experiences in Vietnam—a fear of rurally based revolutions and hence a focused concern with rural poverty. The attention given rural poverty in the 1970s may thus echo earlier shifts by France, Great Britain, and the United States in the late 1940s, as they faced the threats of colonial rebellions and the spread of communism. Finnemore's emphasis, however, was less on the enabling factors than on the institutional interests and capacities of the Bank that made it possible and necessary for it to define a program on which it was capable of acting.

In the case of the ECLA, Sikkink argues that neither institutional transformations nor external crises fully explain why a group of development specialists, whose collective ethos enforced their individual commitment to structuralism, changed their minds. She turns to a concept of institutional learning:[26] ECLA specialists had trouble pointing to a single case in Latin America where their diagnosis and cure for poverty had led to growth and equity, whereas for all their revulsion at Chile's repressive regime since the 1970s, they had to admit that it had achieved growth without inflation, as had East Asian countries whose strategies were as open to the world market as the ECLA's were resistant to it. Equally important was the concern of the ECLA staff to be taken seriously and the risks of isolation in their profession and in the world of providing advice. The ECLA was forced to come to terms with anomalies which challenged its core assumptions. Sikkink's paper gave rise to an important discussion over how one weighs different parts of the causal chain: the violent destruction of the Allende regime and the Chilean left cut off one set of possibilities for policy interventions and for social science, but it is not clear that the repression of 1973 is a sufficient explanation for a process of rethinking that occurred in many places over the course of a decade. The unsettled issue is a reminder that models of development are never very far away from struggles for power.

The Transmission and Circulation of Development Knowledge

The fact that a new orthodoxy emerges within powerful institutions does not by itself explain the wider acceptance of this orthodoxy. It is necessary to examine as well the processes by which development knowledge circulates.

In part the ability of powerful institutions to disseminate ideas arises from their place at the center of development finance.[27] Money talks. Yet this materialist explanation overlooks the specific networks of communications through which ideas circulate internationally. The power of an institution like the World Bank is based as well on its position within overlapping global networks of research, communication, and training. The Bank's employment of a small army of researchers, recruited internationally from developing and developed countries, produces masses of country and project review documents filled with statistical data which are disseminated globally. The recruitment of academics from developing countries to work for short stints in the Bank and the support of training programs for mid-level bureaucrats contributes as well to the dissemination of the Bank's ideas. Sharpless suggests that the Rockefeller Foundation's support of centers for demographic research in the 1950s resulted in the training of a generation of demographers from around the world. By doing so, the Foundation succeeded in creating an intellectual climate for the acceptance of population control programs in the 1960s. In another context, both Anne-Emmanuelle Birn (1992) and John Farley (1991) have written about the Rockefeller Foundation's earlier success in fostering the development of certain models of public health in developing countries through the training of students and funding of schools of public health and nursing. Packard's paper for this volume also suggests that approaches to eradicating tropical diseases after the war reflect the privileging of particular ways of thinking about public health that developed powerful institutional and intellectual backing in the United States and in international organizations such as WHO.

Yet even with their financial and communication power, the knowledge-shaping power of institutions varies over time. The World Bank's influence on the creation of development orthodoxies, as Thomas Biersteker suggested (1993 and in workshop discussions), has been mediated by shifts in the global economy. The availability of credit in the 1970s made it worthwhile for national governments or international agencies to mount efforts for interventionist development programs—paying and empowering a wide range of experts—but the credit squeeze of the 1980s made it seem as if doing anything other than leaving things to the market had to buck financial pressure as well as strong arguments from well-situated economists. Much of the current rhetoric about structural adjustment programs is about the absence of alternatives, while critics of such policies try to get the idea of alternatives back in. In fact, some states have been better able than others to hold off structural adjustment programs; any explanation of their differential acceptance and impact must consider national politics as well as the power of international institutions.[28]

The successful transmission of ideas emanating from powerful development organizations was also fostered by global political shifts. The end of the Cold War narrowed development options by discrediting socialist alternatives. The absence of both financial and ideational options has narrowed the space within which the governments of developing countries can make policy choices. It is perhaps historically significant that the earlier postwar push for market-led development was short circuited by the rising fear of communist expansion and the need for more interventionist development, while the second coming of market-driven development—and the willingness of leaders in the United States and elsewhere to accept whatever consequences the market may have—became politically feasible, in part, through the demise of communism.

The strong stress on market discipline sits rather uneasily with the other major trend among the powerful development institutions: their concern with "governance" and the imposition of political conditions—some form of democratization—on the provision of aid. Compelling as many of the critiques of government corruption, clientalism, and incompetence are, it is not clear that imposed austerity helps to build political capacity. More important, looking at this new trend in historical perspective makes it look less new. The insistence on "good government" reproduces much that was previously said about the "good economy": a bland assertion that the West has defined objective standards for others to meet, a generalized set of categories (elections, multiple parties) that define those standards, irrespective of the actual debates that might be going on in specific contexts over how more people might acquire meaningful voice in their own lives.[29]

The Reception and Appropriation of Development Knowledge

While development ideas may spread out from key institutions, they may not be simply accepted or replicated. They may be transformed or appropriated in ways that were unintended. Akhil Gupta's chapter reveals how populist developmentalist ideas adopted by Indira Gandhi's Indian National Congress and disseminated by international organizations in the mid-1970s were coopted by rural leaders as an ideology of popular mobilization. He suggests that the meaning of would-be hegemonic ideologies is never stable. Conversely, Michael Woost suggested that the appeal of community development and popular participation have been appropriated and subverted in Sri Lanka to serve the interests of market-driven development strategies designed to turn Sri Lanka into a Newly Industrialized Nation (NIC). In the new context, "participation" refers to workers doing their bit to serve industrial and agricultural capitalism. Alberto Arce examined the local appropriation of market-centered development ideas in Chile, Mexico, and Bolivia. He argued that languages of development should not be treated as static frameworks broadcasting cryptic messages from the development apparatus; rather they generate interfaces with processes of change. The language of market-led development generates metaphors which question the traditional sphere of action of the state, creating dissonance and contestation but not necessarily a single set of practices. In contrast to cases where development ideas are appropriated by local populations, Jean-Pierre Olivier de Sardan's paper suggested that development knowledge may not in fact penetrate very far within developing countries. In Niger, he showed, development ideas and language are not shared by local populations, except for certain local citizens who serve as development "brokers" and successfully use development language to appropriate material resources for their own purposes (see also Olivier de Sardan 1995).

How does one analyze stickiness within the reception of development ideas? Language is often stickier than policies. Gillian Feeley-Harnik argued that deeply held images, developed out of specifically American experience with "taming" the wilderness, have a deep, often subliminal, effect on the way issues like conservation and population control are talked about, and which remain powerful even as immediate policy issues shift. The concept of community participation is an ideal which is applied to a wide range of programs, even when that participation is diluted of influence or empowerment. Words like "overgrazing" convey images of conservation problems as rooted in the behavior of "target" populations—making it easy to ignore the social processes that gave rise to these problems.[30] Concepts like sustainability and participation become a kind of shorthand, distilling complex and in many cases highly problematic processes. In this way they are part of a range of template mechanisms through which development institutions function.

Template mechanisms are preconstructed frameworks which are used to simplify and control complex environments. One such mechanism is the "case," reducing a complex instance to a single useful message. A document advocating the need for adaptability in public health programs might present the case of the smallpox eradication campaign; export-driven industrialization evokes the case of Taiwan. The case thus becomes a fact, a given, upon which future planning can be based. For years, the case of the NICs evoked the virtues of export-oriented, industry-centered, market-driven development, and it took the mighty labors of several scholars (Amsden 1989; Haggard 1990; Wade 1990; Stein 1995) to show that the NICs' success was far more complicated and that interventionist states were as important as self-regulating markets. It is still not clear that the case of market-driven development in Southeast Asia has been altogether discredited outside scholarly circles, and it is still less clear whether people from the NICs have been able to make their voices heard about their own conception of the "case" they represent.

Templates can be elaborated into far-reaching cultural paradigms. Hoben argues that first world development practitioners, as much as third world peoples, operate within particular cultural constructs. His own example of the image of the "fall from an ecological paradise" is one of them. Timothy Mitchell's analysis of developers' conceptions of the Nile Valley reveals another: simple images of the overpopulated village—quaint and isolated from the dynamism of world history, its poverty a "natural" feature of geography—demarcates an area distinct from "the economy," where rationality, measurability, and adaptability prevail. Such representations demarcate a space for intervention while precluding analysis of land inequality, hierarchical social relations, structures of power, and mechanisms of production and exchange (Mitchell 1991 and workshop paper; see also Ferguson 1990). Such systems structure options, define relevant data, and rule out alternatives.

The application of templates to real world situations—particularly in the field—serves as well to filter out experience. Stacy Pigg's chapter focuses on a situation in which western development agencies were eager to graft their health care innovations onto the concept of the Traditional Birth Attendant, hoping to train local health care practitioners rather than impose an external structure on Nepalese villages. Yet the development apparatus focused on its desired figures not as they were, but as generic categories. The Traditional Birth Attendant embodied all that was defined as "indigenous," and relations of developers and developees tended to reproduce the dichotomies that the innovative program seemed intent on abrogating. Corinne Kratz's paper on the operation of focus groups within a Safe Motherhood program in Kenya, shows that the actual operation of such groups—intended to elicit popular participation in development planning—reproduced the very hierarchies they were supposed to avoid. What emerged in the field was the category of African Woman, removed from the varied and complex roles which Kenyan women exercised.

Indeed, issues of gender present a striking instance in which a social category both opens up and bounds a complex set of issues. Both academic social scientists and activist organizations have insisted that the majority of the world's poor are women, that women do much of the world's farming, and that the concrete manifestation of industrial development is often the entry of women into extremely low-paid jobs. Yet much writing about development codes women as "traditional" and sees men as the agents of transformation. The program of Women in Development is a response to these critiques, yet this sort of response risks compartmentalizing the problem, as if action directed toward women could be an "add on" to a development process otherwise unchanged. A more radical approach, Gender and Development, focuses instead on the subordination of women and thus forces examination of power and patriarchy. Some writers (for example Shiva 1988) insist that a feminist approach should lead to a rejection of the development framework altogether, as a patriarchal project leading to the appropriation of ever more finite resources— notably water and forests—that only diminish the kind of sustenance-oriented economic activity in which women are most often engaged in practice and which they symbolize ideologically. This argument approaches from a feminist standpoint the rejection of science and development as projects of an oppressive modernity that have come from certain scholar-activists as a critique of imperialism (for example Nandy 1988). But feminist theory has been at least as critical of the substitution of generalized conceptions of "women" for analysis of gender politics in specific instances, and some feminists argue for a complex engagement with the details of development processes and careful discussion of how they can be altered (Moser 1993; Agarwal 1992). All this hardly exhausts the possibilities of analysis of gender, and one of the achievements of the past two decades has been a wealth of research that reveals the fluid and contested nature of gender relations in a variety of situations.[31] The most difficult challenge is to turn such investigation into programmatic initiatives that address the specific circumstances of women without essentializing the category of gender.

Templates, cultural paradigms, and generic representations of the "indigenous" are not about to disappear. Large-scale organizations need to simplify; funding cycles demand replicable project designs.[32] When USAID and other organizations tried to focus on small projects to avoid the problems of giganticism for which past development efforts were rightly criticized, they needed approaches that did not demand deep situational analyses for each project. Academic social scientists should not be dismissive of such difficulties. The historian's or anthropologist's concern with context and complexity is neither more nor less separable from a self-serving professionalism than the development practitioner's concern with the replicability of project design, the desire for stable decision-making frameworks, and the need for a quick and readily graspable analysis of the specificity of each case in which action is being taken.[33] Nor does one get to the bottom of such issues by attributing them to the developer's apparent conceit of remaking the world in the name of modernity: "indigenous" societies are as socially constructed as developers' world views, with parallel tendencies to leave much of social life out of focus, to obscure the operations of power and hierarchy. Development paradigms—from the orthodox to the radical—have at least thrown different frameworks into relation to each other, drawing attention to the fact that at the local level as much as at the global one, what exists is not necessarily what has to be.

Such considerations underscore the need for a frank and far-reaching examination of the politics of development, beyond the general tendency of large organizations to behave in certain ways or of scientific paradigms to be resistant to contradictory evidence. Power entails both arrogance and limits. Agencies working in developing countries delve into local political and economic complexities at their own peril. It is politically more judicious to explain the destruction of the rain forest in Brazil or soil erosion in the West African Sahel in terms of a "tragedy of the commons" model than to analyze the political and economic forces which drive farmers in both regions to expand cultivation into environmentally fragile areas (Peters 1994). Highlighting these forces might embarrass and alienate local national governments and imply interventions which are politically unacceptable to them. Conversely, focusing narrowly on the age-old deficiencies of a "target" population may facilitate the cooperation of an international agency intent on accomplishing something within the limits of the status quo and a national bureaucracy interested in acquiring outside resources to distribute and in perpetuating a view of economic problems as being amenable to the sort of expertise the bureaucracy shares with knowledgeable outsiders (Ferguson 1990).

Academic disciplines as much as development institutions work through paradigms and other template mechanisms which are resistant to change, and the way they select future practitioners often works to exclude rather than encourage forms of knowledge which challenge the discipline's core assumptions. Economics, for instance, operates through the construction of models which by their very nature work to stabilize assumptions used for decision making. Ali Khan suggested that uncertainty can be configured, but the configuring of uncertainties corresponds to the conceptual structure imposed on them, thus limiting their play. As Ben Crow noted in a commentary at the final workshop, there is no notion of "field economics" comparable to the status of fieldwork in anthropology, so that economists work with data mediated through state collection apparatuses and categories that are not fully examined. The economics profession is not unaware of issues such as these, as Carter's chapter suggests. An approach like Carter's in effect blurs the boundary line between economics and economic anthropology—with its stress on the specific—and his focus on the implications of unequal resources and unequal access to information also reveals areas of convergence between the kinds of questions raised by Marxists and innovative work in the neoclassical tradition.

Nevertheless, it is far from clear that the economics profession rewards those who ask nitty-gritty questions in the same way as those who work at a high level of abstraction. Many of the economists who are most involved in development and in the training of students from developing countries are located in the United States primarily at land grant institutions, often in departments of agricultural economics, set apart from the towers of theoretical eminence.[34] In Great Britain, development institutes both encourage interdisciplinary focus on a range of problems in poor societies and present the risk of isolation from disciplinary "mainstreams." In anthropology, Ferguson's argument that development anthropologists are too compromised by the practicality of what they do to achieve high status within the discipline is paralleled by the danger that their research is too painstakingly specific to be at the core of development projects.

Perhaps the most important question of all concerns the knowledge that is generated and disseminated within Latin America, Africa, and Asia (Long and Long 1992). Rosen (1985: 233) argues that the greatest contribution a development effort can make is not so much the concrete projects that result, but the building up of institutions—including the training of local economists—who can "examine, analyze, and suggest solutions for the problems of their own country." Such expertise would also be able to examine, reject, or modify "expert" advice coming from outside. Stephen Biggs (1990) argues that research institutes and government departments located within developing countries actually contribute far more to innovation than they get credit for. Crop research institutes are among the most valuable sites of knowledge production and dissemination that complicate the picture of a one-way movement of knowledge. Such loci of expertise make it possible for debates to take place within developing countries over what precise measures are most desirable in local circumstances and to negotiate more effectively with powerful international bodies. They help make possible a cafeteria approach to development initiatives from abroad—picking and choosing useful knowledge without accepting the package of "modernity"—rather than being stuck with a fixed menu (Boiral and de Sardan 1985: 14–15). But capacities vary greatly: India or Argentina is far better able to participate in such dialogues than Sierra Leone or Burma. An undesirable effect of antistate, pro-market bias in current development programs is losing focus on the fact that education and research require a complex infrastructure and expensive, if not immediately productive, investment.

The issue is deeper than this. The power of western science may be felt even when the institution doing that science is located in Asia. Recently, many development practitioners have acquired a new respect for what is called "indigenous technical knowledge."[35] Yet the very category suggests that such knowledge can be neatly bounded from knowledge of the more universal sort; Africans or Asians are assumed to know certain things by virtue of their birth and culture, whereas the rest of us know certain things by virtue of having gone to the trouble of learning them. In practice, as Pigg and Kratz suggest, the very act of collecting indigenous knowledge is transformative, leading to hybrid forms of knowledge.

Yet concepts of the "indigenous" or the "local" can be politically useful even when they are referring to political and social relationships far less bounded than the terms suggest. It is often in the name of "indigenous rights" that movements—which sometimes connect the allegedly local with national intellectuals in a capital city and support organizations around the world—make a coherent and compelling case for why a dam should be considered harmful or why forestry policy should be made by those affected. While the leaders of such movements may gain stature by linkages to international NGOs as much as by support of a "community," it is by demonstrating the power of the local that they make a case.[36]

It is not hard to deconstruct the modes of discursive power. It is much harder to discover how discourse operates within institutions. One point on which there was wide agreement at the workshops was how little we actually know about the way institutions—from small NGOs to the World Bank—actually operate. Papers like those of Finnemore, Sikkink, and Pigg represent a beginning.[37] In North America, we know even less about the distinct forms of organization, the political issues, and the relations with former colonies that characterize the European Economic Community, Scandinavia, or Japan (see Gendarme 1995). We tend to think of NGOs as a category whose mere existence shows that "civil society" is working to counter the state's dominance of development initiatives, but we also tend to treat those organizations in generic terms, not exploring their varied ideologies, organizational forms, and relations to state mechanisms. The subtle interplay of national policy, foundations with the financial resources to shape intellectual inquiry, and the operations of programs in the field—issues raised in different contexts by Packard, Sharpless, and Pigg—deserves further study. The momentous events of recent years that cast Eastern Europe into a realm of "transition" and "development" raises questions that have long needed more attention in Africa, Latin America, and Asia: how to understand specific dynamics of change without taking the end point for granted (Verdery 1996; Stark 1996).

After all is said, we are still left with dilemmas intrinsic to the enormous inequalities of wealth, power, and access to knowledge in the world: the desperate nature of problems versus the imperiousness of proposed solutions, the specific social relations and struggles in each situation versus the dangers of paralysis before vast and varied problems, awareness of the ways in which global and national structures condition exploitation and impoverishment versus the political dangers of too close an examination of precisely those sorts of issues.

USES AND DANGERS: DEVELOPMENT AS DISCOURSE AND PRACTICE

To argue, as we have been doing, that the development concept can be located in historical conjunctures and that it can be understood in relation to intellectual trends, shifts in global economic structures, political exigencies, and institutional dynamics has important implications for debates about the future. It lends a certain skepticism to assumptions that current fashions—such as "getting prices right" or "sustainability"—represent the triumph of one model over another. The record of the past suggests that theories that seem to be conquering the world are part of shifting patterns, perhaps even a cyclical alternation between approaches that are laissez faire and growth-oriented versus those that are politically interventionist and equity-oriented. The kinds of analysis contained in this volume encourage skepticism over whether "the market" can be neatly opposed to "the state" or to "policy interventions"; once one starts to talk about real markets they turn out to be as messy, as filled with blockages and contradictions, as the real states whose failings have become all too familiar. Market mechanisms, state mechanisms, kinship mechanisms, and other kinds of social organizations are not pristinely separated from one another (Carter, this volume; de Alcántara 1993; Lele in Ranis and Schultz 1988; Chaudhry 1993; Colclough and Manor 1991; Putterman and Rueschemeyer 1992). We are also skeptical of the argument that development represents an instance of the tyranny of modernity, of colonialism by other means, for the history which shows the colonial origins of development initiatives and the development construct is also a history of how that concept was mobilized and deflected for other ends. People around the world are in some way *engaged* with far-reaching structures of power, and those engagements take more varied and complex forms than acquiescence or resistance. Denunciations of modernity or evocations of community are not going to make multinational corporations or representatives of the World Health Organization go away. The question is how deeply the implications of interactions can be discussed, and how wide the range of possibilities for affecting those interactions can be broadened (see also Bose, this volume).

The development framework, as it has existed in the past half century, has excluded many questions that are quite germane to questions of poverty, power, and change. In public contexts, institutions like the World Bank cannot talk too much about the power relations within the sovereign states with which they work. But critics of the World Bank don't necessarily want those questions probed either, for condemnation of Bank-type interventions are often set against notions of "community" or "social movement" that might not look so positive if subject to scrutiny.[38] Neither "universality" nor "community" has a monopoly of virtue, or of evil. What is important is the relationship of the two categories (see Bose, Gupta, and Cooper, this volume). People living within situations of oppression or exploitation—by local tyrants, by multinational corporations, by local patriarchs, by greedy bureaucrats—have the possibility of attaching their cause to something beyond their own borders, of turning rhetoric of human rights, of self-determination, of cultural integrity to political use.[39] Development rhetoric represents one possible framework in terms of which causes can be mobilized. The point is not that development—any more than a list of universal human rights—itself offers answers, but that it shapes possibilities for political mobilization that cross differences of culture, nationality, and geography.

From the 1940s, the power of the development construct lay in its rejection of the past and its aspirations for the future rather than its capacity to address the complexities and the possibilities that lay within ongoing processes. Yet the very controversies within and about the concept also present the possibility that development can be taken apart, that particular projects as well as particular rhetorics can be appropriated, refashioned, and used for a variety of purposes. Development is invoked within

political struggles in a wide range of countries, sometimes by elites insisting that everybody subordinate individual interests to a higher cause
which the state claims to represent, sometimes by oppositional groups
claiming that true development can only be achieved with a change in
policy and leadership. The International Monetary Fund may try to impose a unitary vision of the proper way to run an economy—and it has
financial as well as discursive power to do so—but those visions are subject
to challenge within their own terms and through alternative ideas about
citizenship and progress.

It is as true now as it was fifty years ago that most of what contributes
to productive investments (or destructive exploitation) comes not from
"projects" devised in the name of development, but from the operations
of local entrepreneurs, multinational corporations, banks, and parasta-
tals.[40] Yet the very fact that a development question exists points to the
limitations of capitalist development: it is precisely because large areas of
the world are poor and are not contributing to the generation of surplus
value that there is a development problem which cannot be reduced to
analysis of the immanent logic of capitalism.

Interventionist policies have been advocated on the grounds that they
would bring more people into the sphere of capitalist production, to the
mutual benefit of the people involved and of capitalists. Now, the argument is being made by ultramodernist critics of development economics
that one should leave the entire problem to the undistorted market. It is
far from obvious that doing that would work any better than it did on the
eve of the first wave of colonial development interventions in the 1940s.[41]
Arguments that the market works better than planned interventions are
thus misspecified—it is not clear that this dichotomy corresponds to economic organization in either developed or undeveloped societies. But
such arguments remain powerful ideological statements: they imply that
certain parts of the world will be rewarded by world markets if they do
well, while others can be written off if they do badly. That is what the end
of the development era would mean: to narrow issues that can be the
objects of fruitful debate.

Fifty years of development initiatives and development rhetoric have
laid before the world's population the knowledge that conditions of malnutrition and ill health exist around the world and the insistence that all
of us are implicated and complicit in that fact. Poverty in all corners of
the world has become a discussible issue—an issue around which profound disagreements may exist, which pose dangers of objectification of
"victims," and which may create privileged domains of operation for the
entrepreneurs of poverty eradication. Debate over such issues keeps open
the possibility that local movements can mobilize around pressing issues
and make their cause a wider one. The absence of a grand alternative to

capitalism does not mean that the challenges and the limitations which capitalist production encounters around the world have disappeared. Capitalism is no more likely to have brought all the world's population into useable relations of production and consumption in the year 2000 than it did in 1900. It is certain that poverty and inequality will remain, but whether they will remain issues that can be fruitfully debated, within and across state boundaries, is less clear. The issues that have been at the center of the development framework can be ignored, but they will not go away.

NOTES

1. For a concise review of the succession of theories in economics, see Arndt (1987).

2. Our discussion is limited to the relationships of the first and third world. This is not because the "development" experience under communist regimes is unconnected to the problems being raised here: indeed, communist societies represent the clearest alternative model of development to those discussed here. In many ways, the developmentalist ethos of communism has parallels to the capitalist variant, and there are indeed connections, as in the influence of Soviet planning models on Nehru's India. The present editors would be foolish to do more than call attention to such questions, for communist developmentalism is a subject that deserves to be examined in depth and with sensitivity to its variants and complexities.

3. A valuable introduction to recent debates is Watts (1993). McCloskey (1985) terms conventional economics "modernist" because of its claim to have found universal laws of human behavior, and his arguments with this kind of modernism are discussed below. Ironically, his briefer treatment of development economics (1987) ends up with a position very close to what we call ultramodernism.

4. Such an argument has gone from dissent to dominance. See Bauer (1972) and Lal (1985).

5. The language of death and burial has been much used in evaluations of development economics: Hirschman (1981) and Seers (1979) lament its passing; Lal (1985) gloats over the body; and Toye (1987) and Lewis (1984) insist that reports of development's death are exaggerated. Bardhan (1993) has recently argued that rather than being a deformed and doomed child of mainstream economics, development economics gave the field as a whole its most basic propositions—Adam Smith was really a development economist. Another sort of language to which development has been subject is that of prosecution and judgment, as in Hill (1986). On these issues, see Carter and Ferguson, this volume.

6. This is too vast a field to survey here. But (in addition to studies in anthropology and economics cited below), see Novick (1988), Fisher (1993), Mudimbe (1988).

7. McCloskey's work itself unleashed a conversation: Klamer et al. (1988), Nel-

son et al. (1987), and in particular the scathing critique in Rosenberg (1992: chaps 2, 4).

8. Klitgaard (1990) details the development experts who passed through the tiny country of Equatorial Guinea while he was there: from the United States, Great Britain, Germany, Spain, Argentina, and Chile, working for the World Bank, the United Nations, churches and other nongovernmental organizations, and other aid agencies. Unlike other developing countries, Equatorial Guinea lacked indigenous personnel who shared the foreign experts' training. But "development" was a sufficiently universal value that outside bearers of knowledge and insiders could converse. These connections were laden with power: local officials used their connections to these institutions in their own efforts to deepen state authority and fight turf battles with each other, while the World Bank and the International Monetary Fund used their power to grant or withhold money to demand specific actions by a sovereign state.

9. Among assessments of this experience, see Ranis and Schultz (1988), Adriaansen and Waardenburg (1992), Choquet et al. (1993), Rock (1993), and Rodwin and Schön (1994), plus the pro and con arguments cited earlier.

10. Robert Shenton and Michael Cowen argued that development should in fact be seen as a quintessentially nineteenth-century construct, leading to a debate at the workshop over how much that observation said about the shifting uses of this construct in later years. William Beinart's paper contributed to the discussion of colonial images of nature and management, in pastoralism as well as agriculture.

11. On the tension between the concept of "evolution" and that of "development" in the history of one discipline, see Ferguson's contribution to this volume.

12. The obvious point that economic growth and institutional change took place even where developers did not consciously try to bring it about has been emphasized by defenders of the free market (Bauer 1984) and Africanists who want to show that Africans were themselves agents of progress (Chauveau 1985).

13. Quoted in Escobar (1995: 3). For background, see Rosenberg (1982). See also Sharpless (this volume); Packenham (1972); Lumsdaine (1993).

14. Joseph Love presented a paper on the intellectual roots and historical origins of structuralism. See also Love (1996) and Kay (1989).

15. Some critics of development write as if identifying a "development discourse" shows it to be hegemonic and as if deconstructing that discourse automatically destroys its legitimacy. Discourses are studied in relation to other discourses. People working in the trenches have good reason to believe that something is missing here. For examples of the linguistic critique of development, see Moore and Schmitz (1995), Sachs (1992), and Crush (1995).

16. Anthropology had to a certain extent been chafing at its own borders since the 1930s, finding in questions like labor migration and nutrition problems that did not fit neatly into the Africa of tribes. But it was only in 1951 that George Balandier set out a clear and powerful argument why the "colonial situation" itself should be the object of inquiry, and his intervention came at a time when colonialism was collapsing and scholars were more interested in exploring new possibilities rather than investigating the dying order in the depth that Balandier's argument implied.

17. Lanteri (1985: 217) reports that the training of colonial officials in France once included ethnology and sociology, but the training of development personnel dropped this in the 1960s, focusing almost entirely on economics and management and thereby contributing to a conception of development as a universal process, independent of context.

18. See Martin and Knapp (1967) for papers on the problems of teaching development economics.

19. W. A. Lewis (1954, 1955); see also Arndt (1987), Meier and Seers (1984), Meier (1987), and Cooper, this volume. Stephen Gudeman presented a workshop paper arguing that the Lewis theory obscured the specificity of the "traditional sector."

20. Hirschman has been criticized for failing to put his insights into rigorous mathematical models, and he has been defended for discussing development in a narrativized form which stressed "learning" within societies, the forging linkages among economic actors, and the importance of situation-specific, empirically rich analysis. See the recent symposium on his work published by Rodwin and Schön (1994).

21. The papers of Arturo Escobar, Gillian Feeley-Harnik, Michael Woost, Ivan Karp, Corinne Kratz, Gracia Clark, and Alan Hoben as well as several commentaries contributed to these discussions.

22. Goldstein and Keohane (1993) have previously argued for an examining the role of ideas in international politics, but Finnemore and Sikkink seek to take the discussion toward a deeper analysis of ideas and institutions and away from a perception of interests as givens.

23. Although the inability of modernization theory to deal with the conflictual nature of change, its teleological conception of modernity, and its reduction of "tradition" to an ahistorical foil is widely acknowledged, there are attempts to resurrect it, notably through concepts like "civil society" and "governance," put forward as new stand-ins for the old teleology. See Barkan (1994) and more generally Apter and Rosberg (1994).

24. Such approaches to development are similar to the dichotomous views that have become influential in colonial states, in works ranging from Fanon to James Scott (1990) to Subaltern Studies (Guha and Spivak 1988): the "autonomy" of the "subaltern" or the "hidden transcript" of subaltern discourse is starkly separated from colonial discourse. For arguments for an interactive, nonbinary approach see Cooper (1994) and Cooper and Stoler (1997). David Ludden's workshop paper connected development issues to Subaltern Studies, arguing that the varied ways in which Indian agriculturists took whatever initiatives were available to them raises questions about the usefulness of a category like "subalternity."

25. Thomas Biersteker examined the current movement for democratization and the ways in which it influenced development institutions and national priorities; Kwasi Wiredu also presented a paper on the relationship of democracy and development.

26. The learning concept was used in the classic text of Hirschman (1958: 47, 177) as a way to demonstrate the diverse character of development and the importance of thinking about it in strategic terms: communities learn how to use resources in different way.

27. A stimulating study (Fisher 1993) of an institution that helped to shape social science beginning in the 1920s, the Social Science Research Council (which sponsored this series of workshops), focuses on its relationship to foundations and government and the desire of influential elites to develop a social science that was both rigorous and practical.

28. As Gracia Clark's workshop paper on Ghana in the era of structural adjustment pointed out, this program has been successful as a cultural system, reproducing and propagating itself, while the perception of narrow options which this system fosters allows the effects of adjustment on specific groups—such as market women—to go unexamined. That structural adjustment is not gender-neutral is emphasized as well in Afshar and Dennis (1992). On alternatives, see Stein 1995, and for an important example Diouf, this volume.

29. See, for example, the effort to assign grades to different states based on what preset categories can be ticked off in the African Governance Program of the Carter Center (an exercise repeated in each issue of the Center's newsletter, *African Demos*). For a survey of the effects of political conditionality on African states, see Robinson (1995).

30. Literatures exist about labeling (Wood 1985), development narratives (Roe 1991), and development discourse (Apthorpe 1986, Moore and Schmitz 1995). Deconstructing the power relations behind "keywords" may give the misleading impression that the messages they seem to convey are what is received by their audience (a problem, for example, with Sachs 1992).

31. These issues were raised in the workshops at several instances, most notably in the paper of Arturo Escobar and the commentary of Pauline Peters. For a few recent collections showing the range of scholarly analysis of gender and development, see House-Midamba and Ekechi (1995) and Adepoju and Oppong (1994), while for an instance of innovative research on this topic see Hodgson (1995).

32. A classic study of organizational imperatives in the development field is Tendler (1975). She points out that development entails high uncertainty, particularly over the beneficiary's input, and "the project" is an effort to maintain control over a confusing process, even if this organizational logic contravened the long-range goal of the effort. On the idea of planning as "a body of customs" amenable to anthropological analysis, see Robertson (1984: 2).

33. Emery Roe's criticism of scholars who always find a reason why a development project should be deemed pernicious touched off an interesting discussion of these points. See also his paper and critiques of it in Roe (1994).

34. Some of the tensions between the theoretical aspirations of economics and the down-to-earth problems of agricultural research emerge in the articles in Martin (1992).

35. It has also been shown that different peoples have concepts of change that can be translated as "development." See Peel (1978).

36. These issues were central to two workshops which followed those represented in this volume, held at the Harvard Institute for International Development in 1995–96 under the title "Development Encounters," and organized by Pauline Peters and Frederick Cooper.

37. A more common genre—sweeping denunciations of the World Bank from

leftist critics or blanket dismissals of everything state bureaucracies do from critics on the right—does not get to the bottom of the issues. For a more nuanced view of the Bank, see Laidi (1989).

38. Some critics would like to see initiatives for change coming from social movements rather than from a global framework like development (Escobar 1995). This begs the key question: what distinguishes a "good" social movement, which expands the opportunities for human fulfillment, from a "bad" one, which imposes one sort of particularism on other people? Both are social movements, and implicitly the critic is imposing some sort of general criteria of human progress on them—in short coming back into the same sort of universalizing discourse that they criticize in the development concept. Escobar and others are making a quite valid effort to look for a more modest, more culturally specific, less universalistic "we" implied in the idea that "we can make a better world" than the more totalizing versions of the development framework. Yet their solution no more resolves the tensions of universal and particular than does the development concept— which is also amenable to nuance and recognition of the tensions it embodies (see Gupta, this volume).

39. Since the eighteenth century, both pro-market and antimarket rhetorics have played major parts in political mobilization in Latin America. Free market rhetoric was repeatedly used against entrenched oligarchs in Latin America, just as criticism of the market was invoked against the pain that international commerce inflicted in other situations. Salvatore (1993).

40. This point was emphasized in the commentaries of Michael Watts and Michael Johns at the final workshop.

41. Some recent studies of the effects of structural adjustment in Africa suggest that it reconfigures—but does not lessen—the rent-seeking behavior these programs targeted (Boone 1994; Lewis 1994). Chaudhry (1993) argues that managing a relatively open economy takes more government capacity than controlling a relatively closed one. Stewart, Lall, and Wangwe (1992) present studies that stress the contradiction between short-term adjustment and long-term development. Diouf (this volume) suggests that such programs, for all their hard-nosed, technical aura, are in the end exercises in political rhetoric.

REFERENCES

Adepoju, Aderanti, and Christine Oppong, eds. 1994. *Gender, Work and Population in Sub-Saharan Africa.* London: Currey for ILO.

Adriaansen, Willem L. M., and J. George Waardenburg, ed. 1992. *A Dual World Economy: Forty Years of Development Experience.* Bombay: Oxford University Press.

Afshar, Helen, and Carolyne Dennis, eds. 1992. *Women and Adjustment Policies in the Third World.* New York: St. Martin's Press.

Agarwal, Bina. 1992. "The Gender and Environment Debate: Lessons from India". *Feminist Studies* 18: 119–57.

Amin, Samir. 1974. *Accumulation on a World Scale.* Translated by Brian Pearce. New York: Monthly Review Press.

————. 1993. *Itinéraire Intellectuel.* Paris: L'Harmattan.

Amsden, Alice. 1989. *Asia's Next Giant: South Korea and Late Industrialization*. New York: Oxford University Press.

Apffel Marglin, Frederique, and Stephen Marglin, ed. 1990. *Dominating Knowledge: Development, Culture, and Resistance*. Oxford: Clarendon Press.

Apter, David, and Carl G. Rosberg, eds. 1994. In *Political Development and the New Realism in Sub-Saharan Africa*. Charlottesville: University Press of Virginia.

Apthorpe, Raymond. 1986. "Development Policy Discourse". *Public Administration and Development* 6: 377–89.

Arndt, H. W. 1987. *Economic Development: The History of an Idea*. Chicago: University of Chicago Press.

Bardhan, Pranab. 1993. "Economics of Development and the Development of Economics". *Journal of Economic Perspectives* 7: 129–42.

Barkan, Joel. 1994. "Resurrecting Modernization Theory and the Emergence of Civil Society in Kenya and Nigeria". In *Political Development and the New Realism in Sub-Saharan Africa*, edited by David Apter and Carl G. Rosberg, 87–116. Charlottesville: University Press of Virginia.

Bauer, P. T. 1972. *Dissent on Development*. Cambridge, Mass.: Harvard University Press.

———. 1984. "Remembrances of Studies Past: Retracing First Steps". In *Pioneers in Development*, edited by Gerald Meier and Dudley Seers, 27–43. New York: Oxford University Press.

Biersteker, Thomas J. 1993. "Evolving Perspectives on International Political Economy: Twentieth Century Contexts and Discontinuities". *International Political Science Review* 14: 7–33.

Biggs, Stephen D. 1990. "A Multiple Source of Innovation Model of Agricultural Research and Technology Production". *World Development* 18: 1481–99.

Birn, Anne-Emmanuelle. 1992. "The Rockefeller Foundation in Mexico". Paper for conference on Health and Society in Developing Areas.

Boiral, P., J. F. Lanteri, and J. P. Olivier de Sardan, eds. 1985. *Paysans, experts et chercheurs en Afrique Noire: Sciences sociales et développement rural*. Paris: Karthala, 1985.

Boiral, P., and J. P. Olivier de Sardan. 1985. "Introduction". In Boiral et al. 1985, 7–23.

Boone, Catherine. 1994. "Trade, Taxes, and Tribute: Market Liberalizations and the New Importers in West Africa". *World Development* 22: 453–67.

Callaghy, Thomas. 1994. "State, Choice, and Context: Comparative Reflections on Reform and Intractability". In *Political Development and the New Realism in Sub-Saharan Africa*, edited by David Apter and Carl G. Rosberg, 184–219. Charlottesville: University Press of Virginia.

Chaudhry, Kiren Aziz. 1993. "The Myths of the Market and the Common History of Late Developers". *Politics and Society* 21: 245–74.

Chauveau, J. P. 1985. "Mise en valeur coloniale et développement: Perspective historique sur deux exemples ouest-africains". In Boiral et al. 1985, 143–66.

Choquet, C. O. Dollfus, E. Le Roy, and M. Vernières, eds. 1993. *Etat des savoirs sur le développement: Trois décennies de sciences sociales en langue français*. Paris: Karthala.

Clifford, James, and George Marcus, eds. 1986. *Writing Culture*. Berkeley: University of California Press, 1986.

Coats, A. W., ed. 1986. *Economists in International Agencies: An Exploratory Study.* New York: Praeger.

Colclough, Christopher, and James Manor, eds. 1991. *States or Markets? Neo-Liberalism and the Development Policy Debate.* Oxford: Clarendon Press.

Cooper, Frederick. 1994. "Conflict and Connection: Rethinking Colonial African History". *American Historical Review* 99: 1516–45.

Cooper, Frederick, and Ann Stoler, eds. 1997. *Tensions of Empire: Colonial Cultures in a Bourgeois World.* Berkeley: University of California Press.

Coquery-Vidrovitch, Catherine, Daniel Hemery, and Jean Piel, eds. 1988. *Pour une histoire du développement.* Paris: L'Harmattan.

Crush, Jonathan, [ed.]. 1995. *Power of Development.* London: Routledge.

Dasgupta, Partha. 1993. *An Inquiry Into Well-Being and Destitution.* Oxford: Clarendon Press.

de Alcantara, Cynthia Hewitt, ed. 1993. *Real Markets: Social and Political Issues of Food Policy Reform.* London: Cass.

Escobar, Arturo. 1995. *Encountering Development: The Making and Unmaking of the Third World.* Princeton: Princeton University Press.

Farley, John. 1991. *Bilharzia: A History of Imperial Tropical Medicine.* Cambridge: Cambridge University Press.

Ferguson, James. 1990. *The Anti-Politics Machine: Development, Depoliticization and Bureaucratic Power in the Third World.* Cambridge: Cambridge University Press.

Fisher, Donald. 1993. *Fundamental Development of the Social Sciences: Rockefeller Philanthropy and the United States Social Science Research Council.* Ann Arbor: University of Michigan Press.

Fisher, William F. 1995. *Toward Sustainable Development: Struggling over India's Narmada Dam.* Armonk, NY: M. E. Sharpe.

Gendarme, René. 1995. "La coopération de l'Europe et de l'Afrique: Histoire d'une espérance déçue". *Mondes en Développement* 23, 92: 15–33.

Goldstein, Judith, and Robert O. Keohane, eds. 1993. *Ideas and Foreign Policy: Beliefs, Institutions, and Political Change.* Ithaca: Cornell University Press.

Guha, Ranajit, and Gayatri Chakrovorty Spivak, eds. 1988. *Selected Subaltern Studies.* New York: Oxford University Press.

Haggard, Stephen. 1990. *Pathways from the Periphery: The Politics of Growth in the Newly Industrializing Countries.* Ithaca: Cornell University Press, 1990.

Hall, Peter. 1989. *The Political Power of Economic Ideas: Keynesianism Across Nations.* Princeton: Princeton University Press.

Hannerz, Ulf. 1990. "Cosmopolitans and Locals in World Culture". In *Global Culture: Nationalism, Globalization and Modernity*, ed. by Mike Featherstone, 237–52. London: Sage.

Hill, Polly. 1986. *Development Economics on Trial: The Anthropological Case for a Prosecution.* Cambridge: Cambridge University Press.

Hirschman, Albert O. 1958. *The Strategy of Economic Development.* New Haven: Yale University Press.

———. 1981. *Essays in Trespassing.* Cambridge: Cambridge University Press.

Hodgson, Dorothy. 1995. "The Politics of Gender, Ethnicity, and "Development": Images, Interactions, and the Reconfiguration of Maasai Identities in Tanzania, 1916–1993". Ph.D. Dissertation, University of Michigan.

House-Midamba, Bessie, and Felix K. Ekechi, eds. 1995. *African Market Women and Economic Power: The Role of Women in African Economic Development.* Westport, CT: Greenwood.

Kay, Cristobal. 1989. *Latin American Theories of Development and Underdevelopment.* London and New York: Routledge.

Klamer, Arjo, Donald McCloskey, and Robert Solow, eds. 1988. *The Consequences of Economic Rhetoric.* Cambridge: Cambridge University Press.

Klitgaard, Robert. 1990. *Tropical Gangsters.* New York: Basic Books.

Laïdi, Zaki. 1989. *Enquête sur la Banque Mondiale.* Paris: Fayard.

Lal, Deepek. 1985. *The Poverty of Development Economics.* Cambridge, Mass.: Harvard University Press for the Institute of Economic Affairs.

Lanteri, Jean-François. 1985. "Sciences sociales et formation à la coopération: La permanence d'une interrogation critique". In Boiral et al 1985, 211–22.

Lele, Uma. 1988. "Comparative Advantage and Structural Transformation: A Review of Africa's Economic Development Experience". In Ranis and Schultz 1988, 188–227.

Lewis, John P., ed. 1988. *Strengthening the Poor: What Have We Learned?* New Brunswick, NJ: Transaction Books.

Lewis, Peter M. 1994. "Economic Statism, Private Capital, and the Dilemmas of Accumulation in Nigeria". *World Development* 22: 437–51.

Lewis, W. Arthur. 1954. "Economic Development with Unlimited Supplies of Labour". *Manchester School* 22: 139–91.

———. 1955. *The Theory of Economic Growth.* Homewood, Il.: Irwin.

———. 1984. "The State of Development Theory". *American Economic Review* 74: 1–10.

Long, Norman, and Ann Long, eds. 1992. *Battlefields of Knowledge: The Interlocking of Theory and Practice in Social Research and Development.* London: Routledge.

Love, Joseph L. 1996. *Crafting the Third World: Theorizing Underdevelopment in Rumania and Brazil.* Stanford: Stanford University Press.

Lumsdaine, David Holloran. 1993. *Moral Vision in International Politics: The Foreign Aid Regime, 1949–1989.* Princeton: Princeton University Press.

Mandel, Ernest. 1975. *Late Capitalism.* Translated by Jores de Bres. London: New Left Books.

Martin, Kurt, and John Knapp, eds. 1967. *The Teaching of Development Economics: Its Position in the Present State of Knowledge.* Chicago: Aldine.

Martin, Lee R., ed. 1992. *A Survey of Agricultural Economics Literature. Vol. 4.* Minneapolis: University of Minnesota Press for American Agricultural Economics Asociation.

McCloskey, Donald. 1985. *The Rhetoric of Economics.* Madison: University of Wisconsin Press.

———. 1987. "The Rhetoric of Economic Development". *Cato Journal* 7: 249–54.

Meier, Gerald M., ed. 1987. *Pioneers in Development Second Series.* New York: Oxford University Press.

Meier, Gerald M., and Dudley Seers, eds. 1984. *Pioneers in Development.* New York: Oxford University Press.

Mitchell, Timothy. 1991. "America's Egypt: Discourse of the Development Industry". *Middle East Report* : 18–34.

Moore, David B., and Gerald J. Schmitz, eds. 1995. *Debating Development Discourse: Institutional and Popular Perspectives.* New York: St. Martin's Press.

Moser, Caroline O. N. 1993. *Gender Planning and Development: Theory, Practice and Training.* London: Routledge.

Mudimbe, V. Y. 1988. *The Invention of Africa.* Bloomington: Indiana University Press.

Nandy, Ashis, ed. 1988. *Science, Hegemony and Violence: A Requieum for Modernity.* Delhi: Oxford University Press.

Nelson, John, Allan Megill, and Donald McCloskey, eds. 1987. *The Rhetoric of the Human Sciences.* Madison: University of Wisconsin Press.

Novick, Peter. 1988. *That Noble Dream: The Objectivity Question and the American Historical Profession.* Cambridge: Cambridge University Press.

Olivier de Sardan, Jean-Pierre. 1995. *Anthropologie et développement.* Paris: Karthala.

Packenham, Robert. 1973. *Liberal America and the Third World: Political Development Ideas in Foreign Aid and Social Science.* Princeton: Princeton University Press.

Peel, J. D. Y. 1978. "Olaju: A Yoruba Concept of Development". *Journal of Development Studies* 14: 139–65.

Peters, Pauline. 1994. *Dividing the Commons: Politics, Policy and Culture in Botswana.* Charlottesville: University of Virginia Press.

Pigg, Stacy Leigh. 1992. "Inventing Social Categories Through Place: Social Representations and Development in Nepal". *Comparative Studies in Society and History* 34: 491–513.

Pletsch, Carl E. 1981. "The Three Worlds, or the Division of Social Scientific Labor, Circa 1950–1975". *Comparative Studies in Society and History* 23: 565–90.

Putterman, Louis, and Dietrich Rueschemeyer, eds. 1992. *State and Market in Development: Synergy or Rivalry?* Boulder: Rienner.

Ranis, Gustav, and T. Paul Schultz, eds. 1988. *The State of Development Economics: Progress and Perspectives.* Oxford: Blackwell.

Robertson, A. F. 1984. *People and the State: An Anthropology of Planned Development.* Cambridge: Cambridge University Press.

Robinson, Mark. 1995. "Aid, Democracy and Political Conditionality in Sub-Saharan Africa". In *Economic and Political Reform in Developing Countries*, ed. by Oliver Morrissey and Frances Stewart, 81–97. New York: St. Martin's Press.

Rock, Michael T. 1993. "'Twenty-Five Years of Economic Development' Revisited". *World Development* 21: 1787–801.

Rodney, Walter. 1972. *How Europe Underdeveloped Africa.* London: Bogle-L'Ouverture.

Rodwin, Lloyd, and Donald A. Schön, eds. 1994. *Rethinking the Development Experience: Essays Provoked by the Work of Albert O. Hirschman.* Washington: Brookings Institution.

Roe, Emery M. 1991. "Development Narratives, or Making the Best of Blueprint Development". *World Development* 19: 287–300.

———. 1994. "Against Power". *Transition* 64: 113–69.

Rosen, George. 1985. *Western Economists and Eastern Societies.* Baltimore: Johns Hopkins University Press.

Rosenberg, Alexander. 1992. *Economics: Mathematical Politics or Science of Diminishing Returns.* Chicago: University of Chicago Press.

Rosenberg, Emily. 1982. *Spreading the American Dream: American Economic and Cultural Expansion, 1890–1945.* New York: Hill and Wang.

Rosenstein-Rodan, P. H.. 1943. "Problems of Industrialisation of Eastern and South-eastern Europe". *Economic Journal* 53:202–211.

Sachs, Wolfgang, ed. 1992. *The Development Dictionary: A Guide to Knowledge as Power.* London: Zed Books.

Said, Edward. 1979. *Orientalism.* New York: Vintage.

Salvatore, Ricardo D. 1993. "Market-Oriented Reforms and the Language of Popular Protest: Latin America from Charles III to the IMF". *Social Science History* 17: 485–524.

Scott, James. 1990. *Domination and the Arts of Resistance: Hidden Transcripts.* New Haven: Yale University Press.

Seers, Dudley. 1979. "The Birth, Life, and Death of Development Economics". *Development and Change* 10: 707–19.

Shiva, Vandana. 1988. *Staying Alive: Women, Ecology and Development.* London: Zed.

Sikkink, Kathryn. 1991. *Ideas and Institutions: Developmentalism in Brazil and Argentina.* Ithaca: Cornell University Press.

Stark, David. 1996. "Recombinant Property in East European Capitalism". *American Journal of Sociology* 101: 993–1027.

Stein, Howard, ed. 1995. *Asian Industrialization and Africa.* New York: St. Martin's Press.

Stewart, Frances, Sanjaya Lall, and Samuel Wangwe, eds. 1992. *Alternative Development Strategies in Subsaharan Africa.* London: Macmillan.

Tendler, Judith. 1975. *Inside Foreign Aid.* Baltimore: Johns Hopkins University Press

Toye, John. 1987. *Dilemmas of Development.* Oxford: Blackwell.

Verdery, Katherine. 1996. *What Was Socialism, and What Comes Next?* Princeton: Princeton University Press.

Wade, Robert. 1990. *Governing the Market: Economic Theory and the Role of Government in East Asian Industrialization.* Princeton: Princeton University Press.

Watts, Michael J. 1993. "Development I: Power, Knowledge, Discursive Practice". *Progress in Human Geography* 17: 257–72.

Wood, Geof. 1985. "The Politics of Development Policy Labelling". *Development and Change* 16: 347–73.

Young, Crawford. 1982. *Ideology and Development in Africa.* New Haven: Yale University Press.

The End of Empire and the Development Framework

ONE

Instruments and Idioms of Colonial and National Development

India's Historical Experience in Comparative Perspective

Sugata Bose

An elephant with its feet unchained was the chosen motif on the government's publicity handouts advertising its new "liberalization" policies in 1991 as India seemed poised to make a U-turn from the course it had set since the end of colonial rule in the quest for "national development."[1] Unimpressed by the image of a plodding elephant, a popular and influential western mouthpiece championing robust economic growth likened the Indian economy to a tiger caged and proclaimed that "[t]his tiger, set free, can be as healthy and vigorous as any in Asia" (*Economist* 1991: 5).[2] Whatever the preferred metaphor from the animal kingdom, many Indian commentators and outside observers were wondering aloud whether India had not in the process of freeing itself from British chains unwittingly tied up its development potential in a tangled web of self-imposed constraints.

India at any rate did not seem to offer a developing "third world" model to the ex-communist "second world" that was about to taste the mixed treats of first world–directed development efforts. As Vaclav Klaus, the freest of Eastern Europe's free-marketeer politicians exclaimed, "I have read everything about Indian planning from Mahalanobis onwards. It's wrong, all wrong."[3] This must have sounded a trifle ironic to those who knew something of the history of development. In the halcyon days of development planning in the 1950s and early 1960s, Nehruvian India had "appeared to theorists of reformed capitalism as an answer to the challenge posed by the model of growth presented by Mao's China" (Chakravarty 1987). Now India was being asked to unlearn its long-cherished dogmas of development and be tutored in the lessons of stabilization and structural adjustment by those international paragons of virtuous economic discipline based in Washington.

India's failings in its developmental efforts are many and the disenchantments and disillusionments among its own populace deep and widespread. All but the most churlish would acknowledge that there have been some successes to report as well. What is truly remarkable about the current convergence of criticisms of India's postindependence development efforts is that the volleys have come from diverse and occasionally conflicting sources and premises. The critics range from "neoclassical" and liberal advocates of the "free market" to "postmodern" votaries of the "fragment" and "antidevelopment." In order to make a measured assessment of India's development experience in the midst of this cacophony, there is no alternative but to return to the drawing board of history. It is only by recovering the intellectual and political origins and aims of development and reappraising the strategies and trajectories pursued toward the set goals that it may be possible to ferret out not only the successes from failures but also the legitimate from flawed criticisms. "Any evaluative judgment," as Amartya Sen stresses, "has to be . . . comparative" (1989: 371). The recourse to history immediately opens the way to one comparative dimension—that over time. The other comparative dimension—that with other countries—often has been at least partially blocked by a weighty Orientalist intellectual tradition of essentializing India and its history as plain peculiar. The development paradigm, whatever its other limitations may be, is not on the whole wedded to ahistorical attributes of cultural uniqueness and consequently not hostile to careful and meaningful cross-country and cross-regional comparisons.

Before delving into history in the comparative vein, it may be useful to clarify the senses in which the terms "instruments" and "idioms" are used in this paper. Each term is used in at least two senses. Scholars and practitioners in the field of development economics generally take instruments to refer to "means-enhancing"[4] variables, such as savings rates and investment, foreign exchange reserves, food stocks, and so on. This is the first sense in which the term "instruments" is used in the appropriate contexts of economic analysis. Any attempt to probe the relationship between development knowledge and the social sciences must, however, also deploy a broader definition of instruments that refers to state institutions and policies. This is of the essence since development efforts have been generally conducted over the past half century under the aegis of centralized, late colonial and postcolonial states. Any rethinking about development must include ideas about restructuring the modern nation-state. The term "idioms" in the first place encapsulates the goals, such as removal of poverty and improvement in the quality of life, that assigned the idea of development its normative privilege. Yet in order to avoid the methodological pitfalls usually associated with a sharp separation between means and ends, "idioms" will also refer to the singular concepts of nationhood and particular state forms that came to be favored by the dominant ideology of development as better suited to its purpose. Idioms in this connotation could well serve as political instruments.

HISTORICAL ORIGINS OF THE CONCEPTS OF COLONIAL AND NATIONAL DEVELOPMENT

Two years before the passage of the landmark British Colonial Development and Welfare Act of 1940, the Indian National Congress had set up a National Planning Committee to draw up blueprints for the economic and social reconstruction of India once independence was won. By contrast with Africa, the institutional expression of the concept of "national development" predated that of "colonial development" in India. An economic critique of colonial rule was articulated, of course, in both continents long before colonialism under siege turned to development as an ideology of self-justification. At the turn of the century in India leaders of the Indian National Congress like Dadabhai Naoroji and Romesh C. Dutt wrote powerful critiques of the high land-revenue demand and the drain of wealth funneled through India's export surplus, which they held squarely responsible for poverty and famines in India (Naoroji 1901; Dutt 1904). In 1908 Mohandas Gandhi in *Hind Swaraj* offered his own particular reading of the early tomes of economic nationalism: "When I read Mr Dutt's economic history of India, I wept; and as I think of it again my heart sickens. It is machinery that has impoverished India" (Gandhi 1958: 22–23). While Gandhi condemned modern industrialism as evil, other nationalist critics denounced colonial fiscal and financial policy for stunting India's potential for industrialization, which was a necessary condition if not the panacea for eradicating poverty. Whatever the differences in nationalist positions, Indian nationalism "began as a critique of policy" and "became a critique of British power by its being denied a voice in government" (Ludden 1992: 263).

The precise relationship between colonial and national development marked both by contradictions and imbrications can be clarified and elucidated only by bringing into play the analytical distinctions between instruments and idioms. David Ludden has recently assigned joint authorship and copyright to "colonial capitalism" and "bourgeois nationalism" in the creation of "an institutional complex—a development regime . . . as a vital force in the cultural and material life of India" (1992: 249).[5] This regime with its built-in trend toward more centralized and ramified state power has fairly deep historical roots going back at least to the mid-nineteenth century. "By 1900," Ludden writes, "institutional foundations of the state information apparatus and the surrounding constellation of public debate and expertise *that sustain India's development regime today* were in place" (1992: 261, emphasis added). Such an observation has a measure of accuracy with reference to the inheritance of instruments of development in the form of institutions of state. Yet, as Ludden acknowledges but does not sufficiently emphasize, the trend in India's development regime toward instrumental centralization and expansion of state power was not inevitable or inexorable and had to overcome significant opposition and resistance.

The idiom of national development, on the other hand, might be construed to be the only distinguishing feature of the facade of a postcolonial state that was erected on the authoritarian, institutional foundations of the colonial state.[6] The "transfer of power" in India in 1947 involved the transfer of the colonial military, police, bureaucracy, and judiciary from the British to the hands of the leadership of the Indian National Congress. As Partha Chatterjee aptly notes, "even today one is forced to witness such unlovely ironies as regiments of the Indian Army displaying the trophies of colonial conquest and counter-insurgency in their barrack-rooms or the Presidential Guards celebrating their birth two hundred years ago under the governor-generalship of Lord Cornwallis!" In such a scenario the postcolonial state found its "distinctive content" only in the idiom of national development. Planning for development enabled the postcolonial state to "claim its legitimacy" as an embodiment of "the will of the nation." It was in its "legitimising role" that the idiom of planning for national development "was to become an instrument of politics" (1993a: 57).[7]

As a general proposition it is doubtless true that "goals themselves are very often fixed because certain instruments have to be used" and "instruments in politics can become goals in themselves" (P. Chatterjee 1993a: 52). But in the specific historical context of India, the mischief of invoking legitimizing idioms to privilege preferred instruments was committed, I will argue, at the conjunctural moment of the postcolonial transition. Recent attempts at unraveling Indian nationalist thought, whether construed as "a derivative discourse" (P. Chatterjee 1986) or as "a cultural product of nineteenth-century capitalism, on the same plane with bourgeois nationalisms in the West" (Ludden 1992: 263), have tended toward a teleology that confuses the outcome of 1947 with a long-term, essentially unilinear, trend inherent in the ideology of the political economy of nationhood. Caveats about "noninevitability" and "possibilities" notwithstanding, these teleological views leave little theoretical space for the recovery of historically contested visions of nationhood, alternative ideological frameworks for the postcolonial state and real debates about the instruments and idioms of national development.

These debates deserve a closer analysis, especially since the lines of division did not always reflect the dichotomies of modernity versus tradition, reason versus unreason, science versus superstition, or, most simplistically, Nehru versus Gandhi that many latter-day commentators have read into them. Analyses based on these dichotomous schemes often enable particular critiques of India's development experience to parade as general critiques of science, reason, and development. A consideration of the debates over national planning during the final decade of the British Raj in India may help throw light on the complex relationship of universal values to the particular history of Indian development.

At the third general meeting of the Indian Science News Association on August 21, 1938, Meghnad Saha, a renowned scientist, asked Subhas Chandra Bose, the President of the Indian National Congress, a loaded question:

> May I enquire whether the India of the future is going to revive the philosophy of village life, of the bullock-cart—thereby perpetuating servitude, or is she going to be a modern industrialized nation which, having developed all her natural resources, will solve the problems of poverty, ignorance and defence and will take an honoured place in the comity of nations and begin a new cycle of civilization?

The Congress President said in reply:

> I must say that all Congressmen do not hold the same view on this question. Nevertheless, I may say without any exaggeration that the rising generation are in favour of industrialisation and for several reasons.

The reasons cited were fourfold. Industrialization was necessary for (1) "solving the problem of unemployment," (2) "national reconstruction" based on "Socialism," (3) ability "to compete with foreign industries," and (4) "improving the standard of living of the people at large." What was needed in the cause of national development was "far-reaching cooperation between science and politics" (Bose and Bose 1995: 43–48).

At his Presidential Address at Haripura in February 1938, Subhas Chandra Bose had outlined "the long-period programme for a Free India." The "first problem to tackle," according to him, was "increasing population." As regards "reconstruction" the "principal problem" would be "how to eradicate poverty from our country." That would "require a radical reform of our land system, including the abolition of landlordism." "Agricultural indebtedness" would "have to be liquidated and provision made for cheap credit for the rural population." But to "solve the economic problem" agricultural improvement would "not be enough" and an ambitious plan of state-directed industrial development would be necessary. "However much we may dislike modern industrialism and condemn the evils which follow in its train," Bose declared, "we cannot go back to the pre-industrial era, even if we desire to do so." The state in independent India would "on the advice of a planning commission" have "to adopt a comprehensive scheme for gradually socialising our entire agricultural and industrial system in the spheres of both production and appropriation" (Bose and Bose 1995: 15–16).

In October 1938 Bose announced the formation of the National Planning Committee of which he made Jawaharlal Nehru the chair.[8] Many leading Indian minds, including India's greatest poet Rabindranath Tagore, who was keenly aware of the evils of the modern nation-state, responded with alacrity to the idea of rational and scientific planning for Indian industry and seemed enthused by a "modernist" vision of India's economic and social reconstruction.[9] This vision was at variance with Gandhi's evocation of self-governing and self-sufficient village communities. Gandhi had written in *Hind Swaraj* in 1908, "India's salvation consists in unlearning what she has learnt during the past fifty years or so. The railways, telegraphs, hospitals, lawyers, doctors and such like have all to go, and the so-called upper class have to learn to live consciously and religiously and deliberately the simple life of a peasant" (Gandhi 1958, vol. 10). Over some forty years since 1908, Gandhi only slightly modified his stance. As late as October 5, 1945 he wrote to Nehru:

> I still stand by the system of Government envisaged in *Hind Swaraj*. I have not *Hind Swaraj* before me as I write. It is really better for me to draw the picture anew in my own words. And whether it is the same as I drew in *Hind Swaraj* or not is immaterial. . . . I am convinced that if India is to attain true freedom and through India the world also, then sooner or later the fact must be recognized that people have to live in villages, not in towns, in huts, not in palaces. . . . I do not want to draw a large scale picture in detail. It is possible to envisage railways, post and telegraph offices etc. For me it is material to obtain the real article and the rest will fit into the picture afterwards (Nehru 1989: 505–506).

The sole Gandhian purist on the National Planning Committee, J. C. Kumarappa, almost succeeded in putting the spanner through the works by questioning the committee's authority to plan for industrialization since the national priority ought to be the containment if not the abolition of modern industrialism. Nehru promised safeguards for "cottage industries" but could scarcely conceal his exasperation with such "unscientific" obduracy. On the whole, however, Nehru enjoyed his work on the National Planning Committee, finding it "soothing and gratifying" and "a pleasant contrast to the squabbles and conflicts of politics" (cited in P. Chatterjee 1993a: 54).

Planning, Partha Chatterjee has argued, by being constituted as a domain outside politics, served as an instrument to politically resolve the debate on the need for industrialization in India. There can be little disagreement about the political instrumentality of the planning exercise before and, more pronouncedly, after independence. But that was not all that there was to it. What Chatterjee's critical formulation on development planning misses is that the "modernist" rational idiom of national development was no more and no less visionary as well as no more and no less politically instrumental than the Gandhian utopia. It is worth noting that some of the biggest Indian industrialists of the inter-war era were financial backers of the Gandhian Congress and harbored a sense of deep unease about the agenda of socialist visionaries who were among Gandhi's critics. The Gandhian notion of self-regulating, harmonious village communities and the associated concept of elite trusteeship of common property were designed to politically resolve potentially explosive class and caste conflicts within Indian agrarian society. It requires an analytical sleight of hand to counterpose antimodernist vision to modernist politics.

Another false dichotomy has crept into the scholarly literature on nationalism and development around the issue of authenticity. Gandhian nationalism, it has been argued by Ashis Nandy and Partha Chatterjee in slightly different ways, represented a truly "indigenous," and thereby authentic, form of resistance to the modern West (Nandy 1983, 1989; P. Chatterjee 1986: 85–130). This ahistorical view underplays the extent to which the Gandhian vision of village republics, for example, borrowed from mid-nineteenth-century western misperceptions of India's past portrayed in the writings of Henry Maine and others (Gandhi 1958, 3:332, 341). The unfolding of the colonial encounter as a messy historical process means that the search for wholly "untainted" anticolonial nationalist thought can only end in futility and carry the unfortunate implication of erasing significant strands of resistance that fail to meet the ahistorical litmus test of purity.

This is not to deny that Gandhian thought provided a powerful critique not only of modern industrial civilization but of "fundamental aspects of civil society" (P. Chatterjee 1986: 93). But it would be an error to invest all nonsubscribers to Gandhi's antimodernist idiom with having megalomaniacal dreams of the bourgeois acquisition of power at the apex of a centralized nation-state. To focus on Gandhi's localism and Nehru's centralism is to miss out on the multifarious ways in which nationalist thought construed the relationship between nation and state as well as the role of the state in development. Beyond evoking the utopia of Ramrajya, where the patriarchal ruler was the embodiment of the collective will of his subjects in a way that rendered representative institutions unnecessary, Gandhi did not elaborate on a theory of the state. His was a relentless nihilism, a celebration of extreme—albeit enlightened—anarchy and a pursuit of decentralization to the point of atomization. It was Gandhi's unwillingness "to draw a large scale picture in detail" that explains his current appeal to a particular brand of postmodernism that exults over the "fragment."

Many socialists within India's anticolonial movement, by contrast, favored a strong centralized state which could in theory serve as a better instrument to carry out a radical economic and social program. But even within this camp there were variations. Some seemed more willing than others to build the socialist state on the basis of regional autonomy and an equitable sharing of power among different religious communities. In any case, the bureaucratic and authoritarian colonial state was not the kind of centralized state socialist ideologues had in mind. Science and reason, according to this idiom, would be the servants, not the masters, of the efforts at development. The aim was to reverse the process of rural poverty and urban decay that were seen to have set in under colonial rule. There were other models, such as, C. R. Das's draft Swarajist "constitution" of 1923, which offered something of a blueprint of decentered democracy and planning for economic generation from the local communities upwards. According to this remarkable model, the "ordinary work" of a "Central Government" in free India "should be mainly advisory." It called for "a maximum of local autonomy, carried on mainly with advice and coordination from, and only a minimum of control by, higher centres" (*Das* 1982: 63–80).

In an insightful analysis of nationalist thought at the "moment of arrival" exemplified by Nehru, Partha Chatterjee has shown how the discourse came to be conducted in "a single, consistent, unambiguous voice" and succeeded in "glossing over all earlier contradictions, divergences and differences." Yet a methodological flaw creeps into his approach in seeking to "give to nationalist thought its ideological unity by relating it to a form of the postcolonial state which accords most closely to [his] theoretical characterization" (1986: 51, 49). This device of "taking as *paradigmatic* the most developed form of [the postcolonial] state" (49) unfortunately obliterates "all earlier contradictions, divergences and differences." The ideology of official nationalism adopted at the moment of the acquisition of centralized state power cannot be permitted to obfuscate the important dimension of ideological disunity and discontinuity in anticolonial nationalism and development planning. What got marginalized in 1947 were conceptions of a state of union forged from below that reflected and presided over the balance and harmony of free regional peoples and religious communities.[10] The victory of singular nationalism conflated with a centralized postcolonial state also marked the primacy of instruments over the idioms of national development. It was a paradigm shift in the idea of development brought about by the capture of centralized state power by the machine politicians among the nationalist elite.

NATIONAL DEVELOPMENT AND THE POSTCOLONIAL STATE

The project of planning for national development in the postcolonial phase privileged instruments over idioms, means over goals, in at least two distinct ways. First, the exercise of planning concentrated on questions of means enhancement, such as, ways to increase the rate of savings. Consequently, means came to be confused with goals and the accumulation of capital rather than betterment of the quality of life often turned out to be the end-all of development efforts. Second and more important, an insufficiently decolonized, centralized state structure seized upon national development as a primary source of its own self-justification. Instead of the state being used as an instrument of development, development became an instrument of the state's legitimacy. Even though India opted for a political system based on representative parliamentary democracy, elections based on universal adult franchise were incapable of bridging the gap between a democratic political process and a postcolonial state imbued with a strong element of bureaucratic authoritarianism.

Even in the specific domain of planning, postcolonial India lost sight of the vision of eradicating poverty, morbidity and illiteracy that had inspired the debates on national development in the colonial era. This was not a case of Nehruvian modernism triumphing over Gandhian traditionalism. Some of the fiercest critics of the Nehruvian state were those modernist socialists who deplored the nationalist leadership's eagerness to inherit the colonial mantle. For example, the scientist Meghnad Saha, who had been a stalwart of the National Planning Committee during 1938–1940, had warned on the eve of independence that planning had become a "catchword." The Bombay Plan of 1944 had been hatched by "a syndicate of capitalists," the Department of Planning and Development established later that year was the handiwork of "foreign bureaucrats" and in the case of the Bengal Government Plan of 1945 "the Civil Service provided the philosophy and the direction" (S. Chatterjee 1987: 431, 445). In other words, the official version of development had arisen after and in reaction to the popular, national efforts. Capitalists and colonialists were stealing the idea mooted initially by socialists within the nationalist movement. In the early 1950s, Saha, as scientist-cum-socialist politician, kept up a steady tirade against the sellouts by Nehru's government in the Indian Parliament. He argued in 1953 that if India's First Five Year Plan were "not altered root and branch, it will perpetuate our 'Colonial Status' in the economic field, and greatly jeopardize our hard-won 'Political Freedom' "(Chatterjee 1987: 533).[11]

The early exercise in development planning in postcolonial India drew much more from the colonial Planning and Development Department set up in 1944 than the work of the National Planning Committee during 1938–1940. The First Five Year Plan of 1950–1955 was little more than a collection of public projects that had been under consideration during the last years of the British Raj (Robertson 1984: 20). The Second and Third Five Year Plans drawn up under the direction of the famous statistician P. C. Mahalanobis represented something of a break with the past in its emphasis on capital-goods led import-substituting industrialization. A departure from both the "textiles first" and "export-led" strategies adopted by other industrializing countries, these plans nevertheless relied heavily on influential means-enhancing models of development. The Second Five Year Plan of 1955, "the single most significant document on Indian planning," was "a variant of the Lewis model" (Chakravarty 1987: 3, 14). Arthur Lewis's celebrated comment that development economics was about transforming a country which saved 5 percent of its income to one which saved 20 percent remains a classic statement on development as means enhancement. The Indian variation from the pristine Lewis model related to the role given to a development bureaucracy and not just capitalist industrialists in powering growth in the "modern" sector of the economy.

The Third Five Year Plan built in many important ways on the second, but also placed a special emphasis on agriculture and "distributional considerations." The opening chapter of the plan document, partly written by Nehru himself, talked about reducing income disparities by "raising the level of the minimum." But, as even a staunch defender of Indian planning had to concede, "there was no clearly laid out strategy which could be expected to raise the 'minimum level'—at least, not one that could match the industrialization targets articulated with great eloquence in the first two plans" (Chakravarty 1987: 28). The shift of emphasis from growth to distribution and the new concern with income did not, in any case, entail a sensitivity to entitlements and capabilities of people which, Amartya Sen has forcefully argued, have a much more direct bearing on the means-using goals of development (Sen 1983).

The acknowledged successes of India's first three plans—a dramatic improvement in the savings rate, the establishment of a heavy industrial base, the upgrading of the skill base and the breakout from the agricultural stagnation of the first half of the twentieth century—were major achievements of means enhancement toward which the development effort had been geared. The "crisis of Indian planning" in the mid-1960s is generally put down by its apologists to "external shocks" in the form of war-induced increase in defense expenditure and monsoon failures, and by its critics to either "urban bias" or "neglect of foreign trade." While quirks in the weather pattern may well have compounded India's food situation and the unwarranted export pessimism of the early 1960s may well have been something of a missed opportunity in India's development trajectory, the real problem was that the planners had forgotten the idioms of national development.

In the late 1960s and early 1970s there was a partial recovery of these idioms in the "populist" political and economic program of Indira Gandhi with its emphasis on poverty eradication and rural employment. This particular paradigm shift was triggered by a realization of the limits of the Nehruvian form of oligarchical democracy whose project of "national development" had not cared to address the means-using needs of the poor. In the 1967 elections the party bosses had failed to deliver their vote-banks as before. Indira Gandhi's populist initiative to "abolish poverty" was designed to widen and deepen the party's social base of support. But this attempt to make the center the fount of redistributive justice for those at the bottom of the agrarian hierarchy was not matched by political empowerment at the base and became vulnerable to challenges mounted by middling agrarian groups and rich farmer lobbies in several states. Agrarian development was turned into a fiercely contested site where the center's populist championing of the rural poor was countered by an agrarian populism anxious to gloss over class differentiation in the countryside (Gupta, this volume).

Yet even Indira Gandhi's brand of populism remained tall on rhetoric and short on performance and did not really grasp the issue of capabilities and entitlements of the poor. The Fifth and Sixth Five Year Plans of 1974 and 1980 respectively—marking a "shift in emphasis away from the earlier concept of a 'traverse,' with its so-called heavy-industry bias, to a strategy centring around 'food' and 'fuels' "(Chakravarty 1987: 38)—did not represent a departure from the obsession with means enhancement. Improvements achieved in instrumental variables like savings, foreign exchange reserves, and food stocks in the mid-1970s were consequently not reflected in indicators of the quality of life. As Kaushik Basu points out, "These . . . are all instruments. We must realize that food stocks with the Government is not something which the people eat, the savings rate is not something which you wear and one cannot sleep under the roof of foreign exchange" (Basu 1990: 108). By the early 1980s the center's populist fervor had already waned. Clarion calls for "a sharper focus on employment and poverty alleviation" in the *Approach to the Seventh Five Year Plan* of 1985 was immediately and resoundingly contradicted by the minuscule allocations for employment generation and poverty eradication and a real decline in plan outlay in the very first budget of the plan period (Basu 1990: 110).

In assessing the lessons and nonlessons of the Indian development experience, Amartya Sen makes a clear distinction between what is instrumental and what is intrinsic: "The importance of savings and investment is instrumental rather than intrinsic, and any enhancement of instrumental variables may be washed out, in the tally of final accounting, by a deterioration of the impact of that instrumental variable on things that are intrinsically valuable" (Sen 1989: 374). What post-1947 India lacked, by contrast for example with post-1949 China, was direct and massive public action to improve living conditions. It was this apathy to questions concerning means use which explained the fifteen-year difference in average life expectancy in the two countries by the late 1980s. India's democratic political process, characterized by a relatively free press and political opposition, enabled it to avoid catastrophes like the Chinese famine of 1958–61. This "elimination of famine" was "achieved despite India's food availability per head being no higher than that in sub-Saharan Africa" (Sen 1989: 387). Yet the Indian development effort has launched no major onslaught on chronic malnutrition and morbidity. If India had China's lower mortality rates, "there would have been 3.8 million fewer deaths in India around the middle 1980s." Looked at another way, "every eight years or so more people in addition die in India—in comparison with Chinese mortality rates—than the total number that died in the gigantic Chinese famine" (Sen 1989: 384).

Instead of focusing on these means-using failures, the bulk of self-serving, right-wing criticism of the history of Indian development, seeking to justify the recent "liberalization" policies, has concentrated even more than before on issues of means enhancement (Bhagwati 1993). The development debate in India has witnessed clear lines of disagreement within the rounded circle of such issues as import substitution versus export promotion, industrialization versus agricultural dynamism, and, of course, state direction versus market incentives. Some have recently pointed out, for example, that the fast-growing and high-performing economies of Southeast and Northeast Asia have relied less on the magic wand of the market and more on the whip of strategic state intervention. While such debates are not altogether irrelevant, Amartya Sen has made a compelling case that "the main shortcoming of Indian planning" has been "to wit, not aiming at the ultimate objectives of planning" (Sen 1989: 388).

The question remains, however, whether the Indian state as presently constituted has the will or the capacity to aim clearly and unambiguously at the original goals of national development. This leads us to consider the broader definition of instruments referring to state institutions and policy. Pranab Bardhan has argued that the heterogeneity of dominant proprietary classes in India—industrial capitalists, rich farmers and professionals—has led to "the proliferation of subsidies and grants to placate all of them, with the consequent reduction in available surplus for public capital formation." The scramble among the heterogeneous proprietary classes for a share of the spoils turned India's public economy into "an elaborate network of patronage and subsidies." The "relative autonomy" of the Indian state from any single dominant class is qualitatively different from the "embedded autonomy" of some of the East Asian states which makes for more efficacious public responses to market conditions. One of the "symptoms" of India's spoils system and subsidy "raj," according to Bardhan, has been the rapid decline of "a semi-insulated technocratic institution" like the Planning Commission. A "lack of political insulation from conflicting interests" increasingly kept the Indian state confined to regulatory functions rather than "more active developmental functions" (Bardhan 1985: 61, 65, 73–74; 1992: 324–27).

Bardhan's analysis is insightful in so far as it explains certain macroeconomic inefficiencies arising out of the demand overload in India's political processes. Yet I would argue that the very "political insulation" of the planning apparatus, nestling within a state structure inherited almost intact from the colonial era, may explain the imperviousness of the centralist Indian state to the means-using development needs of subordinated social groups. In other words, an insufficiently decolonized and inadequately democratized state structure can hardly be expected to perform means-using miracles for India's poor. But should the critique of the postcolonial state as an instrument be so extended as to produce an all-encompassing rejection of the idioms of development?

IS DEVELOPMENT HISTORY?

The "neoclassical," "market-oriented" critics of India's development experience have seized upon the more obvious bureaucratic logjams in the path of economic development to justify the search for a "liberalized" economic regime. It is not difficult to argue that in the quest for the label "made in India" the Indian strategy of import-substituting industrialization paid a high price in spiraling costs and plummeting quality. The overall record in the agrarian sector, which witnessed scuttled land reforms and a pale green revolution, was not much more impressive. But the crux of the problem, as we have seen, may well have been the failure of Indian development planners to focus on means-use and concentrate unambiguously and determinedly on the intrinsic values of development.

The free marketeers' attack on the state has found an unlikely convergence with the antimodern traditionalist and postmodern fragmentalist onslaughts on centralized state monoliths. The criticisms have gone far beyond doubting the efficacy of modern nation-states in playing their developmental role to call into question two reasons of state—science and development (Nandy 1988; Apffel Marglin and Marglin 1990). In so far as development planning was an exercise in instrumental rationality, the failures of development have been seen to be have constituted sufficient, legitimate grounds for denunciations of the cunning of reason. I would accept that the centralizing modern state has often resorted to reductionist mega-science to buttress itself, to homogenizing development to legitimize itself and to anesthetizing rationality to transcend the "irrational" arena of politics. It is also undoubtedly true, as David Ludden has stated, that "the national state has like its colonial predecessor turned its guns against those who oppose the trajectory of its development regime" (1992: 279). Nandy goes a step further to claim that "a part of the growing resistance to the ideas of development and modern science in India derives from the contradiction that has arisen between them and the democratic process" (1989: 25). For all this, it is not entirely clear why science, reason, and development should be culpable for the crimes of the modern state. Such a sweeping rejection of "modernity" flows from a failure to take a nuanced and differentiated approach toward, and instead attach a singular label to, complex historical phenomena.

"Development regimes," writes Ludden, "hire historians to make themselves look good" (1992: 278). These are the historians who not only concentrate on, but celebrate, the genealogy of the nation-state. But history, if not historians, can also turn out to be the most formidable enemy of development regimes. As Ludden acknowledges:

> Precolonial political culture produced multiple, overlapping levels and arenas of authority more than centralized states. Even the Mughal state was more patrimonial than bureaucratic, and its centralization was more ideological than operative. From medieval to late precolonial times, centralization was episodic. Precolonial traditions hardly sustain India's "stateness" and may better explain its opposition (1992: 266).

A similar argument could be made about *anticolonial* political culture if we are careful to avoid the conflation of nation and state until its actual historical occurrence at the moment of the postcolonial transition and resist the temptation to give nationalist thought its unity by reading back from the telos of 1947.

The challenge in this connection is to recover from anticolonial thought alternative models of state structures and ideologies that might be better suited to the achievement of democratic development. If the particular postcolonial historical form of India's "stateness" is wholly inappropriate to aiming for means-using developmental imperatives, "statelessness" might be equally antithetical to democratic aspirations. This is why the project of decentering the discourse of development has to do more than resurrect "indigenous" forms of antimodernism with a deeply ingrained aversion to the state. Pranab Bardhan has recently underlined the trace of patronizing elitism running through much of what he has termed the "anarcho-communitarian critique" of the state and development (Bardhan 1996). Undiscriminating denunciations of an ill-defined "modernity" and uncritical eulogies of "tradition," "community," and, most recently, "the fragment," achieve little more than an inversion of the old and worn tradition-modernity dichotomy. The problem of reconfiguring the relationship between nationalism, democracy, and development needs to be relocated in the very different context of the dialectic between domination and resistance, privilege and deprivation at the global, national, and local levels.[12]

The call for a thorough decolonization of both the idea of development and institutions of state may sound like a tall order in the current conditions of drift in civil society and crisis of the centralized state. Yet the atmosphere of uncertainty and flux affords opportunities for a fresh round of rethinking and restructuring fifty years after the decisions of expediency which characterized formal, political decolonization. A major reorientation of the terms of public debate already seems underway to recapture the values that had informed the early initiatives of national development. There is a growing recognition that the development debate in India should be taken "well beyond liberalization" and the spotlight redirected toward "expanding social opportunities" (Dreze and Sen 1995). The economic reforms pursued by the Congress government from June 1991 to May 1996 addressed only the first part of a two-part problem facing Indian economic development. This was largely because a significant paradigm shift in 1991 was triggered by a particular balance-of-payments crisis and not by an overall reassessment of the country's economic trajectory. So the reformers concentrated on redressing the negative effects of overintervention by the state in certain sectors and removing the more stifling bureaucratic controls on industry. They moved tardily, if at all, to rectify state negligence of critical social sectors, notably, health and education. The political costs of pursuing a lopsided reform process appear to be enabling the long-forgotten intrinsic values of development to reenter the discourse, but the failed institutions of state have yet to be imaginatively refashioned. On the one hand, the privileged but besieged defenders of the centralized monolith have resorted to the dangerous course of a bigoted religious majoritarianism. On the other, the new populism of the 1996 United Front government in New Delhi, of which several regional parties are members, is displaying deep taints of localism and agrarianism while proclaiming solidarity with the aspirations of the poor and disadvantaged majority. Actual allocations have not, at the moment of writing, matched the resurgence of pro-poor rhetoric. The successful realization of the idioms of equitable development requires the appropriate instruments, both economic and political. Simple-minded decentralization will provide little help in that direction and mindless anti-statism may well prove counterproductive. Anticolonial thought, if not the actual denouement of nationalist politics, was never so impoverished as to be contained within the stark dichotomies of centralism and localism, Nehru and Gandhi. Indeed, most thoughtful anticolonial activists would have been surprised if they were told that a substantial measure of autonomy for regions and communities could not be combined with a radical, redistributive impulse from a negotiated center. Any number of "constitutions" of the Indian Union—from the hair-brained to the highly sophisticated—had vied in the realm of ideas with the one that was adapted in 1950 from the colonial Government of India Act of 1935. If the dismantling of the structures and ideologies of the postcolonial state is long overdue, it needs to be reconstituted on the basis of careful consideration of proposals, old and new, for a state of union presiding over a multilayered, democratic political system and functioning on terms forged by its various constituent units.

If the postmodern quest for decentered democracy is not to fall into the embrace of a conservative, economic elitism and unbridled capitalism in its attempt to escape the clutches of the antidemocratic modern state, it must be able to come forward with alternative democratic models of state. The history of development had been marred in its early stages by the tainted history of the politics of decolonization, characterized by the inheritance of state structures rather than the rebuilding of new ones from the very foundations. Any attempt to historicize development underscores the imperative to fashion the instruments to realize the idioms which remain as salient as ever to democratic aspirations in the postcolonial world.

NOTES

1. An earlier version of this paper was presented at the workshop on "Historicizing Development," the first of three in the Social Science Research Council series on "Development Knowledge and the Social Sciences," held on December 10–12, 1993, at Emory University, Atlanta. I am grateful to the workshop organizers and participants, especially Fred Cooper, Randall Packard, and Michael Watts for their helpful comments.

2. "The Tiger Steps Out" is the caption of the next "Survey of India," published three and a half years later (*Economist* 1995).

3. Interview of Vaclav Klaus, then Finance Minister of Czechoslovakia and later Prime Minister of the Czech Republic with Sarmila Bose, *Ananda Bazar Patrika*, April 1990, cited in Sarmila Bose (1993).

4. On the distinction between "mean enhancement" and "means use," see Sen (1989: 373–80).

5. Ludden defines a development regime as "an institutionalized configuration of power within a state system ideologically committed to progress that draws its material sustenance from the conduct of development" (1992: 252).

6. On the lasting legacy of the centralized colonial state apparatus in postcolonial South Asia, see Jalal (1995).

7. I am quoting from Chatterjee's essay entitled "Development Planning and the Indian State" in Byres (1993). A slightly modified version of the same essay

appears as the chapter entitled "The National State" in P. Chatterjee (1993b). Chatterjee does not use the word "idiom," which I have introduced to clarify the aspects of legitimacy and instrumentality in the exercise of development planning.

8. "I hope you will accept the Chairmanship of the Planning Committee," Subhas Chandra Bose wrote to Jawaharlal Nehru on October 19, 1938. "You must if it is to be a success" (Nehru 1989: 301). The fifteen-member committee comprised of five scientists (Nazir Ahmed, V. S. Dubey, J. C. Ghosh, A. K. Saha, and Meghnad Saha); four industrialists/businessmen (Walchand Hirachand, Ambalal Sarabhai, A. D. Shroff, and Purushottamdas Takurdas); three economists (Radhakamal Mukherjee, K. T. Shah, and M. Visvesvaraya); and three politicians (N. M. Joshi, a labor leader; J. C. Kumarappa, a believer in Gandhian village communities; and Jawaharlal Nehru).

9. "The other day I have had a long and interesting discussion with Dr. Meghnad Saha about Scientific Planning for Indian Industry; I am convinced about its importance and as you have consented to act as the President of the Committee formed by Subhas for the guidance of the Congress, I would like to know your views on the matter," wrote Rabindranath Tagore to Jawaharlal Nehru on November 19, 1938 (Nehru 1989: 304).

"He [Tagore] has been rather captivated by Dr. Saha's ideas of Rational Planning and he is hoping much from the Committee. He wanted to talk to you, before you took up any *other* work, lest you, by force of events, got yourself cut off effectively from the Planning Committee's work. . . . He also wants a 'modernist' to be the Congress President for next year, so that, the Report when finished would be warmly accepted by the All-India Congress and not just shelved up. In his opinion—and in the opinion of us all too—there are only two genuine modernists in the High Command—you and Subhasbabu. Your active cooperation is already secured by your being Chairman of the Planning Committee and he therefore is very eager to see Subhasbabu again elected the President," wrote Anil K. Chanda to Jawaharlal Nehru (Nehru 1989: 308).

10. I have engaged in a more detailed discussion of alternative models of nation and state in anticolonial thought in Bose (1996).

11. Meghnad Saha was elected to Parliament in 1952 from Calcutta by defeating the Indian National Congress as an independent candidate with the support of the leftist parties. Of particular interest is his pamphlet "Rethinking Our Future: An Objective Review of the Report of the Planning Commission and Its Industrial Programme" (S. Chatterjee 1987: 532–637). In addition to his trenchant criticisms of India's postcolonial development policies, he denounced the Congress government's reneging on its long-standing promise of linguistic reorganization of states in the name of the state's integrity and administrative convenience (S. Chatterjee 1993a: 528–554). He also dissented from the state's decision to "concentrate" nuclear physics research, calling for a more decentralized structure so as not to "smother all fundamental research and choke the growth of knowledge" (S. Chatterjee 1993b: 175).

12. For a more elaborate statement of an argument about ways to reevaluate nationalism, reinvigorate democracy and reconstitute development, see Bose and Jalal (1996).

REFERENCES

Apffel Marglin, Frederique, and Stephen Marglin, eds. 1990. *Dominating Knowledge: Development, Culture and Resistance.* New York: Oxford University Press.

Bardhan, Pranab. 1985. *The Political Economy of Development in India.* Delhi: Oxford University Press.

———. 1992. "A Political-Economy Perspective on Development". In *The Indian Economy: Problems and Prospects,* edited by Bimal Jalan, 321–37. Delhi: Viking.

———. 1996. "The State Against Society: The Great Divide in Indian Social Science Discourse". In *Nationalism, Democracy and Development: State and Politics in India,* edited by Sugata Bose and Ayesha Jalal, 184–95. Delhi: Oxford University Press.

Basu, Kaushik. 1990. "Indian Economy: Performance and Policy". In *The Indian Economy and Its Performance since Independence,* edited by R. A. Choudhury, Shama Ghamkar, and Aurobindo Ghose, 106–112. Delhi: Oxford University Press.

Bhagwati, Jagdish. 1993. *India in Transition: Freeing the Economy.* Oxford: Oxford University Press.

Bose, Sarmila. 1993. "To Market, To Market: Economic Reform and Industry in India and Eastern Europe". Mimeograph (Warwick Manufacturing Group).

Bose, Sisir K., and Sugata Bose, eds. 1995. *The Collected Works of Netaji Subhas Chandra Bose Vol. 9: Congress President, Speeches, Articles and Letters January 1938–April 1939.* Calcutta: Netaji Research Bureau. Delhi: Oxford University Press.

Bose, Sugata. 1996. "Nation as Mother: Representations and Contestations of India in Bengali Literature and Culture". In *Nationalism, Democracy and Development: State and Politics in India,* edited by Sugata Bose and Ayesha Jalal, 50–75. Delhi: Oxford University Press.

Bose, Sugata, and Ayesha Jalal, eds. 1996. *Nationalism, Democracy and Development: Reappraising South Asian States and Politics.* Delhi: Oxford University Press.

Byres, Terence J., ed. 1993. *The State and Development Planning in India.* Delhi: Oxford University Press.

Chakravarty, Sukhamoy. 1987. *Development Planning: The Indian Experience.* Delhi: Oxford University Press.

Chatterjee, Partha. 1986. *Nationalist Thought and the Colonial World: A Derivative Discourse?* London: Zed Books.

———. 1993a. "Development Planning and the Indian State". In *The State and Development Planning in India,* edited by Terence J. Byres, 51–72. Delhi: Oxford University Press.

———. 1993b. *The Nation and Its Fragments.* Princeton: Princeton University Press.

Chatterjee, Santimoy, ed. 1987. *Collected Works of Meghnad Saha Vol. 2.* Calcutta: Saha Institute of Nuclear Physics. Bombay: Orient Longman.

———, ed. 1993a. *Collected Works of Meghnad Saha Vol. 3.* Calcutta: Saha Institute of Nuclear Physics and Bombay: Orient Longman.

———, ed. 1993b. *Collected Works of Meghnad Saha Vol. 4.* Calcutta: Saha Institute of Nuclear Physics and Bombay: Orient Longman.

Das, Chittaranjan. 1982. "Swaraj Scheme, January 1923". *Oracle.* 4, no. 1 (January), reprint.

Dreze, Jean, and Amartya Sen. 1995. *India: Economic Development and Social Opportunity.* Delhi: Oxford University Press.

Dutt, Romesh C. 1904. *Economic History of India.* Vol. 2, *In the Victorian Age* London: K. Paul, Trench, Trubner.

Economist. 1991. "The Tiger Caged: A Survey of India". (May 4).

———. 1995. "The Tiger Steps Out: A Survey of India". (January 21–27).

Gandhi, Mahatma. 1958. *The Collected Works of Mahatma Gandhi.* New Delhi: Publications Division, Government of India.

Jalal, Ayesha. 1995. *Democracy and Authoritarianism in South Asia: A Comparative and Historical Perspective.* Cambridge: Cambridge University Press.

Ludden, David. 1992. "India's Development Regime". In *Colonialism and Culture,* edited by Nicholas Dirks, 247–87. Ann Arbor: Michigan University Press.

Nandy, Ashis. 1983. *The Intimate Enemy: Loss and Recovery of Self under Colonialism.* Delhi: Oxford University Press.

———, ed. 1988. *Science, Hegemony and Violence: A Requiem for Modernity.* Tokyo: The United Nations University.

———. 1989. "The Political Culture of the Indian State". *Daedalus* 118, no. 4: 1–25.

Naoroji, Dadabhai. 1901. *Poverty and Un-British Rule in India.* London: Sonnenshein.

Nehru, Jawaharlal. 1989. *A Bunch of Old Letters.* Centenary edition. Delhi: Oxford University Press.

Robertson, A. F. 1984. *People and the State: An Anthropology of Planned Development.* Cambridge: Cambridge University Press.

Sen, Amartya. 1983. "Development: Which Way Now?" *Economic Journal* 93: 745–62.

———. 1989. "Indian Development: Lessons and Non-Lessons". *Daedalus* 118, no. 4: 369–92.

TWO

Modernizing Bureaucrats, Backward Africans, and the Development Concept

Frederick Cooper

Colonial governments in the 1940s thought of development as an idea which would reinvigorate colonialism, but it turned out to be central to the process by which colonial elites convinced themselves that they could give up colonies. French and British officials believed that their development initiatives would make colonies simultaneously more productive and more ideologically stable in the tumult of the postwar years; they sent waves of experts to Africa to refashion the way farmers farmed and workers worked, to restructure health and education. Postwar imperialism was the imperialism of knowledge. But within a scant ten years, the developmental initiative had lost its reformist zeal, and instead of development being a colonial initiative—requiring authority as well as expertise—it was being discussed as a natural unfolding of a universal social process, which human agents could facilitate but which was driven by history. As such, it could be administered by Africans as well as Europeans. Unlike other justifications of empire, development came to have as strong an appeal to nationalist elites as to colonizers. In the end, Africans took over the development project along with the state apparatus built by the colonial regime, and the departing colonizers could convince themselves that their successors would inevitably trod the path they had laid out.

The question this leaves is why Africa ended up with a development project framed in a particular way. This chapter—which is an early formulation of a new research project—takes up part of that question, focusing on the thinking of imperial bureaucracies in the postwar years. First, I situate the development initiative in the imperial crisis of the 1940s. Then, I begin to explore the conceptual categories through which French and British bureaucrats approached the development problem, looking at the implicit social theory behind economic policy. Here, I run into a striking feature of imperial discourse at the most senior levels: the Africa France and Great Britain sought to develop was not the complex, varied, changing social field African historians have now shown it to be, but a flat, unchanging, primitive landscape. Development was something to be done *to* and *for* Africa, not with it. I next look at the disillusionment with the development drive beginning to become evident in the early and mid 1950s, reflected in the enormity of primitive Africa which both governments felt they had to remake. What emerges from all this is the dualism in colonial thinking: a modern future set against a primitive present. It was a brittle conception of change, but its very abstraction allowed France and Great Britain to preserve their sense of future mission even as they acknowledged that they could not manage its present. Finally, I open up (and no more than that) the connection of the modernizing thought of the colonial bureaucracies to modernization theory in the social sciences, notably the dualistic approaches in economics that came into fashion in the 1950s.

THE IMPERIAL CONTEXT OF DEVELOPMENT

France and Great Britain came to their postwar development initiatives via different paths. In both cases, the idea of economic progress had much deeper roots, and in both cases governments had long supported initiatives to "open" Africa—especially railway, road, and port construction. But more explicit and ambitious schemes in the 1920s were rejected. The colonial ministers of Great Britain and France, Lord Milner and Albert Sarraut, proposed the use of metropolitan funds to overcome the barriers to expanding colonial production. Their initiatives were rejected by governments not ready to give up the tradition of colonial self-sufficiency, believing that limited capital resources were better spent in the metropole, and fearing that development would disrupt colonial societies (Constantine 1984; Havinden and Meredith 1993; Marseille 1984; Coquery-Vidrovitch et al 1988). Both regimes were happy to take what they could get from African cash crop growers or private European initiatives—and colonial states supported (and at times compelled) such efforts in a variety of ways, but at the cost of colonies' resources themselves. They also pioneered what was later assimilated into the development framework: actions, notably in the domains of health, agriculture, urbanism, and transport, that were most often seen as technical but which also constituted authoritarian interventions into African society in the name of the general good (Anderson and Grove 1987; Beinart 1984; Vaughan 1991; Packard, this volume).

The depression deepened this backward imperialism on the ground, even as it began to undercut self-confidence in London or Paris. Declining economies sloughed off their social security problems into the country-side. The misnamed Colonial Development Act of 1929—advertised to Parliament as a social imperialist measure, creating jobs in England making steel for colonial railways—didn't do much to accomplish even that. France and Britain adopted more mercantilist trade policies, seeking to use the empire as a unit that could save itself. This protected the mediocrity of colonial economies. In France, the Popular Front sketched out another plan for colonial investment along Sarraut's lines—both underscored and undercut by claims that such a policy would harmonize the interests of colonial and metropolitan subjects and allow Africans to improve themselves in the context of their own communities. Arguments for the use of planning in order to build a colonial economy "in the general interest" began to be heard. The development fund never received government approval, and the main benefit Africans received from the Popular Front was a temporary easing of the burden of forced labor (Mérat 1936; Cotte 1981; Marseille 1984).

The break occurred first in British colonies, after the economy got better and social conflict got worse. The anxious rethinking among metropolitan leaders that led to Keynesian economics was part of the story. But what explains the timing and the fact that this thinking actually penetrated the political process was what the British called "disturbances" in the colonies. The most critical ones took place in Trinidad and Jamaica in 1935, 1937, and 1938. They began as strikes in key industries, but became general strikes and led to riots, including some in plantation areas of Jamaica. The 1935 copper mine strike in Northern Rhodesia was part of this too: the strike spread from mine to mine, brought in nonminers, including women, in the mine towns, spread without benefit of a trade union via religious groups, dance societies, personal networks, and mass meetings. There were strikes in the Gold Coast in 1939 as well as a cocoa selling boycott in 1937–1938, and a general strike in Mombasa in 1939. All these events were far more than industrial relations problems, bringing in a mass of people sharing common poverty and subordination and lacking permanent jobs and career possibilities. The investigating committee in the copperbelt saw "detribalization" as a danger but thought it could be solved by repatriating workers after contracts; they were wrong and a second strike occurred in 1940. The committee in Mombasa said the opposite but could not do anything about it: port labor should be decasualized, allowing controlled housing to be devoted to a compact, steadily working dock force, and enabling this body of men to be separated from the urban mass with whom it had made common cause (Cooper 1996).

The West Indies Royal Commission report was so critical that it was suppressed until the end of the war—it saw disorder as the result of unremedied legitimate grievances and called for metropolitan efforts both to increase production and employment and to remedy the miserable state of social services.[1] But while the Royal Commission deliberated, Colonial Secretary Malcolm MacDonald was convinced that he could use the consternation caused by the West Indian riots to make a new initiative in colonial economy policy.[2]

The Treasury did not like to spend money and warned, in its wonderful choice of a word, against creating a colonial "dole." To this, the Colonial Office proposed to reply that spending money on education, health, a labor department, and other basic services would improve productivity and lead to growth which would help governments pay their bills—a human capital theory in today's parlance. But in an internal memo not intended for treasury eyes, one of the Colonial Office's top officials, George Creasy, commented that such arguments

> appear to me to lay too much emphasis on the desirability of making the African (or West Indian, etc.) into a more efficient producer or labourer for the needs of the country. This is a point which, of course, will appeal to the Treasury. . . . I feel, however, that so far as the Colonial Office is concerned our real aim should be the more general one of turning the African into a happier, healthier more prosperous individual in which case all the other subsidiary objects will automatically be attained.

MacDonald added "if we are not now going to do something fairly good for the Colonial Empire, and something which helps them to get proper social services, we shall deserve to lose the colonies and it will only be a matter of time before we get what we deserve."[3]

The closet paternalists of the Colonial Office won passage of the Colonial Development and Welfare Act of 1940, and spent its funds largely on services, above all those intended for urban workers—water, health facilities, housing, education—although the constraints on supplies and shipping were such that not much could be used until the end of the war. The Colonial Office argument for a trickle-up effect was no more clearly spelled out than later arguments for trickle down, but it was a breakthrough in spending imperial funds—grants, not just loans—without social imperialist justification. Officials saw the word "welfare" as a disavowal of intention to exploit the colonies more efficiently.[4] Indeed, an implicit theory of the relationship of economic change and social protest lay behind the discussion within the Colonial Office: welfare—social services in the short run and a higher standard of living in the long—was the antidote to disorder. Even as the colonial strike wave exposed the complexity of labor issues, London was trying to shoehorn the labor question into the development question.

But the labor question would not stay put. Chronic labor unrest during the war forced officials on the spot to grapple with labor issues on their

own terms: as complex questions of how workers were to live and reproduce themselves. The government created labor bureaucracies alongside
its growing development bureaucracy and opened a dialogue with African
trade unionists in the hope that workers' protests could be channeled into
a framework similar to that of industrial relations in the metropole.[5]

In the midst of this, the most talented economist within miles of White-
hall, W. Arthur Lewis, resigned as secretary of the Colonial Office's economic advisory committee. He argued that the bureaucrats were narrowly
defining issues that the committee was being allowed to raise, including
studies of the question of whether African farming units were "uneco-
omically small" and how to plan for industrial development. The Colonial
Office did not want such "political" questions even discussed in its advisory committee.[6] Lewis was talking about an issue of discourse: the boundary of what could be debated.

In 1944, as the Colonial Secretary, Oliver Stanley, asked Parliament to
double the funding of the Colonial Development and Welfare Act, he was
still hesitating between bold initiative and limited promises. Stanley noted,
"Nothing could be worse than to give Colonial peoples the impression
that the Colonial Development and Welfare Act was a permanent subsidy
to their social services which the taxpayer of this country would undertake
to pay without thought either of return, or indeed of supervision." He
was moving toward the human capital theory that his predecessors covertly
rejected: metropolitan funding for social services could be justified for
their contribution to colonial production, but that production would
eventually have to pay for those services. He was serving notice that the
British Empire was not a single unit, in which all subjects could claim a
similar standard of living, and he thereby turned attention to the productionist side of the development-welfare nexus.[7]

In wartime France, meanwhile, the Vichy regime revived the idea of a
metropolitan-directed and financed development plan—a ten-year plan
this time—and stripped away much of its predecessors' ambivalence about
it. Vichy officials mocked the timidity of those who feared that development in the colonies, including industrialization, would upset the social
order; they could keep things under control. Jacques Marseille (1984)
asserts that this plan demonstrates that the right-wing Vichy planners were
less trapped in the colonial past and more willing to let Africans share in
social change than their left-wing predecessors and successors who wanted
to maintain Africa in its agrarian role. Actually, what was visionary about
Vichy was pure fantasy, and what wasn't fantasy was brutal.

Corporatist structures in each economic branch would plan the optimal
activities for each region; European techniques would remake African agriculture; firms would "watch over [the worker's] health, his hygiene, and
his comfort." There was a little problem: "the repugnancy of the native

to wage labor." The answer was a legal obligation to work. Claiming that "the problem of labor must nevertheless by studied seriously, scientifically," Vichy's planners thought that corporatist organization and discipline would solve the development and the labor problem together. The end would be rapid growth of "production and income of peoples, not only the evolved people but the two billion individuals who inhabit our planet."[8]

In French West Africa at this time, largely cut off from European commerce by France's defeat, the lack of imports gave workers virtually no incentive to seek wage labor, and production depended more than ever on forced labor. Governor General Boisson kept warning Vichy that the limits of coercion had already been reached, even in the absence of the Ten Year Plan. To Boisson this level of forced recruitment exposed his own administration to danger, and it confirmed his own essentialist reading of Africa: "Africa is peasant, it must in its necessary evolution remain peasant." Boisson was all but threatened from Vichy for suggesting that labor shortages might limit the development initiative. But his reports were mild compared to the evidence of brutality that later emerged from French West Africa (Boisson 1942; Fall 1993; Cooper 1996).

While the Free French, taking over from Vichy, exposed and repudiated the forced labor regime, they insisted that free labor was so hard to get that they could only gradually wean themselves from coerced recruitment. Officials meeting at Brazzaville early in 1944 went back to something like the Popular Front's approach: reducing the importance of French settlers and lowering the pressure on African communities to supply labor over five years. African society was seen to be the remedy for two problems: the insufficiency of production would be countered by letting African communities grow more crops, enhanced by the organization of rural cooperatives, and population shortage would be countered by letting Africans reproduce within the community setting, with their notions of marriage and family. The new-old *plan d'équipement* would improve infrastructure so that African communities would be linked to the colonial marketing network, and mechanization would keep labor demands as low as possible. Conferees debated whether too much industrialization would cause socially disruptive proletarianization or whether too little would condemn Africa to backwardness. The concluding formula—"prudent industrialization"—suggested that the issue had not been dealt with. The conferees did not make a clear break with the old *pacte coloniale*, a division of labor between an industrial metropole and agricultural colonies, and they finessed a crucial issue: Who would make sure that development would be simultaneously beneficial to African welfare and the imperial economy? The claim of mutual benefit depended on an assertion of central imperial control: planning—"une économie dirigée et planifiée"—appears in the Brazzaville texts more as a mantra than a program.[9]

The claim to mutual benefit bolstered the assertion that the empire would remain unified, relabeled the Union Française. The *évolués*— French-educated Africans—would get an increasing voice in the Union's affairs not by the granting of more autonomy to individual territories, but by the possibility to elect representatives (with a limited franchise and a limited number of seats) to the Assemblée Nationale in Paris. Actually, these reforms were more far-reaching than French leaders realized—the logic of shared membership in the Union Française would provide a basis for claims to assimilation and equality that could not be contained. But even here, the particular sociology behind economic development and political reform in the French empire emerges: a two-class model of colonial society, divided into *évolués*, who could be brought into French institutions, and a majority of *paysans* whose conditions of production, reproduction, and political interaction did not have to be examined at all. Neither wage workers nor an African petite bourgeoisie had a place in official sociology.[10]

But France did make one decisive break with the past: in 1946, with little debate in the legislature, it passed the Fonds d'Investissement et de Développement Economique et Social (FIDES), ending the tradition of colonial self-sufficiency and making available metropolitan funds for development projects. FIDES was accompanied by a contradictory rhetoric, claims that a modern infrastructure would integrate African communities into commerce without changing their nature and that modern sectors would be built with simple European-style houses and up-to-date urban amenities. Within that sector, Africans would be "working in European style, that is with output analogous in quality and rapidity to that of workers from the Metropole. *Bricolage* must give way to technique."[11]

The ideological context in which Great Britain and France turned to development—the need to find a progressive basis for continued colonial rule in an era when major powers had made "self-determination" a slogan of international politics—coincided with the heightened needs both had for their empires. Battered by war, with Asian empires veering out of control, Great Britain and France saw Africa as the one place where new resources could be mobilized. Great Britain faced this imperative with particular acuity during the dollar crisis of 1947. The Labour Government's Minister for Economic Affairs, Stafford Cripps told the conference of African Governors in 1947, "the whole future of the sterling group and its ability to survive depends in my view upon a quick and extensive development of our African resources."[12] Great Britain's postwar Labour government embraced a productionist view of development more decisively than its Tory predecessors: so central was its need for African resources and so much did it fear accusations of exploiting the colonies that its ministers no longer discussed the relationship of development and welfare and the two were elided in public and secret discussion into a single concept. As the dollar drive continued into 1948 and 1949, more assertions appeared that colonial and metropolitan economics were "complementary" or "harmonious," although Cripps revealed the hierarchy of values by telling the very people whose poverty was being alleviated that their interests depended on the health of the British economy and they should be willing to sacrifice "unnecessary current consumption" for that end. And when Creech Jones summarized his ministry's achievements at the end of 1948, the "export drive" came first, dollar earnings and savings second, and social programs in Africa and the West Indies thirteenth.[13] Development discourse was increasingly equating development to growth—and not posing too many questions about the units whose growth was at issue.

It was because British Africa developed higher concentrations of workers at an earlier date—in the mines of Central Africa, ports like Mombasa, or complicated colonial systems like Nigeria—that the labor question was faced at an earlier date than in French Africa. Even so, officials—in London at least—kept trying to turn the labor question into something else. French officials, as the war ended, still thought the labor question could be avoided, or rather that the question was whether Africans would work for wages at all rather than what the social conditions of wage labor would be. London's sociology of development at war's end assimilated labor to welfare: if material conditions for workers came to some unspecified level of sufficiency (carefully kept apart from the metropolitan standard of living), then order could be preserved and the expansion of production could not be seen as exploitation. The momentous "and" in the Colonial Development and Welfare Act contained crucial questions that were not being asked, as did the French script for postwar development, run from France with the help of a small colonial elite assimilated to French culture who presided over an economy of peasants, producing and reproducing in ways that did not need to be understood.

THE SOCIOLOGY OF POSTWAR DEVELOPMENT

In London and Paris, African cultivators appeared very African: French colonial officials seemed to have accepted the old British view ("indirect rule") of coherent communities with their way of life, while their British counterparts were just beginning to think of the rural world as offering more dynamic possibilities than that. In both cases, the terms in which high officials generalized about what they perceived to be African backwardness suggest that the notion of development was a highly abstract one, focused on an endpoint, not a process of moving forward from a constrained but dynamic present. The productive cocoa farmers of the Gold Coast or western Nigeria were well known to local officials but did not figure in the intense discussions of "agricultural development" held in London in 1946 and 1947.

Labour's Colonial Secretary, Arthur Creech Jones, referred to Africans as "raw and ignorant"; a Governor in 1947 encompassed the continent as "a great mass of human beings who are at present in a very primitive moral, cultural and social state." When it came to agriculture, officials were willing to damn African practices and think about harsh and crude remedies. Sydney Caine, head of the Colonial Office's economic department, thought "African systems of land tenure and the cultural routines associated with them, if maintained to the full in their traditional form, would effectively prevent any rapid technical change, possibly any change at all." He noted that officials with whom he was conferring were willing to "accept a quite substantial degree of compulsion in the introduction of agricultural and other improvements." He himself thought colonial peoples, West Indians included, were

> inferior in efficiency as manual labourers and in initiative, enterprise and organising ability as entrepreneurs and managers to the average of this and other countries which are advanced in the western sense. We cannot reject entirely the possibility of innate racial inferiority, but there is certainly insufficient reason at present to accept that explanation. Climatic and living conditions and a social structure which . . . is inimical to change, and therefore to enterprise, are at least substantial factors in this inferiority.

Creech Jones—long opposed to forced labor—now agreed that "economic development in the agricultural sphere is at present held back by the low standard of productivity of the African peasant, by his unwillingness to adopt improved agricultural methods and by his failure to take proper measures for the conservation of the soil," and he too concluded that compulsion would have to be used if African peasants didn't shape up.[14]

The architects of postwar development thus wanted Africa to have a completely different agricultural system, and hadn't much idea how to reform the current one. The Governors' Conference of 1947 was informed that the time of "the individual family working with primitive tools" was gone "and that radical changes in the system of agriculture are required to permit operations on a larger scale, with increased use of mechanical assistance and with the basic object of increased productivity." Some thought was given to encouraging plantation agriculture, and some to other ways of increasing scale. But officials pulled back, as contemptuous of the possibility of an African landlord class as of African small-holders.[15]

The quest for the "progressive farmer" sat uneasily with habits of supporting "traditional" authorities, and condemnation of practices of African agricultural techniques coexisted with distrust of the very farmers who separated themselves from past practices. Many rural interventions relied on agricultural extension officers to cajole and coerce African cultivators to conserve the soil, fight plant diseases, and use better tools and equipment. The madcap quality of the British Groundnut Scheme or the French Office du Niger—huge agricultural projects directed like military operations—makes a little sense when one considers how little officials trusted Africans' market responsiveness with the vital task of supplying vegetable oil to the English working class or cotton to France's mills (Low and Lonsdale 1976: 12; Moore and Vaughan 1994: 110–28; Havinden and Meredith 1993: 276–83).

French colonial discourse at times seemed to be looking back to the peasant just as British discourse was looking toward mythic agricultural revolutions. But as expectations within the bureaucracy rose about what FIDES would accomplish, a similar discourse about the "primitiveness" of African cultivators emerged. "Unhappily," commented one report, "the current methods of land usage amount to 'agricultural nomadism'." Technical experts, police methods, and cooperatives were called upon to get the cultivator to stay put. Another official complained of the archaic methods of cultivation and the passivity and discouragement which led peasants to make do with a subsistence existence "without great effort" rather than try for something better.[16] In French Equatorial Africa, top officials felt they "were starting from zero." A conference to review plans was told that, "Unfortunately, this agriculture is entirely in the hands of Africans, and for this reason its development will certainly be fairly slow, because it will be necessary to act on the native, to teach him to rationalize his methods, to improve his product. . . . " A governor insisted that one had to press development projects in the face of a population that remained "frozen in anachronistic and archaic concepts and does not see the necessity to participate by a voluntary and reasoned effort in the progress of their country. *On the whole the masses are not yet socially ready to adapt to the norms of a renovated life.*"[17]

The bright spot was the Ivory Coast, where African farmers—freed since 1946 from the pains of forced labor—were increasing their output of coffee and cocoa. Local officials pointed out that by the early 1950s the Ivory Coast was accounting for over 40 percent of French West Africa's exports by volume and 64 percent of its foreign exchange earnings. But what is curious is how little officials wanted to know about the social and economic initiatives which made this possible. Officials wanted their cocoa and their prejudices too.[18]

In neither French nor British Africa were officials free to bring their visions of a new future to a *tabula rasa*. When they tried, they faced the social and political complexity of African countryside and city. Attempts to impose seemingly modern methods of soil conservation and agronomy on rural Africa led to enormous conflict (Beinart 1984; Throup 1987; Feierman 1990). In cities, British officials were reminded of what wartime inquiries into labor conflict had discovered, that a working class had come into being and its ability to survive and reproduce itself in urban conditions had to be a part of economic planning. When an extended strike movement—including a twelve-day general strike—disrupted Dakar and Senegal's other cities during a two-month period in early 1946, French officials realized that their bucolic dream was an impossibility and they would have to think seriously about the working class (Cooper 1996).

British and French officials both thought that the solution to the social problem lay in European knowledge of how to manage a working class. They began to separate out a compact body of men who would benefit from improved urban housing and resources and higher pay, who would acquire an interest in a specific career line, and who would bring their families to the city and become socialized and acculturated to urban life and industrial labor over generations. Officials thought trade unions would not only mold grievances into defined categories to which employers could respond, but that they would provide institutions through which workers would feel socially rooted in the city. This thinking was first developed in reaction to strike movements; it later became part of an argument for raising productivity articulated in such studies as the Kenyan *African Labour Efficiency Survey* of 1947 or the writings of the French Office d'Etudes Psychotechniques in the early 1950s. It became a rationale for raising minimum urban wages and for paying more to key workers in mines, docks, and railways, as well as for spending on housing and urban facilities under the Colonial Development and Welfare Act or FIDES.

The core of the argument was that the manner in which a working class reproduced itself—and the multigeneration process of altering culture—determined how that class would work and behave itself. In 1954, a conservative Colonial Secretary was convinced enough of the importance of stabilizing workers' families that he argued "even where the 'bachelor wage' still represents the supply price of labor, it may be below the level of wages necessary to secure efficient production."[19]

The wave of strikes of the late 1940s in both French and British Africa—and the major strikes of the 1950s—forced officials into an engagement with social life that went beyond the development framework. But it was not exactly the social life of workers in Africa's cities, ports, mines, and railways that was being thought about. It was the more abstract idea of a working class—bounded, differentiated, and self-reproducing—as well as the idea of a system of industrial relations to regulate disputes that appealed to officials. Officials knew little about urban living conditions, and they mainly wanted to know about budgets: what numbers should be plugged into calculations of what a family needed to reproduce itself.

Yet this mode of knowledge was turned to advantage by trade unionists: the very Eurocentricity of official thinking and the universalistic language in which it was expressed became the basis for claims. If officials wanted Africans to work like Europeans, they should pay them like Europeans. These arguments—especially in the centralized structures of French Africa—were hard to ignore, not least because officials very much wanted to believe Africans could be the predictable, orderly, productive people they thought they had come to know from decades of class conflict in Europe (Cooper 1996).

In the late 1940s, official discourse treated only one class as a class—the working class. If it was more a hoped-for class than one which existed, at least the fantasy was both positive and fairly specific. Neither farmers nor educated Africans were thought of as classes: the former were too caught up in disparate and backward cultures, too unattached to parcels of land or an agricultural vocation, to be analyzed in such terms; the latter were too young, and those who spoke in public were seen as having another sort of relationship—demagogue to mass—that superseded self-identification *as* an upper class. Officials hoped education would mold a responsible upper class while worrying if they would learn the right lessons, and some wished for a petty bourgeoisie—attached to property and to trade—to develop itself, amid skepticism that it would.[20] Still, discussions in London suggest that high-level debate went on with little attention to people like the West African merchants of Nigeria or Senegal who came closest to filling the bill; fantasized classes were more important than existing social groups. Paris gave more credit to its évolués, but like London it tried to bound the terrain of legitimate politics carefully, excluding the rebels of Madagascar or Cameroon, just as Great Britain excluded the forest fighters of Kenya who attacked the very idea of the colonial state's modernizing project.

What colonial governments—in hitching their aspirations for a politically legitimate and economically productive empire to the idea of development—had given up was their old claim to be presiding over immutably distinct peoples, of providing order to savage peoples and slowly bringing them into civilization. The acultural concepts of development and industrial relations presumed that Africans could function as producers, merchants, or workers much like anyone else.[21] There were two problems in this reconfiguring of hegemonic claims: they opened numerous points for contestation within the colonial powers' own discourse, and the claims were measurable in a way that assertions about "civilization" were not. Trade unions could point to inequality in wage rates, while colonial governments' own accountants could tell whether the development drive was paying off.

THE DEVELOPERS' DISILLUSIONMENT

The concept of economic development had been asked to bear an enormous amount of political and economic weight. It could not. It was not the possibility of economic change per se that was under strain, but the particular vision of it that colonial regimes developed: colonial projects were top-heavy, involving large inputs of planning and expert personnel, funneling material through a clogged infrastructure, and inadvertently putting African trade unions in a position where they could effectively block key nodes in the development network and thus claim more entitlements. A comprehensive review in 1952 of the economic and financial condition of French West Africa by a mission headed by Inspector Monguillot painted a bleak picture six years into the development era. French Africa's production costs were high compared with those of British Africa: wages were double, railway charges were higher, the profits of commercial firms were high, and the bureaucracy was large, well-paid, and growing. Exports had barely reached prewar levels despite the accomplishments of the Ivory Coast; they did not cover the cost of imports, considering both consumer items and capital goods. Development projects were often ill-conceived; they often failed to run a profit; and they burdened budgets with high running costs once they were done.[22]

The accountant's conception of the problem was vehemently contested by the Government of French West Africa, particularly in regard to social spending and labor costs. "I believe," said the Governor General, "that technical and social progress cannot be separated and should march together." Officials defended their labor policy, even if it pushed up wages, and insisted that removing racial distinctions from wage and benefit scales was politically necessary. The High Commissioner saw the roots of development as deeper than immediate returns to investment: "Progress, in this domain, can only be foreseen, alas! to be slow and difficult. The effort which is incumbent on the Administration, toward this end, must focus on the essential: to augment bit by bit the productive potential of the country."[23] The government in Paris was told that France was going to have to support Africa's productive "potential," not just its production, and France was not necessarily going to get anything out of this arrangement for a long time.

Even in social terms, the early results were problematic. The Governor

General, Cornut-Gentille, admitted, "the basic objective which was the elevation of the standard of living of the populations, has not been attained in a significant fashion." Deflecting unrealistic expectations onto others and implicitly deflecting blame onto African culture itself, he observed that Africans "are disappointed to find that progress is slower and more difficult than they imagined it to be in their simple and primitive spirit." The economic results of FIDES were meanwhile questioned in public. Tonnages exported from French West and Equatorial Africa had not regained their 1938 levels. The private capital expected to follow public was not forthcoming: only 20 percent of investment was coming from the private sector, versus 55 percent from the French taxpayer, 25 percent from the African.[24] Other inspections, reports, and evaluations showed not just mismanagement, but that FIDES was taking on a basically impossible task. The narrow, inadequate infrastructure that was the legacy of the previous fifty years of rule was choking on the capital goods being brought in; skilled labor was lacking; the weakness of urban facilities and the acute need for urban labor was leading to escalating demands from Africans; and the imbalances of the development effort were producing acute tensions among regions.[25] The "big push," as some economists at the time called the effort to concentrate resources to overcome barriers and break out of the vicious circle of poverty, was leading to a big clog. Not least important, the argument that development could solve a political and economic problem was losing its force.[26]

The commission studying overseas development in 1953 acknowledged that in the current circumstances France's attempt to "fulfill her strategic, political and social duties in the territories she is charged with administering . . . risks to lead us to the exhaustion of the Metropole and to growing difficulties in our territories. . . . " It still held clung to the belief that looking upon France and Africa as a "vast integrated unity" would lead to progress. But that required redoubled efforts "to reform the mores and customs, to lift them progressively from whatever they have of the primitive, and to lead them to a stage closer to civilized conceptions." In short, the planners were still insisting that Africans remake themselves in the name of Greater France. It all rang hollow, and such an argument opened up the possibility that France should give in to its exhaustion.[27]

Such an argument began to be taken seriously in public. In 1954, Pierre Mendes-France asserted that it was necessary to choose between Indochina and economic reform in France. In 1955 and 1956, some French commentators began to write about what they called "the Dutch complex": that the Netherlands became more prosperous when it lost its East Asian colony after the war. The journalist Raymond Cartier published in a popular magazine an account of wasted development spending, of territories so vast and so impoverished that they offered little to France.

He insisted on asking about each of France's African territories, "What is it worth? What does it cost? What does it bring in? What hopes does it allow? What sacrifices does it merit?" With Algeria and Indochina on his mind, he argued that African demands for self-government were growing and could not be prevented: "It is necessary to transfer as fast as possible as much responsibility to Africans. *At their risk and peril.*"[28] Cartier was in effect taking an old theme of colonialist writing—that Africa was poor and backward—and turning it from a rationale for colonizing into a reason for decolonizing.

What became known among France's intelligentsia as "Cartierisme" went against the imperial sentimentality shared in different versions by a right which wanted a wider field for French economic and political operations and a left which wanted a wider field for socialist reform. But as Jacques Marseille (1984) argues, the growing importance of intra-European trade and the prospect of the European Economic Community gradually tilted the argument toward the pragmatists, although it took the imperial figure of de Gaulle to convince the public that empire could be profitably surrendered. As early as 1956, French administrators were taking the crucial steps to devolve power and abrogate responsibility in Africa. The *Loi Cadre* (framework law) in effect gave elected territorial legislatures fiscal authority over their development and personnel budgets, telling them that if the territories wanted better social services and civil servants wanted better wages, the local taxpayers would have to pay for them.[29] But in withdrawing from the front lines of directed change—and reserving the right to decide how and where development aid should be provided—French officials did not deviate from the notion that their blueprint for a modern economy and a modern society retained its validity.

In Great Britain similar issues arose: in 1955, nearly a third of the CD&W funds appropriated in 1945 and 1950 remained unspent, mostly because the system was so clogged that spending more was "physically impossible," even though the original appropriation was regarded as modest in relation to the colonies' needs.[30] Unlike France, Great Britain hoped to manage the politics of declining empire by superintending the gradual evolution of self-government in its individual territories, each at its own pace. Officials made sure to put on the record that approaching self-government implied that territories "should bear an increasing part of the cost of their own development."[31] Imperial obligations were terminal.

Great Britain too moved toward a dispassionate assessment of the costs and benefits of continued imperial rule. As early as 1951, doubts were surfacing about the contribution that development in Africa could make to the imperial economy, and as Great Britain's economic troubles continued, officials looked inward as well as toward growing exchange with continental Europe.[32] As David Fieldhouse (1986: 23) puts it, the British polity, no longer offered "empire on the cheap," was not so sure it wanted the "expensive reformist empire" of the postwar era. Prime Minister Macmillan asked in January 1957

> to see something like a profit and loss account for each of our Colonial possessions, so that we may be better able to gauge whether, from the financial and economic point of view we are likely to gain or to lose by its departure. This would need, of course, to be weighted against the political and strategic considerations involved in each case.[33]

When the Official Committee on Colonial Policy, gave the cabinet its reply to Macmillan's request in September 1957, it concluded that

> the economic considerations tend to be evenly matched and the economic interests of the United Kingdom are unlikely in themselves to be decisive in determining whether or not a territory should become independent. Although damage could certainly be done by the premature grant of independence, the economic dangers to the United Kingdom of deferring the grant of independence for her own selfish interests after the country is politically and economically ripe for independence would be far greater than any dangers resulting from an act of independence negotiated in an atmosphere of goodwill such as has been the case with Ghana and the Federation of Malaya. Meanwhile, during the period when we can still exercise control in any territory, it is most important to take every step open to us to ensure, as far as we can, that British standards and methods of business and administration permeate the whole life of the territory.[34]

Here is what the calculation of interest had come down to: Great Britain could in most cases get little more economically out of a colonial rule than out of a cooperative postcolonial relationship; the once great empire could not, in these circumstances, risk offending the sensibilities of its one-time subjects.

Officials' best hope was that British discourse and practice had framed the question of governance, and that ex-colonies would become western-style nations. But they were not optimistic. In the next colony in line after the Gold Coast, Nigeria, officials decided that "we are unlikely to have long enough to complete our civilising and unifying mission." Uganda's politics were too divisive for decolonization to proceed favorably; Tanganyika was too "backward"; and Kenya needed British rule "for an indefinite period" even though such a position was "very difficult to maintain." Macmillan told a high-level advisory committee, "the long-term future of the African continent presented a sombre picture."[35]

By then Great Britain had already worked out in the case of the Gold Coast how this decolonization would be managed. There, Great Britain had found itself politically trapped, committed to an orderly transition to self-government but convinced that the one group with a claim to a popular mandate, the Conventional People's Party of Kwame Nkrumah, consisted of dangerous demagogues. Unable to find its mythic moderate alternative, officials finally accepted that Nkrumah's advent was inevitable, and their rhetoric underwent a remarkable transposition. The demagogue became the responsible leader, and his left-wing critics, particularly in the labor unions, became the dangerous demagogues.[36] Now, the transition had to be made successful, and the key concept in managing the transition was the "development" idea which had once been intended to make the state impervious to Nkrumah's kind. Andrew Cohen wrote from his high perch in the Colonial Office:

> Politically the object of the new constitution was to create a state of affairs in which representative Africans and European officials could co-operate in the process of social, economic and political development. But if development does not in fact take place, one of the main purposes of the new constitution fails to be achieved. Moreover once a stable African Government is established it is essential that Government should be able to show results in the sphere of economic and social development. Otherwise it was bound to disappoint the people and likely to lead ... to the transfer of power to irresponsible extremists.[37]

The British and Nkrumah—with development as their shared goal—guided the Gold Coast toward independence in 1957. Nkrumah, it turned out, could do some things that the British could not. Nkrumah had tried to use cocoa farmers' hostility toward programs to control plant disease against the colonial government; in power he sought tight control over cocoa producers and advocated disease-eradication programs, winning the grudging admission that he was "not altogether incapable of acting with responsibility and a certain amount of courage."[38] Nkrumah proved equally able to use means—both of co-optation and repression—to out-flank and contain the labor movement in ways his white predecessors had not (Jeffries 1978).

The argument of the Official Committee on Colonial Policy in 1957 for getting "British standards and methods" to "permeate" the life of the colony represented the best of what authorities could hope for in the late 1950s. And they did not expect to get it: being "ready" for independence was no longer a relevant criterion, and dictatorial tendencies or corruption were no longer an obstacle.[39] But a relationship would continue: trade, aid, and capital transfer—as well as continued evocation of development—would mark the hope that the model Great Britain or France had set would stay in place, no longer requiring European officials to implement it.

The bitter pessimism of the cabinet reports from 1957–1959 overlooked clear evidence of growth in exports and marketed output, of improved infrastructure and much expanded school systems, of better paid workers and newly functioning systems of industrial relations in at least some sectors of some colonies—all of which British officials boasted of in other contexts. But the sense of failure has much to do with the way the problem was framed in the first place: a single idea of "development" bringing together the raising of African standards of living and the reconstruction of the British economy, of "responsible" trade unions and respectable politicians, of "scientific" ideas applied by knowledgeable experts. When questioned by Macmillan in 1957, his officials could not demonstrate that colonial development produced any clear economic benefits for Great Britain itself, while it was equally unclear that colonies were emerging from their economic and political malaise. At the same time, officials—focusing on the end point of modernization—interpreted its absence as chaos and danger.

MODERNIZATION, DUALISM, AND ANALYSIS OF THE POSTWAR WORLD

The modernizing discourse of the bureaucrats predates the rise in the academy of what came to be known as modernization theory. The officials, like the scholars, needed a sense of where they were going, even as events were shattering their sense of control. They could read European history as a process of finding rational solutions to complex social problems. In shifting from one form of colonial authority to another, they were rejecting what was "traditional" in their own authority structures—the right to command, the assertion that the good ruler "knew his natives." In holding before themselves a vision of an Africa transformed by European techniques, institutions, and models, British and French planners were saying that while Africans, like anyone else, could become actors in labor unions and legislatures, officials themselves had the essential knowledge to build the stage and write the script. Modernizers were asserting the right to govern Africa for a time, and they did so on the basis that they knew what Africa should be like, even if it eventually governed itself.

My intent in these pages is not to chart the intellectual roots or the varieties of theories of development and modernization (see Arndt 1987 on economic development), but to point to the shared discursive terrain in which officials and scholars operated. Modernization theory, notably in its American variants, went further than most in posing a dichotomy of "tradition" and "modernity" and discussing the modernization process in terms of the end toward which it was moving. Modernization entailed a package, a series of co-varying changes, from subsistence to market economies, from subject to participant political culture, from ascriptive status systems to achievement status systems, from extended to nuclear kinship, from religious to secular ideology. For some leading exponents, this conception of change was an explicit alternative to communist progressivism.[40] The central tension between modernization as a project directed by those who understood it and modernization as a metahistorical process, driven by deeply seated forces, is evident in the scholarly literature as well as in official discourse.

I have analyzed elsewhere (Cooper 1996) the modernizers' vision of labor and industrialization: industrialism as a "way of life" extending itself around the world, providing imperatives for rational decision-making and hierarchical organization to which all must conform. Not all modernizers thought that every "traditional" society would be swept into a homogeneous modernity, but they warned that resistance would not preserve an alternative way of life but would condemn the resistors to the bottom of the labor market. Here, I wish to look briefly at the way in which the dichotomy of traditional and modern shaped the emerging field of development economics. The dual economy—divided between traditional and modern sectors—became a hallmark of 1950s development economics.[41]

The most rigorous dualistic theory was W. Arthur Lewis's "Economic Development with Unlimited Supplies of Labour," published in 1954. Lewis divided the economy of a less developed country in two, a traditional sector and a capitalist sector, and he argued that the central dynamic of development was moving people from one sector to the other. In the traditional sector, the marginal product of labor was often negligible, zero, or negative; in any case labor could be released from it at a wage determined by subsistence needs or by the average product of labor, rather than by the marginal product of labor as in a developed economy. Maintaining wages at that level would keep the surplus generated by the newly employed workers in the hands of capitalists, who would invest their profits in further production and job-creation, until the traditional sector was drained of its surplus labor. At that point, wages, agricultural productivity, and employment demand would assume a relationship characteristic of developed economies.[42]

Lewis's dual economy is strikingly parallel to dualistic industrial sociology: an economist who argues that a society exhibits a zero marginal product of labor is saying something very similar to an industrial sociologist calling a culture "traditional" or "primitive." Lewis himself contrasted the "economic darkness" of the traditional sector with the "fructification" that occurred when capital was applied to labor in the capitalist sector; the two sectors were "other worlds."[43]

The dynamic in Lewis's model was the movement of people from one sector to another—each sector had its characteristics which Lewis treated as given. Yet Lewis had long been (and remained) critical of plantation owners and imperialism generally, for deliberately keeping agricultural revenues down in order to lower wages. He separated the inequality generated by rent seeking and power—which he condemned—from the inequality generated by capitalist profits—which he argued was the key to economic development.[44]

His attack on old-style imperialism and his acceptance of state planning and intervention was consistent with Colonial Office thinking since 1940. He did not elide growth with raising workers' standard of living as British officials had been doing since the war. He argued on the contrary that wages had to be kept constant until surplus labor was absorbed, and economic development would over time have beneficial effects both for workers in the capitalist sector and the traditional sector; he discussed the factors that might or might not allow particular groups to benefit.[45] Lewis helped shape an emerging mainstream of development economics, looking toward a long-term reduction of global inequalities based on a mix of market mechanisms and state planning, both amenable to economic analysis.[46]

Lewis's argument is particularly interesting because of who he was: a West Indian intellectual, born in St. Lucia, educated at the London School of Economics, a man of two continents but not willing to think of himself as of two cultures:

> A low cultural level is one of the associates of poverty; much is made in nationalist circles of African art and music, but Africans are conscious that their music is not so great an artistic achievement as that of Beethoven, that they are without a literature, that their religions are on rather a low level, and that their kinship and other social patterns, which are such a joy to the anthropologist, are too frail to withstand the ferments of the twentieth century.[47]

He, as an economist and as a colonial intellectual, believed in the route he had taken: through education and wholehearted espousal of the social and cultural forms of modern society. Ruthless in his dissection of unproductive privilege, he was simultaneously a theorist of the end of empire and the rise of a universalistic development economics in which the elites of the former colonies and the former metropole could share a common ground.

CONCLUSION

How does one read what this colonial intellectual and social scientist was saying? At first glance, it looks like a parable of neocolonialism: the emergence of an international discourse that reproduces the dualism of the colonial relationship without its explicit racism and without its reliance on the direct exercise of political power by an imperial government. It was more complicated than that. Development ideology was originally supposed to sustain empire, not facilitate the transfer of power. Yet developmentalist arguments—about labor policy as much as economic planning—were something trade union and political leaders in Africa could engage with, appropriate, and turn back. This framework allowed them to pose demands in forms that could be understood in London or Paris, that could not be dismissed as "primitive." Political parties could assert that true development required sovereign control over a development apparatus, and colonial officials—committed now to social and economic progress as the markers of their success—needed to believe enough that Africans really aspired to a recognizable vision of modernity that this language had to be taken seriously, as indeed it was. Much as one can read the universalism of development discourse as a form of European particularism imposed abroad, it could also be read—as it was by Lewis—as a rejection of the fundamental premises of colonial rule, a firm assertion of people of all races to participate in global politics and lay claim to a globally defined standard of living.

One can see how a Lewis model of the dual economy could slip into the kind of orthodoxy that was a tendency within development economics for some years, with its homogenizing categories for the social and cultural trajectories it sought to modify ("LDC," "target population") and its narrow vision of growth. But development discourse did not fit neatly in such a box. An orthodoxy had not even been established when Latin American economists—in the late 1940s—were articulating a version of structuralist economics than denied the smug assumption of mutual benefit between "center" and "periphery" and insisted that less global exchange rather than more was the key to autonomous development (Economic Commission for Latin America 1951, Sikkink, this volume). Structuralism was to give birth to a radical critique of global capitalism—dependency theory—but also to policies of import substitution industrialism that worked their way into orthodoxy; theoretical engagement was far more complex than a dichotomy of neocolonial and anti-imperialist approaches. Within Africa, the developmentalist paradigm took various forms. In Senegal (Diouf, this volume), the first independent government looked away from the acultural dualism of Anglo-American theory toward French corporatist theorists who stressed the harmony of each social group. The Senegalese planning apparatus did the opposite of what French and British experts had done: it compiled a multivolume survey of each of Senegal's regions, emphasizing the ongoing dynamics of economic organization, the possibilities for change within them, and the ways in which local structures could be animated and empowered. This approach—like many "orthodox" projects—eventually failed, a victim of the continued power of

French firms and the ability of Senegalese elites to appropriate new structures for their rent-seeking activities.[48]

But the fact that an approach to development focused on local conditions and community mobilization was tried in Senegal suggests the openings as well as the closures around the elusive and multivalent concept of development. The issue is not simply the intrinsic merits or the intrinsic arrogance of a universalistic discourse. In the last half century, the political significance of development has shifted fundamentally. It did not simply spring from the brow of colonial leaders, but was to a significant extent forced upon them, by the collective actions of workers located within hundreds of local contexts as much as in an imperial economy. Development was supposed to reestablish imperial control over the agenda of government in the postwar era, but the vision of a reformed Africa was seized by African trade unionists, African political movements, and other social movements to insist—often in conflicting ways—that directed change must take into account the social and political needs of the people most concerned. Even as the evolution of national and international development apparatuses and development theories channeled aspirations in specific ways, the underlying belief that people of all origins should aspire to a better world inspired new challenges. In the 1940s and 1950s—and perhaps in the future—the meanings of development reflected the engagement of local mobilization with global discourses, and of local discourses with the global structure of power.

NOTES

1. The recommendations of this commission were published as a Parliamentary Paper in 1940 (Cmd 6174), the report itself in 1945 (Cmd 6607). See also Constantine (1984).

2. "Colonial Development: Note for the Chancellor of the Exchequer," incl. MacDonald to Simon, 11 October 1939, CO 859/19/7475, Public Record Office (hereafter PRO). When the cabinet appointed the Royal Commission, it was warned by MacDonald that if it recommended increased spending on the West Indies, "It would be disastrous to send a Royal Commission and then reject its proposals purely on financial grounds." Extract from Conclusions of Cabinet meeting, 15 June 1938, CAB 28 (38), in CO 318/433/1/71168, PRO.

3. George Creasy, Minute, 30 November 1939, to Draft Outline of Statement of Policy, and MacDonald, Minute, 14 January 1940, CO 859/19/7475, PRO.

4. Minute, H. M. Moore, 12 January 1940, CO 859/19/7475, PRO.

5. Within the Colonial Office, the Economics Department (headed by Sydney Caine) argued that raising the standard of living was impossible except from productivity gains, while political officials insisted that raising the standard of living was a necessity. In Nigeria and Kenya, Africans settled the dispute: strike waves made wage concessions imperative. Caine, Minute, 30 March 1940, CO 859/40/

12901/Part II; Orde Browne to Caine, 13 November 1941, and Caine to Orde Browne, 16 November 1941, Caine, Minute, 20 December 1941, CO 852/506/15; Governor Bourdillon to Moyne, 24 January 1942, and George Gator, Minute, 21 November 1942, CO 583/262/30519, PRO.

6. W. Arthur Lewis, Resignation minute, 30 November 1944, CO 852/586/9, PRO.

7. Minutes of Colonial Economic Advisory Committee, 19 December 1944, CO 852/588/2; *House of Commons Debates* (13 July 1943): cc. 48–64.

8. These comments come from meetings of the Groupements Professionnels Colonials, Comité Centrale, 10 March 1943, Commission des Questions Sociales, 5 February 1943, AE 51, Comité Centrale, 7 April 1943, AE 61, Archives Nationales, Section Outre-Mer (hereafter ANSOM); Mounier (1942: 75, 161–67).

9. Transcript of sessions of 2, 3 February 1944, and report of Commission de l'Economie Impériale, session of 1 February 1944, AP 2295/2, "Role et place des européens dans la colonisation," report to Brazzaville conference, 20 January 1944, AP 2201/7, Direction Générale des Affaires Politiques, Administratives et Sociales, "Programme général de la Conférence de Brazzaville," 28 December 1943, AP 2201/7, Mahé, "Rapport sur l'industrialization des Colonies," and transcript of session of 7 February 1944, AE 101/5, all in ANSOM; conference recommendations in *La conférence africaine française. Brazzaville 30 Janvier-3 Février 1944* (Brazzaville: Editions du Baobob, 1944), 60–61. On the continuities from the Popular Front through Vichy to Brazzaville, see Cotte (1981: 58–63).

10. The need to coordinate development efforts became an argument for political centralization. "Commission chargée de l'étude des mesures propres à assurer aux colonies leur juste place dans la nouvelle constitution française," sessions of 30 May and 27 June 1944, AP 214, ANSOM.

11. Assemblée Nationale Constituante, *Annales* 4 (12 April 1946): cc. 1756–58; Inspecteur Général des Travaux Publics des Colonies, "Plan d'équipement décennal des Territoires d'Outre-Mer. Afrique Occidentale Française, Section I: Dépenses d'intéret social et dépenses diverses. Notice justicative," 8 February 1945, 1Q 162 (74), Archives du Sénégal (hereafter AS).

12. Transcript of *African Governors' Conferenc*e, 12 November 1947, 40. Ernest Bevin, the Foreign Secretary, turned this hope into a developmental fantasy world, envisioning "great mountains of manganese" and other raw materials in Africa and asserting, "If only we pushed on & developed Africa, we could have U.S. dependent on us, & eating out of our hand in four or five years." Bevin quoted in Hugh Dalton diaries, 15 October 1948, cited in Pearce (1982: 95–96). For the *version française* of the we-absolutely-need-Africa argument, see Governor Roland Pré, speech to Conseil Général of Guinea, 22 October 1949, Agence FOM 393/5bis, ANSOM.

13. Arthur Creech Jones and Sir Stafford Cripps, speeches to *African Governors' Conference,* 1947; Creech Jones, Memorandum on "Development of Colonial Resources," CM (47)/75, 6 June 1947, CAB 129/12; Report of the Colonial Development Working Party, 1948, 4–5, CO 852/868/5; Colonial Development Working Party, Interim Report, 19 April 1948, PREM 8/923, PRO; Creech Jones to Stafford Cripps, 19 November 1949, Creech Jones Papers, Rhodes House, Oxford,

44/1, folios 133–36. "The Future Work of the Colonial Development Working Party," EPC(48)35, 27 April 1948, PREM 8/923, Creech Jones, speech, "Development of Backward Areas," 1949, and "Some Practical Achievements in the Colonies since the War," Colonial Office paper, 7 December 1948, Creech Jones Papers, 44/1 and 44/2, Rhodes House, Oxford University. Anxious officials thus were eager to join in the obsession with economic growth that was emerging among economists (Arndt 1978). See also Cowen (1984) and Cowen and Shenton 1991).

14. Creech Jones, speech to Governors' Conference, 1947, 22; Governor Mitchell of Kenya to Creech Jones, 30 May 1947, CO 847/35/47234/1/47; Sydney Caine, Minute, 23 April 1946, CO 852/1003/3; Creech Jones, Circular Despatch, 13 July 1948, CO 852/1003/4, PRO.

15. Report of the Committee on the Conference of African Governors, 22 May 1947, appendix 6: "The Economic Development of Agricultural Production in the African Colonies," CO 847/36/47238, PRO.

16. AOF, Inspection du Travail, Annual Report, 1951; Senegal, Rapport Economique, 1947.

17. Governor General Bernard Cornut-Gentille, "Memoire sur l'exécution du plan d'équipement en Afrique Equatorial Française pendant les exercises 1947–48 et 1948–49" (Brazzaville: Imprimerie Officielle); M. Moreau, from Togo, to Conférence d'Etudes des Plans, 29 November 1950, Compte Rendu, AE 169; "Observations et conclusions personnelles du Gouverneur Roland Pré, Président de la Commission d'Etude et de Coordination des Plans de Modernisation et d'Equipement des Territoires d'Outre-Mer," May 1954, mimeograph in library of ANSOM, emphasis in original.

18. H. de la Bruchollerie, "Note sur la situation économique de la Côte d'Ivoire au 1er janvier 1954," 1Q 656 (171), AS; Ivory Coast, Rapport Economique, 1950, 1951, 1952, 1953. There was a prewar "pro-peasant" literature, notably by Robert Delavignette and Henri Labouret. This was not renewed or superceded in the years after the war.

19. Oliver Lyttleton, Circular Letter, 2 June 1954, CO 859/810, PRO.

20. A coherent vision of an entire class structure imprinted on Africa—African urban property owners and a stable working class in cities, African landowners and rural wage earners in the countryside—appears in the *Report of the East Africa Royal Commission*, 1953–55. The report is notable for the absence of actually existing people in its orderly categories.

21. It is striking how quickly discussion of racial superiority was banned from colonial vocabularies in the 1940s, but arguments about culture took much the same form as earlier arguments about race. The difference was that cultural change seemed open to the individual, but Africans who chose not to make the transition were seen as willfully obstructionist rather than quaintly backward.

22. Monguillot, Report, 13/D 28 May 1952, AP 2306/10, ANSOM. For scholarly assessment of the development era, see Coquery-Vidrovitch (1988).

23. High Commissioner (Governor General) to Monguillot, 17 July 1952, and Directeur Général des Finances de l'A.O.F., to Monguillot, 5 May 1952, AP 2306/7; Directeur Général des Finances, marginal note on "Rapport concernant

l'évolution des dépenses de personnel depuis 1938 . . . " 22 July 1952, AP 2306/8; High Commissioner, marginal comment on Monguillot, "Situation financière du Budget Général de l'A.O.F.," 20 August 1952, AP 2306/16; High Commissioner to Monguillot, 5 August 1952, AP 2306/10, ANSOM.

24. "Allocution prononcée par Bernard Cornut-Gentille," opening of first session of the Grand Conseil de l'Afrique Occidentale Française, 7 May 1953; *Marchés Coloniaux* 416 (31 October 1953): 3053 and 426 (9 January 1954): 65–66.

25. Conférence des Etudes des Plans, 28 November–1 December 1950, AE 169; M. Huet, "Bilan du Premier Plan du Développement Economique et Sociale des Territoires d'Outre-Mer," nd [1952], AE 749, ANSOM; Roland Pré, "Observations et conclusions personnelles . . . "

26. This idea, based on work of P. N. Rosenstein-Rodan in the 1940s, was prominent among development economists of the early 1950s (Arndt 1987: 58).

27. Commission de modernisation et d'équipement des Territoires d'Outre-Mer, "Rapport général de la sous-commission de l'intégration métropole-Outre-Mer," nd [1953], PA 19/3/38, ANSOM.

28. Raymond Cartier, "En France Noire avec Raymond Cartier," *Paris-Match* 383 (11 August 1956): 38–41 (41 quoted), and 386 (1 September 1956): 39–41, (41 quoted); emphasis added. The importance of this debate is stressed in Marseille (1984: 11, 359, 373).

29. On the connection of the French government's inability to control personnel expenses and the "territorialization" effort of the *Loi Cadre*, see Cooper (1996: chapter 11).

30. Secretary of State Alan Lennox-Boyd, Circular, 21 February 1953, CO 852/1365, PRO; Cabinet Office, Agreed Minute of Commonwealth Economic Conference, 11 December 1952, ibid.; and Lennox-Boyd, *House of Commons Debates* 536 (2 February 1955), cc. 1117–18, 1123. On the disappointing record of development initiatives, see Havinden and Meredith (1993: 276–83, 295, 801–817).

31. Henry Hopkinson, *House of Commons Debates* 536 (7 February 1955): c. 1609; Chancellor of the Exchequeur, remarks at Cabinet Meeting, CM (56) 64th Conclusions, 11 September 1956, CAB 128/30, PRO.

32. "Production of Raw Materials in the Colonial Empire," Cabinet Economic Policy Committee Minutes, 9 March 1951, EPC 5 (51)3, CAB 134/228, reprinted in Hyam (1992: Part 2, 187–88). See also Goldsworthy (1994: Part 1, liv–lviii).

33. Prime Minister's Minute, 28 January 1957, CAB 134/155, PRO.

34. "Future Constitutional Development in the Colonies," Report by the Chairman of the Official Committee on Colonial Policy (Norman Brook), 6 September 1957, CPC (57) 30, CAB 134/1556, PRO, 5–6.

35. "Future Constitutional Development in the Colonies," Note by the Secretaries, 30 May 1957, CP (O) 5, CAB 134/1551; Memorandum by Secretary of State, "Nigeria," C 57 (120), 14 May 1957, CAB 129/87; Memorandum by Secretary of State, "Future Policy in East Africa," CPC (59) 2, 10 April 1959, CAB 134/1558; Minutes of Colonial Policy Committee, CPC (59) 1st meeting, 17 April 1959, ibid., PRO.

36. These rhetorical shifts can be traced in the Political Intelligence Reports in the late 1940s through the 1951 election, in CO 537, PRO.

37. Minute by Andrew Cohen, 14 April 1951, CO 96/826/31596, PRO.

38. W. L. Gorrell Barnes, "Some Notes on a Visit to the Gold Coast March 30th-April 5th 1951," 13 April 1951, CO 96/826/31596, PRO. See also Beckman (1976).

39. Minute by R. J. Vile on Gold Coast readiness for independence, 23 September 1954, CO 554/805, reprinted in Goldsworthy (1994: Part 2, 204–205).

40. Tipps (1973: 204). The best known example of anticommunist modernization theory is Rostow (1960). For an interpretation stressing the Cold War, see Gendzier (1985).

41. The dualism of the 1950s drew on, but was fundamentally different from that of J. H. Boeke (originally published 1942, revised in 1953). Boeke saw dualism as the result of "the clashing of an imported social system with an indigeneous social system of another style" following colonial conquest (p. 4). Boeke's concept was part of a critique of colonialism, but economists of the 1950s were concerned with the relationships of two sectors and what brought about their relationship was not their concern. Dualism thus became a seemingly natural characteristic of the underdeveloped economy, and the critical edge of earlier theories was lost. The dual economy concept was given the imprimatur of the United Nations (1951: 9; 1959: 12) as well as that of leading scholars.

42. Lewis (1954). Some of Lewis's ideas about surplus labor—although not the rigorous sectoral dualism—had antecedents in the work of P. N. Rosenstein-Rodan, particularly 1943. Wartime thinking about the postwar era was important to opening questions of planned investment within the economics profession and among policy advisors. See Arndt (1987: 43–48).

43. Lewis (1954: 141, 147–48). The traditional sector could include urban casual workers and petty traders, from whom siphoning off people would not mean loss of labor time collectively expended in doing their previous activities. Lewis (1955a: 193) favored labor stabilization policies, consistent with his desire to build a modern sector labor force.

44. Lewis (1954: 149, 159; 1939). For another view of Lewis's assumptions about the traditional sector—in particular whether repression is needed to maintain a constant wage rate—see Weeks (1971).

45. While locating the motor of development in the modern sector, Lewis (1954: 183–84; 1951; 1979) favored raising productivity and hence wages in the food-producing sectors.

46. See Arndt (1987), and for a study of how some of these ideas were applied in the late 1950s and 1960s to Africa's first independent state, Killick (1978).

47. Lewis (1955b: 97–98). Earlier, Lewis wrote, "The colonies are poor because the colonial peoples have not learnt how to master their environment. Their techniques and their tools are primitive; their hygiene deplorable; and their attitudes too frequently a fatalistic acceptance of their condition as inevitable." He advocated education, but one can read his 1954 theory as accepting that traditional society could not be so modified, and change could come about only by bringing people out of its embrace and into a modern sector. W. A. Lewis, "Principles of Development Planning," memorandum for Colonial Economic and Development Council, 11 April 1948, Fabian Colonial Bureau papers, Rhodes House, Oxford University, 67/1, item 1.

48. See also Sorum (1977) on the range of French thinking on decolonization and development, and for related arguments Bose and Gupta (this volume).

REFERENCES

Anderson, David, and Richard Grove, eds. 1987. *Conservation in Africa: People, Policies, and Practice.* Cambridge: Cambridge University Press.

Arndt, H. W. 1978. *The Rise and Fall of Economic Growth: A Study in Contemporary Thought.* Chicago: University of Chicago Press.

———. 1987. *Economic Development: The History of an Idea.* Chicago: University of Chicago Press.

Beckman, Bjorn. 1976. *Organizing the Farmers: Cocoa Politics and National Development in Ghana.* Uppsala: Scandinavian Institute of African Studies.

Beinart, William. 1984. "Soil Erosion, Conservationism and Ideas about Development: A Southern African Exploration, 1900–1960". *Journal of Southern African Studies* 11: 52–83.

Boeke, J. H. 1953. *Economics and Economic Policies of Dual Societies as Exemplified by Indonesia.* New York: Institute of Pacific Relations.

Boisson, Paul. 1942. *Contribution à l'Oeuvre Africaine.* Rufisque: Imprimerie du Haut Commissariat de l'Afrique Française.

Constantine, Stephen. 1984. *The Making of British Colonial Development Policy 1914–1940.* London: Cass.

Cooper, Frederick. 1996. *Decolonization and African Society: The Labor Question in French and British Africa.* Cambridge: Cambridge University Press.

Coquery-Vidrovitch, Catherine. 1988. "Transfer of Economic Power in French-Speaking West Africa". In *Decolonization and African Independence: The Transfers of Power 1960–1980,* edited by Prosser Gifford and Wm. Roger Louis, 105–134. New Haven: Yale University Press.

Coquery-Vidrovitch, Catherine, Daniel Hémery, and Jean Piel, eds. 1988. *Pour une histoire du développement: Etats, sociétés, développement.* Paris: L'Harmattan.

Cotte, Claudine. 1981. "La politique économique de la France en Afrique Noire (1936–1946)". Thèse de troisième cycle, Université de Paris VII.

Cowen, Michael. 1984. "Early Years of the Colonial Development Corporation: British State Enterprise Overseas during Late Colonialism". *African Affairs* 83: 63–75.

Cowen, Michael, and Robert Shenton. 1991. "The Origin and Course of Fabian Colonialism in Africa". *Journal of Historical Sociology* 4: 143–73.

Economic Commission for Latin America. 1951. *Economic Survey of Latin America 1949.* New York: United Nations Department of Economic Affairs.

Fall, Babacar. 1993. *Le travail forcé in Afrique Occidentale Française.* Paris: Karthala.

Feierman, Steven. 1990. *Peasant Intellectuals: Anthropology and History in Tanzania.* Madison: University of Wisconsin Press.

Fieldhouse, D. K. 1986. *Black Africa 1945–1980: Economic Decolonization and Arrested Development.* London: Allen & Unwin, 1986.

Gendzier, Irene, 1985. *Managing Political Change: Social Scientists and the Third World.* Boulder, Co.: Westview.

Goldsworthy, David. 1994. "Introduction". *The Conservative Government and the End of Empire 1951–1957*. London: HMSO.

Havinden, Michael, and David Meredith. 1993. *Colonialism and Development: Britain and Its Tropical Colonies, 1850–1960*. London: Routledge.

Hyam, Ronald, ed. 1992. *The Labour Government and the End of Empire 1945–1951*. London: HMSO, 1992.

Jeffries, Richard. 1978. *Class, Power and Ideology in Ghana: The Railwaymen of Sekondi*. Cambridge: Cambridge University Press.

Killick, Tony. 1978. *Development Economics in Action: A Study of Economic Policies in Ghana*. New York: St. Martin's Press.

Lewis, W. Arthur. 1939. *Labour in the West Indies*. London: Fabian Society.

———. 1951. "A Policy for Colonial Agriculture". In *Attitude to Africa*, by W. Arthur Lewis, Michael Scott, Martin Wight, and Colin Legum, 70–104. Harmondsworth: Penguin.

———. 1954. "Economic Development with Unlimited Supplies of Labour". *The Manchester School* 22: 139–91.

———. 1955a. "The Economic Development of Africa". In *Africa in the Modern World*, edited by Calvin W. Stillman, 97–112. Chicago: University of Chicago Press.

———. 1955b. *The Theory of Economic Growth*. Holmwood, Ill: Richard Irwin.

———. 1979. "The Dual Economy Revisited". *The Manchester School* 47: 211–29.

Low, D. A., and John Lonsdale. 1976. "Introduction". In *The Oxford History of East Africa*. Vol. 3. Oxford: Oxford University Press.

Marseille, Jacques. 1984. *Empire colonial et capitalisme français: Histoire d'un divorce*. Paris: Albin Michel.

Mérat, Louis. 1936. *L'heure de l'économie dirigée d'intérêt général aux colonies*. Paris: Sirey.

Moore, Henrietta L., and Megan Vaughan. 1994. *Cutting Down Trees: Gender, Nutrition, and Agricultural Change in the Northern Province of Zambia, 1890–1990*. Portsmouth, N.H.: Heinemann.

Mounier, Bernard. 1942. *L'organisation de l'économie impériale par les comités coloniaux*. Paris: Editions Pedone.

Pearce, R. D. 1982. *The Turning Point in Africa: British Colonial Policy 1938–1948*. London: Cass.

Rosenstein-Rodan, P. H. 1943. "Problems of Industrialisation of Eastern and South-eastern Europe". *The Economic Journal* 53: 202–211.

Rostow, Walter W. 1960. *The Stages of Growth: A Non-Communist Manifesto*. Cambridge: Cambridge University Press.

Sorum, Paul Clay. 1977. *Intellectuals and Decolonization in France*. Chapel Hill: University of North Carolina Press.

Throup, David. 1987. *The Social and Economic Origins of Mau Mau*. London: Currey.

Tipps, Dean C. 1973. "Modernization Theory and the Comparative Study of Societies: A Critical Perspective". *Comparative Studies in Society and History* 15: 199–226.

United Nations. Department of Economic Affairs. 1951. *Review of Economic Conditions in Africa, 1949–50*. New York: United Nations.

————. 1959. *Economic Survey of Africa Since 1950.* New York: United Nations.

Vaughan, Megan. 1991. *Curing Their Ills: Colonial Power and Africa Illness.* Cambridge: Polity Press.

Weeks, John. 1971. "The Political Economy of Labor Transfer". *Science and Society* 35: 463–80.

THREE

Visions of Postwar Health and Development and Their Impact on Public Health Interventions in the Developing World

Randall Packard

The period immediately following World War II initiated a new phase in Europe and America's relationship to its colonial and former colonial dependencies. Under the banner of "development," the rationale for western intervention into the social and economic life of emerging nations in Africa, Asia, and Latin America was transformed and depoliticized. Despite this change in rhetoric, the nature and purposes of postcolonial "development" remained remarkably similar to those of colonial interventions. Political and economic self-interest remained a key component in defining the desire of western industrial nations to transform the so-called "third world." Even the leaders of emerging nations used "development" to rationalize policies and programs that served narrow sets of interests. At the same time, the "partnership for progress" remained a very unequal one, with flows of information, knowledge, technology, and expertise, moving predominantly outward from the "developed" to the "underdeveloped" world.

The contradictions embedded in postwar development were shared by the field of international health. In rhetoric as well as in practice, interventions designed to improve the health of peoples in developing countries underwent a significant shift following World War II. Underlying this transformation, however, one can detect a number of continuities in both perspective and practice. These underlying continuities played a significant role in undermining the effectiveness of efforts to improve the health of developing nations.

HEALTH AND COLONIAL DEVELOPMENT

Prewar efforts to deal with the health of developing regions of the globe from the end of the nineteenth century to the late 1920s shared certain characteristics. First they were closely linked to the economic interests of colonizers. Health was not an end in and of itself, but rather a prerequisite for development. Since their initial movement outward into tropical areas of the world, Europeans had been concerned with improving health conditions in the tropics. This interest reflected, for a long time, a concern for the health of Europeans. The ability of Europeans to tap into the wealth of tropical areas depended on their ability to survive in tropical climates. This survival was at best problematic and at worst impossible during the early years of European exploration.[1]

The need to overcome the health barriers to European exploitation stimulated research into the etiology of diseases associated with the tropics. It also led to the development of schools of tropical medicine and hygiene in both Europe and the United States at the turn of the century. The early successes of these schools in the field of malaria and yellow fever helped make possible European colonization in the tropics (Farley 1991). Over the next half century the health of Europeans continued to generate interest in tropical health.

By the end of the World War I, however, the focus of European health initiatives had been expanded to include, in a limited fashion, the health of "native populations" and not just European colonizers. Yet European interest in the "health of the natives," like their concern for their own health, was shaped by fairly narrow economic interests. Colonial economies depended on healthy workers and not just healthy managers. Accordingly, some investment was directed toward combating illness among workers, at least while they were in the employ of Europeans. During much of the 1910s and 1920s, this narrow material concern for worker health defined European health efforts in the tropics. The success or failure of health interventions was measured by their ability to maintain or increase levels of production rather than by actual levels of health. Production losses, defined in terms of days or shifts lost, served as a surrogate measure for the health of the "native" work force.

The distribution of health services reflected this concern for production. Health resources were concentrated near sites of production with little attention given to populations residing outside these sites. Missionary doctors provided some maternal and child care in the rural areas of colonized countries as a way of supporting the reproduction of converts (Doyal 1979). Colonial governments, however, did little to build rural health services. For most rural inhabitants contact with western medical services was limited to occasional medical campaigns.

There can be little doubt that financial constraints dictated the unwillingness of colonial officials to expand health care coverage more broadly. Colonial treasuries, it was argued, could hardly afford the costs of reproducing and expanding preventive and treatment measures beyond industrial settings. The type of land reclamation and sanitation measures that were employed by Malcolm Watson in Malaya, N. H. Swellengrebel in Indonesia, and William Gorgas in Panama could only be achieved if they were underwritten by private capital.

A second characteristic of colonial medical services was that they tended to be narrowly technical in their design and implementation. The dominance of disease, and particularly parasitic models in colonial medical thinking, together with the medical research interests of colonial medical practitioners, led to a heavy reliance on technology to deal with health problems. Broader based efforts to reform social and economic conditions were viewed as both impracticable and unnecessary (Vaughan 1993; Worboys 1976; Farley 1991; Doyal 1979).

Finally, colonial health interventions reflected a view of local populations as inherently unhealthy and incapable of caring for their own health needs. Conversely, great faith was placed in western biomedicine, even when challenged by objective evidence of its limitations (Vaughan 1993; Lyons 1992).

The narrow limits of colonial medical services began to be reexamined in the late 1920s and 1930s. The world-wide depression hit commodity-producing countries hard. It lay bare the marginal subsistence of local producers who could not sell their produce and workers who lost their jobs. There was also a growing awareness that the endless labor supply which capital had envisioned was indeed finite and subject to an array of health threats. These realizations led to new efforts to examine the health conditions within the colonies. Commissions were organized. Numerous studies of colonial health and nutrition were carried out. This was the period when, as Michael Worboys has described, colonial malnutrition was "discovered" (Worboys 1988).

The discourse on colonial malnutrition represented a break with earlier colonial health efforts in that it focused attention beyond sites of production. Moreover it also differed in recognizing that malnutrition was a product of social and economic determinants. Yet the discovery of colonial malnutrition ended with the professionalization of nutritional science which in effect reduced the problem of malnutrition to a narrow biomedical paradigm. Malnutrition became a disease subject to technical correction.

Similar shifts in thinking can be seen in the work of the League of Nations Malaria Commission. The commission rejected narrow vector control approaches to disease and advocated the importance of broad-based social and economic development. By the end of the 1930s, however, malaria, like malnutrition, was redefined as a problem of vector control, thanks largely to the work of Fred L. Soper and the Rockefeller International Health Division in eradicating the *anopheles gambiae* mosquito in Brazil (Packard and Gadelha 1994).

Thus despite a great deal of rhetoric about the health of the empire, little change occurred in the direction or definition of health in the tropics between the wars. Health remained defined as the absence of disease and the control of disease continued to be viewed in narrow technical terms. Moreover, health was closely tied to the needs of industry and concentrated at sites of production.

HEALTH AND DEVELOPMENT IN THE POSTWAR WORLD

The linkage between international health and tropical development continued after World War II. Moreover, postwar health initiatives shared many characteristics with colonial medicine. Yet the postwar vision of health and development differed in significant ways from that which had existed before the war. The postwar vision of health and development was much more pervasive and encompassing than that which had existed before the war. Health policies, as well as rhetoric, reflected a new realization of the need to extend the provision of health care to entire populations, not just select communities of productive workers.

This shift in vision reflected a more fundamental reconceptualization of "development" and its goals following the war, as well as technological developments which for the first time made the extension of certain types of health intervention affordable on a broad scale. It was also fostered by a faith in the efficacy of this technology and it ability to control and even eliminate disease.

Discussions on the health of peoples living in "underdeveloped" areas of the globe in the immediate postwar period emerged from a growing awareness by western industrial nations that their economic future depended on increasing the production of raw materials as well as markets for manufactured goods. The period saw an increased interest by colonial powers in the development of their tropical dependencies and a realization that increases in the productivity of tropical labor would require investments in social and economic infrastructure including greater investments in public health. This enlightened self-interest was reflected in a series of postwar development and welfare acts. Speaking at the third session of a joint World Health Organization (WHO)/ Food and Agriculture Organization (FAO) meeting on malaria in 1948, Alberto Missiroli of Italy noted that the prosperity of Europe depended on the possibility of exploiting Africa. "Africa cannot be fully exploited because of the danger of flies and mosquitoes; if we can control them the prosperity of Europe will be enhanced."[2]

Within the United States, as well, there was a growing awareness that the development of the so-called "underdeveloped world" was critical for the economic health of the industrialized world. Tropical development, in turn, required the control of tropical diseases. This view was expressed by secretary of state George Marshall as early as 1948 in an address to the Fourth International Congress of Tropical Diseases and Malaria.

> The conquest of diseases which hold millions weak and inefficient, the maximum production of foodstuffs on lands now yielding little are tremendously important requirements of the world situation. The tropical regions, in large measure, hold the key to both these necessary advances. They produce large quantities of materials required by the industrial areas of the temperate zones, but the potential of the tropics largely remains to be developed. The tropical countries do import industrial products, but that market is only a fraction of what it should be. . . . Little imagination is required to visualize the great increase in the production of food and raw materials, the stimulus to world trade, and above all the improvement in living conditions, with consequent social and cultural advances, that would result from the conquest of tropical diseases (Marshall 1948).

The secretary's comments reflected a new definition of "development" that coincided with U.S. postwar economic interests. The problem for the United States was not simply the need to increase the flow of raw materials to industrial nations. The United States needed to expand overseas markets for U.S. manufactured goods. They needed a form of development that would lead to broad-based increases in consumption, and not just production in the developing world. The fear of postwar recession resulting from an inability to support the country's greatly increased wartime manufacturing capacity, placed a high premium on increasing the overseas consumption of U.S. manufactured goods.

The need to foster development through health was expressed by participants at the conference on "Health Problems of Industries Operating in Tropical Countries," convened by the Harvard School of Public Health in 1950. They found their strongest and most sustained expression in the writings of economist C-E. A. Winslow, whose book, *Price of Sickness, Cost of Health* was highly influential in shaping official opinion about the need to control tropical diseases. Winslow asserted that,

> When we consider on the one hand the wastage of the fruits of human effort in the rearing of children who will die before they are able to make any economic return to society and in the support by those adults who remain in good health, of a large proportion of invalids crippled by preventable disease, it is difficult to see how one can seriously question the importance of the contribution of public health to global prosperity (Winslow 1952: 193).

In addition to its economic benefits, tropical disease control quickly became viewed as a critical weapon in the war against international communism. By the late 1940s, communism was viewed as a major obstacle to the goal of a revitalized global economy that was envisioned by western economic and political leaders. With time, of course, defeating communism became a goal in and of itself. In his welcoming address to the conference on "Health Problems of Industries Operating in Tropical Countries," Dr. James S. Simmons, Dean of the Harvard School of Public Health observed,

> In these days of mounting international crisis, this conference takes on a significance *far beyond the mere improvement of the health of industrial workers as a means to increase production*. The health and manpower of the free nations of the world are now the most vital resources in our fight against Communism. They are part and parcel of the defense program of the democratic countries (emphasis added) (Simmons 1950).

Simmons's statement contrasted the broader health agenda that the war against communism required with the narrow economic interest that U.S. industries operating overseas had in the health of its workers.

Harry Cleaver has argued that the concern for combating communism was the primary motivating factor behind the Eisenhower administration's support for the WHO global eradication program in 1957 (Cleaver 1977). Yet it is evident from United States Operations Mission (USOM) records from Vietnam[3] and Thailand[4] that in the early 1950s, malaria control programs were very much part of the U.S. war against communism. The apparent speed with which malaria could be brought under control with DDT, together with its short term effects on other household pests, made malaria control particularly attractive for those who saw tropical disease control as an instrument for "winning hearts and minds" in the war against communist expansion. Malaria control programs were defined by the U.S. Special Technical and Economic Missions to Vietnam and Thailand as "impact programs." These were programs that were designed to have a rapid positive effect on local populations in order to build support for local governments and their U.S. supporters.[5] In short, within the context of the war against communism, health interventions needed to be broad based. Protecting the health of a few thousand plantation workers would be of little help in winning support of local villagers subjected to communist propaganda.

The political benefits that had been achieved by malaria control were laid out in the 1956 International Development Administration Board (IDAB) report to the president on malaria eradication

> Thus, malaria control presents an important opportunity to demonstrate through visible action, our common cause with these progressing countries. It helped to do this in the early 1950s, when Iran was caught in a serious

political upheaval. While the situation was at its worst, the U.S. technical assistance program, with malaria control as a major feature, was operating on a large scale. Qualified non-public health observers, many of whom were in Iran throughout the period, credit the malaria component of the U.S. technical assistance program with playing an important role in supporting our diplomatic representations with a concrete manifestation of our sincerity and mutual interest.[6]

Later on, the report notes,

As a humanitarian endeavor, easily understood, malaria control cuts across the narrower appeals of political partisanship. In Indochina, areas rendered inaccessible at night by Viet Minh activity, during the day welcomed DDT-residual spray teams combating malaria. In Java political tensions intensified by overcrowding of large masses of population are being eased partly by the control of malaria in virgin areas of Sumatra and other islands, permitting these areas to be opened up for settlement that relieves intense population pressures. In the Philippines, similar programs make possible colonization of many previously uninhabited areas, and contribute greatly to the conversion of Huk terrorists to peaceful landowners.[7]

Local governments also perceived eradication as a way to gain popular political support. Thus the IDAB Report noted, "The present governments of India, Thailand, the Philippines, and Indonesia among others, have undertaken malaria programs as a major element of their efforts to generate a sense of social progress, and build their political strength."[8] As A. Viswanathan, the distinguished Indian malariologist, pointed out, "No service establishes contact with every individual home at least twice a year as the DDT service does unless it be the collection of taxes."[9] Thus the interests of local elites and their international partners in maintaining political stability created a common commitment to health campaigns that would have broad impact.

The expanding vision of international health in the immediate postwar period was also linked to the development of new technologies which made disease control relatively inexpensive. The most important of these was DDT. Developed just before the war by German scientists, DDT was employed during the war with great effect in combating typhus and malaria. Sprayed on the walls of huts once every six months, DDT could control or even eliminate the transmission of malaria for a small fraction of the cost involved in the use of earlier forms of insecticide, which required much more frequent applications or costly drainage work.

Streptomycin and INH, developed during the 1940s and shown to provide an effective cure for tuberculosis, provided the technical basis for a greatly expanded campaign against this deadly disease. The development of miniature x-ray equipment furthered the attack. The 1950s saw mass x-ray campaigns and treatment programs established throughout many developing countries. Similarly, the development after the war of an effective freeze-dried vaccine for smallpox eliminated the need for expensive refrigeration and the maintenance of a cold-chain. This development made it possible to attack smallpox on a broad scale in the tropics and raised the possibility for a global campaign to eradicate smallpox.

The goal of disease eradication, which emerged after the war, needs to be viewed, as well, as a stimulus to the expanded postwar vision of international health. Eradication as a practical strategy required a broad-based attack on disease which left no untreated pockets. As long as one case remained, the possibility of renewed transmission remained. Yet to say that eradication was a stimulus to a broader vision of international health immediately begs the question, why did eradication models become popular after the war?

The goal of disease eradication was certainly not new. It had been articulated on numerous earlier occasions. Wickliffe Rose of the Rockefeller Foundation viewed hookworm eradication as the goal of hookworm control in the American south during the 1910s. Yellow fever eradication was also envisioned by Rockefeller Foundation workers in Latin America during the 1920s. Fred Soper became a staunch advocate of eliminating malaria through the eradication of malaria vectors in the 1930s. Moreover, his successes against the *anopheles gambiae* in Brazil and later Egypt provided evidence that malaria vectors could be eradicated (Packard and Gadelha 1994). Yet eradication remained a dream so long as the costs of combating disease remained too high to permit a broad-based extension of known methods. In this sense, the technological developments discussed above were a necessary precondition to the development of eradication strategies.

At the same time, the possibility of eradicating a disease need not result in an attempt to do so, no matter how low the cost. As disease eradicators of the 1950s and 1960s were to find, the path to disease eradication was filled with organizational and technical pitfalls. The willingness to venture down this path required a sense of self-assurance and a faith in the ability of available technology to achieve the goal of eradication despite the presence of obstacles.

There can be little doubt that the international health community that emerged from the war possessed the necessary self-assurance and the faith in technology. These were, in fact, traits that were shared by the larger postwar development community.

Disease eradication, as a prescription for social and economic change reflected and was part of this growing faith in the ability of western science and technology to transform underdeveloped countries. This faith was part of what has been called the "culture of development." The attitude of "know how and show how" that emerged out of the war was embodied in President Truman's Point Four Program and in subsequent U.S. technical assistance programs. As Truman noted in his 1949 inaugural address,

> The United States is preeminent among nations in the development of industrial and scientific techniques. The material resources we can afford to use in the assistance of other peoples are limited. But our imponderable resources in technical knowledge are constantly growing and are inexhaustible.[10]

The same confidence can be seen in the following reference to U.S. sponsored malaria control programs from a Department of State report on the Point Four Program.

> The most dramatic results from the employment of a very small number of skilled men and very small quantities of *scientifically designed materials* have been achieved in the field of medicine. In many areas of the world one trained public-health doctor or a group of two or three working with local people *able to follow their guidance* have been able to rout one of man's oldest and deadliest enemies (emphasis added).[11]

Yet the faith in technology and the optimism about our ability to transform the world carried with it certain assumptions about the peoples and societies that were to receive our technology and be transformed. The above passage not only stresses the ability of western technology to effect change, it also privileges the skills and knowledge of the outside expert while placing local populations in a position of dependence and in need of guidance and assistance.

The dependency of tropical populations on western knowledge was a fundamental assumption underlying malaria control and eradication efforts in the 1940s and 1950s just as it was a first principle of all development schemes during this period. It was moreover one of the areas in which international health in the postwar era maintained perspectives that had existed before the war. We will return to this issue below in discussing continuities and their impact.

The goal of disease eradication was thus a product of a vision of technological superiority and a faith in the ability of western technology to solve the health problems of the developing world. The possibility of eradicating disease, in turn, reinforced the expanded vision of broad-scale health intervention that emerged after the war.

CONTINUITIES AND THEIR IMPACTS

Although the postwar era saw a shift in the scale of health interventions, this new vision retained certain characteristics of the prewar era. Thus, continuity with the colonial era, as much as change, marked health interventions in the 1950s and 1960s, and in fact have continued to do so up to the present. These continuities have undermined a number of international health efforts during this period.

Inequalities in Health Care

Inequality in the distribution of health resources, which marked health care in most developing countries before the war, persisted after the war. Despite changes in the scope of health initiatives organized by international health and development organizations, investments in health at the national level remained highly concentrated, focused on urban and industrial centers, and serving the needs of emerging national elites as well as the interests of international capital. The failure to redress these inequalities resulted from several factors. First, budgets of health services were everywhere limited. Second, political and economic elites resisted any redistribution of resources which would diminish their access to relatively high quality tertiary care. Third, health professionals in the private sector demanded maintenance of high-cost hospitals. Finally, the preferences of international donors for providing high-tech equipment which supported donor country industries reinforced this pattern of maldistribution (Doyal 1979).

International health programs with their wide-scale approach and vision contributed to this pattern. Programs in disease eradication and family planning supplemented national health services and permitted national governments to claim that they were providing health benefits to the masses without changing their class-based health system.

A number of postwar international health programs proved unworkable in the face of inadequate rural health infrastructures. This was particularly true of the World Health Organization's Malaria Eradication Program. Initiated in 1955, the MEP envisioned the elimination of malaria as a disease throughout the world, although it was recognized that Africa represented a special problem and would have to await eradication.

The attack on malaria centered on the use of DDT for residual house spraying. This was designed to reduce the longevity of malaria vectors and thus curtail transmission. The interruption of transmission, it was believed, would lead to a disappearance of malaria parasites in human hosts and thus to the elimination of the disease. Almost everywhere the initial attack phase proved successful. Malaria eradication programs, organized vertically and independently of local health services, mobilized house spraying teams which spread out through the countryside attacking malaria vectors. As predicted, malaria morbidity and mortality fell. The problem came in sustaining this victory and eliminating the last remaining cases of the disease. While vertically organized spray teams had been efficient during the attack phase, they proved inefficient in the consolidation phases. Without an adequate health infrastructure, the identification and treatment of remaining cases of malaria was extremely difficult. Pockets of malaria persisted and grew, undermining eradication efforts.[12]

Similar problems hampered postwar efforts to control tuberculosis. It was one thing to sweep the country with mobile x-ray units and to begin treatment of those identified as having the disease. It was quite another to follow up cases under treatment and to track down and treat contact cases. Without a well-developed health infrastructure, tuberculosis control was impossible.

It is worth noting that the only postwar eradication effort that was a total success, smallpox eradication, did not require the existence of a local health infrastructure. This is because the smallpox vaccine provided a lifelong immunity to the disease. There was no need to follow up on patients. In addition, there were no invisible "carriers" of the disease. A person was either infected and had manifest symptoms, or not infected. Finally, the disease proved possible to defeat without identifying and vaccinating every person at risk. Pockets of disease could be identified, isolated, and attacked, leaving surrounding populations untreated. One of the unfortunate legacies of smallpox eradication was the mistaken belief that its success could be easily replicated with other diseases and that health for all could be provided without health services for all.[13]

Economic Benefits of Health

A second continuity between prewar and postwar health perspectives, which undermined postwar international health efforts, was the tendency to link health interventions with social and economic development. As the earlier quotations from Marshall and Missiroli indicate, health interventions after the war continued to be viewed as a prerequisite to development. This link was particularly clear in the United States where nearly all international health initiatives during the 1950s and 1960s were run out of U.S. Agency for International Development (USAID) and its predecessor the ICA (Kitron 1989). The association of health with development was particularly strong in the case of malaria. However it could also be found in arguments about other infectious diseases, such as yaws and tuberculosis, as well as in family planning programs.

From the outset, the goal of global malaria eradication was constructed as a problem of economic development as much as a problem of public health. A number of malaria experts, including George MacDonald, who developed the epidemiological model upon which the theory of eradication was based, underplayed the material benefits of malaria eradication.

They preferred, instead, to stress the elimination of malaria as a goal in and of itself.[14] Nonetheless, malaria control and later eradication efforts gained widespread financial support from both western donor nations and the governments of developing nations because of their presumed economic and political benefits. Arguments in favor of a policy of malaria eradication were couched in the language of economic development. The Malaria Eradication proposal of the Director General to the Eighth World Health Assembly in 1955 stated,

> There can be no doubt about the general economic and social benefits that malaria eradication brings to the countries cleared of the disease. . . . As regards non-malarious countries, obviously they will share in the benefits if they have import or export business with countries once malarious and now freed of this burden.[15]

The director of the Pan American Sanitary Board made the same point in arguing for UNICEF support for malaria eradication in the Americas in March 1955.

> Malaria is a serious burden on the economy of every malarious country. It has been well said that, where malaria fails to kill, it enslaves. *It is an economic disease.* No infected area may hope to meet the economic competition of non-malarious regions. In agriculture and industry labor is inefficient and the output is often reduced by one-third to one half and even more. . . . As a primary basis for economic development, malaria must be suppressed (emphasis added).[16]

In the years that followed the inauguration of the WHO global eradication program in 1955, efforts to maintain support for eradication drew as well on economic arguments and involved efforts to demonstrate the economic benefits that eradication had achieved. Finally, reassessments of the eradication strategy in the late 1960s, leading to its eventual abandonment by the World Health Assembly, centered on the economic costs and benefits of eradication. As part of this reassessment, seven countries were identified for careful examination. Each was visited by an assessment team. A central question addressed by each team in its report was whether and in what ways malaria eradication had affected the social and economic development of the country in question. The first meeting of the Team Representatives of the Advisory Group on Malaria Eradication Strategy, at which the results of the field studies were reviewed and recommendations to the secretary general were made, began their discussions with the following questions:

   a) has malaria in the past been a serious factor in affecting social economic development;

b) has malaria eradication in the past contributed to social economic development;

c) in the present stage of the country's development, is malaria eradication an important factor for social and economic development.[17]

In short, malaria eradication was linked to the problem of underdevelopment and to efforts to achieve social and economic development.

Family planning, or population control, perhaps the longest running international health effort after the war, was also directly linked to development. Numerous authorities argued that there could be no sustainable development as long as the populations of developing countries continued to grow at a pace that outstripped development efforts.[18] During the 1970s, the United States made the creation of population control programs a prerequisite to any USAID development funding.

Smallpox eradication, again appears to have been an exception to this pattern. Although eradicating smallpox was viewed as a financial benefit to developed countries, which annually spend millions of dollars vaccinating their populations against the risk of smallpox introduced from the developing world, the discourse on smallpox eradication was about health not development.

The linking of postwar international health campaigns with development goals marked a continuation of prewar perspectives. Yet there was a fundamental difference. Health interventions before the war, as we have seen, were limited in scale, and confined for the most part to economic enclaves. Within a plantation or mining center it was possible to measure the benefits of disease control in terms of shifts lost and changes in production levels, or worker efficiency. It was these calculations that provided the economic data upon which advocates of postwar health interventions made their arguments concerning the health benefits of disease control.

When the scale of health interventions expanded to the general population, however, such calculations proved extremely difficult, if not impossible to make. Supporters of health interventions, having argued that investments in health would accelerate social and economic development, found it difficult to support their case. This was particularly clear in the case of malaria eradication.

Writing to the chief of malaria eradication for WHO in 1958, the director of malaria eradication for the Pan American Health Organization (PAHO) noted.

It occurred to us from time to time that it would be a good thing to set the appointment of an expert to study the question but the thought of the problems involved caused us to discard the idea.

He continued that there had been progress in areas in which malaria control had been achieved, but noted, that it was impossible to "affirm

that progress has been the result of the control or reduction of malaria."
He concluded that,

> the side effects of the insect campaigns, such as the elimination or reduction
> of flies in the first years, resulted in a considerable reduction in infant mor-
> tality which confused the results of reduction in mortality due to malaria. If
> to this we add the considerable use of antibiotics during the postwar years,
> it becomes very difficult and complicated to distinguish the economic bene-
> fits obtained from antimalarial campaigns.[19]

Writing in 1959, Dr. Paul Russell, one of the fathers of the Global Eradication Strategy observed that,

> As regards social and economic impact, apart from saving in cost of opera-
> tion, there is probably little difference between the influence of good con-
> trol and that of good eradication. It is also noted that questions about eco-
> nomic and social impact of malaria are frequently asked but that accurate
> and authoritative answers are difficult, indeed for the most part impossible
> to formulate. There are three main reasons for this: 1) it is too early in the
> world wide campaign to have learned much about its economic and social
> effects; 2) measuring the social and economic impact of malaria eradication
> is an extremely complicated procedure greatly transcending the scope of
> malariology; 3) very few efforts have been made to measure the social and
> economic impact of malaria eradication and these few have been amateurish
> and limited in extent.[20]

More recently, a 1990 report on "The Economic Impact of Malaria in
Africa," published by the Vector Biology and Control Project noted, "Malaria's significance as a public health problem is undeniable. However, its
significance as an inhibitor of economic growth and development has yet
to be explicitly measured" (Shepard 1990).

Given its close association with development goals, the inability of supporters to demonstrate that malaria eradication had a major impact on
economic and social development made it difficult for them to justify the
costs of eradication. This was especially so once it became apparent that
eradication would be a lengthy and costly business, and not the quick fix
that had been promised. At the same time, the costs of the program were
rising. These increases reflected both increases in material costs and the
fact that as one neared eradication the cost per person protected increased. As completion dates disappeared over the horizon, it became
more difficult to present the costs of eradication as a capital investment
as opposed to another reoccurring cost.

Even the political benefits were often short lived. The opening up of
new lands often helped relieve land pressure. However, as populations
continued to expand, such benefits were lost. Moreover, in many cases,
the opening up of new lands was accompanied by the expansion of plan-

tation agriculture which squeezed out small holders already operating in these lands. In many tropical areas the popularity of spraying had come from the effects of insecticides on houseflies and other household pests which had been killed along with *anopheline* vectors. The link between mosquitoes and malaria appears to have been weakly understood (itself a product of the lack of community involvement discussed below) and so people saw little benefit in mosquito killing. Unfortunately, houseflies developed resistance to pesticides long before *anophelines* did. As houseflies and bedbugs reappeared, villagers became disenchanted with recurrent sprayings which had little immediate benefit (Gramiccia and Beales 1988, 1344). This was especially true where sprayings not only disrupted people's lives, but also appeared to harm household pets and domestic animals.

As both host and donor governments began to question the economic and political benefits of malaria eradication programs in the early 1960s, they began looking for other programs that would have a quicker and more visible impact on development. USAID, which was by far the largest funder of malaria eradication programs worldwide, gradually cut back its support of bilateral malaria programs and shifted responsibilities to the U.S. Public Health Service during the 1960s (Gramiccia and Beales 1988, 1344). In its place, USAID began concentrating on family planning programs. The FAO, which had originally viewed malaria control and eradication as essential to agricultural growth in the tropics and had worked with WHO in developing control programs, grew disenchanted with disease control. By the late 1950s, FAO was pushing instead for the use of green revolution technologies. Tragically, such packages often involved the massive use of pesticides, including DDT, which accelerated the development of vector resistance (Gramiccia and Beales 1988, 1340).

The ability of eradication programs to maintain the gains that had been achieved was seriously undermined by these shifts in priorities and subsequent cutback in support for malaria work. Spraying operations were curtailed or carried out in a more haphazard manner. When USAID ended its annual contribution to the PAHO Special Malaria Fund in 1970, PAHO was force to restrict funding for malaria programs. Subsequently the USAID Latin America and Caribbean Bureau lowered its priority for malaria, which led to the termination of many antimalarial programs in the region (USAID 1985). It is likely that the reduction in support of spraying activities leading to inconsistent application of pesticides also played a role in the development of vector resistance.

The conceptual linking of health with economic and political development made health programs interchangeable pieces in the development puzzle. As such, they were subject to evaluation in terms of their relative cost and benefit vis-à-vis other development initiatives. In the end, few postwar health programs have been able to demonstrate a direct impact on development. Support for international health programs has thus been difficult to sustain.

Disease Models

The third continuity in international health perspectives was in the tendency to view health as the absence of disease. Postwar international health interventions remained focused on disease control and eradication. Until the late 1970s, broader definitions of health, involving social and economic well being, the provision of the basic resources needed to sustain health, clean water, food, and medical services, attracted little attention. So, too, the broader social and economic determinants of ill health, recognized by the League of Nations Malaria Commission in their reports of 1924 and 1927 (Malaria Commission 1924, 1927), and earlier by Angelo Celli and others, were ignored. Encouraged perhaps by the development of new technologies, and perhaps by the political benefits of silver bullet approaches and a faith in technology to master underdevelopment, postwar health interventions remained disease control programs. Even the problem of overpopulation was viewed as if it were a problem of disease control. As Mahmood Mamdani has shown, early population planners working in India defined overpopulation in medical terms,

> Overpopulation is a malady of society that produces wasted bodies, minds and spirits just as surely as have other familiar scourges—leprosy, tuberculosis, cancer. [The] problem in India [is] of epidemic proportions (Mamdani 1972: 38).

Like a disease, overpopulation could be defeated though classical disease control methods: vertical programs designed to disseminate information and birth control technology. Viewed in this way, the broader causes of population growth were never questioned. This perspective produced interventions which left the broad causes of ill health in the developing world untouched and reduced international health efforts to treating symptoms rather than causes.

Technology and Dependency

The final area of continuity with prewar perspectives, as noted above, was the continuation of colonial attitudes toward the people of developing countries and their limited capacities. This attitude was reflected in the following passage from a speech given by P. Dorolle, deputy director general of the World Health Organization, to the opening session of the First

Malaria Conference in Equatorial Africa, held in Kampala, Uganda, in 1950.

> It is true that a great part of the peoples of Africa south of the Sahara are still in an underdeveloped state so far as degree of civilization and culture and social development are concerned. But, on the other hand, it should be remembered that from the Sahara to Cape Agulhas and from the Gulf of Guinea to the Indian Ocean the African populations have benefited over many decades from the technical and scientific experience of very highly developed countries. Belgium, France, Portugal, the United Kingdom, and the Union of South Africa have all contributed, with untiring generosity and an unflagging desire for progress, their methods, their techniques, and their cultural and scientific resources, for the development of less developed peoples for whose administration these great countries have been responsible or for whom they have been trustees, or responsible in varying degrees (Dorolle 1950, 57).

It can also be found in the following passage taken from the first ICA Malaria Manual published in 1956. The manual went to all U.S. Operation Missions and served as a guide to the development of eradication programs. The manual describes the relationship between western expert and local counterpart as follows.

> The U.S. specialists should have "counterpart" personnel or "opposite members" assigned to them by the host government. Ordinarily this will result in a mutually beneficial "symbiosis". The U. S. entomologist, for example, can learn more quickly the local species bionomics and distribution while the host government counterpart entomologist will be given information regarding the latest control techniques (International Cooperation Administration 1956, 6–7).

This is a classic construction of the relationship between the technical advisor and host counterpart. As in the passage previously cited, the U.S. technical advisor is presented here as possessing the latest technical knowledge of control. He has the "know how." The host counterpart is reduced to "native informant" who will receive technical knowledge. There is no acknowledgment that the host counterpart might have knowledge about control that would be valuable. He only has knowledge of local flora and fauna. This was true even where these counterparts were Europeans, as happened in colonial settings such as southern Africa and Vietnam.

Such attitudes caused resistance among local authorities at the same time that it led to a homogenized approach to malaria eradication that ignored local variables. Others have noted that the local knowledge of malariologists built up over decades of experience became irrelevant under the all powerful gaze of the eradicator. I would argue, in addition, that this leveling was a product of a much more pervasive tendency associated with postwar development schemes, a product of the "culture of development" rather than a peculiar failing of malaria eradication. Again, malaria eradication was part of a much larger vision of postwar development and as such shared its weaknesses.

If the knowledge of local malariologists and other medical professionals was undervalued, that of local populations was virtually ignored. Like other development efforts during this period, postwar health improvement efforts made little or no attempts to enlist the cooperation of local populations in the planning or implementation of these efforts. Moreover, like Soper in the 1940s, eradicationists ignored local social and economic forces that were shaping the local epidemiology of malaria.

This tendency is readily apparent when one examines descriptions of malaria eradication procedures as defined by WHO. For example, before spraying operations could begin, areas to be sprayed were supposed to be surveyed—spleen rates and parasite levels recorded, test spraying carried out, entomological data collected. Nowhere was it stated that surveys should consider the social, cultural, and economic setting within which spraying was to occur. The problem of malaria eradication was medicalized, and local populations were defined as subjects of study rather than social beings. Despite recommendations from WHO officials for pre-eradication economic surveys to provide a base line of development against which one could measure the benefits of eradication, few were carried out.

The absence of interest in local social and economic dynamics, however, reflected a more profound problem. It was not simply that eradicationists were uninterested in such issues. Rather they often assumed that they did not exist. They shared with a large segment of the western development community a vision of the "third world" that precluded a need to understand more than was apparent from a superficial reading of the settings within which they worked. The peoples and places to be benefited from malaria eradication were viewed as timeless communities, suffering from a vast range of endemic diseases, and lacking even the rudimentary knowledge of sanitation.

Images such as these, transmitted through development documents, conference proceedings, scientific articles, and field operation manuals, constructed the problem of tropical health in a way that empowered the application of narrow technical solutions and permitted those applying those solutions to ignore local social and economic dynamics. As Tim Mitchell, Arturo Escobar, and James Ferguson have noted in their work on the language of development planning, the objects of development are constructed by those who practice development in ways which legitimate particular approaches to development. At the same time, these constructions obscure important processes that have shaped development problems as well as alternative approaches to development (Ferguson 1990; Mitchell 1991; Escobar 1988).

Postwar efforts to improve the health of peoples living in the developing world thus retained certain elements which had characterized prewar health interventions. These continuities undermined the success of postwar health interventions during the 1950s, 1960s, and 1970s.

BACK TO THE FUTURE: FROM PRIMARY HEALTH CARE TO SELECTIVE PRIMARY HEALTH CARE

Before concluding, it is worth examining the new ideologies of the 1970s and 1980s to see the ways in which they represented a break or continuity with the past. By the late 1960s, the limitations and failures of postwar efforts at improving the health of the peoples of developing countries began to produce a new shift in perspective. The failure of malaria eradication was perhaps the most important contributor to this rethinking. After malaria eradication, health officials were hesitant to embark on such wide-scale campaigns resting on narrow technological methods. Although the success of the smallpox campaign in the 1960s and 1970s would do much to erode this skepticism, for a brief time in the 1970s, the international health community looked for new approaches to international health. It was in this context that idea of primary health care and the notion of "health for all by the year 2000" were born. The need for basic health infrastructure and the redistribution of health resources, as well as a recognition of the broader forces shaping health in developing countries marked a sharp departure from postwar approaches to international health. The link between health and development was reversed.

Even though this shift in thinking was stimulated by the failings of earlier health initiatives, it needs to be viewed as well within the context of a broader rethinking about development. The late 1960s and early 1970s saw a widespread critique of development, emanating both from the western development community and from the developing world. Development agencies, particularly in the United States began to question strategies based on rapid industrialization and investments in large-scale agricultural projects. In their place, an emphasis on basic needs and small-scale projects emerged in the 1970s. As Martha Finnemore shows else where in this volume, this shift was particularly marked in the World Bank under McNamara.

Paralleling this shift in western development thinking, and in some ways influencing it, was a growing critique of underdevelopment. As Kathryn Sikkink's chapter describes, this critique had its origins in the late 1940s in Latin America with the school of structural economics which put more emphasis on national development and less on progressive integration into world markets. Raúl Prebisch and the Economic Commission for Latin America warned that global markets posed dangers as well as opportunities to primary-product producers. Ideas about national economic planning and industrialization provided a starting point for more radical departures leading to dependency theory and a critique of western-driven development agenda's that produced underdevelopment rather than development. These ideas provided much of the ideological infrastructure upon which primary health care, with its emphasis on equity, popular participation, sustainable technology, and the importance of combating the broader social and economic causes of ill health, was constructed.

Without going into the history of primary health care, its success and failings, it is important to note that as the central movement within the field of international health, primary health care (as laid out in Alma Ata) was short lived. While the rhetoric of primary health care continues, and primary health care projects persist, their character has changed in significant ways. The broader social and economic determinants of sickness and health were never taken seriously in terms of the funding of international health initiatives. Financial constraints and political sensitivities made such an emphasis impossible. This became particularly true within U.S. development agencies during the 1980s. The growing global recession, combined with the fiscal and political conservatism of the Reagan and Bush administrations, put a damper on efforts to reverse the relationship between health and development.

At the same time, the successes of smallpox eradication led to a renewed faith in technological approaches to health. WHO expanded its immunization program, and the UNICEF global immunization campaigns took center stage in international health programs.

Primary health care was replaced by selective primary health care, in which vertically organized health programs were piggy backed on to local health infrastructures. Local health promotion became narrowly focused on particular health problems rather than on the broad-based health and well being of the populations at risk. This shift away from broad-based primary health care has been justified in terms of cost effectiveness. Selective primary health care, Combatting Childhood Communicable Disease (CCCD) projects, or Child Survival programs require limited investments in health infrastructure. However, like the campaigns of the 1950s and 1960s, selective primary health care pays little or no attention to the underlying causes of ill health. Moreover, they define health as the absence of disease and ignore a broad range of health problems. The emphasis which primary health care placed on popular participation has been all but abandoned in favor of hierarchical structures in which health knowledge trickles down. Finally, health remains linked to development, as indicated in the recent ministerial conference on malaria. As health officials and ministers of health from 102 countries met in Amsterdam to discuss future directions for dealing with the growing problem of malaria, echoes of the 1950s could be heard in statements about the "staggering economic impact of malaria" and in assertions that malaria control was a "motor force for socioeconomic development."

Thus despite a continued rhetoric of primary health, international health has maintained a number of characteristics which can be traced to the period of tropical medicine and colonial health services. Verticality, the focus on disease, the emphasis on technology, the dominance of western institutions in determining health needs and approaches, the lack of investment in local health infrastructure, continue to shape international health efforts today as they did in the past and represent obstacles to the construction of effective and sustainable health interventions.

NOTES

1. Europeans operating along the West Coast of Africa in the eighteenth century died at an extraordinarily high rate, with mortality rates as high as 750 per 1000. The main killers of Europeans were malaria and yellow fever. Similar mortality rates were experienced by Europeans in South East Asia during the nineteenth century. The role of malaria in stemming early French penetration of Indo-China led Vietnamese nationalists to view the mosquito as a hero of the resistance.

2. WHO Archives, First Generation Files, 1946–1950: 453–4–21 FAO/WHO, Report of proceedings of Third Meeting of Expert Committee on Malaria to Joint FAO/WHO Meeting, 6.

3. U.S. National Archives, USOM, Vietnam, Health and Sanitation Division, Subject Files, 1951–1954.

4. U.S. National Archives, RG469, USOM Thailand, Executive Offices, Subject Files, Malaria Reports, 1954–1955.

5. A Joint Statement on Public Health Priorities issued by Public Health Division of the Foreign Operations Administration and the Public Health Service and Children's Bureau of the U.S. Department of Health, Education and Welfare in March of 1954 provides the following first principles upon which technical assistance health programs would be supported.

Strengthen economy by health benefits which release effective human energy, improve citizen morale, improve environment for local and foreign investment, open new land and project areas; contribute to our political objectives by reaching large populations with highly welcomed personal service programs, by demonstrating our deep human interest in man and his dignity (RG469 Office of Public Services, Public Health Division, 1952–1959).

6. International Development Advisory Board, *Report and Recommendations on Malaria Eradication*, 13 April 1956, [VBC] 008195, p. 8.

7. Ibid., p. 14.

8. Ibid., p. 11.

9. Ibid., p. 8.

10. Department of State, 1949b, *World Economic Progress through Cooperative Technical Assistance. The Point 4 Program* (1949 Pub 3454 Economic Cooperation Series 35, Truman's Inaugural Speech), 2c.

11. Department of State, 1950, *Point Four: Cooperative Program for AID in the Development of Underdeveloped Areas* (Department of State Pub. 3719, Economic Cooperation Series 24, Washington, U/S. Printing Office), 150–51.

12. For an overview of the history of postwar malaria control efforts and the history of eradication efforts, see Gramiccia and Beales (1988).

13. For a discussion of disease eradication strategies and their relevance to a range of health problems, see Yekuteil (1981).

14. In a letter to Dr. Sonti Dakshinamurti, who had been employed in a consultative capacity by WHO to prepare a study on the economic benefits of malaria eradication, MacDonald wrote, "I have always taken the attitude that economic and social matters should be considered as secondary to the fact that individuals suffer from disease which in some cases may prove fatal. Disease deserves to be tackled on its own account. Any other emphasis on writing up the economic and social losses is likely to distract attention from the more important matter." WHO Documents M2/180/4 MacDonald to Dakshinamurti, 19 June 1958.

15. WHO, Malaria Eradication, Proposal by the Director General to the Eight World Health Assembly, A8/P&B/10, 3 May 1955, p. 9.

16. E/UNICEF/282. paras 7–10).

17. WHO, TDR Documents, AGMES 69/Min.1, Notes of Meeting 6 January 1969, 10:00 to 12:00, p. 1.

18. Numerous studies could be cited here. Perhaps the most influential book in pushing the cause of birth control was Paul Ehrlich's *The Population Bomb* (New York: Balantine Books, 1968). See John Sharpless's article in this volume.

19. Alvarado to Pampana, 9 May 1958, WHO Documents File M2–180–4, "Economic Value of Malaria Eradication."

20. Rockefeller Center Archives, Paul F. Russell, Diaries, 1–21 June 1958.

REFERENCES

Cleaver, Harry. 1977. "Malaria and the Political Economy of Public Health". *International Journal of Health Services* 7: 557–79.

Dorolle, P. 1950. (Deputy Director General of the World Health Organization). "Speech to Opening Session of the Malaria Conference in Equatorial Africa, Kampala, Uganda". WHO Technical Series, no. 38.

Doyal, L. 1979. *The Political Economy of Health.* London: Pluto Press.

Escobar, Arturo. 1988. "Power and Visibility: Development and the Invention and Management of the Third World". *Cultural Anthropology* 3: 428–44.

Farley, John. 1991. *Bilharzia: A History of Imperial Tropical Medicine.* Cambridge: Cambridge University Press.

Ferguson, James 1990. *The Anti-Politics Machine: "Development," Depolitization and Bureaucratic Power in Lesotho.* Cambridge: Cambridge University Press.

Gramiccia, G., and P. F. Beales. 1988. "The Recent History of Malaria Control and

Eradication". In *Malaria: Principles and Practices of Malariology*, edited by W. H. Wernsdorfer and I. MacGregor, 1335–77. Edinburgh: Churchill Livingstone.

International Cooperation Administration. Public Health Division. 1956. *Malaria Manual for U.S. Technical Cooperation Programs*, Public Health Technical Series, Manual 1, Washington, D.C.

Kitron, Uriel. 1989. "Integrated Disease Management of Tropical Infectious Diseases". In *International Cooperation for Health: Problems, Prospects and Priorities*, edited by Michael R. Reich and Eiji Marui. Dover, Mass.: Auburn House Publishing Company.

Lyons, Maryinez. 1992. *The Colonial Disease: A Social History of Sleeping Sickness in Northern Zaire, 1900–1940*. Cambridge: Cambridge University Press.

MacLeod, Roy, and Milton Lewis, eds. 1988. *Disease, Medicine and Empire: Perspectives on Western Medicine and the Experience of European Expansion*. New York: Routledge.

Malaria Commission. 1924. *Report on Its Tour of Investigation in Certain European Countries in 1924*. Geneva: League of Nations Health Organization.

———. 1927. *Principles and Methods of Anti-Malaria Measures in Europe: Second General Report of the Malaria Commission*. Geneva: League of Nations Health Organization.

Mamdani, Mahmood. 1972. *The Myth of Population Control*. New York: Monthly Review Press.

Marshall, George. 1948. "Opening Address". *Proceedings of the Fourth International Congress on Tropical Medicine and Malaria*. Washington, D.C.

Mitchell, Tim. 1991. "America's Egypt. Discourse of the Development Industry". *Middle East Report*, March-April: 18–34.

Najera, J. A. 1989. "Malaria and the Work of WHO". *Bulletin of the WHO*, 67, no. 3: 235.

Packard, Randall M., and Paulo Gadelha. 1994. "A Land Filled with Mosquitoes: Fred L. Soper, the Rockefeller Foundation, and the *Anopheles Gambiae* Invasion of Brazil". *Parisitologica* 34: 197–213.

Shepard, Donald S. 1990. "Economic Impact of Malaria in Africa". Unpublished paper, Vector Biology and Control, Arlington, VA.

Simmons, James Steven. 1950. "Welcoming Address. Conference on Industry and Tropical Health". *Industry and Tropical Health* 1: 12.

USAID. 1985. *Malaria: Meeting the Global Challenge*. A.I.D. Science and Technology in Development Series. Boston: Oelgeschlager, Gunn & Haine.

Vaughan, Megan. 1993. *Curing Their Ills: Colonial Power and African Illness*. Stanford: Stanford University Press.

Winslow, C.-E. A. 1952. *The Cost of Sickness and the Price of Health*. Monograph series no. 7. Geneva: WHO.

Worboys, Michael. 1976. "The Emergence of Tropical Medicine". In *Perspectives on the Emergence of Scientific Disciplines*, edited by Gerald Lemaine, Roy Macleod, Michael Mulkay, and Peter Weingart, 75–98. The Hague: Mouton.

———. 1988. "The Discovery of Colonial Malnutrition between the Wars". In *Imperial Medicine and Indigenous Societies*, edited by David Arnold, 208–23. Manchester: Manchester University Press.

Yekuteil, Perez. 1981. "Lessons from the Big Eradication Campaigns". *World Health Forum* 2: 465–90.

Intellectual Communities
and Connections

FOUR

Intellectual Openings and Policy Closures

Disequilibria in Contemporary Development Economics

Michael R. Carter

Two contradictory trends have characterized the evolution of development economics since the early 1980s. The first is the ascendance of a policy orthodoxy of development liberalism.[1] By banishing statist interventionism, development liberalism marked the assertion within development economics of the fundamental neoclassical economic theorems concerning the superiority of private decentralized decision-making guided by competitive, price-making markets. Ironically, the second trend in development economics has been spurred by ongoing disciplinary revisionism which questions the singular generality, if not the relevance, of these same core economic theorems.[2] No less than other subdisciplines within economics, development economics has been part of this revisionist intellectual project even as development policy has simultaneously swung strongly toward *laissez faire.*

These two trends within development economics have taken place on different stages, characterized by different degrees of public access and attendance. The consolidation of the liberal policy orthodoxy has literally been played out on the world stage, with major roles played by international financial institutions and development agencies in Washington, D.C. Reflecting its dominant position within the development policy community, liberal development orthodoxy has been aptly described by John Williamson (1996) as the "Washington Consensus." Its influence appears throughout the world in the form of trade liberalization, privatization, and foreign aid conditionalities and "policy loans." These policies have given liberalizing states money they can use to soften the impacts of liberalization on the government officials and bureaucrats who become unemployed in the wake of state decontrol of the economy. Even that traditional bastion of dependency analysis, the United Nations Economic

Commission on Latin America (ECLA), gave way to the surge of development liberalism with the 1990 publication of its largely neoliberal *Changing Production Patterns with Social Equity* (ECLA 1990), as Sikkink's essay (this volume) explores.

In contrast, the second trend—intellectual revisionism within economics—has played on more obscure stages, with an often obscure professional dialogue, and a cast sometimes uneasy and unsure about how to interpret the new revisionism before policy audiences.

In an effort to better understand the dynamics between the production of development ideas and their transmission into policy, this essay explores these two tendencies within contemporary development economics. The paper first places the shift to development liberalism in the context of the broader sweep of the evolving discipline of economics, including the emergence of revisionist perspectives on the economic adequacy of *laissez faire*. The paper then explores two areas of revisionist disciplinary research within economics—the theory of agrarian institutions and growth, and endogenous growth theory—which offer intellectual foundations from which to question the reigning liberal policy orthodoxy. The essay concludes with reflection on the disequilibrium between policy and these new currents of economic thought, considering the likely future impact of these new intellectual productions on development policy.

OPENINGS AND CLOSURES IN CONTEMPORARY DEVELOPMENT ECONOMICS

The pronounced and highly public shift to liberal development policy over the 1980s was part and parcel of what Cooper and Packard (this volume) describe as the "ultramodernist" critique of the dominant post–World War II development economics which had underwritten the notion that public investment and planning could speed the growth of low-income economies. This critique is ultramodern in the sense that it roots itself in the singular validity and universal applicability of the basic theorems of neoclassical economics which state that private decision making, coordinated by the market price mechanisms, sees to a socially optimal allocation of resources. From this perspective, the hyperactivity and interventionism of the traditional developmentalist state are both unnecessary and usually destructive.

The decentralized, noninterventionist perspective of the ultramodernist critique represents a dramatic change from the prior approaches to development which stressed more active state planning and policies. Development theories placing considerable faith in the ability of states to engineer rapid economic growth (Lewis 1954, Nurkse 1953, Prebisch 1950, Rosenstein-Rodan 1943) were quite in vogue in the 1950s. A central design for engineering such growth was to extract economic surplus from the traditional agricultural sector to finance accumulation in a modern industrial sector. Buoyed by the apparent success of this model of accumulation in underwriting rapid Soviet industrialization in the 1930s, leaders of developing-world nations enthusiastically embraced roles as active economic managers. International donors fully supported this strategy, and the score of years which began in 1960 was consequently a high-water period for micro- and macroeconomically activist policy.

However, from the late 1960s onward, criticism of development economic activism mounted. Economists of monetarist, rational expectations, and public choice schools of thought, as well as political scientists espousing the new political economy of development, intellectually undercut the old development orthodoxy. Motivated by the melancholy experience of countries following the old models, these academic innovations sowed the conceptual seeds of a development strategy reversal. Debt and foreign exchange crises in Latin America and state economic mismanagement in Africa (Bates 1981, World Bank 1981) stood in sharp contrast to the success of the East Asian "tigers" who were broadly interpreted by some to have been early followers of a liberal model (Belassa 1985, Krueger 1978, Bhagwati 1978).[3]

A large part of the liberal critique of development activism revolved around the exhaustion of import substitution and macroeconomically populist models, and their inability to sustain economic growth in the face of foreign exchange and macroeconomic constraints. However noble the goals of development planners may have been, their policies eventually ran up against constraints which made them untenable. Moreover, state planners in general faced distorted private incentives to protect and enhance their own positions regardless of the economic wisdom of doing so. These observations precipitated a striking reversal of economic development strategy in the early 1980s. The "neoliberal" revolution was at hand.

Whether this revolution has been compelled by foreign donors on unbelieving but submissive governments, or has been embraced and engineered from within developing countries is a subject of ongoing, sometimes vitriolic dispute.[4] While untangling this dispute is not a concern here, the duration and passion of the dispute indicate how pronounced the strategy shift has been. Yet, from within the discipline of economics, this pronounced policy shift can be seen as the return of development economics to the fold, a reassertion of microeconomic fundamentals.

The Invisible Hand Theorem and the World of the Welfare Theorems

Much of the history of neoclassical economics can be read as a meditation on Adam Smith's "invisible hand theorem" which claims that the invisible hand of competitive market discipline will see to it that, in Smith's language, the "private interests and passions of men (sic)" are led in the direction "which is most agreeable to the interests of the whole society."[5] A liberal, or *laissez faire*, policy prescription follows naturally from this theorem. There are really two components to Smithian liberalism. The first component is its methodological individualism which posits that atomistic, self-interested individuals are the primary agents and movers of the economy. The second component is the separable analytical claim that individuals' pursuit of their self-interest results in a socially coherent and largely desirable disposition of resources.[6]

These two components of Smithian liberalism—self-interested individualism and social optimality—are bundled together by the invisible hand in Smith's analysis, and they are often treated as inseparable elements of neoclassical economics. Indeed, contemporary social science usage often uses the term "neoclassical economics" to denote an economics which conforms to the bundled Smithian perspective on individualism and the desirability of markets and *laissez faire*. But, as we shall explore momentarily, the methodological individualism is unbundled from the specific claims of the invisible hand theorem in those variants of neoclassical analysis which show that private interests and passions need not lead to outcomes which are most agreeable to the interests of the whole society. For clarity's sake, this essay will therefore use a minimalist definition of neoclassical economics in terms of the methodological postulate of self-interested individualism. That is, "neoclassical economics" will be used here to denote the perspective that an understanding of the economy can be built up on the foundation of the rational, self-seeking choices of individual economic agents.[7] Whether or not these choices, when coordinated by markets, lead to a social optimum is a separate issue. The hypothesis that it does will be here called "Smithian liberalism" or the "invisible hand theorem."

Several intellectual landmarks stand out in the subsequent development of Smithian liberalism. One is the work of the nineteenth-century French economist Leon Walras who developed the "general equilibrium" model of the market economy and mathematically showed that there exists a set of prices which jointly and simultaneously equates demand and supply for all commodities and factors of production. The "Walrasian equilibrium" determined by this specific set of prices is interesting and important for several reasons. First, because all agents in the economy are buying and selling exactly what they would like to, given the set of prices,[8] the Walrasian equilibrium exhausts all opportunities for mutually beneficial exchange in the economy. Second, while Walras relied on the fictive, heuristic device of a multimarket auctioneer to explain the establishment of the specific set of equilibrium prices in an economy, that set of prices (once established) is appealing because it is consistent with the individual self-interest perspective of neoclassical economics. This second point can be understood by noting that any set of prices *other* than the Walrasian equilibrium prices leaves some agents (e.g., unemployed workers who cannot supply all the labor they would like at the going wage) with incentives to try to change those prices (e.g., bid down the wage by offering to work for less). Hence, from a neoclassical perspective, Walrasian prices are attractive as a representation of the economic equilibrium toward which the economy tends.[9] The work of Walras thus tightens the twine around Adam Smith's bundling of self-interest and social optimality in the competitive market economy.

A series of contributions launched in the 1950s deepened the Walrasian analysis and scrutinized in detail the conditions under which the Smithian bundle of individual self-interest and social optimality holds together. The work of Arrow and Debreu (1954) was particularly important in this respect (fairly approachable summaries of this work are given in Geanakoplos 1989, and Broadway and Bruce 1984). Most simply put, Arrow and Debreu formally established that the competitive market economy achieves a social optimality if there are full and complete (price-rationed) markets for all commodities, including markets for future and possibly contingent commodity transactions.[10] This modern restatement of Smith's invisible hand theorem has come to be known as the First Welfare Theorem which is typically stated as saying that under the necessary conditions, the equilibrium of a competitive economy is Pareto optimal—meaning that resources are used well enough that it is not possible to make any individual better off without taking something away from another individual and rendering that individual worse off. (In contrast, note that when resources are used badly, it would be possible to reallocate resources in such a way that more gets produced and at least some individuals can be made better off with the fruits of the reallocation without taking anything away from anyone else.) In addition to the First Welfare Theorem, Arrow and Debreu also established the terms under which the so-called Second Welfare Theorem holds. This theorem states that subject to certain conditions (most particularly the absence of "increasing returns to scale" in production, consumption, or investment) any Pareto optimal allocation of goods among a population can be realized as the equilibrium a competitive economy would achieve following an appropriate redistribution of initial endowments.[11] To help keep things straight, we will refer to a world in which the conditions necessary for these fundamental theorems to hold as the "world of the welfare theorems."

While often seen as the paradigmatic embodiment of the liberal faith in the social efficacy of unencumbered markets, the Arrow-Debreu results can be interpreted in strikingly different ways. Geanakoplos (1989) notes that Arrow himself maintains that the Arrow-Debreu work is most useful for showing how *in*efficient real world market systems are. In oral remarks to the 1988 American Economics Association annual meetings, Joseph Stiglitz noted that the Arrow-Debreu results can be viewed as a glass half-full, or half-empty—the apotheosis of Smithian liberalism, or its unraveling.[12] However it is viewed, the Arrow-Debreu work did clear the way for careful definition and consideration of economies which operate outside the world of the welfare theorems. The term "post–Arrow-Debreu" will be used here for research which, while maintaining the core methodological individualism of neoclassical economics, supersedes the assumptions which Arrow and Debreu showed that Smith's invisible hand theorem requires.

Development Liberalism as Reassertion of Microeconomic Fundamentalism

A number of areas of mainstream economic analysis developed rather apart from the rigorous exegesis of Adam Smith's invisible hand theorem. Both traditional Keynesian macroeconomics[13] and the development economics discussed in the beginning of this section developed models and modes of analysis which began with aggregate economic relationships rather than with the rational choices of individual agents coordinated by economically endogenous market prices. At best, the non-neoclassical methodological foundations of these fields created a disjuncture between these fields and fundamental microeconomics—a disjuncture which Nobel prize winner Paul Samuelson unflinchingly accepted in the 1950s when he wrote that he could (with good, if schizophrenic, conscience) do microeconomics on Mondays, Wednesdays, and Fridays, and do macroeconomics on Tuesdays, Thursdays, and Saturdays.[14] At worst, it left the fields of macroeconomics and development economics vulnerable to the criticism of being ad hoc, logically sloppy, and unable to answer the question of whether and how their aggregate relationships were consistent with the maximization of individual self-interest and a coherent theory of price formation.

The methodological disjuncture between Keynesian macroeconomics and microeconomic fundamentalism began to close with the late 1960s development of what came to be known as the "microfoundations of macroeconomics."[15] Included in this development were efforts to provide microfoundations for the core relationships of Keynesian economics by showing that those relationships were indeed consistent with individual, self-seeking behavior *if* prices were somehow stuck at other than their Walrasian equilibrium levels (see especially Malinvaud 1977 and Barro and Grossman 1971). As discussed in note 9, the Barro and Grossman formulation foundered on its unclear rationale for why prices should ever get stuck at other than their Walrasian levels. While other economists explored alternative theories of price formation, the other and perhaps dominant direction taken by the microfoundations of macroeconomics was the reassertion of the core tenants of Smithian liberalism. Work in this area disputed the ability of a macroeconomically active government to fine tune or even affect the real operation of the economy, ushering in the sorts of fiscally conservative macromanagement which has at least in name dominated economic policy making in the United States and much of western Europe since the late 1970s.

The turn to development liberalism offers striking parallels to this shift within macroeconomic theory and policy. As Cooper and Packard (this volume) point out, P. T. Bauer's 1976 book *Dissent on Development* moved within a decade from being the heterodox critique of traditional interventionist development economics to being the centerpiece of the new policy orthodoxy of development liberalism. From a disciplinary perspective, this shift and its relative rapidity is intelligible as the reassertion of the basic insights of Smithian liberalism. Development economics had come home to the world of the welfare theorems, prompting some to proclaim the end of development economics.[16] But, even as the prodigal subdisciplines came home, and development liberalism went on the policy offensive, neoclassical economic theory was deepening the post–Arrow-Debreu research agenda on the functioning of actually existing market economies which do not conform to the assumptions of full and complete markets and the absence of increasing returns to scale.

Actually Existing Market Economies and the Opening of Intellectual Space in Contemporary Microeconomics

This section reviews several currents in contemporary microeconomics which breakdown Smith's identification of the market-mediated pursuit of private self-interest with the achievement of social optimality. By unbundling the methodological individualism of Smith and neoclassical economics from the social welfare claims, these revisionist currents open up intellectual and policy space within neoclassical economics. The intention in this section's review is not to give a complete accounting of contemporary economic thought, but instead to highlight those currents which have proven most relevant to the further evolution of development economics discussed below.[17]

One important stream of revisionist work emerged from the seemingly benign analysis of the economics of asymmetrically held information. Information is asymmetric when one party to a transaction knows more about the characteristics of the transacted commodity (good or service) than the other. Information asymmetries can arise either because the characteristics of the good are difficult or costly to determine for the nonspecialist (e.g., the quality of a used car, or of health care), or because the transaction in question has a temporal dimension which makes it difficult for one party to ascertain exactly what has been bought and sold. For example, a labor contract could be written in which it is agreed that a fixed salary will be paid for one week of diligent and intensive work effort. However, in many work environments, it would be difficult and costly for the employer to determine if the worker actually delivered the commodity "diligent and intensive work effort." The employer would then find it in his or her self-interest to employ various incentive devices, perhaps increasing the level of the salary (i.e., the price) to influence the qualitative characteristics of the commodity being purchased. But, as numerous theoretical analyses have shown, prices in markets characterized by asymmetric information may be driven away from conventional (Walrasian) equilibrium levels because the price may itself be known to influence the hard-to-ascertain quality of the good being transacted (see the summary in Stiglitz 1992).

A simple example of price influencing quality comes from nutritional wage theory which suggests that wages will not fall to their market clearing level if lower wages mean lower nutrition for the worker and a proportionately large decrease in physiological work capacity (see Bliss and Stern 1978). More complex instances of price effects on commodity quality occur when a behavioral, as opposed to a physiological response, occurs as price changes. For example, a high interest rate, which makes it difficult for a borrower to achieve full repayment and avoid default, might induce borrowers to simply give up and divert funds to consumption uses since default is likely to occur anyway. Since it could be extraordinarily difficult for lenders to monitor the degree of credit diversion over the term of a loan, lenders may become reluctant to raise the interest rate too much lest it induce behavior by the borrower which is adverse to the interests of the lender. Similarly, if the wage rate in a job were to fall to that level at which jobs are easily had (for example, jobs at McDonalds), then the worker may work less intensively knowing that the worst that can happen is that he or she will lose a job which can be easily replaced. In this circumstance, if employers cannot directly or easily enforce work effort and quality over the work week, they may be reluctant to pay too low wages for fear that it will adversely affect the quality of the commodity (labor) they are trying to purchase.

Several things can happen when the impact of price on hard-to-observe commodity quality is strong enough. First, market prices may stick at non-Walrasian levels *because of the private self-interest of one party to the contract.* The individual denied a loan at 5 percent rate of interest is thrown out of the bank when he or she offers to pay the higher price of 10 percent (see Stiglitz and Weiss 1981; Carter 1988). The unemployed worker who offers to work for less than the firm's current wage rate is turned away (Bowles 1985; Shapiro and Stiglitz 1984). In both these instances, the behavior of the bank and the employer is completely consistent with their private interest rationality—they will expect to make less money if they accept the higher interest rate or pay the lower wage. The second thing which can happen is that certain markets may simply not come into existence because there is no price at which transactions can be profitably made. Crop insurance markets are a good example of this phenomenon (Binswanger and Rosenzweig 1986).

Suddenly, from this asymmetric information perspective, a number of the primary markets which constitute capitalism appear intrinsically incomplete or imperfect in ways which violate the Arrow-Debreu conditions for the social optimality of the competitive market economy. Put differently, the world of actually existing capitalism begins to look rather different from the world required for the first welfare theorem to hold. Unlike the efforts of Barro and Grossman and Malinvaud to reestablish Keynesian macroeconomics on microfoundations, this information-theoretic work offers a consistent answer to the question as to why prices should settle at their non-Walrasian levels despite the fact that there are unconsummated, mutually beneficially exchanges. Greenwald and Stiglitz (1986) push the imperfect information line of reasoning furthest with their analysis of the potential suboptimality of the informationally imperfect, competitive market economy. In addition, as will be discussed in some greater detail in the next section, when markets are intrinsically imperfect or incomplete, the distribution of resource endowments (the "means of production") can influence the aggregate productivity (and perhaps the social optimality) with which resources are used. In this situation, a neoclassical economics built on the methodology of rational individualism begins to look like more classical Marxian perspectives which declare the distribution of the means of production to be of primary import to the functioning and evolution of the economy.[18]

In addition to its deep consideration of asymmetric information, neoclassical economic theory over the last decade has carefully considered a broad class of problems connected with increasing returns to scale. Increasing returns to scale occur when the productivity of a production process, or returns to an investment increase as the scale of the process increases, or as more of the investment is undertaken. While a few examples of increasing returns will be discussed in the next section in the specific context of trade and development policy, several implications of increasing returns can be noted at this stage. First, increasing returns can create what might be termed first mover (or first developer) advantages. If, for example, individuals learn by doing, and if learning by doing exhibits increasing returns to scale, then an early industrializing nation whose work force first "does and learns" may develop a dynamic competitive advantage over other, poorer nations. Second, to the extent that the benefits of increasing returns spill over as a public, or externality-laden good, decentralized, private decision making may not be able to support high productivity equilibria which reap the full benefits of increasing returns to scale. Thus, in the example of learning by doing, private firms may underemploy and undertrain the workforce because their consideration of private returns does not value the extra public benefits to the economy of an increasingly skilled workforce. Put differently, the conditions underlying the second welfare theorem are violated, and certain socially desirable allocations cannot be reached through the coordination of the invisible hand alone.

Ironically then, even as development liberalism was moving from dissent to orthodoxy, the continuing disciplinary meditation on Adam Smith spawned two streams of thought which suggest that the fundamental Smithian welfare theorems may be systematically violated in the actually existing world of imperfect and asymmetric information and increasing returns to scale. Interestingly, Bardhan (1993) notes that many of these currents in contemporary microeconomics reproduce insights of the old developmentalist orthodoxy, even if reproduced on firmer microfoundations (see earlier note). While Bardhan seems primarily interested in arguing that contemporary theory has much to learn from the classical development economics it often spurned (see note 14), his argument naturally raises the question about the degree to which the new policy orthodoxy of development liberalism has in fact fallen out of step with the core microeconomics to which it claims to have returned.

EXPLORING NEW INTELLECTUAL SPACE IN POST–ARROW-DEBREU DEVELOPMENT ECONOMICS

This section explores two contemporary development economics research agendas which have been profoundly influenced by post–Arrow-Debreu economic theory. The first is the analysis of agrarian growth and transformation as it occurs under a liberal policy regime. In this area of research, the economics of information have proven to be especially important to the understanding of agrarian transitions which historically have appeared to crystallize and deepen initial levels of rural poverty and inequality. The second area of work explored here is based on so-called "endogenous growth theory" which has confronted evidence on the failure of international income inequality to decline and income levels to converge across countries with a series of insights derived from the consideration of various forms of increasing returns to scale in production and investment. Both research areas speak to the production and reproduction of initial structures of poverty and inequality, one at the micro, household level, and the other at the macro, national level. Both areas of research also carry policy implications which stand at odds with the contemporary liberal development policy orthodoxy. In neither area, however, does the research indicate a return to the old developmentalist agenda—their policy messages are more nuanced, and perhaps uncertain, as this paper will later explore.

Microeconomic Foundations of Agrarian Growth and Transformation

Over the last decade or so, agrarian development policy has followed the general trend toward development liberalism, forcefully swinging toward *laissez faire* throughout the developing world. Two key questions can be asked of the ever-broadening contemporary experience of agrarian liberalism:

1. When does liberalization generate a positive aggregate growth response?
2. If liberalization brings growth, is the growth it brings sufficiently broadly based to be consistent with a socially sustainable agrarian transformation, or does it tend to deepen existing cleavages in undesirable and socially problematic ways?

The first question asks whether and when liberalization generates stimulative market-level price signals to producers; and whether farm-level constraints *uniformly* block a positive supply response. The second question asks whether farm-level constraints *differentially* constrain strata of producers in a way which skews the costs and benefits of agrarian growth and transformation. Ultimately both questions ask whether development policy requires more than liberalization.

These questions are as important as they are contentious. Empirical reviews of the evidence to date ratify the perhaps obvious: reality is more complex and problematic than the liberalization theory of development suggests. In Sub-Saharan Africa, countries which have liberalized are found among both the best and worst economic performers of the last decade (Barrett and Carter 1996, 1997). In Latin America, countries which have vigorously and successfully pursued liberal, export-oriented agrarian growth strategies present a similarly heterogeneous profile

(Carter, Barham, and Mesbah 1996). In some cases, growth has been broadly based, meaning inclusive of small farmers and the rural resource poor. In others, the trajectory of growth has been narrow—based on a subset of wealthier producers—decidedly exclusionary, and socially problematic in the sense that it spills over through land and labor markets and negatively influences other individuals.

Analysis of agrarian growth and transition from a post–Arrow-Debreu theoretical perspective offers a number of insights into the troublesome linkage between agrarian liberalism and agrarian performance. Assuming technology exhibits constant returns to scale,[19] all producers great and small would pursue identical resource allocation and production strategies in the world of the welfare theorems with its full and complete markets.[20] Growth booms occasioned by new prices, technologies, or markets would not be based on, or biased against, any particular wealth class of producers. However, because of the spatially dispersed, biologically based and stochastic nature of agricultural production processes, information asymmetries of the sort discussed earlier are likely to be especially problematic in rural areas. Hired labor, for example, is likely to be costly to supervise, implying that the labor market may reach an unemployment equilibrium with a wage above the Walrasian market clearing level (the higher wage—and the threat of unemployment—creates work incentives as discussed earlier). Among other things, this sort of labor market equilibrium will imply that family labor will be economically cheaper than hired labor. In addition, the sorts of information costs which make rationing in credit markets likely (discussed earlier) apply with particular force to loans to small-scale farmers, especially in high-risk environments (see Carter 1988). Finally, the difficulty of distinguishing the effects of bad luck (e.g., localized weather disaster or bird damage) from that of sloppy effort and management, would make insurance contracts costly to enforce.[21] In the actually existing world of asymmetric information, and intrinsically imperfect and missing markets, a producer's specific endowment of family labor, savings and risk-bearing capacity is likely to shape and distort economic behavior, with different groupings or classes of producers responding differently to apparently identical market or technological opportunities.[22]

Systematic analysis of agrarian economic performance under actually existing market imperfections raises numerous issues about the impact of a liberal policy regime. First, in basically egalitarian economies (e.g., much of Sub-Saharan Africa) economic liberalization may have modest stimulative impacts if price liberalization simultaneously magnifies price variability even as it improves average farmgate prices. As analyzed theoretically and empirically by Barrett and Carter (1996, 1997), the mixed (across countries and sectors) and disappointing record of agricultural liberalization in Africa may reflect the microeconomic naiveté of a policy regime designed around the presumptions of the world of the welfare theorems. Improved agricultural growth will likely require a mix of ancillary, activist policies to complement the putatively stimulative signals induced by market liberalization and exchange rate realignment.

Within inegalitarian economies (e.g., those of Latin America and parts of southern Africa), post–Arrow-Debreu analysis suggests two fundamental breakdowns which distort the process of market-mediated growth and transformation. First, production behavior is likely to systematically vary across wealth-based classes of producers, with low-wealth producers behaving like prototypical peasants (e.g., labor-intensive production, conservative, non-commercial strategies) and high wealth producers behaving like entrepreneurial capitalists (see Eswaran and Kotwal 1986, 1989a; Carter and Zimmerman 1995).[23] In this circumstance, new economic opportunities may become differentially stimulative across classes, making possible the sorts of class-based growth booms referenced earlier.

Second, in addition to this sort of static differentiation in production behavior, dynamic land and asset accumulation strategies can also systematically differ across classes in actually existing market economies. When producer classes pursue distinct production strategies they are likely to value land and other assets differentially and exhibit differential competitiveness in asset markets. To the extent that land markets are well integrated, those producers positioned to competitively accumulate land will generate upward pressure on asset prices which spills over and affects the land access of less competitive producers.[24] Microeconometric analyses of recent export booms in Guatemala and Paraguay indicate that differential production strategies—rooted in informationally imperfect markets— have spilled over into distinctive class-based patterns of land accumulation. In addition, the decisions about how much to save and how to allocate savings across risky (land) and less risky (grain stores) assets become class-differentiated to the extent that market economy has less than the full suite of Arrow-Debreu contingency markets. Thus, for example, low-wealth agents may find it entirely rational to devote their modest savings to low return assets (e.g., grain stores which yield a negative rate of return) even as their current production is sharply capital-constrained and their land base meager (for example, see the theoretical analysis in Zimmerman and Carter 1996a).[25]

Together, the various possibilities of differentiated production and accumulation strategies suggest that the process of agrarian growth and transformation in actually existing market economies can be an unsteady one, and one in which initial levels of inequality are reproduced and deepened by a growth process. Such possibilities introduce the question of the degree to which the trajectory of agrarian growth itself becomes a function of the initial asset distribution in the agrarian economy. Can the relatively egalitarian growth paths of East Asian economies be understood partially as the result of their relatively equal initial distribution of land, as opposed to the continuing reproduction of inequality which has characterized agrarian growth throughout much of Latin America? Another question concerns the breadth of asset inequality which is required to generate differentiated behavior. Hence, while the range of agrarian asset inequality in much of West Africa appears narrow, econometric work suggests that the degree of risk faced by producers across that range is broad enough that it could motivate sharply different production and accumulation strategies in a world of informationally imperfect markets (Carter 1997).

From a policy perspective, these post–Arrow-Debreu considerations indeed suggest that agrarian laissez faire may not suffice to generate growth in either the amounts or the form which is desired. But, can another policy regime do better? Information asymmetries, and the costs of providing capital and insurance to small-scale producers, are real economic phenomenon. That a competitive market finds it difficult to provide those services is decidedly not evidence that state programs and other centralized mechanisms can do it better, as the accumulated rubble of failed small-farm credit and insurance programs testify. There are policies, and well-ordered sequences of policies, which can make sense in particular environments, as Barrett and Carter (1996) and Carter and Barham (1996) discuss.[26] However, there is no magical formula, no slogan to mobilize a postliberal development policy strategy as the phrase "Get the prices right" did for liberalization. As Timmer (1988) remarks, recognition of the information costs and the intrinsic imperfections of fundamental markets renders a policy design complex. It also blunts the transmission of disciplinary development ideas to the policy sphere—a topic to which the conclusion of this essay will return.

Endogenous Growth Theory and the Reproduction of a Core-Periphery Structure

Perhaps traditionally the sharpest divide among students of development is between those who see the international economy as an arena which produces and reproduces the wealth of some nations at the cost of the persistent poverty of others, and those who see a world in which national growth and living standards eventually converge, extinguishing the distinction between developed and less developed countries. While the former receives its perhaps highest expression in the hands of the world systems theorists who explain the international economic perpetuation of core and peripheral countries (Wallerstein 1979), the latter is firmly rooted in the neoclassical economic growth theory spawned by Robert

Solow (1956). Economic growth in the Solow model results from the accumulation of reproducible assets (capital and labor), and, perhaps, from exogenous or unexplained technological progress. Assuming that there are decreasing returns to all factors (meaning, for example, that holding the amount of labor fixed, the returns from additional units of capital decrease),[27] economic growth in the Solow model converges to a constant, or steady state, level. The underlying logic is fairly straightforward—with returns to further capital accumulation diminishing, the rational agent maximizing a stream of present and (discounted) future utility will eventually cease to further sacrifice current consumption (through increased savings) for an ever smaller future return. For a given technology and rate at which the future is discounted, the poorer a country is, the faster it will initially grow, eventually catching up with the living standards of initially wealthier countries.[28] From this perspective, core and periphery are historical, but not future categories.

The mid-1980s saw the intellectual development of what became known as "endogenous growth theory" (Romer 1986 and Lucas 1988 are the classic early contributions—Romer 1994 provides an overview of work to date). From a theoretical perspective, endogenous growth theory emerges from a reconsideration of the mechanics of economic growth when the assumption of "no increasing returns" is purged from the Solow model. The label "endogenous growth" results from the literature's demonstration that the long-run growth of wealthy nations is not pinned down by diminishing returns to capital, but instead can be "endogenously" increased and sustained through the accumulation of reproducible assets which exhibit *increasing* returns. Knowledge and human capital are two assets which figure prominently in the endogenous growth models. Returns to both arguably increase as more of the assets are accumulated— for example. a single scientist in isolation is relatively unproductive, whereas a grouping of scientists generates proportionately large increases in technical knowledge. As explored in endogenous growth models, a world characterized by such increasing returns can be characterized by divergence, not convergence of living standards. While largely unexplored, endogenous growth theory ultimately offers important parallels to the world systems perspective (though see Krugman 1981).

Whatever its theoretical niceties, a huge boost to endogenous growth theory came from initial empirical evidence which showed that national growth rates over the last thirty years have not been converging in simple conformity with the Solow growth model. The result of this evidence has been an outpouring of econometric studies dedicated to testing the convergence hypothesis (see the Romer 1994 review). An interesting recent trend in the empirical literature is the finding of significant heterogeneity in the world economy. Quah (1993), for example, argues that the standard statistical approach in the convergence literature (which looks for a single summary statistic to see whether or not in general poor initially poorer countries grow faster than initially richer countries) is misleading if there is heterogeneity among countries and over time in the growth relationship. He then goes on to estimate the evolving distribution of income across nations, and finds that while there is some upward and downward mobility of countries, the long-term distribution of world income appears to be approaching a stable bipolar distribution of rich and poor. Somewhat similarly, Durlauf and Johnson (1994) find that the global economy is characterized by discrete growth regimes, and that while groups of countries (which they call "convergence clubs") appear to converge towards a common growth rate, the world economy is not itself characterized by convergence. Finally, a recent paper by Carter and Herrera (1995) explicitly explores the heterogeneity of the growth process among countries grouped by their initial (1960) income level. They find that these initial income "clubs" differ in both their mean trajectory and in the variability around that trajectory. In particular, the poorest grouping of countries on average shows a divergent pattern (i.e., they grow more slowly than the world average), although the performance of countries in this group is more variable then the other country groupings, with some countries growing quickly and others collapsing. By contrast, the club of wealthy nations more uniformly follows a growth regime which grows faster than the world average, again in contradistinction to the Solow model.

In its identification of multiple growth regimes and trajectories, this econometric evidence would seem to indicate space for structural factors and policy to systematically shape the impact of the fate of a country within the international economic system. Similarly, the unusually rapid and sustained growth of East Asian countries cries out for explanation and understanding.[29] While rapid East Asian growth was initially portrayed as the result of the liberal trade orientation of these countries (e.g., see Belassa 1985), this interpretation was hard to sustain as evidence mounted on the distinctive and pervasive illiberality of trade policy in these countries. In 1993, the World Bank issued its own accounting of the "East Asian Miracle," as it called it. While thorough in its cataloguing of East Asian interventionism, the Bank's conclusion that East Asia would have grown even faster without such distortions does not appear particularly well founded, even in terms of the assembled evidence (Rodrik 1994a delivers a particularly scathing methodological critique which nicely complements the criticism of Amsden 1994 and others).

Application of endogenous growth theory in fact provides a provocative series of insights into the desirability of trade liberalization. As compactly summarized by Rodrik (1994a), models of trade and growth in the presence of increasing returns can generate results to "satisfy any type of prior, or to rationalize any conventional wisdom," be it strongly free trade or its opposite. Free trade becomes undesirable in these models when a country's (static) comparative advantage lies in the production of goods which do not generate spillovers into other sectors or which do not require inputs or factors which exhibit increasing returns to scale. Thus, for example, as modeled by Matsuyama (1991), if agriculture is a conventional "diminishing returns" sector, while manufacturing is characterized by a "learning by doing" effect which generates an increasing return to scale (i.e., the more the manufacturing sector grows, the more productive it becomes), a country in which free trade points in the direction of agricultural specialization is doomed to lower long-term growth rates and foregone industrialization. Interestingly, Matsuyama's model, and this literature in general, seems to indicate that the ill-effects of free trade are strongest when trading partners are most unequal in their initial levels of capital and industrialization. From the perspective of this literature, free trade becomes most suspect for those countries whom liberal development has pushed most strongly in this direction.

But is free trade suspect enough that an alternative, more interventionist policy regime is called for? Interestingly, despite the boldly revisionist potential of the theory, most economists seem reluctant to stray too far from accepted liberal practice. Krugman's (1993) stance is perhaps archetypal when he closes his ironically named essay "Toward a Counter-Counterrevolution in Development Theory" by noting that it is not his "intention to offer a clarion call for interventionist trade and industrial policy," and instead only wants the World Bank to continue the promotion of trade liberalization with a bit more humility, borne of the knowledge that "it is not true that economic theory 'proves' that free markets are always best." Rodrik (1992) strikes a similar note when he closes his essay on the limits of trade liberalization with a similar observation that a more humble approach to trade liberalization will keep governments from becoming disillusioned with it and hence tempted to recklessly pursue interventionism.

While the transformation of these theoretical *ubermensch* into policy–Clark Kents superficially resembles the World Bank's hasty retreat from the seeming implications of its own study of the East Asian miracle, there is a substantive reason for their reticence. For while it may indeed be the case that the global economy will function to reproduce, rather than erase a center-periphery structure, there is no simple slogan to carry to the barricades of the counter-counterrevolution which says how to do it better. Krugman (1993) notes that the very factor (increasing returns) which underlies the new growth theory means that the market fragmentation and international insulation of blanket import-substitution regimes of an earlier era are likely to be particularly devastating. And yet, a more finely tuned trade and industrial policy which protects, cajoles, and threatens a domestic industry into (scale-efficient) production for the export market requires a credible government competence unafraid to discipline the private sector, yet not so autonomous that it becomes a predatory organism which uses the economy for short-term private gain. (Interestingly, this description of the disciplined developmental state strikingly parallels what Evans 1995 calls "embedded autonomy.") Given the apparent scarcity of such regimes, and relatively little understanding of where they come from, Rodrik (1993) closes his review essay with an essentially quietistic message that we best not pursue old new policy directions until we better understand the conditions for carrying out those policies successfully.

KNOWLEDGE, LEARNING, AND PERSUASION IN THE POLICY COMMUNITY

Economists are fond of quoting Keynes's statement that "Practical men, who believe themselves to be quite exempt from intellectual influences are usually the slaves of some defunct economist" (quoted in Heilbroner 1972). While useful for assuring that academic economists are paid more than historians, this statement suggests no answer to the question of how ideas pass into the practical realm of policy, except perhaps that "defunctness" somehow helps. And yet understanding how ideas influence policy seems especially relevant in the present moment of intellectual disequilibrium within development economics—a disequilibrium which this essay has described as the ironic conjuncture of a liberal development policy orthodoxy with a disciplinary economics in the midst of a "post–Arrow-Debreu" ferment which questions the universal desirability of economic liberalism.

There are a number of reasons for this disequilibrium and its persistence to date. From the outset it should be noted that policy is constantly evolving and that some of the disciplinary ideas discussed here indeed appear to be having incremental policy impacts. The Inter-American Development Bank, for example, called together a group of policymakers and academic economists in an effort to forge a new, self-styled Latin consensus (Birdsell, Graham, and Sabot forthcoming). While largely accepting of the macroeconomic success of the liberal "Washington Consensus" (see above), the call for a Latin Consensus is predicated on the interpretation that the evidence to date shows that liberalism is insufficient to generate a development path which fully incorporates and benefits all social sectors. Interestingly, this call for a post-liberalization Latin Consensus is motivated by the contrast between Latin America and East

Asia—the same contrast used to motivate trade and other liberalizations in the region.

While time and the unfolding of events will tell more about the transmission of post–Arrow-Debreu ideas into policy, the remainder of this essay will focus on the following three factors which may in fact inhibit their transmission over the longer term:[30]

1. the intrinsic complexity and conditionality of the ideas themselves;
2. the incompatibility between the ideas and political incentives; and
3. the loss of intellectual certainty and universality implied by the ideas ironically inhibits the formation of a coherent epistemic community capable of forcefully pressing the ideas forward.

As will be seen, for each of these factors the contrast with the earlier subsumption of microeconomic fundamentalism into a policy orthodoxy of development liberalism is instructive.

In terms of the first factor, while the economic analysis of actually existing market economies reveals the frailty and bias of the invisible hand as a mechanism of social coordination—and thus the abstract potential for doing better then a laissez faire regime—neither endogenous growth analysis, nor the analysis of agrarian growth paths in imperfect market environments, identifies an unconditional, one-size-fits-all, policy response. That is, neither points toward a single big bang idea or novel form of economic reorganization, such as central planning (or *laissez faire*, for that matter). Indeed, these analyses decidedly do not encourage a return to the past of either the sort of blanket protectionism associated with import-substitution industrialization, or the sorts of government price controls and marketing boards associated with *dirigiste* agrarian policy. The contrast with development liberalism is strong, as the latter offered universal policy prescriptions, many of which could be easily sloganized into phrases like "Get the prices right."

There are two reasons for the ambiguity and conditionality of the policy whimper of post–Arrow-Debreu development analysis. The first is that the analysis itself admits multiple trajectories and equilibria. In some structural circumstances and conditions, a liberal regime may perform quite fine, in others not so.[31] In endogenous growth models, the relative starting conditions (in terms of industrial structures and static comparative advantage) of two trading economies matter for judging the impact of trade liberalization. In models of agrarian growth and transformation, the initial distribution of endowments across agents matters for both the rate and distributive consequences of growth under a laissez faire regime—an identical policy may work differently in East Asia, than it would in arid regions of sub-Saharan Africa, than it would in the inegalitarian structures of Latin America. The second reason for the ambiguity and conditionality of the policy implications of these contemporary development ideas is that the analyses themselves are constructed carefully on an understanding of why the invisible hand of laissez faire fares poorly. And yet, the very factors which palsy the coordination of the invisible hand also confront policy responses. Thus, reaping the benefits of increasing returns requires the selective and disciplined use of interventions, as Bardhan (1993) puts it. Broadening the base of agrarian growth in those instances where market processes exclude small farmers means resolving the informational problems which render the market unable to directly exploit the poverty and productive potential of those individuals. In brief, the ideas imply policies which are as complex to communicate as they are to carry out well.

The issue of complexity aside, the second factor which may inhibit the transmission of these ideas to the policy realm is their dubious compatibility with political incentives. Economists have been eager to note that the interventionist policies of the preliberal era served the private interests of state policy makers (e.g., Krueger 1974 on import substitution policy; Bates 1981 on interventionist agrarian policies). At a more nuanced level of analysis, Cooper and Packard (this volume) have suggested that the interventionist policy regimes of the postwar era coincided with decolonization and were motivated by the need for new regimes and new multilateral organizations, to define and legitimate themselves. Interestingly, Krugman (1995) suggests that the eager adoption of the Washington Consensus liberalism by developing country leaders (prior to the Mexican debacle of late 1994) reflected their desire to cash-in on a speculative bubble of foreign capital inflows rather then their deep-seated belief in the long-run virtues of laissez faire.[32]

While it is beyond this essay's scope to push forward a theory of state action,[33] it is obvious that the present moment is clearly different then the immediate postcolonial period. It is also clear that the sorts of complex and nuanced policies implied by the new development economics—which imply a mix of market and state—offer neither the rent-seeking possibilities of the earlier policies, nor the capability of exciting skittish international investors to instigate politically pleasing capital in-flows. So, is there a politics to implement these ideas? Gupta (this volume) seems to imply in his analysis of agrarian populism in India that the answer is "no." For, while he shows that there was a macropolitical logic for Indira Gandhi to construct a populist coalition around the idea of improving the market access of the rural poor, and broadening the base of agrarian growth, he indicates that the relatively well-to-do rural classes eventually co-opted populist institutions and policies to their narrower ends. The competitive advantages of these classes in the political realm would appear to be based on the same scale and wealth factors which advantage these classes in the market realm. Such reinforcing of political biases does not bode well for the success of actually existing political systems as instruments to correct the failures of actually existing markets economies. On the other hand, Taiwan offers the interesting case in which an authoritarian regime pursued a redistributive land reform which has been credited by many as one of the key elements in that country's rapid and relatively equitable growth experience (see for example World Bank 1993).

Given these problems of analytical complexity and political incompatibility, it is perhaps not surprising to find the tentativeness and weak articulation of these ideas into the policy realm where liberalism still reigns. Yet much has been learned, and Romer (1994) and Carter and Barham (1996), among others, sound the call for further work to explore and sharpen the policy implications of these new currents in development thought. However, even presuming the uninterrupted march of normal science, and the derivation of sharper policy conclusions, will these ideas ever reshape policy in a fundamental way? A third factor which stands between these ideas and the policy realm is, ironically, a by-product of the intellectual openings upon which these ideas are themselves predicated. For implicit in these new disciplinary contributions has been the loss of singular universality which characterizes both liberalism and the developmentalist approaches of the post–World War II decades. The disciplinary jargon of the new research agendas—path dependence, multiple equilibria, hysteresis—hides a loss of faith. Rodrik (1994a), quoted above, says that (post–Arrow-Debreu) neoclassical theory can now be used to generate any result, support any ideological predilection. Given that many practicing economists already believed that data can be tortured to confirm most any prior belief, this epistemological delegitimation of theory becomes doubly important. The new currents in development economics thus dampen the prospects for a unified disciplinary consensus around them, even as they challenge policy makers to learn more complex lessons, on evidentiary grounds which seem less certain.[34] Unclear to this author at least is whether an epistemic community (as Adler and Haas 1992 call transinstitutional groupings of policy makers who share a similar understanding about how the world works) can be formed on such a foundation which seems shaky in comparison to that which nurtured the promulgation of development liberalism.

Perhaps in the end, time will close the disequilibrium between policy and ideas as the latter become more precise and certain. Policy might then become a truly nuanced, site specific, time varying sort of proposition. Perhaps, and perhaps then historians will be paid as much as economists!

NOTES

1. This paper is based on a presentation originally made to the Conference on Development Knowledge and the Social Sciences, University of Michigan, May 1994. The author would like to thank Fred Cooper and David Trubek for their critical encouragement and comments, and Kennette Benedict for asking the right questions about new ideas in economics. While not liable for what follows, Brad Barham, Chris Barrett, and Cesar Herrera contributed tremendously to the ideas in this paper. Support from the Global Studies Research Program of the University of Wisconsin under a grant from the John D. and Catherine T. MacArthur Foundation is gratefully acknowledged.

2. As will be discussed below, neoclassical economics has consequently seen an outpouring of models which look at such things as the conditions under which the gap between north and south deepens over time through free trade and other mechanisms, as well as at ways that the domestic distribution of wealth shapes the trajectory of growth and social transformation.

3. As will be discussed later, the liberalness of the East Asian experience has itself become hotly contested.

4. Thomas Biersteker (1995) reviews the mix of ideological, empirical, and material factors which powered this striking shift to liberal development strategy.

5. The quotation in the text is taken from Heilbroner (1972). As Evensky (1994) points out, Adam Smith thought that a particular moral framework was necessary to hold liberal society together, suggesting that Smith would have himself questioned the universality since ascribed to the beneficent operation of the invisible hand.

6. As will be discussed momentarily, this proposition has come to be known as the First Welfare Theorem—all competitive equilibria are Pareto optimal, meaning that there are not reallocations possible among agents which would make one person better off without making someone else worse off. That is, competitive equilibrium exhausts all possibilities for mutually beneficial exchange.

7. This approach is much less restrictive then is sometimes presumed by non-economists. As will be seen, models based on rational choice can generate very structural-looking results in the sense that the initial distribution and definition of property rights are central to shaping the way the economy works.

8. And, of course, given their resource endowments, which the analysis takes as nonproblematically defined and socially legitimate. The inappropriateness of this latter assumption, even in the context of the questions which neoclassical economics considers, is discussed in Carter (1985) and Hart (1986).

9. Eloquent testimony to the intradisciplinary power of Walrasian prices as the reasonable way to think about equilibrium prices is given by Barro's (1979) retraction of his own earlier efforts (Barro and Grossman 1972) to resituate Keynesian unemployment in a neoclassical model in which prices deviated from their Walrasian values. In the end, Barro agreed that non-Walrasian prices cannot be used to represent equilibrium in a market economic system. More generously, he might have said that a neoclassical model needs compelling reasons—consistent

with the self-interested pursuit of the relevant individual actors—which indicate why prices do not evolve toward their Walrasian levels (e.g., reasons which explain why an employer would not accept the low-wage offer of the unemployed, and hence move the price of labor toward its Walrasian equilibrium level).

10. What has become known as "Coase's Theorem" (after Coase 1961) offers an even stronger proposition—namely that even absent formal markets, individuals will make all mutually beneficial transactions, presuming there are no transactions costs. It is not clear how different this theorem is from the Arrow-Debreu results since, as we will see below, it is precisely the transaction costs associated with asymmetric information which make certain markets fail.

11. The Second Welfare Theorem is potentially very powerful since it implies that a decentralized market mechanism is the appropriate instrument to realize any socially desired outcome.

12. The published version of Stiglitz's remarks (Stiglitz 1989) does not contain the references cited in the text. It is probably fair to say that the fundamental intellectual fault line within mainstream economics is between those who see the glass as half full (and therefore tend to accept the universality of Smithian liberalism), and those who see it as half empty (the neoclassical left).

13. Hicks (1937) is generally credited with codifying the insights of Keynes (1935) into a set of aggregate economic relationships whose relationship to a theory of price formation and market equilibrium is murky, though Leijonhufvud (1968) suggests that Hicks himself fundamentally misunderstood Keynes's non-Walrasian microeconomics of information costs and price formation.

14. I do not know of any similarly startling statement on development economics, but the uneasy position of development economics within mainstream economics departments is perhaps the clearest testimony to the disjuncture between the subdiscipline and the fundamental microeconomic core. Axel Leijonhufvud's (1973) tongue-in-cheek essay "Life among the Econs," which describes the different fields within economics as distinctive castes of an anthropologically exotic tribe whose members construct "modls" (models), captures this ambiguity when he writes:

> The low rank of the Develops is due to the fact that this caste, in recent times, has not strictly enforced the taboos against association with the Poliscis, Sociogs and other tribes. Other Econ look upon this with considerable apprehension as endangering the moral fibre of the tribe and suspect the Develops even of relinquishing modl-making.

15. This author's late 1970s graduate education in economics was built around the slogan that "there ain't no such thing as macroeconomics—there is only good (and bad) microeconomics."

16. The demise of classical development economics is sometimes portrayed as the failure of authors such as Hirschman to "formalize" their ideas—that is, embed them in the language of mathematical models (e.g., see the discussion in Rodwin and Schön 1994). While lack of formalism per se indeed cripples an idea's acceptability within economics, an even greater problem occurs when the idea lacks coherent microeconomic foundations, meaning it is unclear what understanding of individual behavior and price formation buttresses the idea.

17. The discussion here ignores instances of conventional externalities in which an individual's valuation of a good does not fully reflect its social value. In the presence of externalities, individuals in a competitive economy tend to overuse or consume goods which negatively affect other people, and underprovide or consume those goods which positively affect other people. While externalities are of central importance to the overall evaluation of the social fitness of the market economy, the analysis here focuses on the degree to which competitive markets can guide the self-seeking behavior of individuals toward a socially desirable state even when there are no externalities. Broadway and Bruce (1984) provide a more comprehensive overview of the conditions under which the welfare theorems fail to hold.

18. Among methodologically neoclassical economists, John Roemer (1982, 1988) has led the way in showing how many of the insights and ideas of classical Marxian analysis can be recovered through the analysis of the correspondences which exist in Walrasian general equilibrium (replete with its "superficial equality of exchange") between an individual's endowment position in the economy and his or her class and exploitation status. Work which has extended Roemer's mode of analysis to economies with informationally imperfect markets (e.g., Eswaran and Kotwal 1986, 1989a, 1989b, Carter and Zimmerman 1995, Banerjee and Newman 1993), becomes perhaps "more Marxist" in appearance because individuals' ability to exercise certain choices, or participate in certain markets, becomes influenced by their initial structural position in the economy—with the rich optimally choosing to become capitalists and the poor, proletarians. The seeming dichotomy between structural and agency-based explanations begins to look more semantic and less real in these neoclassical models in which structure begins to tightly limit and constrain choice and agency.

19. A technology exhibits "constant returns to scale" when the amount of all input doubles (is cut in half), output doubles (goes down by half). This assumption seems appropriate on both empirical and conceptual grounds. Most agricultural technologies (e.g., seeds and fertilizer) are divisible and can be carried out equally well in a flower pot as on a large-scale field. While it is the case that some inputs are indivisible (e.g., tractors), rental markets would in theory make it possible for smaller scale producers to attain equal access to those inputs.

20. This would hold true even presuming that peasant producers are interested in food security and other consumption goals. For in the world of full and complete markets, food security concerns could be independently covered through insurance and forward markets, and the household's productive resources would be optimally allocated to maximize expected income. In the theoretical language of neoclassical peasant studies, production decisions would be fully "separable" from consumption concerns.

21. Of course events such as generalized flooding or drought would be easy to observe for an insurance provider. However, the fact that there are generalized (or covariate) risks means that, as a group, farmers form a bad and costly group for insurance purposes—rather like a group of individuals seeking cancer insurance when it is known that all group members will contract the disease at the same time. Binswanger and Rosenzweig (1986), for example, catalogue the impact of

these information problems on the systematic imperfections and absence of numerous key markets in rural economies.

22. Economic analysis of the organization of agricultural production has long been shaped by consideration of the informational characteristics of agricultural production processes. Brewster (1950), for example, uses the labor supervision story to explain the predominance of family-labor-based firms in agriculture, a theme continued in more contemporary writing (e.g., Binswanger et al. 1995; Lipton 1993). However, as stressed in the remainder of this section, the situation is more complex when one takes into account the countervailing failures which characterize capital and other financial markets.

23. Put differently, wealth strata become economic classes under the force of optimizing individual choice in the presence of systematically imperfect markets.

24. Lachmann's (1987) analysis of the English enclosure identifies increasing land rents as a key factor which displaced and proletarianized the small farm class which was ill-positioned to participate in the more remunerative activities which were driving the land price increase.

25. While such transactions which reshape the structure of land ownership are pairwise rational for the agents involved, they have spillover effects onto other agents and the economy as a whole. A key source of such spillovers is the higher effective or shadow cost of labor on large farms which is created by asymmetric information problems in the labor market. A shift of land to larger farms may thus lower aggregate labor intensity and absorption (and maybe land productivity) and create what Carter et al. (1996) call an "exclusionary" growth process.

26. Many of these policies require solutions to various problems of local cooperation and collective action so that the relatively plentiful and inexpensive information which is available to locally based peers can be mobilized in an incentive-compatible way. Examples from my own work include: an analysis of the failure of agrarian liberalization in Sub-Saharan Africa which suggests that the liberalization agenda must be expanded to include well-targeted and properly sequenced ancillary microeconomic policies (Barrett and Carter 1997); an analysis of the Paraguayan land problem which suggests that if the institutional policy agenda of land markets and land rights is pursued without or before capital market policies, then a highly exclusionary growth process in Eastern Paraguay will reproduce and deepen itself (Carter and Galeano 1995); an analysis of institutional transformation in West Africa which suggests that the privatization of customary tenures will form the basis for an unequalizing spiral of class differentiation given intrinsic imperfections in capital and insurance markets (Zimmerman and Carter 1996b).

27. Note that this assumption of decreasing returns is the same assumption upon which the Second Welfare Theorem is built, as discussed above.

28. "Poorer" here means an economy with less capital per-worker and hence higher ("less diminished") returns to investment or capital accumulation. The faster rate of growth of the poorer economy thus reflects an underlying logic of utility maximizing choice.

29. As explored in World Bank 1993, a large portion of East Asian growth cannot be accounted for by increases in capital and labor. Given that the amount

of this "total factor productivity growth" is much higher than that observed for other countries (and hence cannot be understood as a global improvement in technology), it would seem that the East Asian countries did something uniquely right at the policy level which permitted their economies to reap increasing returns to their factors of production.

30. A fourth factor which could be added to this list is the impact that professional canons of conformity have on the vigor and direction with which individual analysts might push their thinking. Such considerations might be particularly important in the area of trade policy where the professional presumption in favor of free trade is as intimidatingly strong as the comparative advantage case for free trade is simple and elegant. It seems likely that professional conformity and acceptability played a role in the ECLA shift from dependency to liberalism (described by Sikkink, this volume). Certainly this author absorbed the professional norm that ECLA was not a "serious place" in terms of economic analysis.

31. Thus, for example, the ECLA (1990) effort to temper its new-found free trade orientation with support for some level of active government policy comes off as incoherent and intellectually flabby to well-trained economists (e.g., to the author's graduate students, Boucher 1995 and Zegarra 1994) because it does not have a precise theory explaining why, in what industries, and under what circumstances government trade and industrial policy can do better than the market.

32. Note that Krugman's (1995) analysis contrasts with more conventional economistic visions of the adoption of liberalization, such as that articulated by Rodrik (1994b). This latter analysis is predicated on the notion that while trade liberalization is good for most people ("consumers"), its benefits are diffuse in contrast to the benefits of protectionism which are highly concentrated in a few hands. Rodrik thus suggests that liberalization finds a politically viable constituency only when it can be bundled with macroeconomic stabilization measures which hold a broader and stronger immediate political economic appeal.

33. For the record, it should be noted that the statement quoted from Keynes at the beginning of this section goes on to say: "Madmen in authority are distilling their frenzy from some academic scribbler of a few years back. I am sure that the power of vested interests is vastly exaggerated compared with the gradual encroachment of ideas."

34. Thus Krugman (1995), despite his seminal role in launching many of the new agnostic development ideas, takes comfort in the old time theory simply because it withstood the test of time and reigned universal for an extended period of time.

REFERENCES

Adler, Emmanuel, and Peter M. Haas. 1992. "Conclusion: Epistemic Communities, World Order, and the Creation of a Reflective Research Program". *International Organization* 46, no. 1: 367–90.

Amsden, Alice. 1994. "Why Isn't the Whole World Experimenting with the East Asian Model to Develop?: Review of TEAM". *World Development* 22, no. 4: 627–33.

Arrow, Kenneth, and Gerard Debreu. 1954. "Existence of an Equilibrium for a Competitive Economy". *Econometrica* 22, no. 2: 265–90.

Banerjee, A., and Andrew Newman. 1993. "Occupational Choice and the Process of Economic Development". *Journal of Political Economy* 101, no. 2: 274–98.

Bardhan, Pranab K. 1993. "Economics of Development and the Development of Economics". *Journal of Economic Perspectives* 7, no. 2: 129–42.

Barrett, ChristopherMichael R. Carter. 1996. "Does It Take More than Liberalization? The Economics of Sustainable Growth and Transformation". In *Development at a Crossroads: Uncertain Paths to Sustainability after the Neo-Liberal Revolution*, edited by M. R. Carter, J. Cason, and F. Zimmerman, 73–104. Madison, Wis.: Global Studies Program.

———. 1997. "Microeconomically Coherent Agricultural Policy Reform in Africa". In *The Role of the State in Key Markets*, edited by J. Paulson. London: Macmillan.

Barro, Robert. 1979. "Second Thoughts on Keynesian Economics". *American Economic Review* 69, no. 2: 54–59.

Barro, Robert, and Herschel Grossman. 1971. "A General Disequilibrium Model of Income and Employment". *American Economic Review* 61, no. 1: 82–93.

Barro, Robert, and Xavier Sala-i-Martin. 1992. "Convergence". *Journal of Political Economy* 100, no. 2: 223–51.

Bates, Robert M. 1981. *Markets and States in Tropical Africa.* Berkeley: University of California Press.

Bauer, P. T. 1976. *Dissent on Development* Cambridge: Harvard University Press.

Belassa, Bela. 1985. "Exports, Policy Choice, and Economic Growth in Developing Countries After the 1973 Oil Shock". *Journal of Development Economics* 18, no. 2: 23–35.

Bhagwati, J. 1978. *Anatomy and Consequences of Exchange Control Regimes.* Cambridge: Bollinger.

Biersteker, Thomas. 1995. "The Triumph of Liberal Ideas in the Developing World". *Global Studies Working Paper No. 6* Madison: University of Wisconsin.

Binswanger, Hans, Gershon Feder, and Klauss Deininger. 1995. "Power, Distortions and Reform in Agricultural Land Relations". In *Handbook of Development Economics*, edited by J. Behrman and T. N. Srinivassan, 3:2467–3047. Amsterdam: North Holland.

Binswanger, Hans, and Mark Rosenzweig. 1986. "Behavioral and Material Determinants of Production Relations in Agriculture". *Journal of Development Studies* 22: 503–539.

Birdsall, Nancy, C. Graham, and R. Sabot. eds. Forthcoming. *Inequality Reducing Growth in Latin America's Market Economies.* Washington: Inter-American Development Bank.

Bliss, Christopher, and Nicholas Stern. 1978. "Productivity, Wages and Nutrition, Parts I and II". *Journal of Development Economics* 5: 331–97.

Boucher, Stephen. 1995. "Technology, Growth and the International Economy in CEPAL's Latest Proposal: Intuitive Policies in Search of an Analytical Framework". Unpublished paper.

Bowles, Samuel. 1985. "The Production Process in Competitive Economies: Walrasian, Neo-Hobbesian and Marxian Models". *American Economic Review* 75, no. 1: 16–36.

Brewster, John. 1950. "The Machine Process in Agriculture and Industry". *Journal of Farm Economics.* 32, no. 1: 69–81.

Broadway, Robin W., and Neil Bruce. 1984. *Welfare Economics.* Oxford: Basil Blackwell.

Carter, Michael R. 1985. "A Wisconsin Institutionalist Perspective on Microeconomic Theory of Institutions: The Insufficiency of Pareto Efficiency". *Journal of Economic Issues* 19, no. 3: 797–813.

———. 1988. "Equilibrium Credit Rationing of Small Farm Agriculture". *Journal of Development Economics* 28, no. 1: 88–103.

———. 1997. "Environment, Technology and the Social Construction of Risk". *Economic Development and Cultural Change* 45, no. 3: 557–90.

Carter, Michael R., and Bradford Barham. 1996. "Level Playing Fields and Laissez Faire: Post-Liberal Development Strategies in Inegalitarian Agrarian Economies". *World Development* 24:1133–49.

Carter, Michael R., Bradford Barham, and Dina Mesbah. 1996. "Agro-Export Booms and the Rural Poor in Chile, Paraguay and Guatemala". *Latin American Research Review* 31, no. 1: 33–65.

Carter, Michael R., and Luis Galeano. 1995. *Campesino, Tierra y Mercado* Asuncion: Centro Paraguayo de Estudios Sociologicos.

Carter, Michael R., and Cesar Herrera. 1995. "Neither Wallerstein nor Solow: A Random Coefficients Model of Stasis and Mobility in the Economic World System". Unpublished manuscript.

Carter, Michael R., and Frederic Zimmerman. 1995. "Reproducing Inequality: The Dynamics of Asset Distributions in an Inegalitarian Agrarian Economy". Unpublished paper.

Coase, Ronald. 1961. "The Problem of Social Cost". *Journal of Law and Economics* 3, no. 1: 1–44.

Durlauf, Steven, and P. A. Johnson. 1994. "Multiple Regimes and Cross-Country Growth Behavior". SSRI Working Paper No. 9419R. Madison: University of Wisconsin.

Economic Commission for Latin America and the Caribbean. 1990. *Changing Production Patterns with Social Equity: The Prime Taste of Latin American and Caribbean Development in the 1990s.* Santiago: United Nations.

Eswaran, Mukesh, and Ashok Kotwal. 1986. "Access to Capital and Agrarian Production Organization". *Economic Journal* 96: 482–98.

———. 1989a. "Credit as Insurance for Agricultural Risk and Entrepreneurship". *Journal of Development Economics* 31, no. 1: 37–54.

———. 1989b. "Why Are Capitalists the Bosses". *Economic Journal* 99, no. 1: 162–76.

Evans, Peter. 1995. *Embedded Autonomy: State and Industrial Transformation.* Princeton: Princeton University Press.

Evensky, Jerry. 1994. "Retrospective: Ethics and the Invisible Hand". *Journal of Economic Perspectives* 7, no. 2: 197–206.

Geanakoplos, John. 1989. "Arrow-Debreu Model of General Equilibrium". In *The*

New Palgrave: General Equilibrium, edited by J. Eatwell, M. Milgate, and P. Newman, New York: Norton.

Greenwald, Bruce C., and Joseph Stiglitz. 1986. "Externalities in Economies with Imperfect Information and Incomplete Markets". *Quarterly Journal of Economics* 101, no. 2: 229–64.

Hart, Gillian. 1986. "Interlocking Transactions: Obstacles, Precursors or Instruments of Agrarian Capitalism". *Journal of Development Economics* 23: 177–203.

Heilbroner, Robert. 1972. *The Worldly Philosophers*. New York: Simon and Schuster.

Hicks, John. 1937. "Mr. Keynes and the Classics". *Econometrica* 5, no. 1: 147–59.

Keynes, John Maynard. 1935. *The General Theory of Employment, Interest and Money*. New York: Harcourt Brace.

Krueger, Ann. 1974. "The Political Economy of Rent-Seeking Society". *American Economic Review* 64, no. 3: 291–303.

———. 1978. *Foreign Trade Regimes and Economic Development: Liberalization Attempts and Consequences*. Cambridge, Mass: Bollinger Publishing Company for National Bureau of Economic Research.

Krugman, Paul. 1981. "Trade Accumulation and Uneven Development". *Journal of Development Economics* 8:149–61. Reprinted in P. Krugman, *Rethinking International Trade*. Boston: MIT Press, 1990.

———. 1993. "Towards a Counter-Counterrevolution in Development Theory". In *Proceedings of World Bank Annual Conference in Development Economics, 1992*. Washington, D.C.: World Bank.

———. 1995. "Dutch Tulips and Emerging Markets". *Foreign Affairs* 74, no. 4: 28–44.

Lachmann, Richard. 1987. *From Manor to Market: Structural Changes in England, 1536–1640*. Madison: University of Wisconsin Press.

Lal, Deepak. 1983. *The Poverty of Development Economics* London: Hobart Paperbacks.

Leijonhufvud, Axel. 1968. *Keynesian Economics and the Economics of Keynes* Oxford: Oxford University Press.

———. 1973. "Life among the Econs ". *Western Journal of Economics* 11, no. 3: 327–37.

Lewis, W. Arthur. 1954. "Economic Development with Unlimited Supplies of Labor". *Manchester School of Economic and Social Studies* 22, no. 1: 139–91.

Lipton, Michael. 1993. "Land Reform as Commenced Business: The Evidence Against Stopping". *World Development*, 21, no. 4: 641–57.

Lucas, Robert. 1988. "On the Mechanics of Economic Development". *Journal of Monetary Economics* 22, no. 1: 3–42.

Malinvaud, Edmund. 1977. *The Theory of Unemployment Reconsidered* Oxford: Blackwell.

Matsuyama, K. 1991. "Increasing Returns, Industrialization and Indeterminacy of Equilibrium". *Quarterly Journal of Economics* 106, no. 2: 616–50.

Nurkse, Ragnar. 1953. *Problems of Capital Formation in Underdeveloped Counties*. Oxford: Blackwell.

Prebisch, Raúl. 1950. *The Economic Development of Latin America and Its Principal Problems* Santiago: United Nations Economic Commission for Latin America.

Quah, Daniel. 1993. "Empirical Cross-Section Dynamics in Economic Growth". *European Economic Review* 37, no. 2: 426–34.

Rodrik, Dani. 1992. "The Limits of Trade Policy Reform". *Journal of Economic Perspectives* 6, no. 1: 87–105.

———. 1993. "Trade and Industrial Policy Reform in Developing Countries: A Review of Recent Theory and Evidence". NBER Working paper No. 4417. Cambridge, Mass.: National Bureau of Economic Research.

———. 1994a. "King Kong Meets Godzilla: The World Bank and the East Asian Miracle". CEPR Discussion Paper No. 944. London: Centre for Economic Policy Research.

———. 1994b. "The Rush to Free Trade in the Developing World: Why So Late? Why Now? Will It Last?" In *Voting for Reform: Democracy, Political Liberalization and Economic Adjustment*, edited by S. Haggard and S. Webb, 61–88. Oxford: Oxford University Press for the World Bank.

Rodwin, Lloyd, and Donald Schön, eds. 1994. *Rethinking the Development Experience: Essays Provoked by the Work of Albert O. Hirschman.* Washington, D.C.: Brookings Institute.

Roemer, John. 1982. *A General Theory of Exploitation and Class* Cambridge: Harvard University Press.

———. 1988. *Free to Lose: An Introduction to Marxist Economic Philosophy* Cambridge: Harvard University Press.

Romer, Paul. 1984. "The Origins of Endogenous Growth". *Journal of Economic Perspectives* 8, no. 1: 3–22.

———. 1986. "Increasing Returns and Long Run Growth". *Journal of Political Economy* 94, no. 5: 1003–1037.

Rosenstein-Rodan, Paul. 1943. "Problems of Industrialization of Eastern and Southeastern Europe". *Economic Journal* 53, no. 1: 202–211.

Shapiro, Carl, and Joseph Stiglitz. 1984. "Equilibrium Unemployment as a Worker Discipline Device". *American Economic Review* 74, no. 2: 433–44.

Solow, Robert. 1956. "A Contribution to the Theory of Economic Growth". *Quarterly Journal of Economics* 70: 65–94.

Stiglitz, Joseph. 1989. "Markets, Market Failure, and Economic Development". *American Economic Review* 79(2): 197–203.

———. 1992. "The Causes and Consequences of the Dependence of Quality on Price". *Journal of Economic Literature* 23, no. 1: 1–48.

Stiglitz, Joseph, and Andrew Weiss. 1981. "Credit Rationing in Markets with Imperfect Information". *American Economic Review* 71: 393–410.

Timmer, C. Peter. 1988. "The Agricultural Transformation". In *Handbook of Development Economics*, edited by H. Chenery and T. N. Srinivassan, 1:275–331. Amsterdam: North Holland.

Wallerstein, Immanuel. 1979. *The Capitalist World Economy* Cambridge: Cambridge University Press.

Williamson, John. 1996. "The Washington Consensus". In *Development at a Crossroads: Uncertain Paths to Sustainability after the Neo-Liberal Revolution*, edited by M. R. Carter, J. Cason and F. Zimmerman. Madison, Wis.: Global Studies Program.

World Bank. 1981. *Accelerated Development in Sub-Saharan Africa: An Agenda for Action.* Washington, D.C.: World Bank.

———. 1993. *The East Asian Miracle: Economic Growth & Policy.* Oxford: Oxford University Press.

Zegarra, Eduardo. 1994. "ECLA in Search for a New Role In Latin America: From Structuralism to Neoliberalism". Unpublished paper.

Zimmerman, Frederic, and Michael R. Carter. 1996a. "Dynamic Portfolio Management under Risk and Subsistence Constraints in Developing Countries". University of Wisconsin Agricultural and Applied Economics Staff Paper No. 402.

———. 1996b. "Rethinking the Demand for Institutional Innovation: Land Rights and Land Markets in the West African Sahel". University of Wisconsin Agricultural and Applied Economics Staff Paper No. 400.

FIVE

Anthropology and Its Evil Twin

"Development" in the Constitution of a Discipline

James Ferguson

DEVELOPMENT KNOWLEDGE AND THE DISCIPLINES:
A RESEARCH AGENDA

As more and more researchers turn their attention to studying, rather than simply participating in, the twentieth-century global project we call "development," it is beginning to be evident just how formidable an intellectual task stands before us. It seems more and more that our thinking about an object, development, that once seemed familiar (with its recognizable political economic logic, its manifest ideological motivations, its worrisome deleterious effects) must now take the form less of a set of convictions or conclusions than of a series of unanswered, but answerable, questions. Where did this bulwark of mid- to late-twentieth-century common sense come from? How did it end up taking the form that it did? What are the dynamics through which it is changing, and what political strategies might be effective in opposing, disrupting, or reforming it?

To answer such questions, it will be necessary to have good mappings of the conceptual and institutional terrain on which the power/knowledge regime of development has taken root and grown. One key feature of such a landscape is the set of complex, shifting relations that exists between the academic social sciences and the various kinds of knowledge and theory that circulate within the world of development.

What is the nature of this relation? A familiar academic conceit would have it that key ideas are developed and tested by "theorists" in academia before gradually diffusing outward into various "real world" applications. Development practitioners, in contrast, appear more likely to believe that important development ideas tend to be hammered out in practice, and that academic theory is largely irrelevant to what they do. The actual situation, however, may be more complicated than either of these folk models would allow.

A historical view reveals that models and theories developed within academic settings have been far from irrelevant to "real world" development practice, although they have not always been applied and used in the way that their academic originators might have wished. At the same time, though, it is clear that relations between different academic and nonacademic sites for the production of both knowledge and theory have been complex and multidirectional. In anthropology, for instance, no one could deny that academic theories of "functioning systems" and "social equilibrium" guided both the practice of applied anthropologists in colonial Africa, and the formulation of certain official ideas and policies pertaining to "colonial development." At the same time, however, one would be obliged to recognize that the applied research initiatives taken up in the 1940s and 1950s by the Rhodes-Livingstone Institute, for instance, helped in turn to shape the theoretical agenda of British academic anthropology. Clearly relations of this kind are both important and complex.

What is more, it seems clear that the nature of such relations between academic forms of theory and knowledge and those used in development settings varies both over time and across disciplines. In anthropology today, the relation between doing development and doing plain old anthropology is understood to involve a distinction between the pure and the applied—"academic" or "theoretical" anthropology versus development or practical anthropology. Yet, as I will show, the idea that development is an applied issue and not a theoretical one is a fairly recent addition to the stock of anthropological common sense. In other disciplines, meanwhile, the issue appears to be posed quite differently. For political science and sociology, for instance, development appears to be an issue not so much for applied researchers as for "area studies" or "international" specialists—a distinction that has little force in anthropology, where everyone is an area studies specialist.

The kinds of relations that link the academic disciplines to the production and circulation of development knowledge and theory therefore require to be studied with some specificity, taking into account the distinctive configurations of the different disciplines, as well as changing relations over time. Such a project might be important not only as a way of furthering our understanding of the world of development and how it works, but also as a way of understanding our own positions as academics who seek to have some effect on that world. How, for instance, are we to understand the real importance and efficacy of academic critique in the politics of development? Considering how central the project of critique is to many academics who work on development we have remarkably little understanding of what it actually accomplishes. Clearly critique is not as all-powerful a force as we might like to believe. (Consider only how little difference the academic-theoretical destruction of "modernization theory" seems to have had on the practices of many development agencies, where practitioners assure us it remains alive and well.) Yet it is equally clear that what happens in the domain of academic critique is not wholly cut off from the wider world, either. What kinds of flows exist, linking academic theories and knowledges to the world of agencies, policies, and practical politics? What does this mean for the tactics of a critical intellectual activity that seeks to participate in the crucial political struggles surrounding the governing and managing of what has come to be called "the Third World"?

This paper does not seek to answer these questions, but to begin work on one small part of a larger research agenda that might do so. By looking at some of these issues in the context of one discipline, it contributes to a larger project that would systematically investigate the relations between the ideas and practices of development and the disciplinarily configured knowledges of the social sciences.

For the case of anthropology, I will argue, the disciplinary relation to development has been both especially difficult and especially central, thanks to anthropology's historical role as the science of "less developed" peoples. While the underpinnings of such a conception in social evolutionist theory were largely eroded during the course of the twentieth century, the place of anthropology in the academic division of labor (and thus its academic-political need for distinctiveness vis-à-vis sociology, history, political science, etc.) has continued to give "the anthropological" a special relation to the "less developed." In particular, I will try to show that the marked antipathy of much mainstream anthropology for development, as well as the sharp separation of an applied development anthropology from a theoretical academic sort, may be taken as signs not of anthropology's critical distance from development but of its uncomfortable intimacy with it. I will suggest that insofar as the idea of a distinctively anthropological domain of study remains linked (if only implicitly) to ideas of development and its lack, a truly critical stance toward development will require a willingness to question the disciplinary identity of anthropology itself.

THE CONCEPT OF "DEVELOPMENT" AND THE THEORETICAL FOUNDATIONS OF ANTHROPOLOGY

[W]e owe our present condition, with its multiplied means of safety and of happiness, to the struggles, the sufferings, the heroic exertions and the patient toil of our barbarous, and more remotely, of our savage ancestors. Their labors, their trials and

> *their successes were a part of the plan of the Supreme Intelligence to develop a*
> *barbarian out of a savage, and a civilized man out of this barbarian.*
>
> LEWIS HENRY MORGAN, CLOSING LINES OF *Ancient Society* (1877: 554)

The origins of anthropology as a discipline are conventionally traced to the late nineteenth century, and to such "founding father" figures as Lewis Henry Morgan in the United States and E. B. Tylor in Britain. The dominant conception that such thinkers elaborated, and the key idea that gave to anthropology its early conceptual coherence as a discipline, was the idea of social evolution. Against the common nineteenth-century assumptions that "savages" such as the Australian aborigines or Native Americans were either essentially different kinds of creatures than "civilized" Europeans (the racist supposition), or examples of degeneration, showing just how far from God and original perfection it was possible for miserable sinners to fall (a theological interpretation dating back to the middle ages), the social evolutionists insisted that what they called "savages" and "civilized men" *were* fundamentally the same type of creature, and that if "higher" forms existed, it was because they had managed to evolve out of the "lower ones" (rather than vice-versa, as degeneration theory had it).

The project for the new field of anthropology was to trace the different stages of this progression, and to use observations of "savage" and "barbarian" peoples as evidence that would fill in what the earlier stages of human history had been. Thus did nonwestern peoples end up construed as living fossils whose history and experience "represent, more or less nearly, the history and experience of our own remote ancestors when in corresponding conditions" (Morgan 1877: vii). On the one hand, it is important to note that this was a vision of a kind of human unity. But on the other, of course, it was a device of differentiating and ranking different contemporary societies according to their level of evolutionary development, since (in spite of the best laid plans of the Supreme Intelligence) "other tribes and nations have been left behind in the race of progress" (1877: vi).

The idea of "development" was, of course, central to this conception—indeed, Tylor was able to refer to the social evolutionist position simply as "the development theory" (Tylor 1884: 90–91). Development was the active principle according to which new and higher stages of human society might emerge out of older and more simple ones: the driving motive force in human history. The circular logical move from a perceived directionality in history (e.g., a perception that complex civilizations arose from simpler ones) to the imputation of a teleological force that had caused it (i.e., the idea that such "advances" are *caused* or *explained* by a universal principle or "law" of social evolution) cast doubt upon the scheme's explanatory power, as anti-evolutionist critics quickly pointed out. But the idea that human history was animated by a single great principle of directional movement—evolutionary "development"—provided an extraordinarily powerful narrative device for those who would tell a single, unified, and meaningful story of "Mankind." The metaphor of "development" invited, too, a fusing of the idea of evolutionary advance with the developmental maturation of an organism or person, thus facilitating the persistent slippage between the contrasts primitive/civilized and child/adult that played a key role in ideologies of colonialism.

The development theory of nineteenth-century evolutionist anthropology, of course, reflected basic cultural and philosophical themes with a long and deep history in western thought (see also Nisbet 1969, 1980; Williams 1985, Young 1990). Yet it possessed a specificity that goes beyond such generic themes as the idea of progress, or the ontology of monism. In particular, there are three key principles embedded in nineteenth-century social evolutionism that are worth emphasizing. First, there is the central idea that different societies are to be understood as discrete individuals, with each society making its way through the evolutionary process at its own pace, independently of the others. Second is the insistence that although each society is in some sense on its own, all societies are ultimately heading toward the same destination; in this sense, human history is one story, not many. Finally, the social evolutionary schemes posited that differences between human societies were to be interpreted as differences in their level of development. If other peoples differed from the western standard, it was only because, "left behind in the race of progress," they remained at one of the prior developmental levels through which the West had already passed. Taken together, these three principles frame a formidable and durable vision of human history and human difference, "a vast, entrenched political cosmology" (Fabian 1983: 159) that has been of enormous consequence both in anthropology and in the wider world.

Within anthropology, the evolutionary schemes of nineteenth-century theorists like Morgan and Tylor are generally taken to have been definitively refuted in the early twentieth century, most of all by the work of the American relativist and culture historian Franz Boas and his students. In the wake of their devastating criticisms of the empirical adequacy of the nineteenth-century evolutionary schemes, the emphasis on sorting societies according to their level of evolutionary development largely dropped out of anthropology in the first half of the twentieth century. Both in the United States and in Britain,[1] though in different ways, a critique of speculative evolutionism was followed by moves to relativize ideas of progress and development. From whose point of view could one society be seen as "higher" than another, after all? Evolutionism came to be seen not only as empirically flawed, but as ethnocentric as well. The task, instead, came to be seen as one of understanding each unique society "in its own terms," as one of many possible ways of meeting human social and psychological needs (Malinowski), or as one "pattern of culture" (Benedict), one "design for living" (Kluckhohn) among others.

At one level, such shifts did mark a clear break with evolutionist ideas of development:[2] nonwestern cultures, in the new view, were no longer to be understood as "living fossils" trapped in evolutionary stages through which the West itself had already passed. Different societies now really were different, not just the same society at a different stage of development. Yet the break with evolutionism was less complete than it is often made to appear. It is significant, for instance, that mid-twentieth-century relativist approaches (whether Boasian/American or functionalist/British) preserved the old evolutionist idea that different societies were to be conceived as individuals.[3] Even more striking, perhaps, is the way that postevolutionist approaches preserved the grand binary distinction between primitive and modern societies, and accepted that anthropologists' primary specialization would remain the study of primitive societies. No longer would different primitive societies be placed on a ladder and ranked against each other; all were now equally valid, forming whole culture patterns (US) or functioning systems (UK) worth studying in their own right. But they were still seen as a distinctive class set apart from, and in some sense prior to, "modern," "western," "civilized" society. It is telling that both the label, "primitive" (or some close synonym), and the underlying category, were accepted by the leading anti-evolutionist anthropological theorists (e.g., Boas, Malinowski, Benedict, Mead, Radcliffe-Brown, Evans-Pritchard, Gluckman) right up until the 1960s and 1970s (and even later, in some cases). As Fabian (1983: 39) has pointed out,

> Just because one condemns the time-distancing discourse of evolutionism he [sic] does not abandon the allochronic understanding of such terms as "primitive". On the contrary, the time-machine, freed of the wheels and gears of the historical method, now works with "redoubled vigour". The denial of coevalness becomes intensified as time-distancing turns from an explicit concern into an implicit theoretical assumption.

The basic evolutionary dualism of primitive versus modern thus persisted in twentieth-century anthropology, even long after the demise of evolutionism in its strong, nineteenth-century form. Indeed, as recently as 1991, Claude Levi-Strauss (author of perhaps the single most widely-read and far-reaching critique of social evolutionism and its developmentalist premises, "Race and History" [Levi-Strauss 1976]) felt called upon to make clear that his concern for "traditional societies" should in no

way be misconstrued as a form of support for anticolonial movements or
Third World nationalism. As he explained, "I'm not interested in people
as much as beliefs, customs, and institutions. So I defend the small populations who wish to remain faithful to their traditional way of life, away
from the conflicts that are dividing the modern world." People in the
Third World "who leave this [traditional] state and take part in our [*sic*]
conflicts," he went on to explain, "cause political and even geopolitical
problems" (Levi-Strauss 1994: 425). In formulations like this, it is evident
that the idea of an evolutionarily primitive state, prior to the contamina-
tions of "development," remains remarkably central to a certain idea of
both what anthropologists study, and to whom they owe their political
loyalties. Insofar as an explicitly nonevolutionist anthropology through
most of the twentieth century continued to be construed as the study of
(as Levi-Strauss would still have it) "small populations" who "remain faithful to their traditional way of life," the anthropological object continued
to be defined within the terms of a plainly evolutionary dualism that in-
sistently distinguished between a developed, modern "us" and a not-yet-
developed, primitive "them."[4]

"DEVELOPMENT" BECOMES "APPLIED"

"They are too modern. They probably all wear pants."
A SENIOR BRITISH AFRICANIST, CA. 1969, TO SALLY FALK MOORE,
EXPLAINING WHY A STUDY OF THE "MODERNIZING" CHAGGA OF TANZANIA
WOULD BE OF MERELY APPLIED, RATHER THAN THEORETICAL, INTEREST.

Anthropologists had, of course, long recognized the existence of a set of
issues surrounding the interactions of "primitive" peoples with a modern
industrial world that encroached upon them. Some early twentieth-century diffusionists had emphasized such connections (Vincent 1990: 119–
25), and even the most ahistorical sorts of "salvage anthropology" were
obliged to recognize the impact of such things as capitalism and colonialism, if only so that their distorting effects could be filtered out in the
reconstruction of hypothetical "pre-contact" social and cultural forms
(Tomas 1991, Stocking 1991). It was also recognized early that anthropology might claim a place for itself in the world of practical affairs (and,
not incidentally, a share of the funding pie) by providing scientific advice
on the nature of such processes. As early as 1912, Rivers had sought to
obtain Carnegie Foundation support for the new discipline of anthropology on the grounds that anthropological knowledge might help to understand better the "rapid and destructive change" wrought by imperial
rule; in 1917, Rivers again pleaded for an anthropological role in "The
Government of Subject Peoples" (Vincent 1990: 120). Later, Malinowski
would call for a "Practical Anthropology," which would be an "anthro-

pology of the changing Native" and "would obviously be of the highest importance to the practical man in the colonies" (1929: 36). As Stocking has noted, such appeals to practical application were key to the establishment of British anthropology in the 1930s, especially through the securing of Rockefeller Foundation funding (Stocking 1992: 193–207, 255–75; see also Kuklick 1991). In the United States, meanwhile, applied work on change and acculturation flourished in the 1930s and 1940s, as the discipline's emphasis turned away from "salvage anthropology" and toward domestic social problems, poverty, and the war effort (Vincent 1990: 152–222, Stocking 1992: 163–68; see Gupta and Ferguson, 1997).

There are two observations that might be made about such work. First, although the connection may appear self-evident to the late-twentieth-century reader, the idea of development does not seem, in this period, to have been considered especially central to the question of the impact of western expansion on peripheral or colonized peoples. The operative concepts, instead, were "acculturation" and "assimilation" (especially in the United States) and "culture contact" and (later) "social change" (mostly in Britain). The old idea of evolutionary development, after all, had referred to an internal and immanent societal process, analogous to the autonomous development of an organism; the question of the impact one society might have on another was of quite another order. And such evolutionist theories of society were in any case out of favor at this time, on both sides of the Atlantic. In this context, the theoretical concept of development seems to have had very little to do with discussions of social change, acculturation, and applied anthropology.

Second, it is important to note that although studies of culture contact and culture change enjoyed some significant visibility in the field during the 1930s and 1940s, they failed to achieve dominance, or even full legitimacy, within the discipline. As late as 1936, the editor of *American Anthropologist* questioned whether acculturation studies even belonged in anthropology at all, suggesting that they were really a form of political science instead (Vincent 1990: 198; Spicer 1968: 22). Even much later, studies of "acculturation" and "social change" remained mostly low-status pursuits in academic anthropology. The obvious explanation for this is perhaps that applied work in nearly any field suffers from a relatively low academic status, as against loftier theoretical pursuits. But there does not seem to be any intrinsic reason why social change and culture contact should not themselves have been considered theoretical topics. How did such issues come to be seen as primarily *applied* concerns in the first place?

As I have argued elsewhere (Gupta and Ferguson, 1997), the ascendancy of a distinctively localizing, "peoples and cultures" style in anthropology was tied to the rise of fieldwork as a hegemonic and disciplinarily distinctive method. With the Malinowskian revolution in fieldwork methodology (which was really only consolidated in the 1930s) came a newly strengthened expectation that a scientific anthropological study would be a comprehensive account of "a people," "a society," "a culture"—in short, an *ethno*-graphy, an account of a whole social or cultural entity, ethnically defined. Within such an optic, the central theoretical agenda concerned the description and comparison of "whole societies" characterized by their distinctive "social systems" (UK) or "cultural configurations" (US). When societies left this state of wholeness through processes of change imposed from without, they also threatened to leave the domain of anthropology, in a process that was generally considered to be of great practical importance, but limited theoretical interest.[5] Malinowski was ready enough to make grandiose claims for anthropology's expertise in culture contact and social change when it was a matter of beating the drum for more funding (Stocking 1992: 193–207, 255–75), but the actual status that such work enjoyed within the discipline is perhaps revealed more precisely by Mair's recollection that "Malinowski sent me to study social change because, he said, I didn't know enough anthropology for fieldwork of the standard type" (Grillo 1985: 4).

Development, Decolonization, Modernization

A major geopolitical restructuring, and with it a new burst of social engineering, reconfigured the political and institutional landscape of the social sciences in the years following World War II. There is a great deal about this crucially important period that is not yet very well understood, and further research may be necessary before it is possible to get a satisfactory understanding of what postwar developments meant for the academic disciplines. Cooper (this volume) has recently begun to excavate the origins of a global project of "development" from within the postwar planning of the colonial empires (see also Cooper 1996). One important early finding of this work is that, in the process of decolonization, a strategically vague story about development came to provide an ambiguous charter both for retreating colonial bureaucrats *and* for ascendant nationalist rulers (see Bose, this volume). This charter, a broad vision that came to be shared by a wide set of transnational elites, framed the "problems" of the "new nations" in the terms of a familiar (at least to those schooled in nineteenth-century anthropology) developmentalist story about nations (conceived, again, as individuals) moving along a pre-determined track, out of "backwardness" and into "modernity."[6]

It was within the terms of this narrative, of course, that a host of "development agencies," programs of "development aid," and so on, were conceived and put into place in the years following World War II (Escobar 1995). One of a number of consequences of this development was that funding and institutional positions became increasingly available for those with the sorts of expertise considered necessary to bring about the great transformation. The world of academic knowledge could hardly have remained unaffected. Not surprisingly, the first discipline to feel the effects of the new order was economics, and a recognized subfield of "development economics" appeared swiftly in response to the postwar initiatives (Hirschman 1981, Seers 1979). But how did this historical conjuncture affect the practices of anthropologists?

As experts on "backward peoples," anthropologists were clearly well positioned to play a role in any project for their advancement. In the past, anthropologists had often been openly hostile toward social and cultural change, seeing it as a destructive force that might wipe out fragile cultures before they could be properly recorded and studied by ethnographers. Yet development in the postwar era was linked to a much more optimistic mood, and to a universalizing political project of democratization and decolonization (see Cooper, 1996). The new notion of progress was linked not simply to western expansion or emulation, as in the nineteenth century, but to a specifically *inter-national* conception in which formerly "primitive" peoples might proudly "emerge" into the modern world and take their seat at the table of the "family of nations" (Malkki 1994). Where anthropological liberalism had once been most comfortable arguing that nonmodern "others" had functioning, well-adapted social and cultural orders of their own, the times more and more called for a different argument: that "natives" could just as well, given a little time (and perhaps a little help), participate in the modern world on equal terms (see Wilson and Wilson 1945; Mead 1956).

Such impulses are particularly well illustrated in the work of the Rhodes-Livingstone Institute in (then) Northern Rhodesia. Set up as an applied research institute to provide useful information to government and industry, it is often cited as an early example of anthropological engagement with problems of industrialization, migrant labor, and other "modern" issues (Werbner 1984, Brown 1973). Animating such work was an optimistic conception of an emerging modern Africa, and a commitment to showing that Africans were successfully adapting to urban, industrial conditions. Against conservative and racist arguments that Africans did not belong in "white" towns on a permanent basis, and would always remain primitive villagers at heart, anthropologists sought to show that African migrants were settling more permanently in town (Wilson 1941–1942), that they were developing new modes of urban social interaction there (Mitchell 1956), and arriving at new political structures suited to their new needs (Epstein 1958). Such accounts retained some traces of the old anthropological suspicion that economic and cultural assimilation to western ways was not necessarily a welcome development, and they

emphasized the ethnographically particular details of a process that resisted being neatly fitted into a simplistic, universal developmental narrative. But however messy it might be, they left no doubt that what they
called "the industrial revolution in Africa" was an epochal, historically
progressive force that would ultimately bring Africans into the modern
world. Portraying with sympathy and approval the emerging new class of
"modern," westernized, urban Africans (as Magubane [1971] has
charged), the Rhodes-Livingstone Institute anthropologists positioned
themselves not, in the traditional anthropological style, as the chroniclers
of the vanishing old ways, but as the defenders of the right of Africans to
enjoy the modern new one.[7] (See Ferguson 1990).

As decolonization proceeded, the social sciences became more and
more concerned with the problems of the development of new nations.
In the process, the anthropological concern with social and cultural
change became increasingly linked with the idea of development, and
(especially in the United States) with modernization theory as elaborated
in other disciplines (notably Political Science and Sociology). "Social
change" was now to be understood as "development," the evolutionist
connotations of the old nineteenth-century term being newly appropriate
to the mood of the times. Indeed, ideas of linear stages that would have
been quite familiar to Morgan began to reappear in surprisingly explicit
ways in modernization theory (see Hymes 1972: 28–30). Theoretically,
ideas of social evolution began to become respectable again in American
anthropology (starting with Leslie White in the 1940s, and continuing
through the 1950s and 1960s, with figures like Service, Sahlins, and Harris). But even anthropologists with no explicit allegiance to neo-evolution-
ist theory began to bend their work in the direction of modernization.[8]
Indeed, it is striking how many American anthropologists trained in a
cultural relativist tradition that explicitly rejected evolutionist schemes of
stage-wise progressions were by the early 1960s signing on uncritically to
such dubious modernization schemes as Walt Rostow's *The Stages of Growth*
(1960), offering as a distinctive anthropological contribution the locating
of cultural obstacles to economic "take-off" (for a sophisticated example,
see Geertz 1963a, 1963b).

If the earlier anthropological shift from evolutionism to relativism had
resulted in the issue of developmentalist progressions being turned "from
an explicit concern into an implicit theoretical assumption" (Fabian
1983: 39), the postwar era begins to see a shift back to explicit concern.
What had been a background theoretical assumption (a fundamental difference between primitive and modern societies) is abruptly shifted from
the background to the foreground, and from the passive voice to the
active. Increasingly, the question becomes, how do "traditional societies"
become modern? And how can they be helped (or made) to make this

transition? But, significantly, this question has become linked less to abstract theoretical speculation than to explicit programs of directed social
change. The grand project that Morgan (in the passage quoted at the
opening of this essay) saw as reserved for "the Supreme Intelligence"—
"to develop . . . a civilized man out of this barbarian"—was now understood to be a job for the merely mortal intelligence of anthropologists.

For Morgan, of course, the question of how societies developed from
one evolutionary level to the next was nothing if not a theoretical one:
his typology of developmental stages aimed at nothing less than the explanation of both human history and human diversity. Even for evolutionism's relativist and functionalist critics, as I have argued, the distinction between "primitive" and "modern" societies was a theoretically
zmotivated one. But with the new project of official modernization, issues
of development came increasingly to belong (as had the earlier issues of
"acculturation" and "social change") less to the academic world of theory
(which remained largely devoted to comparing and generalizing about
"primitive societies") than to a domain of practical, policy-oriented work
on problems of contemporary economic transitions. "Development" had
become "applied."

Academic anthropology in the 1950s and 1960s mostly kept its distance
from such applied issues of development. The "theoretical" work that
earned high status in the academic world was largely centered on comparing and generalizing about societies and cultures conceived as separate
and autonomous individuals, whether the subject matter was kinship, social structure, or culture and personality. In this larger context, the
change-oriented work of the Rhodes-Livingstone Institute was indeed ex-
ceptional. Yet, even in this case, it is noteworthy that the
Rhodes-Livingstone anthropologists who had the greatest impact on academic anthropology were not those working on urbanization and industrialization (e.g., Clyde Mitchell, who came to be appreciated more by
sociologists than by anthropologists, or Godfrey Wilson, whose *Essay on the
Economics of Detribalization in Northern Rhodesia* was not widely appreciated
until much later). The greatest academic influence, instead, was exerted
by figures like Max Gluckman and Victor Turner, whose best-known works
on the Lozi and Ndembu respectively remained in the classical anthropological mold of the ahistorical, rural, "tribe" study. Studying "modernizing" peoples might well be of considerable applied or policy significance, as the senior Africanist quoted at the top of this section conceded.
But a study of people (men?) who "probably all wear pants" could hardly
be central to the more prestigious arena of anthropological theory, built
as it was upon the description and comparison of societies as little contaminated by development as possible.

Neo-Marxist Critique

A major disruption of the received anthropological wisdom regarding development and modernization came with the rise of dependency theory and a set of neo-Marxist critiques of both modernization theory and traditional anthropology. The nature of these critiques is well known, and they have been discussed extensively elsewhere. (For discussions of the impact within anthropology, see O'Laughlin 1975, Foster-Carter 1977, Seddon 1978, Oxaal, Barnett, and Booth 1975, Wolf 1982, Bloch 1985). I will therefore not review these critiques in detail here, but will simply underline their significance for the developmentalist foundations of anthropology.

The context for the neo-Marxist critique was significantly shaped by the social and political upheavals of the 1960s. Developments in the wider world (especially the rising tide of Third World nationalism and anti-colonial wars of liberation) combined with political upheavals on western university campuses to impress upon anthropologists the need to give more attention to questions of social change, domination, and colonialism. Since, as we have seen, the intellectual resources for dealing with such questions that had developed within Anglo-American anthropology were fairly limited, it is perhaps not surprising that many of the key ideas of this period came from elsewhere. By the 1970s, both disciplinary and national borders seemed to have softened: French structural Marxism (as elaborated by philosophers such as Louis Althusser, as well as by anthropologists such as Claude Meillassoux and Pierre-Philippe Rey), as well as Latin American dependency theory and Wallersteinian world system theory, began to make their way into the Anglo-American anthropological mainstream. The old functionalist orthodoxy began to splinter, as history, political economy, and colonialism began to gain new legitimacy as bonafide anthropological topics.

For anthropology's relation to development, the most significant aspect of the turn to Marxism and political economy in the 1970s was its profound challenge to two key pillars of anthropology's inherited developmentalist cosmology. First, and perhaps most profoundly, the new critical anthropology rejected the picture of the world as an array of individual societies, each moving through history independently of the others. This, as I suggested above, was a vision that was largely shared by the nineteenth-century evolutionists and their twentieth-century critics, who disagreed about whether the different tracks all headed in the same direction, but accepted the idea of different and separate tracks.[9] In place of this conception, anthropologists influenced by dependency theory, neo-Marxist modes of production theory, and world system theory, began to insist that differences between societies had to be related to a common history of conquest, imperialism, and economic exploitation that systematically linked them. Supposedly traditional practices and institutions, rather than being relics of a pre-capitalist past, might instead be interpreted as products of, or reactions to, processes of capitalist penetration, the articulation of modes of production, or world-system incorporation. And poverty, rather than an original condition, might be a *result* of such processes. Instead of being simply "*un*developed" (an original state), the Third World now appeared as actively "*under*developed" by a first world that had "underdeveloped" it (thus Walter Rodney's influential title: *How Europe Underdeveloped Africa*).

This brings us to the second pillar of developmentalist thought that was brought into question in this period: the assumed identity of development with a process of moral and economic progress. Neo-Marxists insisted that what was called "development" was really a process of *capitalist* development: the global expansion of the capitalist mode of production at the expense of existing pre-capitalist ones. And the outcome of such a process might not be "real development," in the sense of a better life for people in the Third World, at all. Development (really, capitalist development), then, might not be "Progress" in any simple way; indeed, for poor peasants, it was likely to make life much worse. The benign moral teleology of the development story (a central feature of nineteenth-century anthropology and 1960s "modernization theory" alike) was radically called into question.

These two breaks with anthropology's developmentalist heritage were of fundamental importance. Indeed, they provide an invaluable point of departure for those who would restructure anthropology's disciplinary relation to development. However, as with the relativists' rejection of nineteenth-century social evolutionism, it is important to recognize not only what the critics were rejecting of the development story, but what they were willing to retain of it as well. It is evident, for instance, that for neo-Marxism, world history still had the character of an evolution, with the march of the capitalist mode of production leading in a linear, teleological progression toward a future that would culminate (if only after a long process of struggle) in socialism. There remained, too, a tenacious attachment to the idea of what was again and again spoken of as "*real* development" (in the name of which "mal-" or "under-" development could be denounced). And if capitalism could not deliver the "real development" goods, neo-Marxism was prepared to promise that socialism could—and even, all too often, to endorse the exploitation of peasant producers by radical Third World states in the name of "socialist development."

"Development Anthropology"

It is ironic, but probably true, that the very popularity within anthropology of the radical, neo-Marxist critiques of orthodox development and modernization theory in some ways set the stage for a new era of closer collaboration between anthropologists and the organizations and institutions charged with implementing capitalist development policy. If nothing else, the radical critiques made it more legitimate, and more intellectually exciting, to study issues of development in the context of an increasingly radicalized and politicized discipline. At a time when university-based scholarship was under pressure to demonstrate its relevance, and when anthropology was particularly challenged to show that it had something to say about change, not just stasis, and about the modern world, not just the "tribal" one, a politically engaged and theoretically challenging approach to development had considerable appeal. For anthropologists in graduate school during the 1970s, "underdevelopment" became an increasingly hot topic.

At the same time, the wider institutional context was changing quite dramatically. Driven by an awareness of the failures of conventional development interventions, and perhaps also motivated by the apparent successes of communist insurgencies in mobilizing poor peasants (especially in Asia and Latin America), mainstream development agencies began to place a new emphasis on the "basic needs" of the poor, and on the distinction between mere economic growth and "*real* development," understood in terms of such measures of human welfare as infant mortality rates, nutrition, and literacy. The World Bank, under the leadership of Robert McNamara (see Finnemore, this volume), and later the United States Agency for International Development (USAID), under a congressional mandate to channel aid to the poor, began to direct more attention to the "soft," "social" side of development policy, and to turn more readily to social sciences other than economics. This conjunctural moment, fitting nicely with an employment crisis in academic anthropology, gave rise to a burst of anthropological interest in development, and a new, recognized subfield of anthropology, "development anthropology." (See Hoben 1982, Escobar 1991 for reviews of the period).

Many anthropologists thus came to development with a strong sense of theoretical and political purpose, determined to bring anthropological knowledge to bear on the great problems of poverty, exploitation, and global inequality. As Escobar (1991) has argued, however, work in development anthropology gradually came to be more and more adjusted to the bureaucratic demands of development agencies, at the expense of its intellectual rigor and critical self-consciousness. In spite of anthropology's long-standing claims of sensitivity to local perceptions, and its principled rejection of ethnocentrism, Escobar's review concludes that development anthropology has for the most part "done no more than recycle, and dress in more localized fabrics, the discourses of modernization and development" (Escobar 1991: 677). Significantly, as this adjustment of anthropologists to the demands of development agencies was proceeding, the strong links with theory that had characterized a more radical anthropology of development in the 1970s gradually weakened. The theoretical engagement with structural Marxism and radical underdevelopment theory—which had once linked such mundane empirical concerns as the dynamics of rural African household structure with the most abstract sorts of theoretical debates (e.g., the Althusserian critique of empiricist epistemology)—slowly slipped from view almost entirely, and with it the idea of a theoretically ambitious anthropology of development. Within academic anthropology, development anthropology came to be seen as a low-prestige, "applied" subfield—recognizably anthropological in its grassroots focus and vaguely populist commitments, but commonly understood to have little to do with mainstream anthropological theory.

Within development agencies, meanwhile, development anthropology was not faring much better. The distinctive disciplinary emphasis on the particularity and specificity of local conditions made it easy enough for the development anthropologist to serve up post-hoc criticism of failed projects (which quickly became a kind of anthropological specialty). But given the institutional needs of development bureaucracies, the anthropological talent for demonstrating the complexity of development problems (and for disclaiming certainty in offering prescriptions) could hardly compete with the universalistic, context-independent projections and prescriptions so confidently dispensed by the economist or the agronomist. Like the challenges to neoclassical orthodoxy generated from within economics (discussed by Carter, this volume), anthropological critiques have made little headway in the policy sphere—not because they lack policy implications, but because those implications are complex, context-dependent, and entail uncertainty. In spite of on-and-off rhetorical commitments to such apparently anthropological principles as "indigenous knowledge," "popular participation," and "local decision-making," development agencies have mostly allowed anthropologists only a very marginal position, with little influence on policy formation (Hoben 1982, Chambers 1987, Escobar 1991, Gow 1993).

ANTHROPOLOGY AND ITS EVIL TWIN, OR, WHY "DEVELOPMENT" IS NOT WELCOME IN THE HOUSE OF ANTHROPOLOGY, AND WHY IT JUST WON'T LEAVE

Anthropologists, for the most part, have taken post–World War II "development" for granted; they have accepted it as the normal state of affairs and have thus

contributed to its naturalization. How unanthropological, one might say, to accept
an entire historically produced cultural field without probing its depths.
ARTURO ESCOBAR, "ANTHROPOLOGY AND THE
DEVELOPMENT ENCOUNTER"

For many anthropologists, there are few things more alarming than applied
anthropology.
GLYNN COCHRANE, *Development Anthropology*

Well, which is it? Has anthropology been guilty of an uncritical acceptance
of development, as Escobar would have it? Or has anthropology sponta-
neously rejected development, fleeing in alarm at the very idea, as Cochrane insists? The answer, curiously, is that it has done both at the same
time. On the one hand, Escobar is surely right: development anthropology
has plodded along as a subfield in a way that even its own practitioners
insist is characterized by a striking lack of self-consciousness or critical
awareness (Chambers 1987, Gow 1993, Redclift 1985). Largely oblivious
to current theory and historically grounded criticism alike, development
anthropology seems hardly to care if its most central assumptions are regarded as untenable or worse in the wider discipline. Indeed, as one practitioner has recently noted, development anthropologists "have studiously
avoided defining the principal objectives of development" (Gow 1993:
382), and have been conspicuously uninterested in the larger theoretical
and historical issues that development interventions raise. In the absence
of attention to such issues, Gow points out,

> the anthropologist can easily become a practitioner of the "quick fix" ap-
> proach, engaged in relieving the more visible symptoms of "underdevelop-
> ment", but in the process inadvertently running the risk of strengthening
> the very forces responsible for the conditions it seeks to alleviate (1993:
> 382).

Yet Cochrane, in the second of the quotations paired above, also has a
point: academic anthropology has indeed looked upon development anthropology and other applied sub-fields with disdain and discomfort, leading one commentator to suggest that "the meaning of applied anthropology is to be found in its rejection by those in the mainstream of the
subject" (Grillo 1985: 9). Development anthropologists commonly report
being treated by academics "with a certain aloofness, if not passive con-
tempt" (Gow 1993: 381). Nor is this reaction a particularly recent one.
An academic skepticism of anthropological participation in "development" goes back at least to Evans-Pritchard (1946; see also Firth 1938),
and the eminent academic anthropologist, Edmund Leach, was only ech-
oing a widespread sentiment within the discipline when he remarked (in
an introductory textbook), "I consider 'development anthropology' a
kind of neo-colonialism" (1982: 50).

Development anthropologists are, of course, acutely aware of the way that such attitudes leave them "isolated from those programs and individuals generally regarded as leaders in constructing and teaching anthropological theory" (Little and Painter 1995: 603). Indeed, some development anthropologists report feeling "doubly damned"—by the prejudices of academic anthropologists, who see them as second-rate anthropologists at best, cynical hacks at worst; *and* by those of development professionals, who see them as the local representatives of a romantic, soft-headed, and obstructionist discipline (Gow 1993). But development anthropologists, of course, have their own disdain for academic anthropology, which they see as irresponsibly detached from the practical problems and struggles of real people, and sometimes so preoccupied with "theoretical" issues of "texts," "discourses," and "cultural construction" as to be unreadable by most Third World colleagues, with little to say about real-world solutions to global tragedies like poverty and violence (Little and Painter 1995: 605).

The result, then, is a field that is divided between those who retain a characteristically anthropological antagonism toward "development" (based chiefly in the academy) and those who have embraced the development world, only to find themselves marginalized and sometimes scorned in the anthropological field at large. What are we to make of this stark opposition, even antagonism, between an applied, development anthropology, and an academic, theoretical sort? And why, as Grillo (1985: 9) has asked, "does anthropology, more than any other social science, appear to make such heavy weather of this distinction?"

To answer this question, we must begin by observing that academic anthropology itself continues to be defined in disciplinary terms that are in some ways continuous with its nineteenth-century roots as the science of the less developed. Indeed, in this sense, development (or its absence), far from defining a mere subfield within the discipline, continues to be at the heart of the constitution of anthropology itself.

Evolutionist ideas have been surprisingly durable in anthropology, as authors such as Fabian (1983) and Thomas (1989) have pointed out. Indeed, it is difficult to read the annual program of the American Anthropological Association meetings (littered as it still is with allochronic papers on this or that "traditional society") without suspecting that Tylor may have been right that aspects of a culture may persist as "survivals" long after they have ceased to fulfill any real function. But surely the anthropological romance of the primitive *is* an anachronism? In the wake of at least two decades of vigorous internal critique—first along the lines of political economy, later via a critique of representation—anthropology can surely not *still* be in the thrall of its old developmentalist metanarratives?

To some extent, to be sure, anthropology's disciplinary object has indeed been transformed, and anthropologists now are routinely concerned with questions of history and transformation, with the way local communities are linked to a wider world, and with a host of nontraditional substantive questions. The extent to which such a restructuring has taken place, however, has been limited by a number of factors. Perhaps the most important of these is the way that what anthropologists do, and what will be taken to be "anthropological," is determined by the conventional division of academic labor between the social scientific disciplines. What distinguishes anthropology from sociology, political science, and other fields continues, in practice, to be largely a matter of the kinds of societies or settings that they study.[10] Anthropologists, in practice (at least those who are trained and hired by "leading departments"),[11] continue to work mostly in the Third World, and to specialize disproportionately in the study of small, rural, isolated, or marginal communities. Indeed, graduate students who wish to work in less traditionally anthropological sites report encountering significant difficulties in finding acceptance and legitimacy for their work, both within their graduate training programs, and in the arena of academic hiring once they complete their degrees ("All very interesting, but what's the *anthropological* angle?"). Anthropologists today are expected, it is true, to address questions of the transformation of local communities, and of linkages with wider regional and global processes; but it remains the case that it is a particular *kind* of people we are interested in seeing change, and a particular kind of local community that we seek to show is linked to that wider world.

The idea of "the local," in fact, has come to assume a remarkably prominent place in anthropology's disciplinary self-definitions. Where once anthropology studied "the savage," "the primitive," "the tribal," "the native," or "the traditional," today we are more likely to say that anthropologists study "the local." More and more, anthropology seems to be defined as a kind of attentiveness to "local knowledge" (Geertz 1983), or a field that specializes in the study of "local people" in "local communities" (thus, not incidentally, a sort of study that must be carried out "in the field").[12] Such a definition does make it possible to study a wider range of phenomena than did the older conception of "primitive" or "traditional" societies. But the difference may be easily overstated. After all, even if it is true that all social processes are in some sense local, it is also clear that, in normal anthropological practice, some problems, some research settings, even some people, are more local than others. A California real estate office, for instance, could surely serve as a site for anthropological, participant-observation research; but would this sort of local site be as local (and thus as anthropological) as, say, a New Guinea village? Certainly, all would politely agree that the anthropologist studying the real estate office was still doing anthropology, but would such work provide the foundation for a successful academic career? Disciplinary hiring practices—which (as I have suggested elsewhere [Gupta and Ferguson, 1997]) rely heavily on authenticating experience in "the field" (archetypically not only "local," but muddy, tropical, disease-infested, and so on)—make such an outcome unlikely.

Insofar as a certain opposition of "us" and "them," "the West" and "the rest," continues to inform the constitution of anthropology as an academic discipline, the concept of development must retain a special salience, sitting as it does astride this venerable binary opposition. For the kind of societies and settings that anthropologists typically study and the kind they do not are separated precisely by development (those that have not experienced development are most anthropological; those that are "developed" are least; and those in between, "developing," are in the middle of the spectrum of anthropological-ness). Indeed, it is clear not only that anthropologists have mostly studied in "less developed countries," but also that they have tended to study "less developed" categories of people within those countries (indigenous native peoples in Brazil, "tribal" and "hill people" in Southeast Asia, foragers in southern Africa, and so on). Likewise, when anthropologists work in the "developed world," they tend to study the poor, the marginalized, the "ethnic"—in short, the Third World within. Indeed, anthropologists in the West usually work in settings that might also make good sites for "community development programs." In all these cases, too, those who lack "development" are those who putatively possess such things as authenticity, tradition, culture: all the things that development (as so many anthropologists have over the years agreed) places in peril.

We are left, then, with a curious dual organization binding anthropology to its evil twin: the field that fetishizes the local, the autonomous, the traditional, locked in a strange, agonistic dance with the field that, through the magic of development, would destroy locality, autonomy, and tradition in the name of becoming modern. Anthropology is left with a distinct resentment of its evil twin, Development; but also with a certain intimacy, and an uneasy recognition of a disturbing, inverted resemblance. How often have western anthropologists "in the field" felt the unsettling need to distinguish themselves, in their forays among the "less developed," from those other white folks one is likely to meet out in "the bush"—the "development people" who (like those other alter egos, the missionaries), are "others" who resemble a little too closely the anthropological self (indeed, for whom one might oneself be mistaken)? How many of us have felt the same embarrassment reported by Eric Worby, who arrived in his remote Zimbabwean village research site only to be informed by the elders who greeted him, "You have come to civilize us!" (Worby 1992).

Like an unwanted ghost, or an uninvited relative, development thus continues to haunt the house of anthropology. Fundamentally disliked by a discipline that at heart loves all those things that development intends to destroy, anthropology's evil twin remains too close a relative to be simply kicked out; "after all," anthropology says to itself, "these issues, even if theoretically suspect, are of great practical importance." Thus we end up with an "applied" subfield ("development anthropology") that conflicts with the most basic theoretical and political commitments of its own discipline (hence its "evil"); yet which is logically entailed in the very constitution of that field's distinctive specialization (hence its status as "twin" to a field that is always concerned with the "less," the "under," the "not-yet" . . . developed). A twin that can seemingly never be embraced, accepted, or liked; but which just won't leave.

To move beyond this impasse will require a recognition that the extraordinarily tenacious vision of a world divided into the more and less "developed" has been, and in many ways continues to be, constitutive of the anthropological domain of study. Critiques of development, however necessary they may be, and however effectively they may be articulated.[13] will not be sufficient to solve the Jekyll-and-Hyde-like conflict between development and anthropology, or applied and academic types of anthropological knowledge (as if an academically based critique of development could simply overturn it, and thus do away with the division). On the contrary, so intimately intertwined is the idea of development (and its lack) with the idea of anthropology itself, that to be critical of the concept of development requires, at the same time, a critical reevaluation of the constitution of the discipline of anthropology itself. Anthropology cannot throw the evil twin out of the house, because the twin remains a part of itself, if only in a repressed and ill-acknowledged way.

CONCLUSION

The larger question of the relations linking development knowledge to the academic disciplines of the social sciences, with which I began, cannot be answered in any general way; a better understanding will await a good deal of quite detailed and specific work on the subject. But if the case of anthropology suggests anything of importance for this larger project, it is that the shape of development knowledge is not unrelated to the shape of disciplinary knowledges. Insofar as this is true, it may be suggested that in order to truly transform the kinds of knowledge that participate in questions of global politics and policy, it may be necessary to start by transforming the shapes of our disciplinary knowledges. If so, some immediate intellectual tasks may be closer to hand, and less utopian, than railing, from within our academic disciplines, against the development monster outside (as we patiently explain, yet again, to an audience of the already-converted, why structural adjustment hurts Africa's poor . . .). A real reconfiguration of the epistemic terrain that makes most academic work so irrelevant and powerless in its encounter with development may require, at least as a beginning, that we engage in some foundational work on our own disciplinary houses.

NOTES

1. Throughout this paper, I concentrate on anthropology as it developed in the United States and Britain (including some significant influences from the French tradition), while ignoring other regional and national traditions in anthropology that may well be significantly different. Such a choice is justified by the global hegemony that Anglo-American anthropology has undoubtedly enjoyed, but it is not meant to foreclose the possibility that the relationship of anthropology to "development" may be differently configured elsewhere. See Gupta and Ferguson (1997) for a discussion of the Anglo-American anthropological orthodoxy of "fieldwork" and its relation to alternate and heterodox regional and national traditions.

2. This is a point which Fabian (1983), in my view, seriously underestimates.

3. This is an idea that the early Boasian emphasis on diffusion in some ways called into question, but which emerged strongly in the more developed relativisms of Benedict and Mead and was quickly written into the collective "peoples and cultures" common sense of the emerging discipline.

4. There is an interesting study to be done of the search by mid-twentieth-century anthropology for a coherent analytic object, as various attempts were made to explain what distinguished "primitive" societies (or those which anthropologists could legitimately claim as their own distinctive object) from others. There seems to have been a fairly general agreement that such societies were "pre-" (another sign that evolutionist ideas are hardly absent); but pre- what? Pre-industrial? Pre-literate? Pre-modern? Pre-westernized? Pre-complex-organization? Was one to include India and China ("traditional" and "nonwestern," but hardly "small scale" or "pre-literate")? What about Ancient Greece ("pre-industrial," but suspiciously literate and western)? Or acculturated American Indians (with irreproachably primitive genealogies, but troublingly modern problems)? Perhaps what is most striking is how easily such difficulties were passed over in practice; in the discipline's hyphenated self-definitions, it may be that the prefix ("pre-") carried more weight than any of the various suffixes.

5. Among the most significant exceptions to this general trend were the anthropologists affiliated with the Rhodes-Livingstone Institute, discussed below.

6. As Chatterjee (1986) has argued, the new nationalist elites did not for the most part challenge this Eurocentric picture, but concentrated instead on speed-

ing the progression that it implied, building "modern" nations out of "backward" ones. See. also Ludden 1992, and the chapters by Bose and Gupta in this volume.

7. The Rhodes-Livingstone Institute anthropologists' conception of their own work as a defense of the urban African against racist colonial conservatism helps to explain the shock and disbelief with which they responded to Magubane's attack (see the comments appended to Magubane 1971). To be sure, the specifics of Magubane's argument were often flawed, and occasionally self-contradictory. But the more striking aspect of the exchange is the utter failure of scholars like Mitchell and Epstein to understand how anyone could possibly see their work as part of an oppressive colonial order. From their point of view, their positive depiction of the westernized, urbanized African was a rebuttal to racist white settlers who would bar Africans from such a status; from Magubane's point of view, on the other hand, such liberal willingness to bestow upon Africans the blessings of civilization was simply a form of cultural colonization.

8. In fact, there seems to have been surprisingly little interest on the part of U.S. neo-evolutionists in the modernization projects of the 1950s and 1960s. This may be, in part, explained by the general alignment of the evolutionism of this period with a cold-war Left politics, in what some have seen as a sort of shadow dance with a politically taboo, and not very well understood, Marxism—it being one of the more surprising accomplishments of McCarthyism to have turned Morgan (the corporate railway lawyer) into a surrogate for Marx.

9. Early twentieth-century diffusionism, both in the United Stated and in Britain, challenged this conception. But with the rise of functionalism and the quest for whole, functioning societies, diffusionism's concerns with history and culture contact were marginalized, only to be rediscovered in a different form many decades later (Vincent 1990: 119–25; see. also Gupta and Ferguson, 1997).

10. The other main point of distinction, the unique anthropological emphasis on fieldwork, is not unconnected to the question of "kind of society," as Akhil Gupta and I have recently argued (Gupta and Ferguson 1997).

11. For some observations about the hegemonic power of a handful of "leading departments" in the United States and Britain to dominate the entire discipline of anthropology, see Gupta and Ferguson, 1997.

12. This discussion reviews a number of points that I have argued elsewhere, together with Akhil Gupta (Gupta and Ferguson 1997).

13. I have in mind here Escobar's important review of "development anthropology" (1991), which convincingly dissects the failings and limitations of the subfield, but does not go very far toward connecting these in any systematic way with what seem to me a related set of failings and limitations of "mainstream" anthropology—thus letting us academics, as it were, off the hook all too easily.

REFERENCES

Bloch, Maurice. 1985. *Marxism and Anthropology: The History of a Relationship.* Oxford: Oxford University Press.

Brown, Richard. 1973. "Anthropology and Colonial Rule: The Case of Godfrey

Wilson and the Rhodes-Livingstone Institute, Northern Rhodesia". In *Anthropology and the Colonial Encounter*, edited by T. Asad, 173–97. London: Ithaca Press.

Chambers, Erve. 1987. "Applied Anthropology in the Post-Vietnam Era". *Annual Review of Anthropology* 16: 309–37.

Chatterjee, Partha. 1986. *Nationalist Thought and the Colonial World: A Derivative Discourse?* London: Zed.

Cochrane, Glynn. 1971. *Development Anthropology.* New York: Oxford University Press.

Cooper, Frederick. 1996. *Decolonization and African Society: The Labor Question in French and British Africa.* Cambridge: Cambridge University Press.

Epstein, A. L. 1958. *Politics in an Urban African Community.* Manchester: Manchester University Press.

Escobar, Arturo. 1991. "Anthropology and the Development Encounter: The Making and Marketing of Development Anthropology". *American Ethnologist* 18, no. 4: 658–82.

———. 1995. *Encountering Development: The Making and Unmaking of the Third World.* Princeton: Princeton University Press.

Evans-Pritchard, E. E. 1946. "Applied Anthropology". *Africa* 16: 92–98.

Fabian, Johannes. 1983. *Time and the Other: How Anthropology Makes Its Object.* New York: Columbia University Press.

Ferguson, James. 1990. "Mobile Workers, Modernist Narratives: A Critique of the Historiography of Transition on the Zambian Copperbelt". *Journal of Southern African Studies* 16, no. 3: 385–412; 16, no. 4: 603–21.

———. 1994. *The Anti-Politics Machine: "Development", Depoliticization, and Bureaucratic Power in Lesotho.* Minneapolis: University of Minnesota Press.

Firth, Raymond. 1938. *Human Types.* London: T. Nelson and Sons.

Foster-Carter, Aidan. 1977. "The Modes of Production Controversy". *New Left Review* 107: 47–77.

Geertz, Clifford. 1963a. *Peddlers and Princes: Social Development and Economic Change in Two Indonesian Towns.* Chicago: University of Chicago Press.

———. 1963b. *Agricultural Involution: The Process of Ecological Change in Indonesia.* Berkeley: University of California Press.

———. 1983. *Local Knowledge: Further Essays in Interpretive Anthropology.* New York: Basic Books.

Gow, David D. 1993. "Doubly Damned: Dealing with Power and Praxis in Development Anthropology". *Human Organization* 52, no. 4: 380–97.

Grillo, Ralph. 1985. "Applied Anthropology in the 1980s: Retrospect and Prospect". In *Social Anthropology and Development Policy*, edited by R. Grillo and A. Rew, 1–36. New York: Tavistock.

Gupta, Akhil, and James Ferguson. 1997. "Discipline and Practice: "The Field" as Site, Method, and Location in Anthropology". In *Anthropological Locations: Boundaries and Grounds of a Field Science*, edited by A. Gupta and J. Ferguson, 1–46. Berkeley: University of California Press.

Hirschman, Albert O. 1981. "The Rise and Decline of Development Economics". In *Essays in Trespassing*, 39–65. Cambridge: Cambridge University Press.

Hoben, Allen. 1982. "Anthropologists and Development". *Annual Review of Anthropology* 11: 349–75.

Hymes, Dell. 1972. "The Use of Anthropology: Critical, Political, Personal". In *Reinventing Anthropology*, edited by D. Hymes, 3–79. New York: Pantheon.

Kuklick, Henrika. 1991. *The Savage Within: The Social History of British Anthropology, 1885–1945*. Cambridge: Cambridge University Press.

Leach, Edmund. 1982. *Social Anthropology*. New York: Oxford University Press.

Levi-Strauss, Claude. 1976. "Race and History". In *Structural Anthropology, volume II*. New York: Basic Books.

———. 1994. "Anthropology, Race, and Politics: A Conversation with Claude Levi-Strauss". In *Assessing Cultural Anthropology*, edited by R. Borofsky, 420–29. New York: McGraw Hill.

Little, Peter D., and Michael Painter. 1995. "Discourse, Politics, and the Development Process: Reflections on Escobar's *Anthropology and the Development Encounter*". *American Ethnologist* 22, no. 3: 602–616.

Ludden, David. 1992. "India's Development Regime". In *Colonialism and Culture*, edited by Nicholas B. Dirks, 247–88. Ann Arbor: University of Michigan Press.

Magubane, Bernard. 1971. "A Critical Look at Indices Used in the Study of Social Change in Colonial Africa". *Current Anthropology* 12: 419–31.

Malinowski, Bronislaw. 1929. "Practical Anthropology". *Africa* 2, no. 1: 22–38.

———. 1930. "The Rationalization of Anthropology and Administration". *Africa* 3, no. 4: 405–430.

Malkki, Liisa. 1994. "Citizens of Humanity: Internationalism and the Imagined Community of Nations". *Diaspora* 3, no. 1: 41–68.

Mead, Margaret. 1956. *New Lives for Old: Cultural Transformation—Manus, 1928–1953*. New York: Morrow.

Mitchell, J. C. 1956. *The Kalela Dance*. Rhodes-Livingstone Paper, no. 27. Manchester: Manchester University Press.

Moore, Sally Falk. 1994. *Anthropology and Africa*. Charlottesville, Virginia: University of Virginia Press.

Morgan, Lewis Henry. 1877. *Ancient Society*. New York: Henry Holt and Company.

Nisbet, Robert A. 1969. *Social Change and History: Aspects of the Western Theory of Development*. New York: Oxford University Press.

———. 1980. *History of the Idea of Progress*. London: Heinemann.

O'Laughlin, Bridget. 1975. "Marxist Approaches to Anthropology". *Annual Review of Anthropology* 4: 341–70.

Oxaal, I., T. Barnett, and D. Booth, eds. 1975. *Beyond the Sociology of Development*. London: Routledge and Kegan Paul.

Phillips, Anne. 1977. "The Concept of Development". *Review of African Political Economy* 8: 7–20.

Redclift, M. R. 1985. "Policy Research and Anthropological Compromise: Should the Piper Call the Tune?". In *Social Anthropology and Development Policy*, edited by R. Grillo and A. Rew, 198–202. New York: Tavistock.

Rostow, W. W. 1960. *The Stages of Growth: A Non-Communist Manifesto*. Cambridge: Cambridge University Press.

Seddon, David, ed. 1978. *Relations of Production: Marxist Approaches to Economic Anthropology*. London: Frank Cass.

Seers, Dudley. 1979. "The Birth, Life, and Death of Development Economics". *Development and Change* 10:707–19.

Spicer, Edward. 1968. "Acculturation". *International Encyclopedia of the Social Sciences* 1: 21–27.

Stocking, George W., Jr. 1992. *The Ethnographer's Magic and Other Essays in the History of Anthropology*. Madison: University of Wisconsin Press.

———, ed. 1991. *Colonial Situations: Essays on the Contextualization of Ethnographic Knowledge*. Madison: University of Wisconsin Press.

Thomas, Nicholas. 1989. *Out of Time: History and Evolution in Anthropological Discourse*. Cambridge: Cambridge University Press.

Tomas, David. 1991. "Tools of the Trade: The Production of Ethnographic Knowledge in the Andaman Islands". In *Colonial Situations*, edited by G. Stocking, 75–108. Madison: University of Wisconsin Press.

Tylor, Edward Burnett. 1884. "How the Problems of American Anthropology Present Themselves to the English Mind". *Transactions of the Anthropological Society of Washington* 3:81–95.

Vincent, Joan. 1990. *Anthropology and Politics: Visions, Traditions, and Trends*. Tuscon, Ariz.: University of Arizona Press.

Werbner, Richard P. 1984. "The Manchester School in South-central Africa". *Annual Review of Anthropology* 13: 157–85.

Williams, Gavin. 1978. "Imperialism and Development: A Critique". *World Development* 6: 925–36.

Williams, Raymond. 1985. *Keywords*. New York: Oxford University Press.

Wilson, Godfrey. 1941–1942. *An Essay on the Economics of Detribalization in Northern Rhodesia, Parts One and Two*. Rhodes-Livingstone Papers 5–6. Manchester: Manchester University Press.

Wilson, Godfrey, and Monica Wilson. 1945. *The Analysis of Social Change*. Cambridge: Cambridge University Press.

Wolf, Eric. 1982. *Europe and the People without History*. Berkeley: University of California Press.

Worby, Eric. 1992. "Remaking Labour, Reshaping Identity: Cotton, Commoditization and the Culture of Modernity in Northwestern Zimbabwe". Ph.D. Thesis, Department of Anthropology, McGill University.

Young, Robert. 1990. *White Mythologies: Writing History and the West*. New York: Routledge.

SIX

Population Science, Private Foundations, and Development Aid

The Transformation of Demographic Knowledge in the United States, 1945–1965

John Sharpless

The geopolitical realities of the postwar world sparked a renewed debate over the economic and political consequences of rapid population growth.[1] Although the intellectual origins of this controversy lay in the eighteenth century, the apparent relationship between rapid population growth, diminishing resources, and the potential for economic and political disorder took on new meaning in the decades after World War II. Even before the war was over, U.S. policymakers linked America's strategic interests with, first, the reconstruction of Europe and Japan and, subsequently, with the economic development of Asia, Latin America, and Africa along capitalist lines. As the United States expanded its programs to promote development, however, it appeared that one of the primary reasons that these efforts faltered was the accelerated population growth brought on by western intervention. This observation rekindled long-standing controversies about the legitimacy and efficacy of government-sponsored birth control programs. A lack of consensus on the issue, however, made a coherent policy response difficult and controversial.

By the Kennedy administration, however, a radical transformation had occurred. Opposition to population control had been muted and the United States embarked on a program to reduce fertility across much of the Third World. Since the 1960s, a sizable portion of our nonmilitary foreign aid has been aimed at that goal. How did such a radical shift in development policy occur? A close examination of the 1940s and 1950s reveals a set of complex linkages between government economic planners, foreign policy experts, corporate leaders, professional demographers, and the directors of major philanthropic foundations. These linkages provided a network for the reworking of demographic knowledge to make it more "user-friendly" to policymakers and created a political climate in which such a profound shift in policy was possible. The story of how that process worked itself out provides some insight into the changing character of development knowledge since World War II.

THE AMERICAN MISSION AND FOREIGN AID: THE CHALLENGE OF POPULATION GROWTH IN POSTWAR IDEOLOGY

With the defeat of the Axis powers, the internationalists in the Truman administration, Congress, and the corporate and private foundation community posed a challenging agenda. If America would take the lead, the world could embrace an era of peace and harmony. The benefits of "progress" would be manifest. Although differences in religion, nationality, and race would remain, humanity would finally rise above petty prejudice and parochialism to affirm the essential and (presumably universal) principles highlighted in the United Nations charter. American technology and "know-how" could free the world from hunger and disease. Finally, America's unrivaled military superiority would provide the unspoken but ultimate potential for a final and just resolution to any globally threatening conflict.

Ultimately, however, it would be dollars rather than bombs which would make all of this work. The essential fabric which would hold new internationalism together would be a new era of world commerce and trade. An advanced form of capitalism would prevail. The volatility of the business cycle and imperialist excesses of the past would give way to an orderly and humane corporatism based on cooperation and consensus.[2] In his famous Point Four Program, President Truman assured a skeptical leadership in the developing nations that "new economic developments must be devised and controlled to benefit the peoples of the areas in which they are established. Guaranties of the investor must be balanced by guaranties in the interest of the people whose resources and whose labor go into these developments. The old imperialism—exploitation for foreign profit—has no place in our plans. What we envisage is a program of development based on the concepts of democratic fair dealing."[3]

There was a "dark side," however. If America retreated into isolationism, the forces of disorder would prevail. Totalitarianism thrived in an atmosphere of ignorance, economic stagnation, poverty, and political instability. If the United States failed to resolve these problems it would eventually find itself embroiled in another, even more destructive world war.

Given the choice, Americans reluctantly embraced an unprecedented program of economic assistance. This massive expenditure of aid involved both public and private foreign assistance. Some of the economic and technical support was routed indirectly through international agencies but much of it was directly administrated by U.S. agencies, private charities, and foundations. Regardless of the aid's source or destination, there would be an impressive unanimity of purpose. The "Grand Vision" was shared by the leadership across the wide spectrum of American institutions: in government agencies, philanthropic foundations, major corporations, and among most academics in America's leading universities.

There were many obstacles to overcome. First and foremost, the emergence of the Soviet Union as America's great adversary was the most serious threat to this vision for a new world order. Obviously, communism posed a countermodel for world development. But, at a more visceral level, Americans feared that left unchecked, communism could threaten the American homeland itself. Soviet communism, therefore, only added urgency to the mission. Its challenge certainly did not dissuade Americans from their task.

Equally distressing, however, were the mundane and seemingly ever present problems which had plagued humanity for centuries—famine, deprivation, and disease. While Americans had great confidence in the promise of technology and the ability of scientific experts to resolve problems, there was now a sense of desperation. It was in this setting that the population issue emerged so significantly. The idea that rapid population growth could pose a threat to peace and progress was not new.

The propaganda of the Axis regimes *seemed* to leave little doubt that population pressures had, in part, driven their expansionary desires.[4] While no one seriously believed that it was the sole or even the primary cause of the war, the rhetoric of *lebensraum* had made its impact. Equally important was the widely accepted notion that rapid population growth could result in persistently high unemployment, declining incomes, and economic stagnation—an atmosphere ripe for political disorder. There were as well a host of humanitarian issues directly related to rapid population growth—health and medical problems, agricultural development, and resource conservation.

The "population question" which had been largely an academic issue prior to the war, gained an immediacy in the context of postwar development assistance. The directors of the major philanthropic foundations, as well as the government economic planners who guided postwar reconstruction in Asia and Europe, were forced to confront the possibility that their intervention would only make matters worse. This meeting of concerns would foster an alliance between the public and the nonprofit sector in the immediate postwar period; one which would lay the basis for a full-scale, direct involvement by the U.S. government in population control in the Third World in decades after 1965.

THE NONPROFIT FOUNDATIONS AND POSTWAR
RECONSTRUCTION: THE LIMITS OF POPULATION POLICY TESTED

The prewar history of modern Japan was highlighted with the first signifi-cant attempt by a nonwestern nation to industrialize through overt state and corporate intervention. Its efforts to promote industrial development were a source of fascination and considerable apprehension among West-ern analysts.[5] Indeed, it was in this context that the detrimental effects of population growth on economic development were first identified. Not surprisingly, the American planners administering the Japanese recon-struction were keenly aware of the seriousness of the "population ques-tion." It was, however, an issue fraught with controversy in both Japan and the United States.

A fortuitous convergence of interests allowed the Allied Command (SCAP) to air the issue of population control while keeping the contro-versy at arm's length. John D. Rockefeller, III, who had been interested in the development of safe, effective birth control since the early 1930s, was pressuring the Rockefeller Foundation to move more aggressively in this area. His travels in Asia following the war confirmed his view that population growth was to become a major issue in the next decade (Harr and Johnson 1988: 452–65). Although the staff at the Rockefeller Foun-dation had been debating the prospect of establishing a program for pop-ulation assistance, nothing had come of the discussions. In the hope of clarifying the issue, the Foundation sent a delegation to Asia to meet with military and political leaders, medical and public health officials, and aca-demic professionals.

The group included two prestigious professional demographers, Frank Notestein and Irene Taeuber (both of the Office of Population Research at Princeton University). Along with Marshall Balfour and Roger Evans, who represented the Foundation, they were to assess the "demographic situation" in Japan, China, Korea, and Indonesia. Their interests, however, conveniently merged with those of Allied Command. General William Draper, Under Secretary of War, gave the mission his personal blessing, which no doubt opened doors inaccessible to the ordinary traveler. While the group was careful not to suggest any agenda for intervention, by their very presence they gave credibility to growing concerns over population growth.[6]

Anticipating their arrival, General Crawford F. Sams, head of the divi-sion of SCAP responsible for public health, wrote a long memo offering his reflections on population, economic growth, and political stability in Japan. To his mind a single essential principle drove the logic of population growth: "in a country primarily agricultural, the birth rate follows what is called the Malthus Law, which results in a population increasing more rapidly than the increase in capacity of the country to produce food." In contrast he observed, "in a country which becomes industrialized with accompanying urbanization, the birth rate drops rapidly, population becomes stabilized and, as the country becomes predominantly industrialized and urbanized, the death rate eventually exceeds the birth rate and the total population begins to decline."[7]

He judged that industrialization and accelerated urbanization had been slowly moving Japan to a low fertility society when the pronatalist policies of the imperial government and the war itself had interrupted these trends. Moreover, the initial policies of SCAP itself to severely limit Japan's industrial growth posed the likelihood of further reversing the process. In Sams's estimation this would lead "to an explosive situation, as all incentives to limit families would be denied and that the 'Malthus Law' would become operative in Japan and a peaceful, stable country could not be established." He was pleased to report, however, that "the present policy, approved by FEC in February 1947, of permitting an industrial level equivalent to 1930–34 will re-initiate the population shift from rural to urban." He predicted that this change in policy would "provide the incentive for limitation of the size of families and the downward trend in birth rates should be rapidly resumed."[8]

Sams stated bluntly that "the idea that populations of a country can be increased or decreased by fiat, law or propaganda alone, as advocated by many of the uninformed, is ridiculous." Nonetheless, despite his suspicion of fertility control "by fiat," he was pleased to note that the Japanese Diet had passed legislation which rescinded measures limiting the dissemination of birth control information and the establishment of birth control clinics. In fact, the Diet also enacted a new Pharmaceutical Law which permitted the manufacture and distribution of contraceptive devices. He concluded, "the world's outstanding authorities on demography . . . will [soon] visit Japan . . . and I believe that they will agree that all measures which are practical and sound have already been undertaken by SCAP to provide incentive and means whereby the population of this country may become stabilized and the long-range objective of the Occupation for establishing a peaceful, stable, democratic country may be obtained, with the incidental accomplishment of removing this country from becoming an increasing financial burden to the United States taxpayers."[9]

Although they had their criticisms of SCAP policies, the Rockefeller delegation generally confirmed Sams's assessment of the demographic situation in Japan. Moreover, there seems little doubt that the subtle interaction between American nonprofit foundations, professional demographers, and U.S. policymakers was instrumental in assisting a transition to a more liberal environment for fertility control in Japan.

But there was more to their visit than assisting policy change. After their visit to Japan the Rockefeller Team proceeded to Korea, Taiwan, Hong Kong, and Indonesia. Upon returning home, they produced a lengthy report along with a list of recommendations for possible Rockefeller Foundation support. While the report had a restrained scholarly tone, there was no doubt about the message: Asia faced growing problems due to population pressure. Despite the academic prose, there is a very real sense of crisis in the message presented by its authors.

Of course, the Rockefeller Foundation could not directly intervene in such a controversial area as family planning. Moreover, there was some disagreement among its advisors over whether intervention could make much difference. Although he posed his objections in more academic terms, like General Sams, Frank Notestein was not yet convinced that anything short of major economic transformation would alter the forces of population growth. Given the constraints, the best the team could recommend was expanded support for demographic training and research.

The document they produced was not meant solely for internal consumption, however. Less the recommendations to the Foundation, it was distributed to the academic and policy making community. Copies were sent to leading scholars in a variety of disciplines, Washington bureaucrats, foundation directors, and military officers (Balfour et al. 1950).[10]

This scenario became a common ritual throughout the 1950s. There would be a number of foundation-sponsored "demographic missions" to Third World countries lead by prestigious demographers. The U.S. government, while keeping its distance, would quietly assist them in their passage. They would meet with high-level officials highlighting the importance of the "population problem." They would return home to produce a report which would be distributed free of charge to the policy making elites in the United States and overseas. This process of internationalizing demographic knowledge was essential in establishing an intellectual climate for a major public policy change.

CODIFYING DEMOGRAPHY: INSTITUTION BUILDING AND THE PRODUCTION OF KNOWLEDGE

Beyond their role as expediters of knowledge, however, the question of what direction the major philanthropic foundations should take remained open to debate. They were charting new ground. Immediately after the war, the old-line foundations like Rockefeller and Carnegie sought to redefine their role in an environment of international philanthropic competition. Younger and more aggressive, the Ford Foundation was more willing to intervene on controversial policy issues but its directors, too, debated the nature of overseas philanthropy.

It is not surprising. U.S. foreign aid programs expanded into the developing world with Truman's Point Four Program. Although humanitarian rhetoric surrounded these efforts, much of this aid was, of course, tied to Cold War objectives.[11] At the same time, international agencies like WHO and UNESCO increased their support for health and agricultural projects. Finally, an increasing number of charitable private relief agencies sought to bring the apparent benefits of western technology and expertise (in the parlance of the time, "American Know-How") to the developing nations of the world. In this setting, the mission of the private foundations was unclear.

Equally important, donor institutions—both public and private—were forced to confront the possibility that their aid would be wasted in this rising sea of humanity. As fast as the international gift-giving grew, the needs of developing nations always seem to out pace the flow of resources. Despite the apparent success of the Marshall Plan in western Europe, the challenge of economic and social development in Asia, Africa, and Latin America seemed to defy all efforts. The solutions to problems posed by poverty, deprivation, and political instability appeared less obvious than those confronted by foundations before the war. Many of the problems confronting the postcolonial world were not so obviously tractable (Sharpless 1993).

The intransigence at the Rockefeller Foundation on the population issue pushed a small group of scholars and "population activists" (led by John D. Rockefeller, III) to found the Population Council in 1953. A "special purpose" foundation, the Population Council allowed foundations like Ford and the Rockefeller Brothers Fund to assist population research while remaining distant from any potential controversy. Although the stated purpose of the Population Council was to support *scientific* research in both demography and reproductive biology, under the directorship of Frederick Osborn, it aimed at promoting a consensus among political, religious, academic, and business elites on the population issue. Its directors disdained the politically charged rhetoric of the birth control groups, but there was no doubt about their strong conviction that rapid population growth posed a serious challenge to social and economic progress in the developing nations of the world (Population Council 1978).

The conservative course charted by the directors of the Rockefeller Foundation, however, is understandable. While there was little doubt that rapid population growth was making economic development more difficult in such places as India and China, the complexity and magnitude of the problem posed a serious challenge to anyone who proposed a policy solution. Limiting population growth implied the distribution of birth control. And even at this late date, the issue of birth control was still a very touchy one. Therefore, it was partly the potential for controversy which lead to their hesitancy but it was also the lack of consensus on what the solutions were. Foundations wanted demographers to propose some kind of program of action, similar to the kinds of public health programs that the foundations had found so attractive in the 1920s and 1930s. There was a deep division among experts on whether it was possible to alter reproductive behavior in an environment in which "traditional value systems" still placed a premium on large family size. There were practical considerations as well. Few of the existing means of contraception were effective or morally acceptable.

In this context, support for demographic research increased but most of this support was aimed at "institution building" (Caldwell and Caldwell 1986). Population Council and Ford Foundation sponsored a network of population studies centers based on the Princeton model. The idea of university "studies centers" was not a new one. Since the end of the war, government and foundation funding was used to establish semiautonomous training and research programs in U.S. colleges and universities. The advantage for scholars was greater independence from university bureaucracies. The advantage for government agencies and foundations was the formation of a direct connection with the scholarly research establishment.[12] By the end of the decade there were few major universities which did not have a program in population studies.

At the same time, money was provided for the training of foreign scholars at American institutions. Not surprisingly, they returned home to head government agencies or demographic research centers at their national universities. The latter, of course, often found sponsorship by U.S. foundations as well.

The important point is that the institutionalization of demography in this period, in large part, determined how "the population problem" would eventually be defined by the end of the decade. The American vision of population studies became the global vision. Alternative conceptions of population dynamics were marginalized. Moreover, it was the American vision of the population problem which would guide *public* policy when the U.S. government decided to support family planning programs in the Third World.

It was primarily in the nonprofit sector where the policy debate over "the population problem" played out in the 1940s and 1950s. And this process ultimately defined how the policy issues would be viewed in the period of expanded public funding which followed. The field of professional demography was the vehicle through which this effort was manifest. The philanthropic subsidy of demographic research in the immediate postwar years was not simply an exercise in pure science but was specifically aimed at policy. The foundations helped to create a generation of experts who were to serve as advisors to the U.S. foreign aid programs in population assistance when they emerged in the 1960s. What happened, in essence, was not only the legitimization of the "science" of demography but also the acceptance of demography as a *policy science.*

Equally significant, the process of institutionalizing population studies and codifying demographic knowledge took place not only in the United States and Europe but across the developing world. Indeed, in the 1950s a world wide network of "population experts" developed with a core body of knowledge and a common mode of discourse. They codified a shared set of assumptions about how population dynamics worked, how the phenomenon was to be studied and, most important, the terms under which intervention was appropriate. A consistency in methodology, analysis and language was forged by an impressively small group of scholars located primarily in the United States but also in Britain, India, and Asia. The power to accomplish this task was based on their relationship with the philanthropic community.

The foundations were, of course, primarily concerned with the success of their philanthropic efforts in the Third World and not U.S. national security. Nonetheless, since they funded research which focused on the interconnection between economic development, modernization, and population growth, it clearly carried implications for U.S. policy overseas (if for no other reason than the possible failure of our public foreign aid efforts). Policy makers in Washington kept close track of this research throughout the decade. Professional demographers were confronting basic issues surrounding the role of western intervention in the developing world. There could be little doubt that demographic research, therefore, would have important Cold War implications.

THE QUEST FOR LEGITIMACY: COLD WAR DEMOGRAPHY AS SCIENCE AND POLICY

Social scientists had been advising politicians and bureaucrats since the turn of the century but never more so than in the postwar era. This was decidedly the case in the area of strategic policy making at the international level. The Department of State, the military, the CIA, and National Science Council all had social scientists on their staffs. But they also contracted regularly with "think tanks" and universities research centers (Lyons 1969: chap. 6; Smith 1991: chaps. 3–5).

Initially, demographers were limited in what they could offer the national security establishment. Not only was their science (apparently) less precise, but its immediate application was less obvious. It appeared that demographers had little to contribute to solving the most pressing problems of the day. They were given the mundane task of providing the raw material for the "real" social scientists who could offer serious advice and council to the policy elite. The Department of State and the military, of course, had their own statistical offices. In the Department of State, the obscure Office of Functional Intelligence monitored changes in the economic, demographic, and political character of nations across the world. Occasionally, however, projects were contracted to universities. During the war, for example, the Department of State asked Notestein to produce a series of reports on Asian populations. The final reports on India, Taiwan, and Japan were published over the next decade (Davis 1951; Barclay 1954; Taeuber 1958).

Therefore, while population specialists had yet to convince policymakers that there was an immediate crisis which they were particularly suited to resolve, they did have a continuing relationship with the federal government, even if it was only in a support capacity. In addition, with the absence of a clearly defined academic niche for employment in America's universities, the federal government offered an opportunity for career advancement to the would-be "population scientist." Many of the leading demographers of the 1960s began their careers in government. Dudley Kirk moved from the Department of State's Office of Functional Intelligence to head the Demographic Research Division of the Population Council. He was followed in the same position at the Department of State by Christopher Tietze who, in turn, on his retirement from government service, became a leader in birth control research. The Princeton demographer, Edgar M. Hoover, who coauthored the highly influential *Population Growth and Economic Development in Low Income Countries* (1958) was formerly a senior economist at the CIA (Coale and Hoover 1958).[13]

Being relegated to a statistical support capacity played to the bias of the more conservative actuarial types who wanted the profession to divorce itself from its highly politicized past. (They were actually relieved that no one asked their opinion on anything other than the accuracy of the data!) One of the primary goals of the leading figures in demography was to break with the strong tradition of advocacy which had underscored population research and discourse back to the eighteenth century.

The efforts were destined to fail. The unique mix of morality and science in the field of demography could be traced back to Thomas Malthus (1766–1834) whose writings sparked a three-century debate over the capacity of human beings to breed beyond their ability to feed themselves. His infamous *Essay on Population* (1798) was influential not only for its scientific insight but also for its strong moralistic pronouncements. It was this rich mixture of science, morality, and public policy which was to nourish a heated debate into the postwar era. Most notably, the Malthusian controversy would take on new meaning in the discussions surrounding America's economic development programs in the Third World.

Postwar efforts to make population studies more scientific and less moralistic stemmed from a small group of economists, sociologists, and statisticians who saw the primary purpose of demography to be the collection and analysis of social and economic information (Hodgson 1991). Among the advocates of the "scientific approach," the driving but naive assumption was that population experts should provide governments with accurate statistical information without any political bias. There are, however, few issues involving population which are not without a moral or political component. It is a rare government which collects data with no political intent. All data have a sociopolitical context. Analysis, no matter how technical, carries direct implications for policy. Despite deliberate attempts to render demography politically neutral, therefore, its ideological origins consistently re-emerged.

Two particularly forceful groups which remained important well into the twentieth century were the eugenics movement and the birth control crusade. Each would take on different forms in the 1950s but demography continued to be affected by both.

The eugenics movement arose in the context of generally declining population levels across Europe and declining fertility among the native-born populations of northern European heritage in the United States. In the United States, the concomitant rise in immigration from southern and eastern Europe added a deeper concern over a shift in ethnic mix. For the eugenicists, the most pressing population problem was that the most productive, talented, and capable were in decline while the "wrong kinds" flourished. While there was a board spectrum of people who at one time or another were associated with the eugenics movement, the bulk of eugenics writings were concerned with race and nationality issues, immigration restriction (in the case of the United States), and the incidence of mental illness and criminality among various subgroups in the population. Much of this, to the extent that it was scientific at all, was based on the rather crude genetic models of the time. Despite a thin veneer of scientific rhetoric, most of the eugenics literature had elitist overtones and more often than not was unabashed in its racist implications (Kevles 1990; Haller 1963; Gould 1993).

Confident that their prejudices would be confirmed, many of the eugenicists promoted demographic studies, regardless of the focus, as being an important first step in establishing a scientific basis for eugenic legislation. A few of the more scientifically oriented eugenicists later held prominent places in the professional demographic circles of the 1940s and 1950s. Some like Frederick Osborn, Robert Cook, and Warren Thompson, were major institution builders for the field of professional demography in its formative years. Osborn, for example, was instrumental in establishing the Population Center at Princeton and later served as the first Director of the Population Council (Critchlow 1995: 5–7).

Adolf Hitler's Third Reich would give eugenics a bad name. But even by the early 1930s many of those urging a more scientific approach to the study of population were uneasy with the overly racist rhetoric of their colleagues in eugenics. Their claims were condemned as unscientific, biased, and unsupported by the data. While the word "eugenics" was used with less frequency in the postwar period, the "ghost in the closet" remained an ever-present figure in modern demography. Particularly sensitive to the challenge that its scientific theories were racist doctrines in disguise, professional demographers were very hesitant to propose population control solutions in the Third World without sound empirical data to back up their views. The nonprofessional advocates of population control were less constrained, however, and strong hints of racism remained an aspect of postwar demographic discourse despite efforts to the contrary.

A similar uneasiness surrounded the relationship forged between the social reformers who crusaded for unrestricted access to birth control and their professional colleagues in demography. Initially, the birth control movement was associated with radicalism, sexual liberation, and feminism (Chesler 1992; Gordon 1976; Kennedy 1970; Back 1989; Reed 1983). At first, the birth control movement aimed at simply reforming restrictive legislation which prevented open exchange of information on the topic. By the 1930s, however, the leaders in the movement were more bold in their demands, pressing New Deal administrators to include birth control assistance as part of government health and welfare programs.

In the early forties, however, there were profound changes in the public image of the movement as it evolved toward the *family planning* campaigns of the postwar decades. It was more than a change in organizational nomenclature.[14] The movement's essential ideology divorced it from its past. Increasingly, the idea of contraceptive use was to merge with notions of the well-ordered, responsible middle-class family. The "more respectable" elements in the birth control movement had found a successful avenue to convince the American people that fertility control was no longer to be associated with its earlier image of radicalism and sexual deviance.

The consequences were subtle but significant. Given the prescribed role of the housewife in the "typical American family," embracing family planning was not liberating but actually more constraining. Birth control was to be used *only* in the context of marriage. The primary purpose of contraception was to limit the family size. The presumption was that with fewer children, the American housewife could be a better, more efficient mother. It was definitely not anticipated that it would free her from her traditional role as housewife.

Family planning, therefore, played a pivotal role in the public ideology of the "family" in America's domestic Cold War politics. The suburban, white, middle-class family became identified as a major bulwark against communism (May 1988: chap. 6). Moreover, these presumptions were often carried into the analysis of Third World population problems in which it was often assumed that the rise of "modern attitudes" and a decline in family size would not only promote economic development but erode support for communist-inspired revolution.

It was also assumed that the children would be better off in the smaller family setting. A married couple could invest more in each child rather than dissipate their resources over many. This supposed tension between quantity and quality embedded itself not only in the popular imagery of the period but also in the scholarly models for fertility behavior. (The link to the earlier eugenics literature is, I think, obvious here.).

Similarly as this vision was transported overseas, one of the unchallenged presumptions was that the lives of people in the Third World would be bettered if their families came to look as much as possible like middle-class American families. Traditional family structure and premodern attitudes about the "investment value of children" limited "development" not only for the individual but also the community and the nation.

THE REWORKING OF TRANSITION THEORY: DEFINING THE POPULATION PROBLEM IN PUBLIC POLICY DISCOURSE

If smaller families were better for all concerned (including policymakers at the Department of State!), then how should one go about promoting such a thing? The real issue was ultimately one of changing attitudes. People had to "think modern" for fertility change to occur. But serious questions immediately presented themselves. How did this process happen in the past? And could it be made to happen today? As the expert advice to General Sams suggested, the answers to these questions were ambiguous. Demography had succeeded in inventing a theoretical apparatus to explain family size and historical change, but the policy implications of that theory were not obvious.

The *demographic transition model* provided the theoretical nexus which tied mortality theory to fertility theory and embedded it in a model of historical change. It was for demography what modernization theory was for sociology and economic development models were for economics.

The idea of "demographic transition" was originally based on an impressive similarity in patterns of population change across Europe over the previous three hundred years. The historical evidence suggested a sequence of events which originated in a hypothesized "premodern period" when high mortality levels kept a lid on population growth. High fertility was necessary for couples to achieve their desired family size in the face of poor diet, disease, war, and famine. In addition, the *labor value* of children in a rural, low technology environment was substantially greater than in the modernized urban world where children cost more than they were worth. Finally, in a world without pensions or social security, having children who survived to their middle years was essential for the survival of the parents in their aging years.

At some point, however, in nearly every region of Europe this cycle was permanently broken. Mortality rates declined. Of equal importance, the trend persisted despite the harsh conditions of industrial urban life. For an intermediate period, therefore, population levels surged. The increase resulted because of a "momentary" lag in expectations about the likelihood of survival. As it slowly became apparent that more children were surviving into adolescence and that adult (particularly maternal) mortality was declining, couples began to readjust their expectations about the necessity for high fertility. Moreover, as people moved to the cities, the "value of children" changed, placing a further premium on small family size. Postponing marriage, declining marriage altogether, and the use of "primitive methods" of birth control and abortion all served as mechanisms for encouraging an overall decline in fertility rates. A posttransition phase finally emerged marked by a new equilibrium of low mortality and low fertility.

None of the early proponents of the transition theory presumed a uniformity of experience in the details. Nor did anyone assume that the timing and speed of these processes would be the same across regions. There was, however, a presumption of inevitability. In fact, while some areas in northern Europe went through the process early on and other areas in the east and south experienced this process quite late, there was an impressive uniformity of across time and space.

Although it was a historically based model with an impressive claim to universality, the precise timing of these social and economic processes was unclear. The explanatory "variables" are not really variables at all but generalizing concepts such as "industrialization," "modernization," and "urbanization." The concepts have meaning, of course, but as intellectual constructs which cluster variables, they may have conflicting interpretations. The transition model, therefore, is at once complex and at the same time, deceptively simple.

Policy makers, therefore, could find little solace in transition theory. Clearly, the early decline in mortality was *not* the result of overt intervention. Improvements in sanitation systems, introduction of modern health practices and the scientific discoveries affecting disease control came *after* the initial drop in mortality levels. All these factors served, subsequently, to sustain mortality decline into the era of high urban concentration. Nonetheless, the overall trend was established over a very long period of time and was deeply imbedded in changes in agricultural practices, shifts in dietary mix, and subtle changes in life style. Likewise, the European fertility transition occurred *without* modern methods of birth control and despite religious and civil opposition to limiting births. At the individual level, variables like education, income potential, and changing attitudes about sexuality and the role of women in society appeared to be important.

Since demographers in Europe and America were primarily concerned with their own declining populations in the 1930s, the policy implications of transition theory seemed remote. The postwar period, however, brought serious empirical challenges to the efficacy of transition theory outside Europe and America. There had long been indications that population levels in South Asia and the Far East were growing rapidly. It was only in the postwar era, however, that the consistency and the quality of the data were sufficient to reveal these trends with any precision. The conclusion was unavoidable that for the colonial and postcolonial areas of the world, population growth was reaching levels which were never found in Europe during the transition period. Moreover, population growth was occurring without a concomitant rise in industrial development or any apparent shift in attitudes toward western belief systems. Declining mortality levels seemed to result from introducing western advances in health science without significant adjustments in social structure or economic development.

While it was possible to modify the theory to account for colonial situations (see, for example, Notestein 1948), it took some effort to propose a policy response. The transition model predicted that *someday* change would come but we would have to be patient. The process of historical change was slow, deep, and subtle. Without the prospects of massive immigration there seemed few policy options available. Although the fertility rates in these areas had not changed substantially, with the "artificial" drop in the mortality rate the overall population levels were rising rapidly. In the 1940s there was little unanimity among demographers on the prospects for successful intervention.

The pressure for a policy solution, however, forced a fundamental reinterpretation of theory. Less restrained by scholarly consistency, birth control advocates had long argued that it was possible to intervene to limit fertility. They claimed that just as mortality levels had been altered with western intervention, fertility levels presumably could be affected with the systematic distribution of birth control. Now the social scientists were increasingly converted to this view and over the next decade there was an impressive convergence of opinion among professionals toward the new orthodoxy.

That demographers were willing to advocate policies which seemed inconsistent with their major theoretical paradigm shows the degree to which the political context of their research drove their presumptions. Ironically, transition theory was turned on its head. By the end of the 1950s most demographers had come to argue that changes in attitudes at the individual level (presumably through educational programs advocating contraception) could alter the macrodevelopment situation. This was quite the opposite of what they had argued a decade earlier (Hodgson 1983).

But it is also important to remember that hopes for intervention were pegged on improved birth control technologies. By the end of the 1950s, the investment made by private foundations and wealthy benefactors in biological research came to fruition (Onorato 1991; Djerassi 1992). Both the contraceptive pill and an effective IUD were being tested. It was possible, therefore, to rephrase the discussion in essentially technical and logistic terms. This made the problem not only tractable but the solution was wonderfully American with its focus on a simple technological "fix" to a complex problem.

As the decade closed, therefore, the stage was set. With science, technology, and public policy united, there seemed little doubt that it was possible to control the fertility of developing nations. The next logical step was to move out of the realm of nonprofit assistance and academic discussion into governmental action. For that to happen, however, it was necessary to integrate this vision of world population control with U.S. national foreign policy.

"WAR, STARVATION AND COMMUNIST INTRIGUE": WORLD POPULATION GROWTH AND NATIONAL SECURITY

Given the national security discourse of the 1950s, the "world population crisis" had to be mapped into Cold War rhetoric if it was to become an area for public funding. The language of the academy needed to be transformed into the politically charged discourse of anticommunism. Here the role of the nonprofessional population "expert," the popular press, and those academics who spoke to both audiences became important.

The idea that rapid population growth in developing countries could contribute to communist revolution can be found in the population literature of the early 1930s, but it was in the context of the Cold War that the connection took on a particular urgency. Kingsley Davis, who was a major figure among professional demographers, argued that "the demographic problems of the underdeveloped countries, especially in areas of nonwestern culture, make these nations more vulnerable to Communism." In his view, "an appropriate policy would be to control birth rates in addition to such activities as lowering death rates, the provision of technical assistance and economic aid. Such a combination of policies, if carried through effectively, would strengthen the Free World in its constant fight against encroachment" (Davis 1956: 356; see also Davis 1958: 296). These views were echoed by Philip Hauser; the leading population sociologist at the University of Chicago went so far as to claim that Marxist opposition to Malthusian doctrines were a contrivance to encourage further hardship and political disorder (Hauser 1958: 14–15).

Among the professionals, however, the population growth/communist connection was still highly debatable. Frank Notestein and Dudley Kirk, for example, opposed linking anticommunism to population control efforts. Their concern was that leaders of the unallied nations, upon hearing that American policymakers were acting primarily to stop communism, would then resist efforts to institute population control programs.

The scholarly complexities, therefore, needed to be reduced to simple unambiguous nostrums for politicians to rally to the cause. It was left to nonprofessional "population activists" to translate the guarded scholarly prose into overtly Cold War rhetoric. Their influence with policymakers often rivaled that of the most prestigious demographers. Whether they were business men, retired military officers, or diplomats, they found the cause for world population control an area to focus their public service enthusiasm. Each, of course, had their own personality. Some were more extreme and vocal than others but what they shared was the ability to influence powerful men in the business community with the idea that rapid population growth was detrimental for America's corporate interests (Piotrow 1973: chap. 2).

Notable among these figures was Hugh Moore, president of the Dixie Cup Corporation. In 1953 he attended a meeting of the Steering Committee for the Western Hemisphere Region of the newly formed International Planned Parenthood Federation (IPPF). Although Moore described his role at the meeting as "observer," he was actively involved in the discussions. He argued aggressively for shifting the emphasis of the organization away from its image "as a women's organization, primarily for the protection of motherhood and the family." The world population problem, he felt, "should be approached from the new angle of the preservation of peace." What he meant was that the message should be reworked and refocused at the "executives of American corporations whose operations would be crippled if the Communists were to take over their sources of raw materials in Asia, Africa and South America." In his opinion, if IPPF was to get the funding it needed, it meant not only a more strident message but one aimed at the *men* who had the money to make a difference.[15]

Apparently encouraged by these discussions, he published a short pamphlet entitled "The Population Bomb." Initially about 700 copies were printed and distributed to corporate and political elites around the country. Subsequently, the addresses in *Who's Who* were added to the list of nearly some 10,000 names and free copies were sent to high school, college, and public libraries. Eventually, Moore claimed nearly 200,000 copies in circulation. Some editions were more aggressive than others in linking rapid population growth with communist intrigue, political disorder in developing countries, and the potential for a World War III. In nearly every edition, however, he proclaimed that "the population bomb threatens to create an explosion as disruptive and dangerous as the explosion of the atom, and with as much influence on prospects for progress or disaster, war or peace."[16]

Although they may have supported his calls for intervention, professional demographers and the administrators in the more reserved foundation establishment were critical of his approach. Most of their criticism focused on the offensive and potentially controversial presumption that population control should be aimed at Asians and South Americans with the primary goal of halting the spread of communism. As early as 1954, John W. Gardner, president of the Carnegie Corporation, cautioned Moore that, "the Communists can make fine use of our anxiety that we will run out of raw materials. Putting the words War, Communism and World Population in a 'deadly triangle' may be dramatic, but I really doubt whether it is the way to further the cause of rational planning of family size in the Asiatic countries. These countries will have to make their own decisions, and they will do so in the light of their own interests and of their own knowledge."[17]

Moore remained unredeemed in his enthusiasm, however, and at the end of the decade Frank Notestein found it necessary to remind Moore that "the Communists are doing an excellent job of picking up quotations from the West that they can exploit to our disadvantage . . . [and] it is particularly important that educational material on population, if it is likely to reach the underdeveloped areas, be based strictly on humanitarianism and not on the political fears of the Western World."[18] Moore, revealing his marketing savvy, responded to these criticisms by producing two editions—one censored for foreign audiences and an unrestrained version for the American market.[19]

Moore appeared to be interested in meeting criticism if it was aimed at factual information, but he would not abandon his highly politicized and inflammatory style. While acknowledging their help, Moore never saw the demographic experts as his primary audience. He wanted to influence

America's business community and Washington's policy elite. And there is some evidence he did so. He brought the rarefied discourse of the professional demographer into the public arena, cut away all ambiguity, and made population growth a strategic issue of serious importance. His little booklet was, for example, assigned reading at the Department of State's Foreign Service School. And it is significant that General William Draper turned to him rather than the professional demographers for advice on the problem when the President's Committee on Foreign Aid held hearings in 1958.

CLOSURE: THE DRAPER COMMITTEE AND AFTER

In the late 1950s, a series of setbacks in international affairs provoked Congress once again to examine the effectiveness of America's foreign aid program. Responding to congressional calls for action, President Eisenhower appointed yet another "blue ribbon" committee to examine the purpose and effectiveness of America's foreign assistance program. One of their primary interests, of course, was the political fate of the developing countries of Asia, Africa, and Latin America. These were the regions that Washington analysts increasing saw as the battleground for the Cold War.

Retired General William Draper was chosen to head the committee. One of the white-collar generals of World War II, he later went on to serve as a high-level administrator in the postwar reconstruction programs for both Europe and Japan. As Under Secretary of War he had approved the Rockefeller population mission to Asia in the late 1940s. After retiring from the army, he returned to investment banking, serving on the boards of several major international corporations.

Although Draper's committee was delegated only to look at military foreign aid, he read his mandate broadly and in the course of their investigation the committee's staff examined both military and nonmilitary foreign aid. They focused in some detail on the social, economic and political forces facing recipient countries. With the assistance of Robert Cook of the Population Reference Bureau and Hugh Moore (neither of whom were professional demographers), Draper's staff prepared a brief section in the final report which focused on the problem of rapid population growth (Piotrow 1973: chap. 4; Critchlow 1995: 10–11). By arguing that such growth could erode all efforts at development and negate the impact of our foreign assistance efforts, Draper validated what Hugh Moore, Kingsley Davis, and Philip Hauser had been arguing in the public press. While not all members of the committee were in agreement on the population issue, the committee's official recommendation was that the

United States should provide assistance to developing nations who sought to control their population growth.[20]

There was a momentary flurry of controversy when the committee presented its findings. The obvious implication that the United States should offer advice and, perhaps, technical support for fertility control was not lost on the policy making community. Eisenhower, while accepting all other aspects of the report, publicly rejected the idea that the government had any role in affecting population dynamics.[21]

It is impressive how quickly official policy changed, however. Only a few years later, Richard Gardener, Deputy Assistant Secretary of State for International Organization Affairs announced before the United Nations General Assembly that the United States would support expanded programming in the area of population research and development advising.[22] And by the end of the Johnson administration, the reduction of fertility levels in developing countries became an important component in U.S. foreign assistance. U.S. government appropriations for family planning and contraceptive services rose to an unprecedented level of $60 million by 1970. Of that, about 10 percent went to training, institutional development, and demographic education; 7 percent assisted the collection of demographic and social data; and roughly 3 percent went to "population policy and social science research."

A modest 3 percent allocation was as close as this funding every got to "pure" demographic research. But the influence of federal funding was significant. It moved through the institutions created by the nonprofit sector in the 1950s, reinforcing the power and prestige of the demographers who dominated these networks. The effect of this growing dependency on federal funding, therefore, continued the biases in demographic research. Like so many other areas of postwar government-directed funding in the social sciences, research in demography became increasingly tied to policy considerations. Since U.S. population policy focused on fertility control, demographic research followed funding.

Moreover, since this federal subsidy came at a key stage in the development of the field as a whole, it had a profound effect on the character of the discipline for years to come. The institutionalization of demography as a social science as well as the definition of the basic discourse domain occurred in this period. Because the primary *policy* concern was rapid population growth in developing countries, there was inordinate emphasis on fertility research, family planning attitudinal analysis, and birth control program effectiveness. Overseas research received precedence. Domestic demographic issues, migrations studies, research on aging and differential mortality analysis, for example, all were to receive secondary consideration.

The infusion of public funding revealed the degree to which the national security interests had been fused with the idea of population control in the Third World. There seems little doubt that Cold War imperatives serve in large part to justify these expenditures. The impressive gains in the prestige of demography were truly remarkable and clearly a result of its role as a "policy science." Had it remained an area solely of scholarly interest it is unlikely that this level of funding would have been forthcoming nor would its leading scholars have achieved the fame they did.

We should be cautious not to overstate the impress of strategic concerns on the implementation of population policies aboard. As with many areas of our foreign aid assistance, our motives were mixed. Certainly, one sees references to health and welfare issues but, at least in this early period, the major policy justification was in terms of promoting economic growth and preserving political stability. Later, the ecology movement added further impetus to the cause for population control. It seems unlikely, however, that the United States would have become so deeply committed to fertility control in Asia, Africa, and Latin America had not the competition with the Soviet Union in these areas been so keen.

The merger of national security interests with population growth issues did not occur in a political vacuum nor was it a sudden transformation. Since the early 1940s there had been discussion among policy elites both inside and outside the government over the effect of rapid growth on economic and political development. Not surprisingly, throughout this discussion demographers played a pivotal role. They provided the research base for these discussions and the scientific rhetoric to lend strength to the various contending arguments. As professional demographers became convinced that intervention was both practical and appropriate, policymakers embraced the idea that population control was a legitimate area of government intervention. At the same time, it was necessary to bring the issue into the vernacular of the popular media. The meshing of the language of the social science with Cold War ideology, therefore, was the final link in this process of transforming social scientific knowledge into the discourse domain of foreign policy and political action.

NOTES

1. Support for this project was provided by the Social Science Research Council, the Rockefeller Archives Center and the Graduate School of the University of Wisconsin. These institutions are not responsible for the opinions expressed in this essay.

2. Secretary of the Treasury Henry Morgenthau, Jr., who was chair of the American delegation at Bretton Woods in 1944 set out the essential justifications for American postwar internationalism:

There must be a reasonable stable state of international exchange to which all countries can adhere without sacrificing the freedom of action necessary to meet their internal economic problems.

Second, long-run financial aid must be made available at reasonable rates to those countries whose industry and agriculture have been destroyed by the ruthless torch of the invader. . . . [and] made available also to promote sound industry and increase industrial and agricultural production in nations whose economic potentialities have not yet been developed (Morgenthau 1944: 112).

3. *The Public Papers of the Presidents of the United States: Harry S. Truman* (Washington, D.C.: Government Printing Office, 1964), 112–16.

4. In truth these claims were more fiction than fact. Fertility had slowed in all the Axis nations despite aggressive pronatalist campaigns. While shortages in raw materials *may* have contributed to their drive for expansion, population pressure certainly did not. Nonetheless, the connection between population growth and war was a common theme in the academic literature before and after the war. See, for example, Thompson (1946) and Nef (1950).

5. The prewar literature on Japan's economic development, population pressures, and possibility of military expansion is voluminous. A few examples are Pitkin (1921); Nasu (1929); Crocker (1931); Dennery (1931); Penrose (1934); and Ishii (1937).

6. M. C. Balfour, "Preliminary Note on the R. F. Population (Public Health and Demography) Reconnaissance in the Far East," January 1949: *Rockefeller Foundation Papers*, Record Group 1.1 (Projects), Series 600 (ASIA), folder 9, page 6, Rockefeller Archives Center, North Tarrytown, New York.

7. Memorandum, Sams to Almond, Subject: "Population in Japan," National Archives, Washington, D.C. RG 331 *Supreme Commander for the Allied Powers*, Natural Resource Section, Administrative Division (General Subject Files), Box 2928, p. 1.

8. Ibid., p. 3.

9. Ibid., p. 2. This comment was obviously aimed at American birth control advocates who saw Japan as a "target of opportunity." Margaret Sanger, the renowned crusader for birth control, was to apply for a military permit to visit Japan in the following year. She would be turned down by SCAP authorities fearful that her visit would be "used for political purposes." See Taeuber (1958: 370 n 25).

10. Irene Taeuber, who had the strongest connections in Washington, was asked to produce a list of the most powerful men in the policy making community. It included Admiral Roscoe Hillenkoetter, Director of the CIA; Dr. Holis Peter, Chief of the Division of International and Functional Intelligence at the State Department; and Paul Hoffman, Chief Administrator of the ECA (the predecessor to USAID). They were all sent free unsolicited copies of the Rockefeller report. Memo, Irene [Taeuber] to Roger [Evans], *Rockefeller Foundations Papers*, Record Group 1.2, Series 600 (Asia), Box 2, Folder 9, Rockefeller Archives Center.

11. For a good review of the conflicting goals of U.S. foreign doctrine in this era, see Hagen and Ruttan (1988).

12. For a general discussion of this process, see Lyons (1969: 170–79). The

History of population studies centers has yet to be written but a good start is Caldwell and Caldwell (1986: 59–76, 143–50).

13. This study was perhaps the most influential work in demography in the postwar period. It was sponsored, in part, by the International Monetary Fund. The Population Council provided free copies to Third World scholars, health officials, and political leaders.

14. The idea of changing the name is generally attributed to D. Kenneth Rose, who had worked with a public relations agency before coming to the birth control movement. Margaret Sanger's well-known hostility to the term did not affect its quick and wide-spread acceptance among activist who sought to legitimize the movement with conservative middle-class constituencies.

15. The gathering included Margaret Sanger, Lady Rama Rau (President of the Indian Planned Parenthood Association), Eleanor Pillsbury (President of American Planned Parenthood), William Vogt (Director of American Planned Parenthood), and Frederick Osborn (President of the Population Council). Moore related the details of this initial IPPF meeting some years later at a luncheon he convened at the Harvard Club in New York. The minutes of that meeting (taken by T. O. Griessemer) can be found in the *Population Council Records*, Record Group IV 3B4.2, General File Box 22, Folder 344, Rockefeller Archives Center.

16. Despite its wide circulation in the 1950s, there are surprisingly few copies available. The one in the Library of Congress, for example, is missing! Another problem is that Moore did not put publication dates on any of the five major reprintings which occurred over the 1950s. Various versions can be found at the Rockefeller Archives Center collection (see accompanying footnotes). There were various covers on the pamphlet over the decade but the bomb analogy was always maintained. Sometimes it depicted the earth as a bomb with tiny human figures crowding every continent, the burning fuse at the top about to be snipped by a scissors labeled "population control." Another version showed the classic mushroom cloud of an atomic explosion hurling thousands of people out into space.

17. Gardner to Moore, December 2, 1954, *Records of the Population Council* Record Group IV 3B4.2, General File, Box 22, Folder 344, Rockefeller Archives Center.

18. Notestein to Moore (July 21, 1959), *Records of the Population Council*, Record Group IV 3B4.5, Organization File, Box 101, Folder 1893: page 1, Rockefeller Archives Center.

19. Moore to Notestein (August 20, 1959), *Records of the Population Council*, Record Group IV 3B4.5, Organization File, Box 101, Folder 1893 Rockefeller Archives Center.

20. William Draper et al., "President's Committee to Study the United States Military Assistance Program," *Final Report* (Washington, 1959): 94–97.

21. Draper would later claim that Eisenhower had asked him to "look into this population matter." See Piotrow (1973: 38–42). Some years later, the retired president at his home in Gettysburg told Draper that, in retrospect, he was pleased Draper had brought the issue into the policy debate. Eisenhower later served, along with Harry Truman, as honorary co-chair of the Planned Parenthood Federation.

22. Richard Gardner, "Population Growth: A World Problem, Statement of U.S. Policy," *Department of State Bulletin*, January 1963. For a discussion of this transition period see Piotrow (1973: chaps. 6–9) and Sharpless 1995).

REFERENCES

Back, Kurt W. 1989. *Family Planning and Population Control.* Boston: Twayne.

Balfour, Marshall C., Roger F. Evans, Frank W. Notestein, and Irene B. Taeuber. 1950. *Public Health and Demography in the Far East: Report of a Survey Trip, September 13–December 13, 1948.* New York: The Rockefeller Foundation.

Barclay, George. 1954. *Colonial Development and Population in Taiwan.* Princeton: University Press.

Caldwell, John, and Pat Caldwell. 1986. *Limiting Population Growth and the Ford Foundation Contribution.* Dover, N.H.: Pinter.

Chesler, Ellen. 1992. *Woman of Valor: Margaret Sanger and the Birth Control Movement in America.* New York: Simon & Schuster.

Coale, Ansley, and Edgar M. Hoover. 1958. *Population Growth and Economic Development in Low Income Countries: A Case Study of India's Prospects.* Princeton: Princeton University Press.

Critchlow, Donald T. 1995. "Birth Control, Population Control, and Family Planning: An Overview". *Journal of Policy History* 7: 1–21.

Crocker, W. R. 1931. *The Japanese Population Problem: The Coming Crisis.* New York: Macmillan.

Davis, Kingsley. 1951. *The Population of India and Pakistan.* Princeton: Princeton University Press.

———. 1956. "Population and Power in the Free World". In *Population Theory and Policy,* edited by J. Spengler and O. D. Duncan, 342–56. Chicago: Free Press.

———. 1958. "The Political Impact of New Population Trends". *Foreign Affairs Quarterly* 36 (January 1958): 293–301.

Dennery, Etienne. 1931. *Asia's Teeming Millions.* London: Jonathan Cape.

Djerassi, Carl. 1992. *The Pill, Pygmy Chimps and Degas' Horse.* New York: Basic Books

Gordon, Linda. 1976. *Woman's Body, Woman's Right.* New York: Grossman.

Gould, Stephen J. 1993. *The Mismeasure of Man.* 2nd Ed. New York: Norton.

Hagen, James M., and V. W. Ruttan. 1988. "Development Policy under Eisenhower and Kennedy". *The Journal of Developing Areas* 23: 1–30.

Haller, Mark. 1963. *Eugenics: Hereditarian Attitudes in American Thought.* New Brunswick: Rutgers University Press.

Harr, John E., and Peter J. Johnson. 1988. *The Rockefeller Century.* New York: Scribner's.

Hauser, Philip, ed. 1958. "Introduction". *Population and World Politics,* , 9–23. Glencoe, Ill.: Free Press.

Hodgson, Dennis. 1983. "Demography as Social Science and Policy Science". *Population and Development Review* 9: 1–34.

———. 1991. "The Ideological Origins of the Population Association of America". *Population and Development Review* 17: 1–34.

Ishii, Ryoichi. 1937. *Population Pressure and Economic Life in Japan.* London: King.

Kennedy, David M. 1970. *Birth Control in America: The Career of Margaret Sanger.* New Haven: Yale University Press.

Kevles, Daniel J.. 1990. *In the Name of Eugenics.* New York: Knopf.

Lyons, Gene M. 1969. *The Uneasy Partnership: Social Science and the Federal Government in the Twentieth Century.* New York: Russell Sage.

May, Elaine Tyler. 1988. *Homeward Bound: American Families in the Cold War Era.* New York: Basic Books.

Morgenthau, Henry, Jr. 1944. "The United Nations Monetary and Financial Conference: Address by the Secretary of the Treasury". *Department of State Bulletin,* 11, no. 266 (July 30): 112.

Nasu, Shiroshi. 1929. "Can Japan Solve Her Population Problem?". In *Population: Lectures on the Harris Foundation,* by Corrado Gini, Shiroshi Nasu, Robert R. Kuczynski, and Oliver E. Baker, 187–207. Chicago: University of Chicago Press.

Nef, John. 1950. *War and Human Progress.* Cambridge: Harvard University Press.

Notestein, Frank W. 1948. "Summary of the Demographic Background of Problems of Underdeveloped Areas". In *International Approaches to Problems of Underdeveloped Areas: 1947 Annual Conference of the Memorial Fund (November 19–20, 1947),* 9–19. New York: Milbank Fund.

Onorato, Suzanne A. 1991. "The Population Council and the Development of Contraceptive Technologies". *Rockefeller Archive Center Research Reports* (Spring): 1–3.

Penrose, E. F. 1934. *Population Theories and Their Application with Special Reference to Japan.* Stanford: Food Research Institute, Stanford University.

Piotrow, Phyllis. 1973. *World Population Crisis: The United States Response.* New York: Praeger.

Pitkin, Walter B. 1921. *Must We Fight Japan?* New York: The Century Company.

Population Council. 1978. *The Population Council: A Chronicle of the First Twenty-Five Years, 1951–1976.* New York: The Population Council.

Reed, James. 1983. *The Birth Control Movement and American Society: From Private Vice to Public Virtue.* Princeton: Princeton University Press.

Sharpless, J. B. 1993. "The Rockefeller Foundation, the Population Council and the Groundwork for New Population Policies". *Rockefeller Archives Center Newsletter* (Fall): 1–4.

———. 1995. "World Population Growth, Family Planning and American Foreign Policy". *Journal of Policy History* 7: 72–102.

Smith, James A. 1991. *The Idea Brokers: Think Tanks and the Rise of the New Policy Elite.* New York: The Free Press/Macmillan.

Taeuber, Irene B. 1958. *The Population of Japan.* Princeton: Princeton University Press.

Thompson, Warren. 1946. *Population and Peace in the Pacific.* Chicago: University of Chicago Press.

Ideas and Development Institutions

SEVEN

Redefining Development
at the World Bank

Martha Finnemore

Notions about development—what it is and how one does it—have changed over the past fifty years.[1] When development first emerged as a transnational mission in the 1950s, the goal of development was understood to be raising GNP. Now that goal has been expanded to include concerns about income distribution and poverty, environmental degradation and sustainability, the status of women, maintaining cultural integrity of indigenous populations, and human rights. Strategies for achieving development goals have also shifted from concerns about capital accumulation, foreign exchange earnings, and construction of large infrastructure projects like dams and power plants to concerns about small farmers, renewable resources, and the provision of social services in urban areas.

In this chapter I explore this process of change by examining one shift in development goals—the incorporation of poverty alleviation as a defining feature of development in the 1960s and 1970s. Prior to 1968 poverty received scant attention in international development institutions, in academic development writings, or even in national development plans. By the mid-1970s, poverty had moved front and center stage in all three arenas of development work. Further, poverty moved from being a condition of states to a condition of people. To the extent that poverty was discussed in the international development community prior to the 1970s, the discussion was about "poor countries;" beginning in the early 1970s, the poor were widely understood to be individual human beings. States were disaggregated in these new development policies and the poor were targeted *within* states.

What caused this change? There was no significant change in the numbers or condition of the poor during this short period. Nor was there any widespread political change that empowered the poor in LDCs and allowed them to demand attention from national and international development bureaucrats. Nor does there appear to have been any sudden rise of powerful organized philanthropic interests in developed aid-donor countries who were pressing for new development policies that would target poor populations.

Instead, I trace the definition of poverty as an essential element of the transnational development mission to an international organization, the World Bank. The Bank was instrumental in this change in two ways. First, a new Bank President, Robert McNamara, brought poverty concerns with him and institutionalized them at the Bank. Concern about poverty had been around for centuries and arguments that development activity should be attending to distributional issues had begun to appear in the new discipline of development economics for several years. However these views did not become globally influential until they found a powerful organizational home, as they did when McNamara brought them to the Bank. Ideas needed to be institutionalized for maximum effect.[2]

Second, the organizational structure of the Bank and the professional norms of the staff (mostly economists) working within it acted as a selection mechanism or filter through which different ideas about poverty alleviation had to pass and from which only a few ideas emerged for implementation. Once poverty was identified as a development "problem," a wide variety of solutions were proposed both inside and outside the Bank to address it. The fact that poverty-alleviating development became synonymous with projects focused on small farmers and provision of urban services reflected the organizational needs of the Bank rather than any intrinsic merit of these approaches over others.

This chapter begins with a brief sketch of development activity and the place of poverty alleviation in that effort prior to the late 1960s. The bulk of the analysis then explores the Bank's role in defining and promoting poverty-oriented development in the 1970s. I focus on two issues: first, how the poverty orientation became established at the Bank and, second, how the Bank interpreted and defined poverty alleviation for practical programmatic purposes through its own bureaucratic structures. In addition, the analysis shows reciprocal effects: the organizational structure of the Bank influenced the shape of antipoverty concerns globally but the poverty alleviation agenda also had a profound effect on the Bank, making it bigger, more bureaucratic, and more professionally eclectic.

Before going further, I should make clear what the chapter does *not* do. It does not argue that the World Bank or anyone else has succeeded in alleviating poverty in the developing world. Assessments of the success of development efforts have been undertaken by a large number of experts and critics. My purpose here is not to assess the success of development efforts but to try to understand more clearly what this massive development effort *is* that consumes so many national and international resources. What is it that those involved in development are trying to do? How does what they are trying to do change over time, and why does it change?

In addition, I do not argue that the World Bank invented poverty as a concern, either of individuals, of governments, or even of international institutions. As will be shown below, concerns about global poverty had been expressed in a variety of quarters prior to McNamara's appearance at the Bank. What McNamara and the Bank did do was to institutionalize this concern; they made it an inextricable part of what development was all about. Before 1968, being "developed" meant having dams, bridges, and a (relatively) high GNP per capita (Mason and Asher 1973: 152; Ayres 1983: 2–3.) After 1973, being developed also required the guarantee of a certain level of welfare to one's population.

BACKGROUND: POVERTY AS A CONCERN IN DEVELOPMENT PRIOR TO 1968

Poverty was never entirely absent from development thinking. As Cooper discusses elsewhere in this volume, colonial powers were concerned with social welfare issues in their colonies but both the concern and the policies it produced differed markedly from the poverty-alleviation focus of development that emerged in the 1970s. The British, in particular, voiced concern in the 1940s about raising the "standard of living" in their colonies but the problem was perceived primarily as a problem of labor and social order, not a poverty problem per se. Wages and social services were inadequate to ensure a sufficient standard of living and too few people were in the wage economy. The task was to "develop" enough industries and create enough jobs so that people could move out of the (presumably) impoverished non-wage economic sector and into the (presumably) more prosperous wage-labor sector producing for the metropole.

The development policies that emerged from this vision of the problem were, not surprisingly, couched in reasoning that more nearly resembled human capital theory than the human rights discourse which formed the background to the 1970s attacks on poverty. Poverty alleviation was not an end in itself but a happy byproduct of expanded production and efficient industrialization. It was also a necessary condition for social calm and continued imperial rule. Fear of political disorder may not have been the only reason to implement social welfare policies in the colonies but it was an important one and the connection between poverty and unrest was frequently noted. In any case, colonial policies slipped by the late 1940s into a growth-oriented mold, assimilating the distinct interests of colonial peoples and imperial economies into a singular concept of "development" (Cooper, this volume).

Perhaps the most important difference, though, between colonial debates about social welfare and subsequent debates about poverty alleviation was that the former were domestic debates in ways the latter were not. Colonial debates were debates within a single government about policies to be implemented inside a territory under its control. As decolonization progressed and these regions became states in their own right, debates over their development moved from what was essentially a domestic arena to an international one in which norms of sovereignty dictated noninterference by governments in the social affairs of other states.

Prior to World War II, concern with poverty across national borders was largely the province of religious and private philanthropic groups. Governments might occasionally supply relief aid in response to a natural disaster, famine, or war but they did not concern themselves with chronic structural poverty in other countries until after 1940.[3] Following the Great Depression and World War II, states began to articulate a more internationalist sense of community that included poverty alleviation. Roosevelt included "freedom from want . . . everywhere in the world" in his Four Freedoms speech justifying the war in 1941, and the Atlantic Charter reiterated this aim.[4] United Nations activity expanded and codified the goal of alleviating poverty, most notably in the *Universal Declaration of Human Rights*, adopted by the General Assembly in 1948; and the *Covenant on Economic, Social, and Cultural Rights*, adopted by the General Assembly in 1966.

These expressions of concern about poverty were not, however, connected to understandings of development or development efforts immediately following the war. The lack of connection is clear from the Bretton Woods discussions and the way in which the World Bank was founded. While the Bank's Articles of Agreement do mention (but do not emphasize) assisting countries in raising standards of living, they do not mention or target poor countries in particular, nor do they mention any kind of guarantee of minimum standards as does the *Universal Declaration*. Rather the articles emphasize productivity, investment, capital accumulation, growth, and balance of payments.

In fact, development received little international attention in the years immediately following the war and was not a major concern at the Bretton Woods conference which structured the postwar economic order.[5] Even representatives of LDCs seemed unconcerned, insofar as their views were expressed in international organizations. Developing country governments at Bretton Woods defined themselves as "raw materials producing nations" rather than as countries with development problems. Certainly they did not view themselves as poor countries or countries with large poor populations for whom the international community should take some responsibility. Developing country proposals at the conference centered around stabilizing prices in commodities markets. They did not mention poverty (Meier 1984: 12–14).

During the 1950s and 1960s development activity began to move from war-torn Europe (where it was called "reconstruction") into LDCs with the creation of the International Development Association (IDA) and bilateral aid programs in industrialized states. However, the "development" activity that was undertaken in this period was not poverty alleviation as that activity was subsequently conceived nor was it understood as poverty alleviation by those who were undertaking it. Development, during these years, was understood to be increasing GNP or, perhaps, GNP per capita. Raising GNP (or GNP per capita) was *the* indicator of development success. Increasing GNP, in turn, meant industrialization and the obstacle to industrialization was capital accumulation. The proper aim of states (and of development) was to promote savings (often through protection against imports), direct investment toward industrialization and, where possible, secure external aid. The "development projects" undertaken by states in this period were large industrial infrastructure projects, such as dams or highways, designed to have large secondary industrialization-promotion effects.[6]

This development orthodoxy was widely held. It permeated academic economics circles and the emerging discipline of development economics (Meier 1984: chap. 6; Lewis and Kallab 1986: chap. 1; Mason and Asher 1973: 481–87). It underlay the national development plans formulated by state planning ministries, the staff of which were often educated by the above-mentioned academic economists (Bhagwati and Desai 1970; Pangestu 1971; ul Haq 1976; Ghana Planning Commission 1964; Indonesia Department of Information 1969; Nigeria Federal Government 1962; Honduras Committee of Nine 1963; Thailand National Economic Development Board 1961). It dominated thinking in multilateral lending agencies like the World Bank (Mason and Asher 1973).

Within this development orthodoxy, poverty was not a visible concern. The approach was not opposed to poverty alleviation in any way. To the extent that anyone thought about poverty, they thought about the salutary effects of GNP growth for all. But mostly, they simply did not think about it. Poverty is almost never discussed in the academic literature. It does not even receive lip service in most of the national development plans of the period, and had virtually no impact on multilateral lending policies or practices.[7]

This is not to say that no one cared about poverty prior to 1968; many individuals, NGOs, and perhaps even some colonial and social democratic governments in Europe did care and acted on those concerns (Cooper, this volume; Lumsdaine 1993). But poverty alleviation was not development. Consequently, it was not an explicitly articulated and internationalized goal of states, multilateral financial institutions, or academic economists.

This changed in the years between about 1968 and 1975. By the late 1970s, everyone involved in development was talking, writing, and structuring policies around poverty issues. Academic treatises were being published, international conferences were being organized, national development plans were reoriented, international aid efforts were retargeted. Data began to be collected on the impact of development efforts on poor populations and these results were the object of intense scrutiny. The goal of poverty alleviation became *institutionalized* as part of the international development effort.

The driving force behind this new understanding of development was the World Bank. Critiques of the reigning development orthodoxy that called for more attention to poverty had been appearing in academic circles for several years but these were controversial and had had little impact on policy. It was not until these critiques were adopted by a powerful institution, the Bank, that they became politically consequential. However, as the following analysis shows, the Bank's own history and organizational requirements left their stamp on these notions. The kinds of poverty-oriented development programs eventually pushed by the Bank looked the way they did, not because they were obviously or objectively best-suited to the task of poverty alleviation but because they met the organizational needs of the Bank.[8]

REDEFINING DEVELOPMENT TO TARGET POVERTY

Intellectual Shifts

Concern about poverty among economists began to surface in the 1960s. Gunnar Myrdal published *Asian Drama: An Inquiry into the Poverty of Nations*, which focused on poverty problems in India and Pakistan, in 1968.[9] That same year, a group at the newly founded Institute for Development Studies at the University of Sussex, including Dudley Seers, began talking about poverty as part of development (Seers and Joy 1971: preface). Written products of these discussions began appearing shortly thereafter (e.g., Seers 1969). Prior to that time the field of development economics had been otherwise occupied. Much of the 1950s and 1960s had been spent on the very basic tasks of fashioning reasonable models of how LDC economies worked. Development economists recognized that their inherited assumptions about the behavior of factors, price mechanisms, and social institutions were inapplicable to developing countries, but rejecting these left the new discipline of development economics scrambling for alternatives. The alternatives these economists came up with in the first instance did not focus on poverty. Arthur Lewis, Raúl Prebisch. and the other pioneers of the 1950s were preoccupied with industrialization and lifting capital constraints; their policies did not target the poor.[10]

The poverty concern among development economists had several sources. The United Nations and other international secretariats had been collecting data on employment, income distribution, and various aspects of social welfare during the 1960s as part of the "Development Decade." As these were disseminated in the second half of the decade they made the scope of world poverty startlingly clear. Gunnar Myrdal also suggests that the domestic "unconditional war on poverty" declared by Lyndon Johnson in the United States may also have prompted interest in poverty overseas (Myrdal 1970: xii–xiii).

The result of these new data and the domestic example was a stinging critique of neoclassical development orthodoxy by many prominent development economists. The problem was not that these efforts had failed to do what they set out to do, that is. promote growth. The problem was that, despite impressive growth records among LDCs during the 1960s, these policies had "failed" because they had failed to eliminate poverty, the critics argued.

The critique was explicit about its normative element. The aim was to "thrust debates over economic and social development into the arena of ethical values" (Goulet 1971). " 'Development' is inevitably a normative concept" and massive poverty was "objectionable by any religious or ethical standards" (Seers 1969). In light of this, the goals of the entire development effort needed to be reassessed (Adelman 1975).

While these attacks on neoclassical orthodoxy were being launched in the late 1960s and early 1970s, they were not immediately embraced by the larger development community. These writings were resisted or ignored by development experts in many quarters. That alleviating poverty was desirable was easy to agree upon; that alleviating poverty was the job of development and development economists was not. How wealth was distributed inside societies was considered a political, not an economic, problem. Decisions about distributing wealth involved making explicit value judgments in ways that were supported neither by traditional economic analytic techniques nor by the professional norms of economics as a discipline.

The critiques did, however, create a permissive environment for change. Seers, Joy, and Myrdal drew attention to the failings of previous development policies. They did not, however, provide a clear consensual blueprint for alternative development policies. They offered no single or simple solution to poverty problems nor did they offer assurances to economists that these problems could be modeled and solved technocratically. Consequently, these writings provoked concern and discussion in the development community but did not, by themselves, indicate a clear course of action. It was in this environment that Robert McNamara assumed the presidency of the World Bank.

Changes at the Bank under George Woods

A number of changes in Bank policy and organization set the stage for the McNamara agenda when he arrived. When Eugene Black retired as Bank president in 1962 he suggested that the Bank "was approaching the peak of its career and that bankable projects were running out because most potential borrowers had enough debt to carry" ("Mr. Woods" 1963: 59; see also, Schechter 1988: 353; Mason and Asher 1973: 458–69, 470– 71).

The Bank's next president and McNamara's immediate predecessor, George Woods, disagreed. To keep money flowing, he raised the "hemline of bankability" for projects by extending grace periods. Under his leadership, the Bank also began siphoning off funds to support IDA loans (which would benefit the poorest countries), despite earlier promises to the financial community holding World Bank bonds that there would be no such mixing of Bank and IDA funds. In an attempt to create more sympathy among Bank staff for LDC projects, Woods sharply increased the proportion of Bank and IDA professional staff who were non-U.S. citizens. He also began to expand the substantive scope of World Bank lending, particularly into education and agriculture. Under Woods, lending for tertiary education, particularly technical training, came to be seen as an essential part of LDC industrialization. Similarly, agriculture was recognized as a "directly productive" sector (akin to industry) whose stimulation would similarly promote growth (Schechter 1988; Adler 1973). Tertiary technical training obviously did not target the masses of poor. Neither did large loans designed to help "farm business."("Mr. Woods" 1963: 59).[11] But these early forays into lending for social and agricultural projects helped set the stage for, and create World Bank organizational structures for, later lending for poverty alleviation.

The Arrival of McNamara

Robert S. McNamara came to the Bank in 1968 with a different background and a different agenda than any of his predecessors. He was the first Bank president who was not a banker. He was a manager.[12] He had been an assistant professor at Harvard Business School before joining Ford Motor company of which he was named president in 1960. From 1961 to 1968 he served as Secretary of Defense under Presidents Kennedy and Johnson (Schechter 1988). He was a "classic Kennedy activist" who believed "very obviously in the 'exercise of power' "("Robert McNamara" 1968) and brought to the Bank a clear set of goals toward which that power was to be directed.

Those goals revolved around a deeply held belief in the virtues and efficacy of foreign aid. McNamara believed both that aid was a moral obligation of rich nations and that such aid could and did work. He was an internationalist driven by internationalist morality and optimism. By helping the poor, rich nations could answer the moral imperative and serve their own interests at the same time. Poverty caused violence, internationally as well as domestically. By alleviating the poverty of others, rich nations could create a more stable and secure world for themselves (McNamara 1973: 15–17; McNamara 1968: chap. 9).[13]

McNamara had expressed these views well before he arrived at the Bank. In a speech to the American Society of Newspaper Editors in Montreal in 1966, while still Secretary of Defense, McNamara argued the importance of ending poverty in the developing world for both humanitarian and security reasons, emphasizing the limitations of military power to achieve security goals in a world of such gross disparities of welfare (Shapley 1993: 381–82). While still at the Pentagon McNamara wrote:

> I am increasingly hopeful that at some point soon . . . [t]he wealthy and secure nations of the world will realize that they cannot possibly remain either wealthy or secure if they continue to close their eyes to the pestilence of poverty that covers the whole southern half of the globe (McNamara 1968: 161–62).[14]

Moving to the Bank was thus in keeping with McNamara's overall internationalist vision. Wars of insurgency were the result of frustrations born of poverty. The obvious imperative was "to cure the malady at its source" (McNamara 1968: 161). Thus, far from being contradictory, McNamara viewed his direction of the Vietnam War and his campaign against world poverty to be two related tasks in the quest for a secure and prosperous world.[15]

McNamara's attack on world poverty came on two fronts. The first of these was to increase dramatically the volume of Bank lending, specifically to double lending in his first five years in office. McNamara was concerned that, after the initial enthusiasm of the early 1960s, developed countries were becoming disillusioned with foreign aid. He cited a "mood of frustration and failure" surrounding the efforts of the Development Decade and feared that developed countries would begin to reduce aid as a result. His response was to use both the Bank's financial resources and political position to ensure and increase aid flows to poor countries (McNamara 1973: chap. 1; McNamara 1981; Maddux 1981).

McNamara's concerns about bilateral giving were well founded. While Official Development Assistance (ODA) from the OECD's Development Assistance Committee (DAC) grew steadily in constant dollars until about 1965, from 1965 through 1972 DAC giving remained flat. Indeed, as a percentage of GNP, ODA for DAC countries declined steadily during the 1960s (OECD 1985: 95, 14).[16]

In addition to increasing the quantity of aid, McNamara wanted to change the way in which aid was used. As a self-perceived manager of a development agency (rather than a commercial banker) McNamara took a much more active interest in what LDC states actually *did* with the money they received from the Bank and in the kinds of effects (if any) aid was having.[17] He loved charts and figures (Shapley 1993) and was strongly struck by the new data, mentioned above, revealing the extent of world poverty.

From his first speech to the Board of Governors in his second month in office, McNamara put poverty issues on the table. He spoke, not only of GNP per capita, but of directing World Bank lending toward improving the living conditions of individual poor people. He proposed expanding education lending to *all* levels of education, emphasizing fundamental illiteracy problems as well as more advanced technical training. He spoke of basic nutritional requirements for individual health and well-being. He spoke of lending for the benefit of individual peasant farmers as well as farming business.[18] A month later, in a speech to the Inter-American Press Association McNamara made "economic and social policies which will permit a more equitable distribution" of wealth the first of his demands from borrowing countries.[19] Unlike his predecessors, he talked about "the poor" as individual human beings rather than as countries, and emphasized poorer segments *within* societies rather than simply classifying entire countries as poor (Reid 1973: 794).

Thus, from the time he arrived in 1968 McNamara understood his central mission to be to do something about world poverty. The questions were "what" and "how." Between 1968, when he arrived at the Bank, and 1973, when he outlined a comprehensive program in Nairobi, McNamara wrestled with these problems of securing the means and developing a strategy for attacking poverty.

Retooling the Bank for Poverty Alleviation

To make a dent in a problem as massive as world poverty McNamara clearly needed a bigger and a somewhat different World Bank.[20] In his maiden speech to the Board of Governors he therefore proposed doubling Bank lending in his first five years.[21] This meant that the Bank would lend nearly as much in the 1969–1973 period as it had in its entire twenty-two year history (Schechter 1988: 362). Doing this required McNamara to borrow more and borrow at rates above its current lending rate, policies that made many in western governments and financial circles uncomfortable and were opposed by more than half of McNamara's senior Bank staff ("Robert McNamara" 1968; Ayres 1983: 61–64).

But simply having more money did not ensure that more money was going to the poor. To tackle this problem, McNamara reconfigured the financial relationship between the Bank and the IDA, whose responsibility it was to serve the poorest countries. Given the global recession and donor states' lack of enthusiasm for aid (especially the United States), securing large replenishments for the IDA proved difficult for McNamara. His response was to begin funneling International Bank for Reconstruction and Development (IBRD) surplus to the IDA. Again, senior staff and world financial figures were unhappy and predicted dire consequences for confidence in the Bank's operations and the Bank's ability to raise funds on world markets (none of which where borne out.) Further, he endorsed proposals to provide the IDA with three billion dollars per year in special drawing rights (SDRs) from the International Monetary Fund (Reid 1973: 805).

In addition to expanding the size of the Bank, McNamara also had to change its organizational structure and style. Prior to McNamara's arrival the Bank had operated with a style termed by one high-level staffer, "leisurely perfectionism." Staff followed projects in minute detail and took months to make decisions.[22] Doubling the volume and changing the direction of lending quickly made this style unworkable. Both required more staff, more work, and less attention to detail.[23] The "new style" of poverty-oriented lending (described below) entailed lending for more small projects based on less information, using less well-developed techniques, and involving more costs and benefits that were difficult or impossible to quantify using standard economic analytic tools. The results were predictable: resistance among staff to new methods and policies, conflicts between old and new staff, conflicts among project staff and program staff, and uncertainty among both staff and borrowers.[24]

McNamara's response to these demands on his institution was to turn what had been a club into a bureaucracy. The World Bank was always a very "presidential" institution. McNamara used those extensive presidential powers and expanded them. He turned the Bank into a much more hierarchical place, gathering to himself the reigns of power and streamlining organization. His consolidation of power extended even to his relationship with the executive directors, the representatives of the member countries who must approve Bank actions (Schechter 1988; Ayres 1983: 64–67; Shapley 1993).

Operationalizing "Poverty Alleviation"

At the same time that McNamara was building this expanded instrument for attacking poverty, he was also thinking about strategies for the attack. Studies coming out in 1968–1969, including the Pearson Report initiated by the Bank, made it abundantly clear that the benefits of growth were not trickling down to the poorest (Johnson 1970; Mason and Asher 1973). However, there was little consensus on an alternative policy that would improve the lot of these poor populations. Defining and articulating this policy alternative became a principal preoccupation of McNamara's initial years in office.

In true whiz kid style, McNamara sought out new ideas and new solutions and brought people who articulated these ideas into the Bank's orbit. They were, for the most part, not lawyers or bankers, but economists or managers.[25] Hollis Chenery, for example, was a Harvard economist who put the Bank on the cutting edge of research in development economics and made essential connections with Dudley Seers and the Sussex crowd. Their collaborative book, *Redistribution with Growth*, a joint effort between World Bank staff and academics, redefined intellectual thinking in the field (Chenery et al. 1974). Mahbub ul Haq, who became head of Policy, Planning, and Program Review at the Bank, was a former finance minister of Pakistan who, having been a strong advocate of growth strategies earlier, became a passionate spokesman about the need to rethink development to solve poverty problems in the late 1960s and early 1970s (ul Haq 1976; Shapley 1993: 508–509). Fabian-inspired British development thinkers, notably Barbara Ward and William Clark, had McNamara's ear from early in his tenure at the Bank. Clark was already at the Bank when McNamara arrived and the two hit it off. He was extremely well-connected in the British development circles concerned with poverty issues and made sure that McNamara met and heard from these critics of development orthodoxy, particularly Ward. McNamara had been "spellbound" by Ward when he first heard her speak during his Kennedy Cabinet years. "She influenced me more than anyone in my life," McNamara said later (Shapley 1993: 505–507).

In addition to hiring new full-time senior staff, McNamara commissioned reports, brought in people to give seminars, or brought them in on short consultancy contracts to work with in-house task forces he set up. For example, McNamara met Alan Berg, an expert on nutrition issues, at a Brookings Institution seminar and was sufficiently interested in his ideas to bring him in to the Bank for a time.[26]

Thus, between 1968 and 1970 a large number of different kinds of poverty-oriented policies were proposed at the Bank. Population control was an early favorite: if only something could be done to control the population explosion in these developing countries, there would be more wealth to go around. Nutrition projects were suggested as a focus of World Bank activity: many of the world's poor were so malnourished that they could not do productive work and raise themselves out of poverty. Health projects were proposed under much the same rationale. Education was explored in great detail as a means of increasing labor productivity. Labor-intensive industries were discussed as a means of alleviating unemployment.

The particular set of policies the Bank settled on in 1970–1971 had less to do with any intrinsic merit of one policy over another and more to do with which policy would best answer the organizational requirements and fit the organizational competencies of the Bank. Population control was McNamara's personal early favorite. He made several high-profiles speeches about it in his early months in office in which he made it clear that he believed population was *the* overriding cause of poverty in the developing world.[27] The demographic characteristics of these policies were easily quantifiable and so appeared congenial to him.

But population control did not match the organizational requirements of the Bank. First, it was too political. It inserted the Bank into a debate that was fundamentally about values and religion in a way that World Bank staffers (as well many outside the Bank) found objectionable. As William Ascher's (1983) study makes clear, the professional norms of Bank staffers were enormously important in determining their reaction to policy changes. Most of the Bank staff were economists by training and understood their roles as technical or managerial. They prided themselves on being able to provide rigorous analyses of development problems and many became profoundly uncomfortable when asked to make what they perceived to be value judgments without sound technical guidelines and methods. (Ascher 1983; Ayres 1983: 38–41).

Further, while population control represented a new poverty-oriented direction for lending, it did not help the Bank meet its other goal of doubling the volume of lending. Population projects simply did not absorb much money, certainly not in comparison with power plants and dams, and moving money was a major preoccupation of the Bank during McNamara's first five years.

Finally, the Bank lacked expertise, experience, and therefore credibility in the field of population control. This made staffers uncomfortable, for the reasons noted above. It also made borrowers suspicious. The World Bank, it will be remembered, plays an active role in the design and supervision of projects it funds. Entering the politically sensitive area of population control was unattractive enough to borrower governments; doing so as the Bank's guinea pigs was even less so.[28]

Proposals that the Bank begin major forays into the areas of health and nutrition also made little headway. In part this was a result of the lack of World Bank expertise and credibility. In part it was because these areas were understood to be the specialization of other international organizations, such as the Food and Agriculture Organization and World Health Organization.[29]

Education fared somewhat better. The Bank had already established a track record here under George Woods. What was needed was a shift in direction toward lending for mass literacy campaigns as well as the more narrow lending for tertiary technical training that the Bank was already funding. However, the relationship between literacy and poverty alleviation was somewhat indirect. Teaching people to read did not, by itself, feed or shelter people. A more direct set of poverty alleviation policies was needed.

The policies that the Bank finally hit upon involved rural development and aid to small subsistence farmers. The World Bank estimated that between 550 and 700 million people were living in rural poverty, most in some kind of subsistence (or sub-subsistence) farming situations. The technology of the Green Revolution, then becoming widely known, could be used to help these very large poor populations. What was needed was an integrated, multisectoral approach toward developing an entire impoverished region. By simultaneously providing agricultural credits, limited irrigation, roads to markets, improved seed stock, education, and training in new cultivation techniques, in ways that would be mutually reinforcing, entire areas could be lifted out of poverty (Ayres 1983; van de Laar 1980).

The organizational attractions of this approach were many. First, the Bank had experience lending in agriculture, even if not to small farmers. Second, these regional projects could absorb a lot of money (thus satisfying the volume goals) and channel it directly toward the world's poorest populations. Third, many if not all of the aspects of these rural regional development projects could be addressed with professional skills possessed by the Bank staff—certainly more so than with the population projects. Finally, these projects were attractive to borrower governments. While LDCs had not shown any particular interest in channeling World Bank funds directly toward the poor, these multisector projects did have the advantage of offering something for a variety of different governmental ministries in borrower states—agriculture for the agriculture ministries, roads for the transport ministry, training for the education ministry.[30]

This set of policies did not emerge overnight. While the poverty focus was present from the beginning of McNamara's tenure at the Bank, the focused rural development program did not appear until 1970 and 1971. It was not institutionalized until 1972 when the Bank set up a specialized unit for rural development and did not arrive on center stage of the world development community's debates until McNamara outlined it in his famous 1973 Nairobi speech.[31]

From the Nairobi speech onwards, the momentum behind the anti-poverty program snowballed. Having achieved his goal of doubling funds since 1968, McNamara was able to shift that money very quickly into these rural development projects. He had created a new branch of the Bank a year earlier to deal directly with rural development and trends in lending shifted quickly away from the old industrial sectors toward agriculture and rural development. The share of agriculture increased from 12 percent of total World Bank lending in 1961–1965 to 16 percent in 1971–1972 and 24 percent in 1973–1974 (World Bank 1975: 11, 58).[32] Rural development lending increased from 2.9 percent of total bank/IDA lending in 1969 to 4.9 percent in 1972, 7.5 percent in 1973 and 11 percent in 1974 (World Bank 1975: 88). As these percentages rose, the share of World Bank lending going to infrastructure projects (power plants, dams, roads) fell. In 1967 such projects consumed 55 percent of Bank lending; by 1977 they consumed on 30 percent (ul Haq 1976: 13). In addition to this sectoral shift the Bank increased the share of its loans to the poorest countries. Of its agricultural lending, the Bank had previously allocated 22.5 percent of its loans to its poorest class of countries (those with GNP per capita of less than $150) and 49.3 percent of its loans to countries with GNP per capita above $376 during the period 1964–1968. In 1969–1974 that poorest class of countries received 38.2 percent of loans while those above $376 received only 31.7 percent (World Bank 1975: 85).[33]

Robert Ayres (1983) provides an excellent overview of the expansion and evolution of the Bank's anti-poverty activities. The most important addition to the Bank's program were the urban poverty projects to provide "sites-and-services," such as potable water, food and medical care, to the urban poor as opposed to building large structures, like apartment buildings, which inevitably ended up costing more than the poorest could afford (Lipton and Shakow 1982; Jaycox 1978). These projects shared the organizational advantages of the rural development projects—ability to absorb lots of money and a multisectoral character that created wide appeal in borrower government bureaucracies.

Spreading the Antipoverty Focus

Ayres (1983) also provides extensive documentation of the Bank's efforts to promote and spread its notions about poverty to its borrower states. He describes implementation of rural development projects despite resistance from entrenched large agricultural interests in Nigeria, land tenure problems in Latin America, and weak national institutions in Tanzania,

Haiti, and Paraguay. In some cases, the Bank's methods of implementation were coercive, as in the Mexican Papaloapan River Basin Project, when the Bank simply withheld funds from Mexican officials who wanted a dam instead of a rural development project in the region (Ayres 1983: 116). More often, the Bank seems to have used methods of persuasion and co-optation. The use of locals rather than expatriates to staff projects, as in West Africa and in Bolivia, created new groups within LDCs who were actively committed to the Bank's antipoverty goals and its programs. More important, the poor beneficiaries of World Bank projects often mobilized and organized as a result of their contact with the Bank and its ideas, pressing for further antipoverty measures. Ayres documents cases of this in Haiti, Bolivia, the Philippines, and Tanzania (Ayres 1983: 139–40).

The World Bank's activities also influenced the shift in intellectual development circles toward a poverty orientation. As was mentioned earlier, the growth-oriented intellectual orthodoxy was under attack in 1968 from poverty-focused critics like Seers and Myrdal. The Bank's switch in approach did much to legitimize the critics and institutionalize the new wisdom as essential to development. The World Bank's research work was widely respected even before McNamara's arrival. With his gravitational pull of academic talent into the Bank, its reputation and influence increased further and was brought to bear on the problem of providing intellectual support for the antipoverty effort. Bank policy papers, which began circulating in the early 1970s, drew large audiences and influenced thinking in both national and international development agencies.[34] Chenery's collaboration with development scholars at Sussex to produce *Redistribution with Growth* (Chenery et al., 1974), mentioned earlier, was influential in reorienting both academic and international policy specialists toward poverty-focused development.

The Robustness of the Antipoverty Focus

Once established, alleviating poverty remained a central part of the development mission, even in the face of exogenous shocks and other changing economic fashions. The whole antipoverty effort might have been still-born within weeks of the Nairobi speech when OPEC members quadrupled the price of oil, sending the industrialized world into a panic and making it harder for McNamara to put poverty high on the agendas of rich nations. He was able to counter this blow and save his Nairobi program by turning, not to the West, but to OPEC states as a source for the Bank's commercial borrowing.[35]

Antipoverty work continued to survive and even expand despite the second oil shocks and global recession of the late 1970s and early 1980s.

While the international economic community, including the Bank, re-trenched during this period and began promoting "structural adjust-ment" in LDCs, it did so with an eye to the effects on the poor and even justified these policies at times as the best way, in the long run, to help the world's poor (Clausen 1985). The World Bank continually did studies of the effects of structural adjustment policies on the poor and debate raged, both inside the Bank and outside, about the effects these policies were having on the poor.

Further, the Bank continued to shift its lending more and more toward the poorest countries during the late 1970s and early 1980s. In 1975, 29 percent of total bank/IDA lending was going to the poorest countries (in this case those with annual per capita incomes below $420 in 1985 dollars). While this figure fell slightly during the late 1970s it rose steadily during the 1980s—the heyday of structural adjustment (Sanford 1989: 152). Structural adjustment policies certainly did affect poverty policies in important ways. However, what is important for purposes here is that there was no return to the status quo ante. Lending continued to target poverty. In fact, the vigor of the debate over structural adjustment's effects on poverty shows how deeply entrenched poverty had become as part of the development mission.[36]

CONCLUSIONS AND IMPLICATIONS

The picture that emerges from the foregoing analysis is one of the World Bank as an arbiter of development norms and development meanings. Prior to 1968, most states and even most development experts did not understand poverty alleviation to be central to the development effort. By 1975, poverty had moved to center stage. The World Bank was not solely responsible for this change. It did not invent the poverty concern nor was it the only actor promoting a poverty orientation. What the Bank did was to pick up this new approach to development and institutionalize the poverty focus so that it became a necessary part of development efforts by both states and international development agencies.

The Bank's ability to do this stemmed from a combination of prestige and power. The intellectual prestige of the Bank's staff facilitated persua-sion of national, international, and academic development experts as to the viability as well as the moral necessity of a poverty focus. The impor-tance of the Bank as the largest multilateral development agency gave it power to apply coercion to recalcitrant borrowers where persuasion failed. In addition, the fact that the Bank was a multilateral entity created less suspicion about its moral and humanitarian motives than might have been applied to similar actions by a single powerful state.

To say that the Bank institutionalized poverty alleviation as a central part of development does not mean that LDC governments now act consistently for the benefit of the poor or even that the Bank consistently acts for the benefit of the poor. LDC governments may be corrupt and incompetent and therefore unable or unwilling to do anything about poverty, just as they were often unable or unwilling to deliver development in development's previous incarnation—as growing GNP. The World Bank, itself, has been criticized for doing more harm than good with some of its poverty alleviation projects and has directed funds toward structural adjustment lending that many argue could (and should) have gone toward poverty alleviation projects. But even in the context of structural adjustment, "development" continues to direct attention to distributional concerns and poverty—a focus not present in development activities in the 1950s. Structural adjustment advocates must now argue that their programs ultimately serve the poor better and must produce data on results that bear out their claims; they cannot ignore poverty.

The redefinition of development to include alleviating poverty has changed the collective international understanding of what development is and the kinds of development activities that are undertaken. Prior to the changes documented here, poverty was a condition of countries, not individual human beings. Development was designed to create modern, industrialized, growing economies in poor countries. What those states *did* with the fruits of growth was their own business. The existence of large impoverished populations in Asia, Africa, and Latin America was deplorable but it was, in political terms, the problem of Asians, Africans, and Latin Americans.

Making poverty alleviation a part of the international development effort changed that. It *internationalized* responsibility for the world's poor. Development agencies now target poor populations within states and are unwilling to leave distributional issues to LDC governments. This change can be seen as part of a much broader internationalization of social concerns since World War II. Rights to food, shelter, education, a safe and sustainable environment; freedom of movement, freedom from torture; women's rights, children's rights; all have been defined by and are being promoted by international institutions, often over the objections of developing states. The internationalization of these concerns is politically controversial because it runs counter to well-entrenched international norms about national self-determination and, to some extent, state sovereignty. Independence, for these developing states, was about running their own affairs. However, intervention based on these social claims, especially by international institutions, appears to be expanding. As the preceding analysis suggests, we can only understand the shape this intervention activity will take—the programmatic meaning of "poverty alleviation" or "sustainable development" or "refugee protection"—if we understand the organizational workings of the institutions that promote these ideas.

NOTES

1. An expanded version of this chapter can be found in Finnemore 1996, chapter 4.

2. Kathryn Sikkink also documents powerful effects from a similar combination of ideas coupled with strong leadership from an organizational base in her study of Raúl Prebisch's use of ECLA to reorient development in the 1940s and 1950s. See Sikkink, this volume.

3. It might be argued that socialists, specifically Soviet Russia, are exceptions to this; however, the Soviets were concerned more with revolution and political power than poverty alleviation (since the former, in their view, were requirements for the latter.)

4. Although, as Lumsdaine points out, it is doubtful that Roosevelt really envisioned massive capital flows to Asia and Africa for development purposes when he made this speech, even though this kind of foreign aid is implicit in the logic of his statements (Lumsdaine 1993, 202).

5. In fact, the bank was originally called the Bank for Reconstruction. The word "development" was not even in its title. It was added later only when E. M. Bernstein pointed out that the bank would need a more permanent function and suggested that that function be development. Bernstein later wrote that he "used this term without being aware that it would become of importance in the future" (Meier 1984; Sanford, 1982).

6. This brief description does not begin to do justice to the extensive writings in development economics of the period or to the intense debates about policy choices within the general development framework. For overviews of development economics in this period, see Meier (1984, chap. 6); Lewis and Kallab (1986: chap. 1); Mason and Asher (1973: 481–87); Adler (1973). For examples of writings from this period about development goals and indicators of success, see United Nations Department of Economic Affairs (1951) and United Nations Conference on Trade and Development (1970). These two reports bracket this period nicely. While the second is much more detailed than the first in its econometric measures, both unequivocally focus on savings, investment, and industrialization. Neither mentions poverty. To be sure, alternative approaches emerged *within* certain LDCs, sometimes embodying more radical versions of national growth efforts, more rarely embracing concerns with community and poverty (Bose, Diouf, Gupta, this volume).

7. In fact, Mason and Asher's (1973) twenty-five-page index to their 900-page history of the World Bank does not have a single entry for "poverty." (Despite the 1973 publication date, this history was written to honor the twenty-fifth anniversary of the bank in 1971 and thus ends just as the shift discussed here begins in the bank.) Richard Webb, who is writing on poverty for the World Bank History Project, counted only three mentions of the word in the 900-page text. Richard Webb, personal communication, 9 June 1993.

8. For an empirical demonstration that the bank did, in fact, lead the way in this shift toward a poverty orientation, changing its focus ahead of both LDC governments and OECD foreign aid, see Finnemore (1996: chap. 4).

9. Myrdal continued to push poverty issues on the agenda with the 1970 publication of *The Challenge of World Poverty*, which probably had a larger impact because of its explicit policy focus.

10. Growth, itself, was relatively new as a concern of economics. Writing about *The Theory of Economic Growth* (published in 1955) Arthur Lewis commented that "no comprehensive treatise on the subject has been published for about a century. The last great book covering this wide range was John Stuart Mill's *Principles of Political Economy*, published in 1848" (quoted in Meier 1984: 127.) For an extended discussion of the evolution of the persistence of static, nongrowth models in the field, see Meier (1984, chap. 5).

Lewis's recommendations are probably more poverty-focused than others' in their emphasis on the need to absorb surplus labor before any benefits will trickle down to the poor. Lewis also stressed the importance of agriculture early on, arguing that low productivity in agriculture was a chief source of economic drag and advocated spending money on rural programs as early as the 1950s. While these recommendations do not appear to have caught on in policy circles, they so provide some precedent for later shifts in thinking about poverty. For more on Lewis see Cooper, this volume.

11. According to one bank staffer, "until the arrival of Robert McNamara, lending for agriculture remained of the traditional types, predominantly plantation or commercial agriculture, largely influenced by the experience of former colonial agricultural officers who constituted a large proportion of the bank's agricultural staff. By the time I came to the bank's Western Africa Regional Office in 1968, the bank had financed only one agricultural project in the 24 countries of the region" (Chaufournier 1984).

12. McNamara was very clear that he regarded the World Bank primarily as a development agency rather than a bank. "If I had wanted to run a bank, I would have been a banker." As quoted in Schechter (1988: 363). See also McNamara (1973: 15).

13. There is also a thesis that McNamara's antipoverty crusade at the World Bank was a form of expiation for his "sins" in Vietnam. See, for example Trewhitt (1971: 38). This thesis does not explain, however, the earlier articulations of concern about poverty in McNamara's pre–World Bank days, before the recognition of his "sins."

The precise origin of McNamara's anti-poverty commitment would require a psychobiography that reaches beyond the scope of this paper. Deborah Shapley, in her recent biography, treats this subject only briefly, mentioning McNamara's own boyhood poverty as an influence (Shapley 1993: 513–14).

14. McNamara expands on these views in his later publication (McNamara 1973).

15. "Everything we have done in Vietnam won't count for a thing if Indian democracy goes down the drain," McNamara remarked to Chester Bowles, U.S. ambassador to India, during the battle to secure additional IDA funding for that

country in the early months of McNamara's tenure at the bank (Shapley 1993: 465).

The Economist's profile of McNamara in June of 1968 also mentions this long-term attention to foreign aid during his seven years at the Pentagon as well as McNamara's concern for the poorest countries rather than "those countries who already happen to have a good chance of lifting themselves out of the mire" [to whom *The Economist* would prefer to lend] ("Robert McNamara" 1968).

16. For more of bilateral aid trends see OECD (1975: 154), Meier (1984: 46).

17. McNamara was the first president of the bank to routinely order evaluations of bank activities and to create a standing branch of the organization for this purpose.

18. Speech to the Board of Governors of the World Bank, Washington DC, September 30, 1968. Reprinted in McNamara (1981: 3–15).

19. Speech to the Inter-American Press Association, Buenos Aries, October 18, 1968. Reprinted in McNamara (1981: 25).

20. Thinking big was clearly McNamara's style. During his Department of Defense days, McNamara became accustomed to having large institutional resources at his disposal with which he could have large effects on the world stage. The relatively small size of the bank was something new to him. "At first he kept talking in billions and then he would correct himself and say 'I meant millions,' "recalls one bank staffer. Quotation is from William Clark's diary as quoted in Shapley (1993: 471).

21. Speech to the Board of Governors of the World Bank, Washington DC, September 30, 1968. Reprinted in McNamara (1981: 3–15).

22. The old style also clashed with McNamara's own. It left the bank underutilized and was "an inefficient way to run a planet" (Shapley 1993: 477). Quotation is from William Clark's diary as cited by Shapley.

23. In fact, doing both simultaneously proved difficult. Escott Reid, a former World Bank employee, describes the frustrations of bank officers. They could meet the volume goals more easily by processing old-style infrastructure loans for dams and roads which were big ticket projects requiring relatively little oversight. Alternatively, they could explore new kinds of lending projects that targeted poor populations, but these projects tended to be lower cost and higher supervision projects that moved less money with more effort (Reid 1973: 796).

24. William Ascher (1983) gives an excellent discussion of the organizational impact of the poverty orientation on the bank. Jonathan Sanford (1989: 159) also discusses some of these issues and Robert Ayres (1983) provides extensive discussions of the organizational dimensions of implementing poverty policies.

25. Shapley (1993: 471–72) recounts the story of McNamara's recruitment of former Securities and Exchange Commission lawyer Eugene Rotberg. During the interview, McNamara ascertained that Rotberg knew nothing about international finance; that his education was in English literature, history and law; and that he thought most investment bankers should be jailed under the Sherman Antitrust Act. Learning this, McNamara asked him if he would accept the post of Treasurer of the World Bank. Rotberg did.

26. Richard Webb, World Bank History Project, personal communication, June 9, 1993.

27. Most notable was his speech to the largely Catholic audience at the University of Notre Dame, Notre Dame, Indiana, May 1, 1969 (reprinted in McNamara 1981).

28. Population control was, however, picked up and promoted by other development organizations with some interesting results. See John Sharpless's chapter in this volume.

29. Interview, Richard Webb, World Bank History Project, June 1993. Population, health, and nutrition projects were ultimately funded as part of the overall antipoverty effort but they never absorbed more than 1 percent of the bank's total lending (Lipton and Shakow 1982: 18; Ayres 1983: 6).

30. Interview, Richard Webb, World Bank History Project, June 1993.

31. McNamara speech to the Board of Governors, Nairobi, Kenya, September 24, 1973 (reprinted in McNamara 1981).

32. In absolute terms, the increase is even more striking. In fiscal years 1969 through 1971, the bank and IDA loaned as much for agriculture as they had in the previous two decades (Mason and Asher 1973: 204).

33. These World Bank (1975) tables do not specify the year for which GNP per capita was calculated or what was done to control for inflation as countries migrate out of GNP per capita categories over time, not due to increasing wealth, but due to inflation. The DAC data, used below, are similarly unclear. In both cases, percentage of World Bank lending or DAC ODA flows to countries with GNP less than $150 in 1969 prices might be given one year; percentage of DAC ODA flows to countries with GNP more than $199 in 1976 prices are given another year. This recurring problem makes it difficult to comparing lending by recipient income group over time.

In this case, however, if countries are migrating out of the GNP per capita < $150 group due to inflation, the shift in Bank lending is all the more impressive.

34. Many of the early poverty policy papers are collected in World Bank (1975).

35. McNamara's attempts to obtain OPEC funding on concessional terms failed (Shapley 1993: 516–19).

36. For a detailed discussion of the bank's balancing of poverty concerns with structural adjustment policies see (Sanford 1988). Sanford, in fact, supplies extensive data showing that World Bank policies have continued to reflect an antipoverty orientation.

REFERENCES

Adelman, Irma. 1975. "Development Economics: A Reassessment of Goals". *American Economic Review* 65: 302–309.

Adler, J. H. 1973. "The World Bank's Concept of Development—An In-House *Dogmengeschichte*". In *Development and Planning: Essays in Honour of Paul Rosenstein-Rodan*, edited by Jagdish Bhagwati and Richard S. Eckaus, 30–50. Cambridge: Massachusetts Institute of Technology Press.

Ascher, William. 1983. "New Development Approaches and the Adaptability of International Agencies: The Case of the World Bank". *International Organization* 37: 415–39.

Ayres, Robert L. 1983. *Banking on the Poor: The World Bank and World Poverty.* Cambridge: Massachusetts Institute of Technology Press.

Bhagwati, Jagdish N., and Padma Desai. 1970. *India: Planning for Industrialization.* New York: Oxford University Press.

Chaufournier, Roger. 1984. "The Coming of Age". *Finance and Development* 21: 32–35.

Chenery, Hollis, et al. 1974. *Redistribution with Growth: Policies to Improve Income Distribution in Developing Countries in the Context of Economic Growth: A Joint Study [Commissioned] by the World Bank's Development Research Center and the Institute of Development Studies, University of Sussex.* London: Published for the World Bank and the Institute of Development Studies by Oxford University Press.

Clausen, A. W. 1985. "Absolute Poverty Can Be Eliminated". *Pakistan and Gulf Economist* 4 (February 16): 45–46.

Finnemore, Martha. 1996. *National Interests in International Society.* Ithaca, N.Y.: Cornell University Press.

Ghana Planning Commission. 1964. *Seven-Year Plan for National Reconstruction and Development, Financial Years 1963/4–1969/70.* Accra, Ghana: Office of the Planning Commission.

Goulet, Denis. 1971. *The Cruel Choice: A New Concept in the Theory of Development.* New York: Atheneum.

Honduras, Committee of Nine. 1963. "Alliance for Progress. Evaluation of the National Plan of Public Investments, 1963–1964, of Honduras". Mimeo. Joint Bank/Fund Library.

Indonesia Department of Information. 1969. *Development: Summary of Indonesia's First Five-Year Development Plan, April 1, 1969 — March 31, 1974.* Djakarta, Indonesia: P. T. Garda.

Jaycox, Edward. 1978. "The Bank and Urban Poverty". *Finance and Development* 15: 10–13.

Johnson, Harry G. 1970. "Pearson's 'Grand Assize' Fails". *Round Table* 237: 17–25.

Lewis, John P., and Valeriana Kallab, eds. 1986. *Development Strategies Reconsidered.* New Brunswick, N.J.: Transaction Books.

Lewis, W. Arthur. 1955. *The Theory of Economic Growth.* Homewood, Ill.: Richard D. Irwin, Inc.

Lipton, Michael, and Alexander Shakow. 1982. "The World Bank and Poverty". *Finance and Development* 19: 16–19.

Lumsdaine, David Halloran. 1993. *Moral Vision in International Politics: The Foreign Aid Regime, 1949–1989.* Princeton: Princeton University Press.

Maddux, John L. 1981. *The Development Philosophy of Robert S. McNamara.* Washington, D.C.: World Bank.

Mason, Edward S., and Robert S. Asher. 1973. *The World Bank Since Bretton Woods.* Washington, D.C.: The Brookings Institution.

McNamara, Robert S. 1968. *The Essence of Security: Reflections in Office.* New York: Harper & Row.

———. 1973. *One Hundred Countries, Two Billion People.* New York: Praeger.

———. 1981. *The McNamara Years at the World Bank: Major Policy Addresses of Robert S. McNamara, 1968–1981.* Baltimore, Md.: The Johns Hopkins University Press.

Meier, Gerald M. 1984. *Emerging from Poverty: The Economics That Really Matters.* New York: Oxford University Press.

"Mr. Woods Looks for New Business". 1963. *The Economist* 209 (October 5): 59–60.

Muscat, Robert. 1966. *Development Strategy in Thailand: A Study of Economic Growth.* New York: Frederick A. Praeger.

Myrdal, Gunnar. 1968. *Asian Drama: An Inquiry into the Poverty of Nations.* New York: Twentieth Century Fund and Pantheon Books.

———. 1970. *The Challenge of World Poverty: A World Anti-Poverty Program in Outline.* New York: Pantheon Books.

Nigeria Federal Government. 1962. *Federal Government Development Programme, 1962–68* Lagos, Nigeria: Federal Printing Division.

OECD. 1975. *Development Cooperation: Efforts and Policies of the Members of the Development Assistance Committee, 1975 Review.* Paris: OECD.

———. 1976. *Development Cooperation: Efforts and Policies of the Members of the Development Assistance Committee, 1976 Review.* Paris: OECD.

———. 1985. *Twenty-Five Years of Development Cooperation: A Review.* Paris: OECD.

Pangestu, J. P. 1971. *Economic Planning Experience in Indonesia* Singapore: University Education Press.

Reid, Escott. 1973. "McNamara's World Bank". *Foreign Affairs* 51: 794–810.

"Robert McNamara, Banker". 1968. *The Economist* 227 (June 8): 70–71.

Sanford, Jonathan. 1982. *U.S. Foreign Policy and Multilateral Development Banks.* Boulder, Colo.: Westview Press.

———. 1988. "The World Bank and Poverty: The Plight of the World's Impoverished Is Still a Major Concern of the International Agency". *American Journal of Economics and Sociology* 47: 257–75.

———. 1989. "The World Bank and Poverty: A Review of the Evidence on Whether the Agency Has Diminished Emphasis on Aid to the Poor". *American Journal of Economics and Sociology* 48: 151–64.

Schechter, Michael G. 1988. "The Political Roles of Recent World Bank Presidents". In *Politics in the United Nations System,* edited by Lawrence Finkelstein, 350–84. Durham, Duke University Press.

Seers, Dudley. 1963. "The Limitations of the Special Case". *Oxford Institute of Economics and Statistics Bulletin* 25: 77–98.

———. 1969. "The Meaning of Development". In *International Development Review* 11. Reprinted and expanded as "What Are We Trying to Measure?" in *Measuring Development,* edited by Nancy Baster, 21–36. London: Frank Cass, 1972.

Seers, Dudley, and Leonard Joy. 1971. *Development in a Divided World* London: Pelican Books.

Shapley, Deborah. 1993. *Promise and Power: The Life and Times of Robert McNamara.* Boston: Little, Brown and Company.

Thailand National Economic Development Board. 1961. *The National Economic Development Programme, B.E. 2504–2506–2509 (1961/2–1966).* Bangkok, Thailand: The Board.

Trewhitt, Henry. 1971. "The Agony and the Expiation of Robert McNamara". *Washingtonian* 38 (November): 35–38.

ul Haq, Mahbub. 1976. *The Poverty Curtain: Choices for the Third World.* New York: Columbia University Press.

United Nations. Conference on Trade and Development. 1970. *The Measurement of Development Effort.* New York: United Nations.

United Nations. Department of Economic Affairs. 1951. *Measures for the Economic Development of Under-Developed Countries.* New York: United Nations.

van de Laar, A. M. J. 1980. *The World Bank and the World's Poor.* Boston: Nijhoff.

World Bank. 1975. *The Assault on World Poverty.* Baltimore, Md.: The Johns Hopkins University Press.

EIGHT

Development Ideas in Latin America

Paradigm Shift and the Economic Commission for Latin America

Kathryn Sikkink

Latin America has been a laboratory for changing development models.[1] In the late 1940s, Latin America gave birth to one of the most influential ideologies of development, the "structuralist" model of development associated with Raúl Prebisch and the Economic Commission for Latin America (ECLA or CEPAL in Spanish). Between 1980 and 1990, ECLA experienced a profound shift in its ideas about development, a shift that paralleled but did not simply duplicate the more general move in Latin America toward neoliberal economic policies. The story of how ECLA went through this shift in development thinking is illuminating for this volume on the production and transmission of development ideas, and for broader questions of the relationship between social sciences and development. Many of the standard explanations for changing development models are unsatisfactory in explaining the new ideas at ECLA. This paper surveys the major explanations for changing ideas—power, learning, and institutional change—in relation to the case of ECLA.[2] I conclude that an approach which stresses a process of learning within institutional and material constraints is the most useful for understanding changing development ideas in ECLA. Because ECLA has been the most important regional economic institution in Latin America, shifts in ECLA thought can be an important microcosm for understanding broader shifts in development ideas in the region.

In the 1950s and 1960s, ECLA was not only the most important economic institution in Latin America, but probably the most influential economic institution based in the Third World.[3] ECLA and Prebisch essentially originated and disseminated two key concepts for understanding underdevelopment: the paired concept of center/periphery and the argument that declining terms of trade for primary products were the main sources of Third World underdevelopment (Love 1980). These concepts became some of the principle metaphors or theories though which many policymakers and academics interpreted underdevelopment. ECLA also embraced and provided theoretical justification for import substituting industrialization (ISI) as a growth strategy. The name ECLA became virtually synonymous with ISI and structuralist economic thought.

Between 1980 and 1990, however, ECLA made an important shift in its approach to development, moving away from its earlier emphasis on ISI to a new focus on international competitiveness. This change was sufficiently dramatic to qualify as a paradigm shift.[4] Dramatic ideational change within an institution becomes a puzzle that needs explanation, because institutional theory suggests that institutions and the individuals within them resist change even when the initial factors that created the institutions have changed (Ikenberry 1988). Although most of the staff are professional economists who engage in research, ECLA is not an academic institution but an intergovernmental organization that answers to the governments of the region. With its major training program of government bureaucrats, its influential publications, and its missions that advise governments, ECLA has been intimately involved in economic policy making over the last four decades.

This chapter has a number of parallels with Martha Finnemore's chapter on the World Bank in this volume. Both explore a paradigm shift within an international organization, and attribute this change more to new ideas or learning than to the pressures of states or international structures. Likewise both chapters stress the role of internal organizational structures and key leaders as central parts of the explanation for changing models within institutions.

TYPES OF IDEAS

In their introduction to their edited volume, *Ideas and Foreign Policy*, Judith Goldstein and Robert Keohane (1993) distinguish between principled beliefs and causal beliefs. Principled beliefs specify criteria for distinguishing right from wrong while causal beliefs are ideas about cause-effect relationships, which provide strategies for the attainment of goals. Because causal ideas are about cause-effect relationships, they are open to falsifiability in a way that principled ideas are not. Most economic ideas are causal ideas, but new economic models do not enter an ideological vacuum, but rather a highly contested political space full of preexisting beliefs and values about the economy. These more general beliefs and values form the context in which debates over new economic models take place, which in turn shapes the nature of the debate over economic ideas and policy.[5] Although ECLA is primarily in the business of producing causal beliefs of a professional or disciplinary nature, the success or failure of economic models in Latin America owes much more to an intersection of different types of beliefs. Particular economic models were often linked to principled ideas or ingrained cultural beliefs and values, which is one reason why it is often more difficult to switch causal ideas when confronted with contradictory evidence. For example, in Latin America, the principled ideas about the importance of Latin American nationalism and autonomy have been historically linked to the causal ideas about the effectiveness of ISI. Not only was ISI believed to offer the most rapid route to economic growth, but it was also valued because it was seen as providing Latin American countries with autonomy and a national sense of pride.

CHANGING IDEAS ABOUT DEVELOPMENT IN LATIN AMERICA

Two central shifts in economic paradigms or economic models have taken place in Latin America over the last sixty years. The first shift in the direction of ISI emerged in the period of the 1940s and the early 1950s. A number of different economic models were equally viable in Latin America in the postwar period. But ISI was the model most captivating to a continent traumatized by memories of its vulnerability during the Great Depression and World War II (Sikkink 1991). ECLA did not lead the move toward this new policy, but it was important in legitimizing the policy and providing the theoretical justification for changes already underway (Hirschman 1961, Bielschowshy 1985).

The second major shift was the neoliberal turn toward greater openness to international trade in the 1980s. In essence, these policies called for trade liberalization, a reduced role for the state in the economy, privatization of state-owned companies, reduced fiscal deficits, and competitive exchange rates. Initially, there was a strong association between these neoliberal policies and authoritarian governments, since the original advocates of neoliberal policies in the region were the bureaucratic authoritarian regimes of the 1970s, especially Chile under Pinochet, and the military juntas of Argentina and Uruguay (Foxley 1983). These policies were later continued by many of the democratic governments that took over in the 1980s and 1990s in Latin America.

CLASSIC ECLA THEORY

The United Nations' creation of ECLA in 1948, against the will of both the United States and the Soviet Republic, reflected the desire of Latin America and other Third World delegations for the United Nations to address the issues of development and industrialization. ECLA set up shop in Santiago, Chile, and enlisted Argentine economist Raúl Prebisch to prepare a study of Latin America's economic situation for the 1949 ECLA Conference in Havana. This text, a ringing critique of the international division of labor and declining terms of trade for producers of primary products, called for industrialization as the only path to development in the underdeveloped countries of Latin America (Prebisch 1950).

There are a number of excellent discussions of ECLA theories and work (Hirschman 1961; Cardoso 1977; Love 1980; Sunkel 1979; Rodriquez 1981; Bruce 1977). Although ECLA work is extremely diverse and has been transforming slowly over time (Pinto 1983), a few central assumptions and arguments presented in the early documents became associated with ECLA thought throughout the continent. Most of these central propositions were laid out in the 1950 Prebisch document, which Albert Hirschman has called the "ECLA manifesto." The first central assumption is that the domestic economies of Latin American countries needed to be analyzed in the context of a global economy divided into center and periphery. The development of the periphery could not be expected to follow the development patterns of the center and, as such, special types of analysis and rules governed development in the periphery. According to Prebisch, the primary mechanism through which the development of the periphery was conditioned by development in the centers was through the declining terms of trade for primary products. Key policy prescriptions followed from this analysis. Only through industrialization would the periphery achieve development and obtain its share of the benefits of technical progress. ECLA argued that because protection in the center interferes with resource allocation and shrinks world trade, protection and import restrictions in the periphery were required to increase industrial output and add to the total product (Hirschman 1961). ISI focused on the internal market; *desarrollo hacia adentro*, or inward-oriented development became the hallmark of ECLA thought. Later, in the 1950s and 1960s, ECLA also placed increased emphasis on economic programming or planning techniques as a means for the state to direct more rationally the development process, and on the importance of regional integration to escape the barriers of small domestic markets.[6] Although classic ECLA thought emphasized inequality among countries, it did not have an explicit focus on poverty or equality within countries, although many of its proponents were deeply concerned about these issues. Rather, ECLA thought, much like liberal thought in this sense, assumed that greater income equality within countries would follow naturally from the ECLA's other policy prescriptions.

Classic ECLA thought had more influence in some Latin American countries than in others. Achieving the most influence in Chile and Brazil, it met with enthusiasm in Central America and the Caribbean, but enjoyed less influence in Mexico, Peru, Colombia, and Argentina (Sikkink 1988). Much like other schools of thought, once put into practice, ECLA prescriptions often were taken beyond the intentions of their originators. Prebisch had stressed that industrialization was not incompatible with the efficient development of primary production nor with more active Latin America foreign trade (Prebisch 1950); but in practice the ECLA ideas were often implemented in a way that led to the neglect of and even discrimination against the primary export sector, and to a gradual decline in Latin American participation in world trade. Likewise, Prebisch and ECLA never ruled out the possibilities that industries would expand and eventually move beyond the internal market into industrial exports. But the manner in which ISI was applied in Latin America often led to what ECLA would later call "elevated and indiscriminate protectionism." If ECLA didn't have an "antiexport" bias, as some of its critics charged, it did exude a certain "export-pessimism" that led to a relative deemphasis on industrial as well as primary exports.

The ideas of ECLA resonated with many strongly held cultural views in Latin America. In addition to its consonance with nationalist sentiment on the importance of being able to produce one's needs domestically, ECLA thought gave Latin Americans an explanation for the frustrating experience of backwardness, which could now be attributed to the international trading system, rather than to some internal failing. It also presented a relatively simple recipe for success.

SHIFTING IDEAS WITHIN ECLA

Between the publication of the so-called "ECLA manifesto" in 1950, and the most recent documents in the 1990s, ECLA has experienced a clear shift in its economic model and the resulting policy prescriptions. This shift from classic ECLA thought to the "new" ECLA thought is clearly revealed by interviews with ECLA staff members and by comparisons of a key early document with important documents from the 1980s and 1990s.[7]

A key ECLA document from 1990 reveals a totally different vocabulary and analysis from classic ECLA thought. The one striking continuity is the importance placed on industrialization and technical progress, but the other dominant themes have changed. The 1990 report does not mention the terms "center" or "periphery" or the concept of "declining terms of trade," although there are some discussions of the influence of the external economic environment on domestic development.[8] New ECLA thought stresses export promotion, international competitiveness, and international openness, while downplaying ISI and the domestic market.[9]

The overall thrust of the 1990 document is on the importance of domestic policy to transform domestic production structures rather than on the external conditioning of Latin American development.

This shift is particularly surprising in an organization like ECLA which was so closely identified with an earlier paradigm that its name has been virtually synonymous with ISI. A superficial reading of the new ECLA reports would lead one to believe that ECLA had "gone over to the other side." Although new ECLA thought consciously tries to set itself apart from an ISI model and neoliberalism, the alternative model they propose sounds more like neoliberalism than classic ECLA thought (ECLAC 1990). One ECLA theorist has called the new approach neostructuralism. Whereas ECLA before advocated *desarrollo hacia adentro* (inward-oriented development), the new approach now calls for *desarrollo desde dentro* (development from within) (Sunkel 1991).

The new titles don't quite convey what is unique about the new ECLA approach, and how far it has changed from classic ECLA thought. By 1990, ECLA was trying to correct both what it saw as the main errors of the ISI approach *and* of neoliberalism. More than any neoliberal analysis, ECLA stresses the problems of poverty in the region, and the importance of finding a development strategy that increases equity while leading to growth. This is what ECLA is now calling "an integrated approach," which emphasizes that growth, social equity, and democracy can be compatible (ECLAC 1992).

In order to promote growth with equity, ECLA supports the general move in the direction of trade liberalization, competitive exchange rates, and export promotion, while still advocating a more central role for the state in directing the new economic policy (Wise 1990). The 1990 ECLA report points out that the goal is not economic openness per se, but rather competitiveness, and that such competitiveness requires, above all, the deliberate and systematic incorporation of technical progress. ECLA thought differs from neoliberal ideas by advocating that the state adopt an industrial, technological, and educational policy to help manage and direct the liberalization and development process. In particular, ECLA emphasizes the importance of the state helping industry to assimilate new technology, supporting healthy linkages between private firms and public institutions like universities, and improving the intersectoral linkages between industry and agriculture.[10]

When exactly did this paradigm shift occur at ECLA? ECLA itself highlights the 1990 document as "a milestone in a process of analysis and reflection that had begun long before," and "a central point of reference for the thinking of the institution" (ECLAC 1992). The analysis of ECLA documents from the 1960s, 1970s, and 1980s (ECLA 1972, 1973, 1983; ECLAC 1990, 1992) confirms this point. Although subtle shifts constantly

occur in ECLA thought, the 1981 report still has more important continuities with the paradigm of the 1950s than with the new thinking of the
1990s. In the 1981 *Economic Survey for Latin America*, the concepts of center,
periphery, and declining terms of trade are as pronounced in 1981 as
they were in 1950. There is no mention of trade liberalization or of the
need for economic openness. Given the continuity of ECLA analysis from
1950 through the early 1980s, the changes recorded in the 1990 document represent a paradigm shift that took place sometime in the mid- to
late-1980s at ECLA. This is confirmed by ECLA staff, who discuss a long
process of transition, which nevertheless did not culminate until the publication of the 1990 document and its presentation at the ECLA meeting
in Caracas.[11]

EXPLANATIONS FOR PARADIGM SHIFT: POWER/INTERESTS

How can we explain such dramatic shifts in development models? The
most common answer in comparative studies of paradigm shift in the
Third World has been that ideas are imposed by power, especially by economic and military power. This approach has led to the deemphasis of
ideas in and of themselves, since they are seen mainly as a thin disguise
for the play of interests and power. This is what Clifford Geertz has called
the "interest theory" of ideology, where ideas are seen as a "mask and a
weapon" (1964). This is still the dominant approach for understanding
economic policy and paradigms in Latin American politics. Dependency
theory and other theories of economic interest groups embrace this con-
ceptualization of the role of ideas, as does much recent work on the political economy of Latin America. As Cooper and Packard note in the
introduction to this volume, such an approach to development discourse
is also shared by some postmodernist critiques, which see development
discourse as "an apparatus of control and surveillance. . . . —a knowledge-
power regime," imposed by the West upon the developing world. Such
interpretations have seen the shift to neoliberal economic ideas in the
1980s either as resulting from powerful international economic interests
imposing their model on Latin American countries in the wake of the
debt crisis (with the International Monetary Fund (IMF) playing the role
of the organizer of the interests of the international capitalist class), or
resulting from the realignment of domestic economic coalitions. There is
little room in these models for "learning," for changing minds, or for
changing perceptions of interests. A particularly compelling version of the
power explanation, points to the chilling impact that severe repression
under military rule in the 1970s and 1980s in Latin America had on the
debate over economic policy in many Latin American countries.

EXPLANATIONS FOR PARADIGM SHIFT THAT
STRESS "LEARNING"

The other main explanations for changing ideas focus on the processes of learning in situations characterized by complexity, failure, anomaly, and new information. Hugh Heclo (1974) sums up this approach when he says "Governments not only power . . . they also puzzle."[12] The learning approaches perceives humans as engaged in reasoning about and processing new information from the environment in an attempt to make sense of their world. The unit of analysis is the individual, the community of individuals sharing common ideas, or the institutions in which ideas become embodied. But this approach as yet lacks the coherent set of assumptions and research programs that characterize some of the other approaches to comparative politics and development.

Recent work on ideas in international relations has focused on the concept of epistemic communities—"networks of knowledge-based experts"—to understand the process through which experts introduce new ideas that can lead to changing patterns of behavior (Haas 1992). With its clearly identified common paradigm and its tightly knit group of economists, ECLA fits the definition of an "epistemic community."[13] Because economic issues are always characterized by a technical complexity and distinct communities of experts that closely resemble "epistemic communities," a learning approach seems initially plausible. The complexity argument alone, however, does not offer a compelling explanation for why an ideational shift occurs at ECLA in the 1980s. The complexity of Latin American economies did not change in such a pronounced or sudden form in the 1980s as to explain the shift in economic paradigms at this time.

Other authors using a "learning approach" have pointed out that new ideas often emerge in response to dramatic policy failures or crises, where past policies have failed to resolve problems, leading to a search for new conceptions upon which to base new policies.[14] This relationship between crisis and failure and the adoption of new economic ideas has been found in a number of different countries and time periods. The two types of crisis or failure most often mentioned include major depressions and war (Furner and Supple 1990).

A useful supplement to the simple notions of failure or success as ways of thinking about why people adopt new ideas is Peter Hall's notion of "persuasiveness." Hall argues that what makes an idea persuasive is the way the idea relates to the economic and political problems of the day (1989). This appears to suggest that there is never a single definition of success and failure, but that both success and failure are interpreted in terms of what are perceived as the most pressing problems facing a country at a particular time.

A third prominent "learning" explanation for the influence of new ideas focuses on the accumulation of anomalies—i.e., outcomes that don't fit the expectations induced by the existing paradigm. Rather than dramatic failure or crises, the anomaly argument suggests that it is the accumulation of small discrepancies that cannot be explained with the old model that eventually leads to the adoption of new ideas. Similar to the process that Kuhn suggests is common in the natural sciences, policy paradigms are resistant to anomalies and may at first suppress them, but the accumulation of unresolved puzzles eventually leads to an increased questioning of the model (Kuhn 1970: 64–65).[15]

INSTITUTIONAL EXPLANATIONS

The strength and continuity of new ideas often depend on the degree to which they become embodied in institutions. The ideas that have been successfully implemented and consolidated are those which have been instilled within an institutional home, where a team of like-minded people transforms their individual ideas into institutional purpose.[16] Many of these institutions were state institutions, part of the economic apparatus of the state, but other institutions outside the state, such as ECLA or the World Bank (Finnemore, this volume), have also played important roles in the transmission of ideas. The importance of institutions for embodying ideas also means that institutional factors will affect paradigm shift.

One of the main claims of institutional analysis is that institutional change is episodic and "sticky" rather than continuous and incremental (Ikenberry 1988). Similarly, we would expect ideas in institutions also to have a "sticky" quality. What is most interesting about the case of ECLA over the first forty years of its existence is that it illustrates the possibility for paradigm shift within an institution. Usually we think that ideas change when new epistemic communities with new ideas come to the fore. This was an important part of the story in Latin America, as the new neoliberal economic ideas of the 1970s and 1980s were associated with the influence of a group of economists trained at U.S. universities, especially at the University of Chicago. But the shift of the 1980s is due to more than just the influence of a new epistemic community, the "Chicago Boys." It also reflects a broader shift in disciplinary knowledge and in cultural values and beliefs. The changing ideas within existing communities of scholars like ECLA are indicative of this broader trend.

How can we consider and evaluate the explanations discussed above to explain changing ideas at ECLA? Clearly power is at play. Economic policy changes in developing countries usually involve more external coercion than those in industrialized countries because the decisions of external economic actors can have a more powerful effect on these more vulnerable economies. The IMF, the World Bank, and bilateral lenders have used stiff conditionality requirements to oblige borrowers to adopt neoliberal policies. Yet, to chalk up such a major ideational shift solely to the power of external forces clearly misses an important part of the story. Contrary to some of the governments of Latin American countries, ECLA was not "forced" to make the ideational shifts that it made. It was not severely in debt; it did not require IMF approval; it was not dominated by U.S. banks or by domestic economic lobbies. Looking at idea shifts in ECLA separates us to some extent from the brute force of power and interest politics, and leads us to inquire about how more insulated intellectuals and international civil servants change their minds. The repression/power argument is initially more convincing. Among the countries most represented among the staff at ECLA were Chile, Brazil, Argentina, and Uruguay, because of their proximity to the ECLA headquarters in Santiago, Chile, and because the teaching of economics was relatively well developed in their universities, as compared to other countries in Latin America. All four of these countries experienced severe military rule in the 1960s and/or 1970s. Faculty members associated with leftist thought were removed from their positions in universities, activists were tortured, imprisoned, disappeared, and murdered. A generation of scholars and potential scholars was lost, as students were targets for repression.

And yet, this explanation is not entirely satisfactory. The initial stages of repression in Brazil, for example, actually contributed to radicalizing ECLA thought, as scholars in exile joined the ECLA staff in Santiago. The Brazilian sociologist Fernando Henrique Cardoso, forced into exile after the coup in 1964, together with Enzo Faletto wrote the seminal text of dependency theory, *Dependency and Development in Latin America*, while they were working at ECLA (Kahl 1988).

The most intense years of repression in Brazil, Uruguay, Chile, and Argentina came well before the paradigm shift at ECLA. During the height of repression, ECLA steadfastly maintained its ideological identity as an island of structuralist thought in a sea of Southern Cone authoritarian countries adopting neoliberal and monetarist policies. In Brazil, the height of repression came during the Médici administration (1969–1974); in Argentina, repression peaked during the period 1976–1979; in Uruguay, from 1972–1977; and in Chile from 1973–1977.[17] During these years, the authoritarian regimes committed the bulk of human rights violations, including executions, disappearances, torture, and political imprisonment. Paradigm shift in ECLA occurred a decade after the end of these intense waves in repression, and indeed after redemocratization had occurred in Argentina, Uruguay, and Brazil in the mid-1980s.

Repression left deep marks on these societies. A generation of future leaders and scholars was lost or scarred. In Chile, for example, of the 2,279 cases of death and disappearance that the Rettig Commission investigated, 60 percent of the victims were under thirty years old. In these 2,279 cases, twenty were professors and 324 were students.[18] These numbers do not include the thousands of individuals who were imprisoned and tortured but later released. Although the report doesn't tell us about the beliefs of the victims, we can assume that many of them were supporters of President Allende, and identified with progressive or socialist beliefs. Many of the students and intellectuals who disappeared might have identified themselves as believers in dependency theory, structuralism, or classic ECLA doctrine. Of the other many thousands that went into exile, a significant percentage never returned to their home countries.

Repression alone, however, cannot necessarily explain the paradigm shift within an economic institution like ECLA. Such an explanation would suggest that a wide range of ideas associated with the left would have been suppressed in these societies. Yet individuals and groups in these countries continued to advocate unpopular ideas of many kinds during and after the military governments. Human rights organizations in all of these countries continue to press for justice for victims of human rights abuses, while new feminist, environmental, and neighborhood organizations emerged and expanded. There was an explosion of civil society and social movement organizations in the waning days of the military regimes, and some of these social movements have continued to grow in their numbers and demands. We have examples in Latin America where savage repression, such as the repression in Nicaragua under Somoza, or in El Salvador in the 1980s, led not to silence but to radicalization of the population. Repression alone cannot explain the ideological content of ideas after that repression is lifted.

Political repression, together with the pressures of international financial institutions, foreign governments, and the changing expectations and demands of the governments of the region formed one part of a regional and international context within which the process of paradigm shift occurred. Repression was one part of the "material matrix of affirmations and sanctions" in the language of Goran Therborn, within which the debate in ECLA took place in the 1970s and 1980s (Therborn 1980).

But the international context was not only one of "material" affirmations and sanctions, it was also one of symbolic, interpreted, and contested meanings. The symbolic impact of the demise of socialism in Eastern Europe and the Soviet Union appears to have had more influence on ECLA thought than the physical facts of repression.[19]

The connection between economic crisis or failure and changing economic policy is also clear in the case of Latin America. The two most important shifts in economic policy making in Latin America both occurred in the wake of the two largest economic crises of the twentieth century. The first move to national populism occurred as a result of the experience of both the Great Depression and World War II, while the second was consolidated in response to the crisis of the 1980s, the most serious economic decline in the region since the Great Depression.[20]

In the case of Latin America, most authors agree that the original adoption of national populist ISI was a response to the perceived failure of the liberal model during the Great Depression and World War II. The opening paragraphs to the ECLA manifesto assert the importance of crisis for contributing to paradigm shift. "In Latin America, reality is undermining the out-dated schema of the international division of labor. . . . Two world wars in a single generation and a great economic crisis between them have shown the Latin American countries their opportunities, clearly pointing the way to industrial activity" (Prebisch 1950). The Great Depression and the war led many Latin Americans to believe that the international economy was unpredictable and undependable, and was likely to remain so in the future.

In an interview, Prebisch confirmed the role of crisis in leading to a shift in his own ideas about development. As a brilliant young student of economics in Buenos Aires, Prebisch had been a believer in free trade, the gold standard, and the international division of labor. Later, as an economic policymaker in the Argentine government and director of the Central Bank during the Great Depression, Prebisch began to question his ideas. "During the Great Depression, in spite of the fact that I had been a neo-classical economist, I realized that faced with the crisis, it was necessary to industrialize. And I did it with a qualm of conscience because it ran against all my ideas. But in light of the events and the intensity of the crisis, I said that there was no alternative. Then I began to theorize."[21]

This statement by Prebisch is very telling, especially in relation to theories of knowledge that argue that there is no "reality" independent of our interpretations of it. Yet Prebisch "saw" things that his existing intellectual apparatus (neoclassical economics) did not anticipate or explain. Despite his firm belief in the free market, he believed that the intensity of the crisis of the depression forced him to reevaluate his existing ideas and search for alternatives. He first advocated new policies (industrialization), and later developed a new theoretical construct to explain what he had seen.

Current ECLA staff describe a very similar process during the paradigm shift in the 1980s. One ECLA economist tracing the sources of shifting ideas within the institution said it came in response to "a challenge that reality set forth," referring to lagging economic growth, hyperinflation, and worsening inequality in Latin America in the 1980s. No matter how much ECLA theories predisposed it to search for the external sources for the crisis, it could not wish away or ignore that Latin America's crisis was far deeper than that of other continents operating within similar external constraints. ECLA was occupied offering advice on short-term crisis management to member governments. In this context, some orthodox economic ideas and tools entered into the ECLA repertoire. Only later did ECLA begin a systematic and conscious effort to revise its theoretical framework.[22]

This explanation still begs the question, however, since "reality" or "failure," like beauty, is partly in the eyes of the beholder. What is it that permits the analyst to interpret a particular reality as the failure of an economic model? In order for the concept of failure to be more useful in explaining paradigm shift, we have to have more precise definitions of what constitutes failure or crisis. Let us begin with the most simple assumption: that perceptions of economic failure are conditioned by a rapid fall in levels of economic growth. Economic development is much more than economic growth, but most of this "much more" is dependent on a minimum level of economic growth.

The Great Depression in Latin America was a period of rapid fall in levels of economic growth. The decline in GDP was most severe during the 1929–1932 period, after which it began to improve. Most countries had recovered 1929 levels of real GDP by 1935, although some, such as Chile, Honduras, and Nicaragua, suffered a more severe recession for a longer time (Thorp 1984: 334). Figures on gross domestic income, taking into account the relative fall in export and import prices, reveal that Chile and Cuba were the worst hit countries in Latin America, and Chile was the worst hit in the world (Kindleberger 1984).

The most striking failures in the 1930s and 1940s for Latin America, however, were substantial external shocks during the Great Depression and World War II, including the loss of export markets and severe supply shortages. These supply shortages exacerbated the deterioration of the physical capital base and the shortage of basic goods. Export levels in some countries suffered more during World War II than they had during the Great Depression, while the fall in imports in many countries was much more drastic than was the decline in exports.[23]

This suggests that we need to refine the concept of failure or disillusionment. The nature of the failure perceived can modify the type of lesson learned from the failure. In the case of the great Depression and World War II in Latin America, the failure was seen more as a breakdown of the international trading order than a crisis of growth. These events did not determine the nature or content of policies; they only created certain predispositions and attitudes. A decade of trying to revive traditional export markets, and almost fifteen years of shortages of foreign industrial imports, undermined faith in free trade and comparative advantage.

DRAMATIC FAILURE FOLLOWED BY INITIAL SUCCESS

But the same experience of failure was simultaneously perceived as an opportunity. The initial wording of the ECLA manifesto states that the major crises of war and depression "have shown the Latin American countries their opportunities." A second perception generated by the experience of World War II and the Great Depression was that the efforts to "go it alone" through ISI had been surprisingly successful, and were the most promising route for future economic policy. The success of the heterogeneous policies adopted by Latin American states in the 1930s and 1940s created confidence in alternative paths to development (Diaz Alejandro 1982). Rather than simple failure, it was the *combination* of perceived failure and initial success that contributed to the adoption of import substituting policies.[24]

During the twenty-year period from 1950–1970, the region's total gross domestic product grew at an average annual rate of close to 5.3 percent. International comparisons showed that the growth rates achieved in the region as a whole were above the average achieved in other developing regions and close to the rates achieved by the industrialized countries (ECLA 1972). Although population growth made the per capita figures much less favorable, the overall trend was uniformly one of positive growth. Latin America had become so accepting of relatively high levels of economic growth that the main debate in the *Economic Survey of Latin America 1970* was whether Latin America should accept the growth target of 6 percent set by the international development strategy of the second U.N. Development Decade, or should set a higher target rate of 7 or 8 percent annual growth. In the early 1970s, economic growth was almost taken for granted. "One thing that is being demonstrated by Latin America's experience is that the economies of the region are capable of attaining high growth rates; this is most propitious and should encourage them to persevere in their efforts to reach more ambitious targets" (ECLA 1972).

Growth levels alone, however, can't explain perceptions of development, because despite the relatively high levels of growth during the period 1950–1980, many Latin American intellectuals continued to be highly disillusioned with Latin American development. Much of the political economic analysis of this period exudes pessimism. Hirschman, among others, has grappled with this topic and offered engaging answers ranging from "fracasomania" to the belief that people never recognize success until it is behind them (Hirschman 1981, 1987). Those critical of the economic model of the 1960s focused on ongoing income inequalities in the region, and dependence on foreign capital. The thrust of these criticisms, often lumped together under the title of dependency theory, was that Latin America needed to find more autonomous and more egalitarian forms of development. Although the foremost work on dependency theory was written while the authors were working at ECLA, dependency theory as such was never clearly advocated by ECLA publications.[25] The disillusionment of the late 1960s and early 1970s expressed by dependency theory did not lead to a paradigm shift, either within ECLA, or in most of the countries of the region.

Not until the 1980s did Latin America experience the kind of dramatic failure that the literature would suggest should lead to a paradigm shift. The decade of the 1980s was referred to as the "lost decade" because of the debt crisis and the resulting stagnant and declining levels of economic growth throughout the region. At the end of 1989, the region's average per capita GDP was 8 percent lower than it had been in 1980, and was the same as that of 1977 (ECLAC 1990).

While the economic crisis of the 1930s was perceived as a failure of the international trading order, the crisis of the 1980s was interpreted differently. In the 1930s, Latin America's economic crisis was part of a huge global economic crisis. In the 1980s, the regional crisis in Latin America was much greater than elsewhere.[26] The crisis was intimately connected to the level of debt, and Latin American countries topped the list as the largest debtors. These differences in the level of economic failure in Latin America, as compared to economic trends elsewhere in the developing world, contributed to the shift in economic ideas at ECLA.

Yet, just like the 1940s, it was the combination of success and failure that consolidated changing ideas about development. As in the 1930s, when necessity was turned into virtue when ISI appeared to offer a more dynamic model of growth, so in the 1980s, neoliberal stabilization policies eventually began to yield some important benefits in the form of reduced inflation, improved balance of trade, and expanded investment. They also brought heavy costs, especially to the working groups and middle sectors who often bore the brunt of the stabilization in the form of unemployment, declining wages, and increased prices.

The initial successes of neoliberal programs won converts to the cause. The case of Chile is most illuminating in this respect. Under a neoliberal economic program, Chile experienced rapid growth and relatively low inflation during the period 1985–1991, although these were accompanied by high unemployment and other social costs.[27] The shift within ECLA mirrored a simultaneous shift going on among many intellectuals who identified with the Chilean left. In the first democratic elections after the end of the Pinochet dictatorship, Patricio Aylwin, supported by a center-left coalition of Christian Democrats and Socialists, reached the presidency on campaign promises to maintain many aspects of the neoliberal economic model inherited from the military government, while addressing the social costs of that program. After taking office, the Aylwin administration launched an aggressive antipoverty program using a combination of tax increases, heavy social spending, and a continuation of many of the vigorous free-market economic policies of the Pinochet government. The policy succeeded in lifting an estimated one million people from poverty during the first three years of the Aylwin administration.[28] The Frei government continued the economic policy direction of Aylwin.

The ECLA central offices are located in Santiago, Chile, where the ECLA staff was able to closely observe the Chilean economic experiment. The debate within ECLA was fueled in part by differing evaluations of the economic "accomplishments" of Chilean neoliberalism. The power of the Chilean example for new ECLA thinking, despite that many of the neoliberal policies were initially implemented under extremely repressive political conditions, is shown in the positive examples given in the illustrative boxes of the 1992 report. Diverse Chilean social and economic policies are referred to as positive examples in eleven of these boxes, more than any other single country in Latin America (ECLA 1990). Some of these policies were implemented by the new democratic government, but others were carried out under Pinochet.

By the mid- to late-1980s, a series of economic indicators led many ECLA insiders to question the validity of classic ECLA doctrine. ECLA, as a community of experts, self-consciously tried to evaluate the strengths and weaknesses of its hypotheses in light of this data. The major anomalies that ECLA staff confronted included 1) the dynamism of the world economy from 1950–1970 (ECLA 1973); 2) the better-than-average performance of Latin American countries during the economic crises of the 1970s; and 3) the worse-than-average Latin American performance during the economic crisis of the 1980s.

ECLA in the 1940s had anticipated a global economy after World War II similar to the economy after World War I. Instead, the world economy expanded dramatically between 1950 and 1970. During this period of tremendous expansion of international trade, Latin America's proportion of world trade deteriorated even more than the norm for developing countries, falling from 11 percent in 1948, to 7 percent in 1960, and to 5 percent in 1970 (ECLA 1973).

By the early 1980s, ECLA economists looking at the development patterns in Latin America began to question a second central hypothesis of the ECLA causal model: that the development of Latin America could be explained mainly by reference to economic events in the center. The dominance of causal thinking and the reliance on empirical evidence is clear in these ECLA reports. The better-than-average performance of the Latin American economies in the 1970s, despite the oil price hikes of 1973 and 1979 and the recession of 1974–1975, first led ECLA economists to question the external conditioning hypothesis. "Somehow, the region seemed to be successfully defying its external conditioning," said ECLA in its 1981 report (ECLA 1983).

The *Economic Survey of Latin America 1981*, however, vacillates on the external conditioning theory. One paragraph begins, "The developing countries today no longer merely respond to, or simply reflect events in the developed world." Yet this same paragraph ends saying, "On balance, the evolution of most non-oil exporting developing nations was heavily conditioned by the sluggish performance of the central economies" (ECLA 1983). These internal contradictions within ECLA documents reflect a debate going on within ECLA at the time, as each document was "negotiated" by different perspectives.[29]

A third important puzzle first appeared in the 1981 survey, and reappeared with greater emphasis throughout the decade of the 1980s: the poor performance of Latin America during the economic crisis of the 1980s in light of the extraordinary economic performance of some countries of East and Southeast Asia. Discussing development trends in developing countries in 1981, ECLA mentions that "only the developing countries of South and East Asia deviated from these trends, registering a remarkable growth rate of over 6 percent which far outdistanced not only other developing countries but the developed economies as well" (ECLA 1983).

One ECLA theorist, Fernando Fajnzylber, was particularly influential in contributing to changes in thinking within the institution. Using a simple but powerful two-by-two table, he demonstrated that although growth and equity can be complementary objectives, in the case of Latin America there was not a single contemporary case where this had happened, despite three decades of ISI.[30] Fajnzylber referred to this category of growth with equity as the *casillero vacio*—the empty box or cell—in Latin America. Nevertheless, Fajnzylber argued that elsewhere, especially in Asia and Southern Europe, growth with equity had been achieved.

The example of Fajnzylber illustrates Donald McCloskey's (1985) point, discussed in the introduction to this volume, about economic arguments as conversations and exercises in persuasion. Fajnzylber was a gifted expositor and writer, and he engaged in an exercise of persuasion within ECLA that was apparently very compelling. He didn't have better data than that offered by other ECLA colleagues or opponents. But in the context of increasing data questioning the classic ECLA doctrine, he came up with a powerful metaphor to convince his colleagues. The table with the "empty box" helped intellectuals separate their original goals— "growth with equity" from the policy strategies they believed would lead to those goals, and to consider why the strategies had not allowed Latin American countries to reach those goals.

This led, in turn, to a form of self-criticism for ECLA, since the main difference between the situations in Latin America and Asia was not the international situation, but rather different domestic policies. This comparison contributed to new thought at ECLA where the relationship between growth and equity was seen to depend largely on the domestic policies chosen, an emphasis that reiterates the move from the external conditioning hypotheses to a new focus on the centrality of domestic economic policy.

By 1992, this puzzle led ECLA to make a causal argument countering part of the external conditioning hypothesis.

> The absence of even a single case in the [Latin American] region in which economic growth has been combined with social equity raised the question . . . of whether the exacerbation of the situation during the crisis of the 1980s might not be attributable to the international context. However, other newly industrialized countries have obtained different results. An examination based on the same comparative indicators of GDP growth and income distribution shows that numbers of European and Asian countries having quite different economic and institutional makeups have been more successful in reconciling satisfactory levels of growth and certain goals in respect to social equity, and many of them were also able to surmount the adverse international conditions existing in the early 1980s (ECLAC 1990).

This process of puzzling that went on at ECLA prepared the ground for the later paradigm shift, but might not have led to a major change had it not been for the major economic crisis of the 1980s. But in the context of a major economic crisis, a series of unresolved puzzles and contrasting cases elsewhere in the world led to a questioning of the model and to a self-described process of learning, similar to that discussed by Heclo in his study of social policies in Europe (Heclo 1974). Of the major explanations for paradigm shift considered here, the combination of failure or crisis with the initial success of the new model appears to be the most useful for understanding the change of economic models at ECLA. Although failure can tell us about receptivity to paradigm shift, it cannot tell us the content of the new paradigm. Failure leads to movement away from the failed paradigm. In Latin America, the crisis of the 1980s guaranteed movement away from import-substituting industrialization. But there are very few economic models that have dominated the economic debates in Latin America.

In the mid-1980s some new democracies adopted "heterodox" policies which were seen as a middle ground between the neoliberalist and structuralist policies of the past. Both Argentina and Brazil experimented with a "heterodox shock" as a means of bringing down inflation and reestablishing growth. Peru also experimented with its own version of heterodoxy. These heterodox programs were loosely associated with ECLA thought, and their progress was closely followed by ECLA staff. Based on the belief that Latin American inflation was partly inertial—feeding on the expectations of future inflation—the heterodox shock programs offered a moderate alternative to the orthodox shock programs of the IMF. Wage and price controls helped protect working people, while at the same time breaking inflationary expectations (Bresser Pereira and Nakano 1987). While these programs were often very successful and politically popular in the short term, as soon as wage and price controls were lifted, inflation (and sometimes hyperinflation) reestablished itself (Sola 1989; Smith 1989). The respective economic crises resulting from the failure of the heterodox plans go far in explaining why Raul Alfonsin in Argentina, Jose Sarney in Brazil, and Alan Garcia in Peru left office with a total lack of popular support.

The apparent failure of these moderate experiments appeared to have closed off yet another alternative, and sealed the return to orthodoxy. ECLA concluded that the effects of heterodox stabilization plans will "not be long-lived unless it is coupled with policies that attack the 'fundamental' imbalances: the fiscal and external deficit" (ECLAC 1990).

ISI ideas were persuasive in the 1940s and 1950s because they addressed directly and forcefully the issue that was seen by many as the central economic problem of the time in Latin America: the need for rapid industrialization. ISI was also appealing to policymakers because it offered a compromise program between the demands of the international economy and the demands of domestic groups. For new models to be adopted, they needed only be persuasive to a fairly small group of policymakers and intellectuals; for a model to be sustained over time, however, it had to be persuasive to a broad range of societal groups.

Neoliberal economic ideas ran counter to the nationalism and statism ingrained in Latin American political and economic discourse. Although they initially faced opposition, neoliberal ideas eventually began to appear more persuasive because they also addressed some of the most pressing problems of their time: inflation and the resumption of growth. In the 1960s and 1970s, many Latin American policy makers saw inflation at worst as a bothersome but not debilitating side effect of their policies—

and at best, as a disguised means to transfer incomes from lower priority sectors to higher priority sectors. By the 1980s, extremely high levels of inflation led to inflation itself being perceived as the central economic problem. The failure of heterodox shocks to address inflation made the orthodox neoliberal ideas more persuasive. The experience of high inflation convinced policymakers and publics alike that economic stability was a precondition for all economic policy making.

The other central problem of the 1990s is the resumption of growth. The relatively rapid growth in Latin America in the postwar period had been taken for granted, as regional economists focused on problems of dependency and inequality. But the absence of any economic growth in the 1980s made people refocus on growth as a necessary precondition for all other kinds of economic change.

Because external events impinge on Third World countries more strongly, the notion of persuasion as externally coerced is more evident here than in Western Europe or the United States. Policymakers may initially adopt economic policies based on ideas that are not internally persuasive, as is often the case with the economic policies advocated by the IMF, but eventually these ideas must generate domestic support or they will not be sustained. The initial success of new models at addressing pressing economic problems may help generate the necessary domestic support.

ECLA, as an intergovernmental organization, also was motivated by bureaucratic concerns, such as maintaining its relevance and usefulness to its government members, and thus maintaining its budget and institutional existence. When ECLA was created in the late 1940s, it was the first organization of its kind, and virtually the only important source of economic data, analysis, and training in Latin America. By the 1980s many other economic institutions had emerged, and ECLA now had to compete with national and regional economic institutions. One concern of ECLA leadership was that if ECLA thought didn't transform in reaction to changes in the world, it would be relegated to "the museum of ideas" and lose its relevance, and thus its support from member governments. As one ECLA staff person observed, "If we cling to old ideas we could end up being irrelevant and that is something we cannot afford. We are creatures of governments."[31] Another staff economist pointed out that the governments of the region were asking for alternative models to those being presented by the IMF and the World Bank, not so much to fight with these but to fill in what was missing.[32]

These suggestions, however, exaggerate the degree to which ECLA simply responded to pressures from governments. If ECLA was truly a "creature of governments" it would have changed its position in the mid-1970s, when most of the countries of the region had military governments adopting neoliberal economic policies. ECLA was able to withstand considerable pressure to change in the 1970s because it believed in its positions, and because the pressures were coming from authoritarian regimes. By the late 1980s, the pressures and requests were coming from democratic governments with considerably greater legitimacy and at a time when staff within ECLA were facing puzzling development anomalies.

ECLA brought its perspective more in line with the neoliberalism of the 1980s, while at the same time it tried to maintain a distinctive voice or vision. This distinctive vision, which is the link connecting current ECLA thought to the concerns of classic ECLA thought, is the focus on poverty and equity in the region. Having agreed with some of the basic presumptions of neoliberalism, ECLA nevertheless insists that there can and should be no growth without equity, and that the welfare of the poorest 40 percent of the Latin American population, who live under the poverty line, must be taken into account. ECLA has also developed some innovative policies for addressing poverty in the framework of free-market economic policies.[33]

Certain ideas also have affinities with particular state or institutional structures (Sikkink 1991).[34] Developmentalist policies were more likely to find an institutional home within planning ministries and development banks. The "external conditioning of development" thesis held an affinity with the institutional needs of ECLA. As a United Nations body responsive to Latin American governments, ECLA was able to sustain more consensus among its members by emphasizing external obstacles to development rather than focusing on difficult internal reforms and redistribution (Dosman and Pollock 1991). This may help explain why it was difficult for ECLA to give up the external conditioning hypothesis. Only when new democratic governments themselves appeared to be demanding a new approach was ECLA able to complete the process of paradigm shift.

Powerful individuals within institutions often play important roles in the adoption and shift of ideas. Just as McNamara played a key role at the World Bank (Finnemore, this volume) Prebisch was a strong intellectual leader and a superb institution builder. He gathered a dynamic team of like-minded economists in Latin America to work with him at ECLA. His fame as a theorist, negotiator, and institution builder at ECLA led to his appointment during the 1960s as the first director of the new United Nations trade organization, the Conference on Trade and Development (UNCTAD). After Prebisch left ECLA, it never recaptured the same institutional prominence it had during his period of leadership, even when he later returned as a senior theorist and editor of the *ECLA Review* in the 1970s and 1980s.

Leadership changes can contribute to ideational shifts within institutions. Prebisch's succeeding executive secretaries, Enrique Iglesias and

Norberto Gonzales, both set into motion processes that contributed to the later paradigm shift.[35] They did not impose their own ideas upon the organization, but rather, through hiring decisions and a series of technical conferences, brought into ECLA the ideological and intellectual debate over economic policies going on within the region in the 1970s and 1980s. Once this ideological debate was occurring within ECLA, it created an intellectual energy and dynamism that contributed to the later paradigm shift.

The actual transformation in ECLA thought corresponds temporally to the tenure of the new executive secretary, Gert Rosenthal, who took office in 1986 and was responsible for overseeing the preparation of the key 1990 and 1992 transition documents. Connected to the question of institutional leadership is the issue of generational shifts within institutions. One factor that facilitated paradigm shift within ECLA was the process of the retirement of the "old guard" and its replacement by a new group of staff less personally invested in the maintenance of classic ECLA positions. The new staff members were more likely to have been trained in U.S. universities than the old staff and to have more mathematical and technical training. Most of the economists from around the region who had been hired to staff the new institution in the early 1950s had reached retirement age in the 1980s. New United Nations budgetary regulations that enforced retirement at sixty years of age speeded that process. Prebisch's death in 1986 was symbolic of the passing of a generation.

CONCLUSIONS

Much more research needs to be conducted on how and why ideas acquire meaning in a political setting and how meanings are transformed. This study focuses on a subset of this larger question by inquiring how paradigm shift occurred in a small, albeit important economic institution. The study suggests some interesting conclusions for the more general study of ideas in comparative politics.

The case evaluated here provides strong support for the "failure" argument that has been frequently raised as an explanation for changing ideas. It also suggests that the combination of failure and the initial success of a new model make a more persuasive explanation of ideational shift. Neither "failure" nor "success" however, are obvious causes in all cases. Both the perception of failure and success is an interpreted response. The persuasiveness of new ideas relates to their ability to address what are perceived to be the most pressing economic and political problems of the day (Hall 1989). And yet, even within this highly interpreted world, theorists can change their minds based on evidence to which their models may not even direct their attention.

Even an institution like ECLA, which was closely identified with a particular paradigm, has significantly shifted its paradigm. These shifts neither come easily nor without debate, but major crisis and failure can provoke a process of reevaluation and learning that leads to internal policy shift. ECLA was consciously involved in a process of evaluating its hypotheses in light of the large amounts of economic data that it was constantly generating. The dramatic economic failure of the 1980s led the organization to reevaluate its ideas, to engage in a process of puzzling and of learning, and to adopt a significantly modified economic paradigm by the 1990s. The metaphor of the "empty box," countries that had achieved growth with equity in Latin America, helped ECLA economists to take a hard look at their model, and to revise and discard the parts of the model discredited by events. The failure of the "heterodox" experiments in Brazil, Argentina, and Peru in 1986 and 1987 closed off a perceived moderate alternative to neoliberalism, and the increasing economic success of the Chilean economic model after 1987 enhanced the power of aspects of the neoliberal model.

In ECLA, the process of paradigm shift was assisted by leadership and generational changes within the institutions as the old guard associated with classic ECLA thought retired and was replaced by a new generation of economists. In addition to "political learning" ECLA was also motivated by its desire for institutional survival. By adapting itself to the changing economic thinking of the day, while trying to keep a distinctive vision with its "integrated approach," ECLA hoped to stay relevant and maintain the support of member governments.

The process of paradigm shift within ECLA is troubling for both the more standard power explanations of policy shift in the Third World and for the postmodern critique (Cooper and Packard, this volume). New thinking at ECLA was not imposed from outside, but theorists at ECLA were aware of the changing nature of development discourse in Latin America, and realized that they would have to adapt if they were going to continue to be relevant and to survive in the new atmosphere. At the same time, they observed anomalies in the world that led them to question their previous models. Although events in the "real world" never exist independently of an interpretive structure, neither can these events fully be manipulated by any world view. Eventually real world events that consistently appear to be at odds with standard interpretations begin to call into question these interpretations, especially within disciplinary communities formed around shared causal ideas.

NOTES

1. The author would like to acknowledge the useful comments of Emanuel Adler, Peter Hall, Peter Johnson, and Carol Wise; the research assistance of Jen-

nifer Lee Smith and Kristina Thalhammer on earlier versions of this paper; and the comments of Frederick Cooper, John Sharpless, James Ferguson, Martha Finnemore, Thomas Biersteker, Arturo Escobar, and other workshop participants on the more recent version.

2. ECLA later changed its name to the Economic Commission for Latin America and the Caribbean (ECLAC), but I will retain the earlier name in this paper to avoid confusion when I compare the 1950s with the 1990s.

3. When Raúl Prebisch, the Executive Secretary of ECLA, was invited in 1964 to become the Director of UNCTAD (the U.N. Conference on Trade and Development), it was symbolic of his stature as a leading development theorist from the nonaligned world.

4. Peter Hall (1992) has distinguished three different levels of economic policy change. Following Kuhn (1970), he refers to the broadest of these as a "paradigm shift," or a "radical change in the overarching terms of policy discourse."

5. Hall (1989) has called these general ideas a nation's "structure of political discourse." In my earlier work, I have referred to them as "historically formed ideologies" (Sikkink 1991).

6. Classic ECLA thought is sometimes linked indirectly to the emergence of Keynesian ideas in the north. A number of key ECLA theorists were well versed in Keynesian thought, although they rarely described it as a source of ideas for ECLA. For example, Raúl Prebisch (1986: 164) wrote one of the first introductory texts to Keynesian thought in Spanish, although he later argued that he was never a Keynesian. Albert Hirschman (1981: 6) argues that the influence of Keynes was indirect. By suggesting that there were two kinds of economics, one which applied to the fully employed economy and another in which there was substantial unemployment of human and material resources, Keynes opened the door for the possibility of a special kind of economics for underdeveloped areas as well.

7. The documents analyzed are: Prebisch (1950), ECLA (1982), and ECLAC (1990). The content analysis was conducted by doing word and phrase frequency counts and examining key words in the first long introductory section of the 1950 document (approximately the first 7,000 words) and comparing the results with analyses of similar sections of ECLA documents from the 1980s and 1990s. For a discussion of methods, see Weber (1985).

8. This compares to the section of the 1950 document analyzed, in which the words "center" and "periphery" or the "center-periphery relationship" are mentioned fifty-nine times, the theme of declining terms of trade is referred to fifteen times, and the issues relating to primary products and raw materials are mentioned thirty-six times (Prebisch 1950).

9. In the analyzed portion of the 1990 document, the word "competitiveness" appears thirteen times, exports are mentioned nineteen times, trade liberalization and economic openness appear seven times, and references to changing production structures or production patterns appear twenty-six times (ECLAC 1990).

10. New ECLA thought has some similarities to and overlap with new theories of growth and trade in U.S. academic economics circles, such as new trade theory and endogenous growth theory (Krugman 1989; Romer 1994), but there is no evidence of obvious linkages between these schools of thought, and ECLA docu-

ments do not makes references to this large body of economic literature. I am grateful to Michael Carter, David Trubek, and Steve Boucher for alerting me to these similarities.

11. Interview with Oscar Altimir, Director of the Economic Development section of ECLA, November 2, 1992, Santiago, Chile.

12. Heclo (1974: 305) discusses uncertainty as one of the main sources of policy learning. Also see P. Haas (1992) for a discussion of the importance of complexity in the epistemic communities' literature.

13. One author defines epistemic communities as "Professionals . . . who share a common causal model and a common set of political values" Ernst Haas, (1990: 41). Peter Haas (1990 and 1992) has developed further the concept of epistemic communities.

14. John Odell (1982: 370–71) argues that a "major failure of past policy, or rather, extreme or accumulated evidence that can be readily interpreted as a consequence of past policy" is an important impetus to cognitive change. Albert Hirschman (1982) makes a related argument when he discusses disappointment as one of the main factors motivating social action. Ideational arguments have also been used to explain why policies remain unchanged despite repeated failure, as in the case of U.S. counterinsurgency policy in the Third World (Shafer 1988).

15. Kuhn (1970: 67) says that when the awareness of anomalies lasts long and penetrates deeply, one "can appropriately describe the field affected by it as in a state of growing crisis." This crisis of the paradigm, however, is different from the notion of dramatic failure or crisis discussed above, which describes a crisis or failure of policy.

16. Both Peter Hall and Emanuel Adler also have stressed the importance of institutions for carrying and disseminating ideas (Hall 1986: 276–80). In his study of the science and technology policy in Brazil and Argentina over the last twenty years, Adler presents a convincing argument that technocrats in institutions who hold collective understandings can "catalytically affect" events, leading to outcomes that would not otherwise occur (1987: 11, 327–29).

17. On Brazil, see Dassin (1986: 79, 234–38); on Argentina, Comisión Nacional Sobre la Desparición de Personas, *Nunca Mas: The Report of the Argentine National Commission on the Disappeared* (New York: Farrar, Straus, Giroux, 1986), xi; on Uruguay, Servicio Paz y Justica, Uruguay, *Uruguay: Nunca Más: Informe Sobre la Violación de Los Derechos Humanos (1972–1985)*, 116–17; and on Chile, Comisión Nacional de Verdad y Recónciliacion, *Sintesis del Informe de la Comisión Verdad y Reconciliación* (Santiago: Comisión Chilena de Derechos Humanos y Centro IDEAS, 1991), 93.

18. *Síntesis del Informe de Comisión Verdad y Reconciliación*, p. 92–94.

19. In interviews with ECLA staff on the sources of ideational change within ECLA, no one mentioned repression. A number of staff referred to the impact of the demise of socialism and to the desire of ECLA, as an intergovernmental organization, to maintain its relevance to member governments.

20. "Worst Year in Half a Century For Latin America's Economy," *UN Chronicle* 21 (March 1984): 16.

21. Interview with Raúl Prebisch, 23 October 1985, Buenos Aires. Translation by author.

22. Interview with Dr. Oscar Altimir, 2 November 1992, Santiago, Chile.

23. For example, in Argentina the average annual import quantum in 1940–1945 was 48 percent below the annual level in 1935–1939 and per capita quantum fell by a full 50 percent. The fall of imports in Brazil, while serious, was significantly less than in Argentina; depending on the source, the average annual import quantum in 1940–1945 was 12 percent to 20 percent below the level for 1935–1939 (Villela and Suzigan 1973: 441), and (ECLA 1951: 111, 211).

24. This relates to Judith Goldstein's argument that "nothing establishes the legitimacy of a policy like success. Policies become institutionalized because they work" (1989: 71).

25. In the preface to the English edition of *Dependency and Development in Latin America*, Cardoso and Faletto point to differences between ECLA thought and the more radically critical Latin American thought associated with dependency theory (1979: viii-ix).

26. Diaz Alejandro points out that Argentina, Brazil, Colombia, and Mexico register GDP growth rates steadier and higher than those of Canada and the United States for 1929–1939. In some Latin American countries, recovery from the Great Depression started as early as 1932, while in the 1980s, most countries did not start recovery until the early 1990s (Diaz Alejandro 1982).

27. "Chile: En el Umbral del Desarrollo?" *El Mercurio* 8 November 1992, B1.

28. Nathaniel C. Nash, "Chile Advances in a War on Poverty and One Million Mouths Say Amen," *New York Times* 4 April 1993, A6.

29. Interview with Isaac Cohen, Director, Washington Office, Economic Commission for Latin America and the Caribbean, 10 August 1992, Washington, D.C. The opinions expressed in the interview are personal and do not represent the position of the institution.

30. Fajnzylber's two-by-two table placed Argentina and Uruguay in the box of equity but low growth; Brazil, Colombia, Ecuador, Mexico, Panama, and the Dominican Republic in the box of growth with little equity; and the rest of Latin America in the box of low growth with little equity; no Latin American countries appeared in the growth with equity box, although Fajnzylber argued that countries like South Korea, Spain, Yugoslavia, Hungary, Israel, and Portugal fit in this box during the period under study (1970–1984). Growth was defined as more than 2.4 percent annual growth in per capita GNP during the period 1965–1984 (Fajnzylber 1990: 12–13).

31. Interview with Isaac Cohen, 10 August 1992, Washington, D.C.

32. Interview with Dr. Oscar Altimir, 2 November 1992, Santiago, Chile.

33. Interview with Isaac Cohen, 10 August 1992, Washington, D.C.

34. This is similar to the discussion of "administrative viability" by Peter Hall (1989: 373, 379), who argues that ideas were more likely to be accepted if "they accorded with the long-standing administrative biases of officials responsible for approving them and seemed feasible in light of the existing implementational capacities of the state." For example, where the central bank played a powerful role in the process of economic policy making, it was likely to inhibit the pursuit of Keynesian policies. Finnemore has made a similar organizational argument in her contribution to this volume. Once McNamara introduced a poverty focus to

the World Bank, organizational features of the Bank determined how that focus would by expressed in bank-lending policy.

35. In particular, Iglesias and Gonzalez began to place increasing emphasis on data collection and analysis as a central part of ECLA work. ECLA had always generated economic data, but in the mid-1970s, it started producing economic data in a more timely and systematic fashion. This data generation then served as a new source of legitimacy for ECLA. In addition, the staff in charge of data collection and analysis became the kernel of new thinking within the organization. Interview with Isaac Cohen, 10 August 1992, Washington, D.C.

REFERENCES

Adler, Emanuel. 1987. *The Power of Ideology: The Quest for Technological Autonomy in Argentina and Brazil.* Berkeley: University of California Press.

Bielschowsky, Ricardo. 1985. "Brazilian Economic Thought (1945–1964) The Ideological Cycle of Developmentalism". Ph.D. Thesis, University of Leicester.

Bresser Pereira, Luiz, and Yoskiaki Nakano. 1987. *The Theory of Inertial Inflation: The Foundation of Economic Reform in Brazil and Argentina.* Boulder, Colo.: Lynne Rienner Publishers.

Bruce, David Camermon. 1977. "The U.N. Economic Commission for Latin America and National Development Policies: A Study of Noncoercive Influence". Ph.D. Dissertation, University of Michigan.

Cardoso, Fernando Henrique. 1977. "The Originality of a Copy: CEPAL and the Idea of Development". *CEPAL Review* 3, no. 2: 7–40.

————, and Enzo Faletto. 1979. *Dependency and Development in Latin America.* Berkeley: University of California Press.

Dassin, Joan, ed. 1986. *Torture in Brazil: A Report by the Archdiocese of Sao Paulo.* New York: Vintage Books.

Diaz Alejandro, Carlos. 1982. "The 1940s in Latin America". Yale University, Economic Growth Center, Center Discussion Paper no. 394, mimeo.

Dosman, Edgar J., and David H. Pollock. 1991. "Raúl Prebisch, 1901–1971: The Continuing Quest". Prepared for the conference, Latin American Economic Thought: Past, Present and Future" organized by the Inter-American Development Bank, Washington, D.C., November 14–15, 1991.

Economic Commission for Latin America. 1951. *Economic Survey of Latin America 1949.* New York: United Nations.

————. 1972. *Economic Survey of Latin America 1970.* New York: United Nations.

————. 1992. "Introduction: Epistemic Communities and International Policy Coordination". *International Organization* 46: 1–35.

Hall, Peter A. 1986. *Governing the Economy: The Politics of State Intervention in Britain and France.* New York: Oxford University Press.

————. 1992. "Policy Paradigms, Social Learning and the State: The Case of Economic Policy-Making in Britain". *Comparative Politics* 24: 275–96.

Hall, Peter A., ed. 1989. *The Political Power of Economic Ideas: Keynesianism across Nations.* Princeton, N.J.: Princeton University Press.

Heclo, Hugh. 1974. *Modern Social Policies in Britain and Sweden.* New Haven: Yale University Press.

Hirschman, Albert O. 1961. "Ideologies of Economic Development in Latin America". In *Latin American Issues,* edited by Albert O. Hirschman, 3–42. New York: Twentieth Century Fund.

———. 1981. *Essays in Trespassing: Economics to Politics and Beyond.* Cambridge: Cambridge University Press.

———. 1982. *Shifting Involvements.* Princeton, N.J.: Princeton University Press.

———. 1987. "The Political Economy of Latin American Development: Seven Exercises in Retrospection". *Latin American Research Review* 22, no. 3: 7–36.

Ikenberry, G. John. 1988. "Conclusion: An Institutional Approach to American Foreign Economic Policy". *International Organization* 42: 220–43.

Kahl, Joseph. 1988. *Three Latin American Sociologists.* New Brunswick, N.J.: Transaction.

Kindleberger, Charles P. 1984. "The 1929 World Depression in Latin America— From the Outside". In *Latin America in the 1930s,* edited by Rosemary Thorp, 315–29. London: MacMillan Press.

Krugman, Paul. 1989. "New Trade Theories and the Less-Developed Countries". In *Debt, Stabilization, and Development: Essays in Honor of Carlos Diaz Alejandro,* edited by G. Calvo et al., 347–64. New York: Basil Blackwell.

Kuhn, Thomas. 1970. *The Structure of Scientific Revolutions* 2nd ed. Chicago: University of Chicago Press.

Love, Joseph L. 1980. "Raúl Prebisch and the Origins of Unequal Exchange". *Latin American Research Review* 15, no. 3: 45–72.

McCloskey, Donald. 1985. *The Rhetoric of Economics.* Madison: University of Wisconsin Press.

Odell, John. 1982. *U.S. International Monetary Policy: Markets, Power, and Ideas as Sources of Change.* Princeton, N.J.: Princeton University Press.

Pinto, Aníbal. 1983. "Centro-periferia e industrialization: vigencia y cambios en el pensamiento de la CEPAL". *El Trimestre Económico* 50, no. 2: 1043–1076.

Prebisch, Raúl. 1950. *The Economic Development of Latin America and Its Principal Problems.* Santiago, Chile: United Nations Economic Commission for Latin America.

———. 1986. *La crisis del desarrollo argentino.* Buenos Aires: Buenos El Ateneo.

Rodriguez, Octavio. 1981. *Teoria do Subdesenvolvimento da CEPAL* Rio de Janeiro: Forense-Universitária.

Romer, Paul. 1994. "The Origins of Endogenous Growth". *Journal of Economic Perspectives* 8: 3–22.

Shafer, D. Michael. 1988. *Deadly Paradigms: The Failure of U.S. Counterinsurgency Policy.* Princeton, N.J.: Princeton University Press.

Sikkink, Kathryn. 1988. "The Influence of Raúl Prebisch on Economic Policy Making in Argentina, 1950–1962". *Latin American Research Review* 23, no. 1: 115–31

———. 1991. *Ideas and Institutions: Developmentalism in Brazil and Argentina.* Ithaca, N.Y.: Cornell University Press.

Smith, William. 1989. "Notes on the Political Economy of Alfonsinismo". Paper prepared for the Fifteenth Congress of the Latin American Studies Association.

Sola, Lourdes. 1989. "Choque heterodoxo y transición política sin ruptura: un enfoque transdisciplinario". *Desarrollo Económico* 28, no. 112: 483–523.

Sunkel, Osvaldo. 1979. "The Development of Development Thinking". In *Transnational Capitalism and National Development*, edited by Jose Villamil, 19–30. London: Harvester.

————. 1991. *El Desarrollo Desde Dentro: Un Enfoque Neoestructuralist para la América Latina*. Mexico City: Fondo de Cultura Económica.

Therborn, Goran. 1980. *The Ideology of Power and the Power of Ideology*. London: New Left Books, Verso.

Thorp, Rosemary, ed. 1984. *Latin America in the 1930s*. London: Macmillan.

Villela, Annibal, and Wilson Suzigan. 1973. *Política do governo e crescimento do economia brasileira, 1889–1945*. Rio de Janeiro: IPEA/INPES Monografia 10.

Weber, Robert Philip. 1985. *Basic Content Analysis*. Beverly Hills, Calif.: Sage Publications Series, Quantitative Applications in the Social Sciences &ns;49.

Wise, Carol. 1990. "U.S.-Latin American Relations and the Changing International Context—Phase Two of the Research Project". Memorandum for the Inter-American Dialogue, 17 September 1990.

Development Language and
Its Appropriations

NINE

"Found in Most Traditional Societies"

Traditional Medical Practitioners between Culture and Development

Stacy Leigh Pigg

Our own staff don't even boil their drinking water. How are we going to educate villagers?

A FRUSTRATED EXPATRIATE ADVISOR IN NEPAL

[T]raining has created almost as many problems in Nepal as it has solved. The most highly trained are reluctant to work in the countryside, while middle-level training of villagers tends to raise their ambitions and cause them to leave their own villages. . . . [W]hen Nepalese receive their development training outside the country or from foreigners, they learn concepts and the jargon of development professionals, and their own local perspectives are lost or suppressed; they even find it difficult to communicate with their own people.

FORMER USAID OFFICIAL IN KATHMANDU (CITED IN BLACK 1991: 170)

Development implementation abounds in paradoxes. It is not unusual for seemingly sensible development solutions to go awry due to "social factors." The problem of technical training that creates people who don't want to do the job they have been trained to do is certainly a familiar one. The explanation is not particularly mysterious: when people aspire to upward social mobility in places like Nepal, they want to leave villages, not go to them. This can cause problems for those development programs committed to working closely with local communities, though. Hence the concerns expressed by foreign development advisors about Nepali development workers who seem unable or unwilling to act as brokers between development programs and village life. Their "own" perspective is replaced by the alien one of development; they can no longer "communicate with their own people." What frustrates foreign advisors is that it seems every time a person with the "local perspective" is enlisted in development work that person switches sides (Black 1991: 170).

I use this image of side-switching as a way into a discussion of the processes of social differentiation, placement, and displacement that occur in and through development activities. Side-switching is not an idiom explicitly used by either development planners or by Nepali villagers. But both these groups of people act and speak as if two sides exist, and for both the relation between these sides is a salient concern. As an ethnographer, I begin with the distinctions people use to interpret themselves and other people, and then follow their implications through social interactions. It happens that in Nepal—a country where the idea of development looms particularly large in public consciousness—the distinction between people who work to implement development projects and the people these projects are intended to reach is fundamental in people's minds. Even as it structures interactions, it also produces a range of complex positionings that, though intelligible through this difference, are not reducible to it. Thus we encounter Nepalis who reject models of culturally appropriate development and foreign advisors who urge that "local culture" must be better understood. We find trained villagers who want government jobs and development agency staff "from the village" who can't communicate effectively with villagers. And, as well, we find villagers who themselves do not conform to the image of villagers constructed in development reports written to convey the local situation to planners.

Programs in Nepal to train Traditional Medical Practitioners (TMP) and Traditional Birth Attendants (TBA) provide one example of institutional attempts to work with and through "local perspectives."[1] What could be a more authentic representative of the local perspective than an indigenous healer? Proposals for these training programs begin with an assumption about how the sides are already drawn up, and training programs attempt to bring the two sides together. The plan they devise for doing so is itself a representation of difference that reiterates the very divisions these programs ostensibly seek to bridge. This model reflects a specific set of development desires—a desire not only for a certain kind of development practice, but also a desire for a certain kind of "traditional" person to be first the object and then the product of development efforts. This essay examines the implementation of this model.

In discussing implementation, development planners use a specific kind of social science language in which "social factors" and "cultural beliefs" figure as variables extraneous to the development project itself (Stone 1992). In this view, the smooth trajectory of project implementation can be constrained, skewed, or hampered altogether by these "sociocultural factors." This essay, in contrast, offers a parallel ethnographic account of development implementation, one that views development activities as they are constituted in and through social interactions. A comprehensive ethnography of development activities would be a vast undertaking, given the multiple and dispersed sites that become linked through policy and implementation. What I do here is piece together an admittedly partial picture. My information on training programs comes from documents and from interviews in 1992 with program personnel in Kathmandu; my information on villagers' perceptions of medicine and development comes from ethnographic research in one village in 1986–1988.[2] I make these two sources speak to each other in order to explore the relation between development conceptualizations of villagers' culture and villagers' conceptualizations of development. By bringing these two perspectives together in this way, I hope to show something of how development ideas actually work in a society that is already profoundly shaped by ideas about development.

THE MODEL: TMPS IN HEALTH POLICY

In the 1970s, two new figures appeared on the scene: the TMP and the TBA.[3] Colonial medics and missionaries were, of course, familiar with the various kinds of curers, diviners, and midwives of the societies in which they worked, and they often regarded these practitioners as the quintessence of tradition. It was but a small transformation to coin a technical term by which to label all non-biomedically grounded practitioners in all nonwestern societies, and to turn the TMP and the TBA into a feature of an abstracted notion of "culture" itself. According to the World Health Organization (WHO),

> Traditional medical practitioners and birth attendants are found in most societies. They are often part of the local community, culture, and traditions, and continue to have high social standing in many places, exerting considerable influence on local health practices. With the support of the formal health system, these indigenous practitioners can become important allies in organizing efforts to improve the health of the community. Some communities may select them as community health workers. It is therefore well worthwhile exploring the possibilities of engaging them in primary health care and of training them accordingly. (WHO 1978: 63)

What interpretive framework makes it possible to "find" something called a TMP or a TBA, when the sorts of roles and practices that might fall under these broad categories vary so widely? TMP and TBA are labels for a generic category, invented to fulfill a bureaucratic function by providing a language of generalization. These terms provide a way of referring to certain practices in the diverse societies in which development activities are carried out, a way that is useful for development policy because it effectively strips those practices of any messy traces of contextual specificity. Such generalization is necessary to the extent that development policy is formulated as a form of transnational expertise. After all, the point of development theories, policies, frameworks, and lessons is that they can be formulated in general and put to use any place that is underdeveloped. Development approaches that seek to work from a recognition of "local beliefs and practices" are thus in the paradoxical position of having to put forth a general model for what can only be locally known. TMP and TBA operate as mediating terms in situations where there is an institutional need to narrow the gap between the myriad local practices and the international world of health service management.

It was in the context of the much touted Primary Health Care (PHC) initiative announced by WHO in 1978 that TMPs and TBAs became suddenly visible and important. The PHC policy emphasized the delivery of essential health care through "socially acceptable" methods, with "full participation" that would maintain "a spirit of self-reliance and self-determination" (WHO 1978: 16). One very concrete way to incorporate local realities into health services is by enlisting "indigenous" or "traditional medical practitioners" into the national health care system. Together with the broader reaction against what was called top-down development, PHC policy helped create a context in which working with local practitioners made sense.[4]

But the antecedents for the idea of training indigenous healers in the techniques of cosmopolitan medicine go farther back, to the policies debated by colonial medics and administrators. In India, debates about whether medical education should integrate western and indigenous systems of knowledge began in the early nineteenth century. For many British officials, medicine and science were symbols of a civilizing progress, while for Indian nationalists, indigenous medicine became a site for anticolonial struggles for autonomy.[5] In colonial East Africa, medical missionaries depicted themselves to their supporters in England as engaged in a battle against the darkness of ignorance with the light of benevolent medical reason. Others argued in favor of tolerance, warning that African healers should be treated with "professional respect" (Vaughan 1991). Also debated in colonial medical policy was whether "natives" should be trained in western biomedicine to serve as health auxiliaries: Would they distort or alter biomedicine in dangerous ways? The more recent proposals advocating the training of TMPs draw from and are positioned within the metropolitan memory of these varied colonial stances.

More fundamentally, the rationale behind the training of indigenous practitioners makes use of a reified notion of "culture" that had become habitual in the discourse of colonial medicine. As historian Megan Vaughan has argued, cultural explanations of health and disease had, by the 1930s, become common among colonial medical authorities "preoccupied with difference." These explanations pointed to characteristics of "the tribe" or "the culture" as a collective entity. By some accounts the ill-health of Africans was attributable to the practices of traditional culture, while others argued the opposite—that it was the erosion of traditional institutions among modernizing Africans that led to the greater incidence of disease. Whether culture was invoked to emphasize the difference between Africans and Europeans or to signal the problems that arise when they cease to be different enough, it became "a subject of a distinct pathologizing account" (1991: 53). While this thinking led to a kind of fatalism among many colonial medical practitioners, and provided, as well, a convenient justification for the failure of inadequate health services, it also prompted some colonial physicians to actively seek out ways to translate health measures into local terms and categories. W. T. C. Berry, for instance, realized that to make public health measures acceptable to ordinary people, it was necessary to understand that they had very different notions of disease causation. But his stance toward these customs and traditions was ambivalent. While he regarded the social cohesion of traditional society as a positive force, he saw certain customary practices as bad for health. In the 1930s, Berry's attention to the cultural understandings that influenced local responses to public health initiatives was innovative. It has since jelled into one stream of received wisdom in international health development planning.

Anthropology also helped set the terms in which the idea of training TMPs would be presented in the 1970s and 1980s. Not only is "culture" now routinely isolated as a distinct factor relating to health, but the attention to differences is readily asserted on relativist grounds. Anthropologists who began working in international health in the 1950s insisted that technological solutions alone would fail unless the social and cultural characteristics of target groups—and the "barriers" these posed to the acceptance of health programs—were taken into account (see Foster 1978). Many anthropologists sought to emphasize the simple point that these target groups were not "empty vessels" waiting to be filled with medical knowledge, but people who already had ways of managing health (Polgar 1962). Some anthropologists have taken on the professional task of enumerating these existing ideas and practices for planners. The popularized notion of culture is now commonly used in planning circles to speak of local perspectives that differ from those of development institutions. Meanwhile, the analytical limitations and political repercussions of this highly reified and static view of culture have come under critical scrutiny among many academic anthropologists. Though few if any would argue with the very basic points made by applied anthropologists, these critics have drawn attention to the ways the use of this concept of culture reinforces and naturalizes socially produced conditions of difference (Gupta and Ferguson 1992); homogenizes variation within groups (Abu-Lughod 1992); invents a nonwestern "other" who is treated as separate from "us" in both time and space (Fabian 1983); and mistakes complex, historically fluid configurations as fixed traits of groups (Appadurai 1988). At issue are the sociopolitical implications of the widespread use of "a conventional concept of culture based on a quasibiological analogy in which a group of people are seen as 'having' or 'possessing' a culture somewhat in the way an animal species has fur or claws" (Jackson 1995a: 18). When what anthropologists hope are more complex, dynamic, and subtle analyses of ways of life are, of necessity, pared down for use in planning, the problems inherent in explanations in terms of "culture" become disturbingly apparent. Arguments about differing points of view, grounded in relativism, slide with alarming ease into highly essentialized depictions of innate differences. Discussions of the local social context are readily reduced to a cataloging of discrete factors or customs of a "culture."[6] Specific examples tend to feed already established stereotypes of nonwestern "others."

For instance, a WHO publication on how to use and train TBAs for maternal and child health programs begins with the premise that:

> Birth practices within a particular culture or sub-cultural group within a larger one, are influenced by the way of living and thinking of the people who share that culture or sub-culture. Although some common elements may be found, these practices, as a rule, vary considerably among societies (Verderese and Turnbull 1975: 23).

This guide emphasizes "the importance of obtaining information on Traditional Birth Attendants practices, in each local situation, when planning and conducting training programmes for this type of personnel" (10). The authors then go on to use an eclectic survey of isolated examples from around the world to illustrate a general discussion of the types of prohibitions, beliefs, and ceremonies that are "likely" in "most" or "some" "traditional societies." Planners are encouraged by this manual to look for isolable "cultural practices," but the language through which they are to frame them first removes "practices" from the context of action and then blurs these particularities into an undifferentiated image of "traditional societies." At work here is a fetishized image of cultural difference that substitutes for contextually grounded accounts. The current model for training TMPs and TBAs encapsulates a tension between these generalized assumptions about the features of "traditional culture" and attention to the actual situation of specific places.

The other key feature of this model is the notion that TMPs and TBAs are a special kind of cultural insider. Discussions concerning the potential value of training TMPs and TBAs have focused on two issues. One is the shortage of health personnel, especially outreach workers, in many countries. The other is the problem of cultural acceptability in the communication of health messages. Advocates felt that TMPs and TBAs were a good practical solution to both problems, since they are "already there" doing the work and are by definition culturally appropriate messengers. These thoroughly pragmatic discussions are carried out in a language saturated with spatial metaphors of separation. The "local culture" is spoken of as an enclosed world on which development acts as an external force. This "culture" is fixed and static; development reaches it with "new" ideas and practices. These metaphors reinforce a tacit view of how the social world is arranged and they stand in contrast to the more complex and ambiguous sociogeographic imagery Nepali villagers use when envisioning their relationship to development. It is the presumed clarity of this boundary between local culture and development that makes mediators and brokers necessary. TMPs and TBAs, as constructed in the 1970s and 1980s, were to play this role.

These, then, were the expectations surrounding the various training programs established in Nepal by a few NGOs, beginning in the late 1970s. As in most countries, training programs for TBAs enjoyed more backing than do similar programs for indigenous healers such as shamans (Pillsbury 1982). Training projects for TBAs were begun independently in Nepal by several organizations, but now, twenty years later, they have mushroomed into an established program with a standard curriculum.[7] The activist-planners who helped build these programs view this history as an uphill battle, a fight against the prejudices of bureaucrats and top-down type planners. "It's a classic example of the hare and the tortoise," one foreign coordinator said of the persistence and slow growth of TBA programs. "We're the tortoise, steady and slow. Everywhere else it's a case of program-of-the-month."

Training programs for shamans in Nepal, in contrast, have remained more haphazard. That the ritual healers referred to generically in Nepali as *dhāmi-jhānkri* are the main healers throughout Nepal is patently obvious to all. Whether people who go into trance, call spirits, give divinations, and perform exorcisms can usefully be incorporated into health services is a matter of divided opinion, however. Because of the persistent assumption that shamans are the main obstacle to persuading villagers to take their illnesses to the health post, these programs have had to make strong claims about the exciting possibilities and surprising results of working with shamans. None of these programs has expanded on a scale comparable to TBA training, though the sponsoring organizations for the most part consider these programs to be "successful."[8]

What happens when this model for using traditional healers in health programs is put into practice? To answer this question, it is important to understand the situation of Nepali villages that contributes to how such programs might be viewed by the people they recruit for training.

THE CONTEXT: A CLOSE-UP VIEW OF ONE VILLAGE

Chandithan (a pseudonym) is a village about an hour's walk from Bhojpur Bazaar, in the middle hills of eastern Nepal. To a foreign observer recently arrived in Nepal, it appears to be a "typical" impoverished village. It is a place of packed mud-and-brick houses and narrow, steeply terraced fields from which families eke out a meager living. The adults look tired; many of the children have worm-swollen bellies; people with chronic coughs and infected sores are not hard to spot. A few questions reveal how common infant deaths are here. These observations confirm what we already know from the statistics. Observers more familiar with Nepal, however, might be less likely to find their images of a traditional village reflected back in this scene. People here seem a bit too educated, too sophisticated, too well-traveled to fit the image of the isolated farmer in a remote village. They have easy access to several clinics, veterinary services, seed and fertilizer distribution centers, a high school and post-secondary branch campus, and a number of government offices. These more seasoned observers are inclined to treat conversations with some villagers as good sources of information on their mentality, while regarding the views of other inhabitants as atypical because their ideas are too much like those of development workers.

People in Chandithan do not discuss themselves in terms of typicality. They see themselves as people who are more cosmopolitan and more modern than people in more remote villages; and as more traditional, and certainly as poorer and worse off, than the merchants, absentee landlords, and government employees who populate towns and cities. Yes, they can, when necessary and if funds permit, go to shops in the bazaar well-stocked with imported vitamin tonics, batteries, and plastic sandals, and they can sell produce, liquor, and milk to the government functionaries renting rooms in Chandithan. But, people are quick to point out, the doctor is almost never in residence at the hospital, the medicines they hand out are second rate, the fertilizer never shows up in time and when it does arrive it is only made available to a few people with inside connections anyway. They point out that they have been repeatedly deprived of electrification schemes and road projects. Development is a promise that has not been fulfilled.

It happens that the district of Bhojpur is located in what can only be called a development rainshadow. Other districts in eastern Nepal are targeted for pilot projects and the big integrated development schemes managed by foreign donors. When money and facilities and opportunities shower down on the two easternmost zones of Nepal, the clouds are mostly spent by the time they blow over Bhojpur. This is why it is all the more interesting to note that despite the comparatively low profile of

individual projects, development figures so conspicuously in the local social imagination. Chandithan offers an instructive window onto the ways
that a four-decade-long national push for development has affected how
people think about their situation and their society.

As the Nepali geographer Nanda Shrestha has pointed out about his
own experience, it is one thing to know that you are poor and hungry,
and another altogether to think of yourself as underdeveloped (Shrestha
1993). One has to learn to be a development category, he says, and that
learning has taken place in Nepal intensively over the past forty-five years.
Villagers see themselves depicted as the most underdeveloped segment of
one of the world's most underdeveloped nations. This way of understanding who they are is not difficult to accept, for it is obvious to villagers that
their life is hard and that others elsewhere have more. Images of life in
"developed countries" come to them juxtaposed with portraits of villagers
who are targeted for development because they lack it.

Villagers thus come, increasingly, to define themselves in and through
the terms that objectify them. What does it mean to be a villager in an
underdeveloped nation and a modernized world? This question now concerns people in Chandithan, though for some it presses more acutely than
for others. Locality, tradition, and custom have become objects of attention and reflection for villagers who must contend with the way others see
them. They engage in comparison and contrasts between the here of the
village and the there of developed places [bikasit ṭhāun].

This idiom of global social differentiation is replicated at another level,
closer to home. People in Chandithan see themselves as people who differ
not only in terms of wealth, caste, ethnicity, gender, and generation, but
also, increasingly, in terms of who is a "modern" [ādhunik, bikāsī] type of
person and who is more traditional, who can manage to exploit opportunities to make a life far from home and who is stuck with his or her lot
in the village. Those positioned closer to the institutions and mode of life
seen as modern speak of others as people "who don't understand" [kurā
bujhdainan] or as people "who lack awareness" [kansas (conscious) chhaina].
Those whose lives are tied more firmly to farming speak of people "who
don't have to carry loads" [bhāri boknu pardaina] or "who don't have to
walk" [hiḍnu pardaina]. Although clearly reflective of economic disparities,
these idioms express the widespread sense that development both creates
and requires a new kind of person, someone who understands and can
maneuver in the world beyond the village. This new kind of person is
often spoken of as an "educated person" [paḍhnelkhne, paḍhne mānchhe].
Schools are an important site for the production of modern identities,
and not only because they are the main places where ideas about nationalism and development are taught. School children view their schools as
vehicles for social emancipation: as symbols of struggles against the past

political oppression that denied villagers schooling; as sites from which systems of gender and caste privilege can be challenged; and as a base for the formation of critical commentary on the government (Skinner and Holland 1996). As school children fashion themselves as "moral persons and social selves," though, they also help produce the image of the un-educated person as an object of pity and scorn (ibid.).

This kind of distinction is by no means unique to Nepal, but it has a special salience there because state-sponsored, international donor-funded development efforts have such a high profile in public rhetoric about citizenship and nationalism. Popular understandings of "development" reveal an historically specific social experience of how this thing called *bikās* has come to villages: as state-sponsored services, intimately tied to politics and patronage; as imported manufactured commodities; as people, things, and ideas from a distant elsewhere. People come to see their villages as places to which *bikās* is brought.[9] They perceive that development will only "come" to those with the status to secure connections with the world from which development emanates (Stone 1989: 210). This leads villagers to wonder whether a village can ever become a "developed place." It is also what makes being a "developed" sort of person so important, both within local social hierarchies and those of the national society at large.

In this context, no discussion of medicine can be socially neutral. Cosmopolitan medicine signifies modernity in powerful ways, while involvement with shamans embeds people in a local world of entangled social obligations to the living, the dead, and the supernatural. A training program for TMPs sponsored by a development organization inserts itself into a highly charged symbolic field, for illness and healing are sites where the cultural politics of development are especially evident. The nuances of this social symbolism are too complex to deal with fully here. But it is clear that when people are in the process of seeking therapy—often a situation of crisis—they confront social inequality head on in the practical problems of gaining access, when they want it, to biomedical health services. They wrestle with the politics of social change when they face questions about the legitimacy of differentially authorized systems of medical knowledge. Moreover, physical conditions such as illness are implicated in sociomoral definitions of personhood.[10] On one level, shamans and doctors figure in villagers' discussions, speculations, and jokes as symbols par excellence of tradition and modernity. On another level, illnesses raise important questions not only about which sorts of treatments to pursue, but also about which aspects of a person's context are most relevant in accounting for it. Most illnesses can be explained and treated in a number of ways, and each explanation implies something different about who a person is.

What is the relationship between local medical knowledge and cosmopolitan medicine? This is as much a question for villagers in Chandithan as it is for health development planners. Villagers envision this relationship in two ways, each of which carries a different implication for the social placement of the village in a landscape of development. Villagers insist, on the one hand, that cosmopolitan medicine fits smoothly into local practices as one option among many. This incorporative model reflects the on-the-ground eclecticism with which people approach healing. It also evokes an image of a developed village and it portrays villagers as people who judiciously weigh their options and reasonably choose what is best under the circumstances. But villagers also offer another version of the relationship between therapies in their commentaries. They frequently stress the contrast between shamans and doctors, and between village ways of doing things and the routines of hospitals and health posts. They describe the deplorable conditions of life in villages by pointing out how inaccessible cosmopolitan medicine is for poor people who lack the status or personal connections to gain entry into the world of offices and clinics. When people stress the difference between shamans (held up as the quintessential village healer, though several other kinds of therapy also exist locally) and doctors (a figure associated with "developed countries" and hospitals, though rarely encountered in the flesh in rural Nepal)[11] they are also expressing their sense of the chasm between two social worlds. Ways of envisioning medical relationships are simultaneously ways of envisioning relationships of social difference. Two accounts of the place of cosmopolitan medicine in village life commingle in villagers' discussions because both have a grounding in their ambivalent experience of development.

Health-related training programs, therefore, can represent a number of things to people whose perceptions are shaped by this context. First, they come to people who are quite used to being chastised by health workers for consulting shamans and other local healers, and who enter the world of the health post expecting this condescending antagonism. Villagers do not accept the notion that health post medicines and shamanic rituals are incompatible options, however. Their approach is pluralistic. Second, these programs come to people who view the universe of potentially useful therapies to be open-ended, who assume that the healing knowledge in any given locale is but a fragment of all possible therapeutic knowledge, and who therefore eagerly seek out shamans from other places, a new mantra, tips on medicinal plants, and commercial medicines. Training programs hold the promise of an opportunity to expand a local knowledge that is already assumed to be incomplete. Third, training programs convey biomedically based knowledge to people who already have some experience with this style of medicine. Some of its treatments are known to be superior to the local remedies, yet many complaints brought to the hospital never receive satisfactory treatment there. Further, most villagers are generally unimpressed by preventative health education—which is what is emphasized in most health outreach programs. They look to institutions of health development for access to curative resources (Stone 1986, 1992). For the most part, they see themselves as people who know how to look after themselves and who make careful, pragmatic choices according to the circumstances, and this stance keeps them from ever fully identifying with the subject position of ignorance development messages often create for them. Last, villagers encounter these programs as individuals who are variously positioned as persons with greater or lesser claims to being the "developed" or "educated" modern type. As we will see in the next section, training programs present them with a situation in which this social position is at issue.

IMPLEMENTATION

A development project starts out as a plan but turns into a context, for instance, when a set of people is brought together to interact around the activity of training. In most cases, this context is structured by planners' models, models not only of the project itself, but of local society, its needs, and the role development can play in meeting these needs.[12] In particular, the expectations planners have about the knowledge and practices that are "out there" in "the culture" become manifest in the organization of programs. The recruitment of trainees, the choice of teaching techniques, the construction of visual aids, and the decisions about the information to be transmitted in a given training are all concrete expressions of accepted ideas about *who* training programs should reach, *why* those targeted should want to be trained, and *what* these programs should accomplish.

The expectations embedded in program design sometimes coincide with, and sometimes diverge from, those of the people involved in the trainings. The problems planners and project directors report, the frustrations they experience in getting these programs up and running, their perceptions of how and why things go wrong index the mixed agendas of the many people involved. Implementation, though often imagined as a straight line from program design to program impact or effect, works more like an attempt to orchestrate a multiplicity of agendas, assumptions, and desires. Consider the following instances of "problems" and "successes."

When NGOs take on the task of training TMPs and TBAs, they apply to the realities of Nepal the theoretical construction of a role that is believed to exist in traditional societies. They look for the Nepali roles that correspond to the image of TBA and TMP, and they attempt to find ways of making "new" medical knowledge understandable to villagers.[13] Sometimes this process of finding a fit looks like a stubborn pounding of square pegs into round holes, while other times it involves a more subtle adjustment. This play between expectations and the conditions in Nepal is evident in two illustrations: the unanticipated difficulties in establishing just what counts as a TBA and the surprising ease in encouraging shamans to work with health posts.

The programs for training TBAs must constantly respond to the criticism that TBAs do not exist "traditionally" in Nepal. This criticism arises because in many parts of Nepal, women are assisted in childbirth by other women—usually a relative—rather than by a recognized specialist. How, then, are TBAs to be recruited for training? Where no traditionally defined TBA role exists, programs seek "respected and influential women." Program organizers complain, however, that frequently these women have little or no interest in midwifery, or that "inappropriate" people (such as unmarried daughters of local politicians) are selected by communities for training. The institutional need to have TBAs to train leads to a program that in many cases produces "trained TBAs" out of women who do not identify themselves as any sort of "birth assistant."

The situation is further complicated by the ambiguities created by translation. Both Nepali and expatriate program advisors commonly use the single umbrella term "TBA" to talk about the women their programs target, even though the programs are reaching a wide variety of women with quite varied forms of involvement in other women's childbirth. They also interchange "TBA" with the Nepali word *sudeni*, even though there are many terms in numerous languages for the various specialist roles that do exist. The word *sudeni* in Nepali is generally associated with a woman who has special skills (particularly the ability to intercede when labor is not proceeding normally), and many women who fit the program vision of a TBA are not, in their own view, *sudeni*. Some are reported to vehemently reject this label. Further, it was found that in areas where TBA training has been carried out regularly, people are much more likely to identify their local *sudeni*, while responses in areas where there have been no training programs often fail to identify any local women as *sudeni* (Levitt 1987). It appears that training programs are creating *sudeni* by using the word to refer to the women they train. Thus one of the first steps in tailoring a training program to "local culture"—putting the message into local terms—proves not only to be more ambiguous than generally assumed, but also to be a practice that actually helps create the equivalencies that the model presumes to already exist.

Another fundamental step in implementing training for TBAs involves finding out what the local practices are so that training programs can address them. WHO guidelines recognize that birth assistance can take many forms other than that of the midwife who cares for women before, during, and after childbirth. In Nepal, nonetheless, the very existence of TBAs remains a vexing question because there are a number of different roles that could be called birth assistance. Generalizations about "traditional" roles and practices do not hold up. Most health development programs employ a form of reasoning about cultural practices that attributes distinct traditions, taboos, rules, beliefs, and so on to clearly bounded, internally homogenous "cultures" that are assumed to be coterminous with ethnic or tribal identities or with the regions of a nation-state.[14] This vision of a nation carved up into neatly defined blocks of "sub-cultures" does not work very well in Nepal for predicting what people in a given locale actually do and think, for many communities are multiethnic and the practices in all are shaped by factors other than ethnically defined traditions. Though the people who carry out the training in localities often have a good understanding of local practices and birth-related concerns, discussions in policy and planning circles about traditional birth practices bring to mind the parable of the blind men and the elephant.

Because trainings are "for TBAs," the impression that there are Nepali midwives "out there" to be trained persists. General expectations about what a traditional midwife would be like continually enter into program design, despite widespread planning knowledge about the nature and variability of forms of birth assistance.[15] Thus, newly arrived foreign advisors repeatedly discover with dismay that TBA trainings are not for "real" TBAs, or that the women involved do not do what it is assumed that "midwives" in "traditional societies" do. Some planners argue that it doesn't matter whether they are finding TBAs or creating them through training. Either way they are introducing important health knowledge into communities, and they are working with the realities of local culture in Nepal. For advocates, the awkward disjunctures between the abstract model of TBA training and the form their work takes in Nepal is of small concern because the training itself matters more than the indigenous roles and customs to which it is to connect.

While the TBAs that are assumed to exist in some form everywhere turn out to be difficult to pinpoint in Nepal, the shamans who are thought to be the bastions of a competing traditional belief system prove surprisingly open to collaboration with health posts.

Since the 1970s, anthropologists and planners have been voicing opinions about whether or not shamans could or should be enlisted in health service delivery (Maskarinec 1995; Miller 1979; Oswald 1983; Parker 1988; Peters 1979; Shrestha and Lediard 1980; Stone 1986). The concern centers on two questions: whether shamans are open to new ideas and practices and whether shamanic healing is too different to lend itself to integration. The terms of the discussion about shamans, most of whom are men, and TBAs, who are always women, reveal how perceptions of local culture are gendered. Notably, shamans are treated as agents who are expected to defend their authority if health workers take an oppositional stance toward them. In contrast, discussions about the trainability of TBAs have tended to focus on whether illiterate women can follow instructions properly and on the gentle persuasion required to make medical information "acceptable" to these women. Expectations about the comparative activity or passivity of male and female TMPs correspond to a gendered hierarchy of cultural knowledge as well. Where local knowledge about pregnancy, birth, and infant care is regarded merely as a set of customs, shamanic knowledge is accorded the status of an alternative belief system central to local culture. As such, it is granted more importance.

The most carefully planned and evaluated program to date—that run by Save the Children Fund-United Kingdom (SCF-UK)—shows an explicit concern with the medical beliefs of shamans. They worked self-consciously to design their training as a dialogue that would foster collaboration, because

> We felt that we could teach the *dhāmi-jhānkris* to recognize signs and symptoms of common illnesses, and to give first aid. The aim was not to undermine their traditional practices and status, but to provide them with new additional techniques to make them more effective village healers (Dhakal et al. 1986: 15).

The training begins with a discussion of recent cases the healers have seen of people with diarrhea. They are led to speculate on the causes of this symptom, and during this discussion the facilitator "expounds his own view . . . using visual aids where relevant" (21). Participants "are encouraged to say whether or not they feel convinced by the trainer's explanation" and examples of successful treatment are used to further convince them. The most important session is the one entitled "germs and spirits." The *dhāmi-jhānkris* are told a story about a man who suffers from diarrhea and vomiting after drinking water from a well. When asked for their "diagnosis," the shamans attribute the illness to bad spirits. After a discussion of the ways water sources can become contaminated,

> We next explain our theory of "kira" (germs, or bugs) in water which can cause disease, and we say that although they are invisible to the naked eye we can see them through our microscopes. The similarity of both spirits and germs both being invisible is again stressed (22).

The analogy establishes an alliance among experts by comparing the *dhāmi-jhānkris'*supernaturally endowed ability to see spirits with the health post staff's ability to divine the presence of microbes. Then

> Further discussion follows on how the *dhāmi-jhānkris'*attempt to treat people by appeasing the spirits, while we point out that we try to kill the germs. The groups agree that "killing" is preferable to "placating" as the problem will be less likely to recur if the cause is totally removed (22).[16]

In evaluating the pilot phase of this program, the organizers reflect on the *dhāmi-jhānkris'* reactions:

> We were surprised at how little resistance there is to this "germ theory." But in fact it does have much in common with their own theoretical notions as to disease causation caused by evil spirits. Invisible beings which lurk in dirty places and attack first one person in a household and then spread through the family seemed perfectly credible as explanations for disease when superimposed on their notions of purification and pollution. They also easily understand the idea that modern medicines eliminate germs, and seem attracted by the thought of a medicine helping the body's own battle against the causative agent of disease. This is similar to the rationale for herbal treatments with which some of them are already familiar. And they know enough about the speed of action of some western cures to acknowledge them as extremely powerful (23).

In the SCF training program for *dhāmi-jhānkris*, the "beliefs" of *dhāmis* become a tool to be used for communication of new health ideas. The dialogue is organized around this very difference: you think that, we think this. This is a dialogue only in the most limited sense, however. In the final analysis, the trainers are convinced that they know the real reasons behind the illnesses the *dhāmis* treat through ritual.[17] All concerned understand the message implicit in the structure of the program: that the *dhāmis* are there to learn about the superiority of medicine.

The training programs treat shamans as if they performed a function analogous to that of doctors, and in doing so they project on to *dhāmi-jhānkris* a certain model of medical practice. They assume that shamans diagnose illnesses by examining symptoms and that shamans have unquestioned authority to instruct patients. Neither of these assumptions holds up to ethnographic research (Maskarinec 1995; Sagant 1987; Stone 1989). Anthropologists have repeatedly pointed out that *dhāmi-jhānkris* are intercessors in a sociomoral cosmos, and though as such they deal with bodily afflictions, it is a mistake to reduce their role to merely that of curer. The contrast between the many anthropological interpretations of shamanism and the assumptions guiding development planning reveals just how difficult it can be for these two sets of professionals to communicate with each other. They differ in their assumptions about how and why culture matters. In training programs for shamans, *dhāmi-jhānkris* are acknowledged to have different beliefs, and even a different knowledge base, but the idea that they are not first and foremost diagnosticians and curers—*medical* practitioners—is not entertained. The program itself is based on the idea that they engage in a cultural variation of the medical acts of biomedicine.[18]

Two problems with this assumption concern anthropologists. One is the resulting inattention to the power dynamics of the social relationships in which the practices of TBAs and TMPs are actually embedded.[19] The other is the distortion in cross-cultural interpretation that occurs when shamanic practice is simply assumed to be based on the same modern, western categories that undergird biomedicine (Gordon 1988). Yet the apparent success of training programs for shamans raises a question few anthropologists care to face: Can bad social analysis result in good development programs? However flawed the development understanding of shamans and their activities might be as cultural description, the comparison they make between shamans and doctors appears to be plausible to all the people involved in the trainings.[20] In fact, this comparison is commonly made in Nepal, and not only among certain development professionals—villagers in Chandithan, as I've mentioned, use a similar rhetoric of comparison and contrast in discussing the relationship between local knowledge and cosmopolitan medicine. That the shaman-doctor comparison is compelling to many people is an ethnographic fact, even if anthropologists find it a poor basis for ethnographic analysis.[21] Though the vision guiding the training of shamans arguably elides knowledge about what shamans do with an idea about how they could fit into health development priorities, shamans appear willing to cooperate, whether or not they are misunderstood.

Some of problems planners describe stem from conflicting views on whether working with local practices is really the way to achieve health development objectives. The manual for the training of the Assistant Nurse Midwives who are to train TBAs contains but one brief passage on tailoring the training to local customs. The nurses are admonished to use simple language and to "show respect for the *sudeni.*" The classes should take "community opinion" into account. The nurses are urged to "observe and promote" those customs that "are not harmful to health," while those that "do pose a harm ... should be discouraged slowly and gradually." "It is important," the nurses are cautioned, "to listen to what the *sudeni* have to say" (Ministry of Health/HMG 1990). Overall, the manual emphasizes the information planners think the trainees need to be taught. This, then, was the fate in Nepal of the framework put forth in WHO documents that give detailed instructions for how to incorporate local beliefs and customs into culturally appropriate training for TBAs.

This manual is itself a product of debates, conflicting agendas, and compromises hammered out for the sake of the larger goal. When I commented on the discrepancy between the theory and the final product to one foreign advisor who had been involved somewhere along the line, she told me that yes, many of them were unhappy with the end result. "It was the Nepali nurses who objected to any mention of customs and traditions," she told me. She suggested that these nurses were unwilling to accept the model of working with local custom. Though I was never able to confirm her version of events with others (and one wonders what complaints the Nepali nurses might have about the expatriate advisors' agendas), her comment is significant for what it suggests about who has what kind of interest in a development approach that seems to side with villagers.

Opinion is split as to what makes a training better—supplying villagers with "correct" information, or conducting the training in a "culturally respectful" way. At issue is what "development" means, not just in theory, but in the lives of positioned actors. Nepalis working in development participate in a system that operates by scrutinizing Nepali life in order to identify its problems. This is a discourse that attributes problems of development alternately to what Nepal lacks and to what is there, and it instills in many Nepalis an acute sense of the failings of their society. It is not uncommon for Nepali development workers to express the attitude that the development of Nepal entails expunging from it precisely those customs that have retarded its progress—the customs of the poor. Those in positions of professional power, whether they come from urban elite backgrounds or whether they come from villages, achieve their position through their ability to know what villagers need, just like any other development expert. Not surprisingly, one of the most direct ways to exercise and communicate this authority is by contrasting expert knowledge with what villagers do and think. These professionals work within a highly racialized form of bureaucracy in which, as Nepalis, they are called upon to represent and know Nepal. Their authority rests on knowing villagers without aligning themselves too closely with them. In contrast, foreign advisors can enhance their authority by talking about the importance of culture and tradition, even if their Nepali counterparts regard them as romantics. They play to a different audience. Criticism of local customs leaves them open to charges of ethnocentrism, while enthusiasm for working "with" people's "culture" is a vouchsafe of their commitment and a guarantor of a place within a well-defined wing of development professionalism. To be a foreigner advocating culturally appropriate development on principle is one kind of identity, while to be a Nepali professional responsible in some small way for bringing about improved conditions in one's country is another. Both positions, however, share an investment in a firm distinction between "their culture" and "our knowledge."

This distinction can itself be the source of problems. "We want the trainings for the *dhāmis* to be a two-way communication," a British project coordinator told me, "but over time it tends to drift into a one-way communication of information. It turns into teaching *dhāmis* the 'right way.'" She hesitated before admitting that this is mostly a problem with the Nepali staff. "It's odd, but more often it is the expatriate doctor who is more likely to see the usefulness of the *dhāmi-jhānkris*. In my practice back home, about 75 percent of my patients could have done with the services of a *dhāmi*." What she meant was that the psychological component of an illness is often the most important, especially since many illnesses are self-limiting. "I hate to say it, but we find there's a clear correlation between the attitude of the trainer who gave the training and the number of shamans who are eager to attend a refresher course."

Program directors also spoke of having to overcome the initial reluctance of Nepali staff and health post workers, who were often dubious about the very idea of a health development program dealing with shamans. That it would be health outreach staff who would be reluctant participants, and not the shamans, was an irony not lost on planners. Their reluctance is not surprising, though, for the programs are asking people who have staked a position for themselves on the side of development to now act as champions of local knowledge by playing a mediating role. Though the structural position of moderately educated, locally based health workers and elite Nepali planners differs, the stake they have in siding with development is analogous.

"Is it easier to train the shamans or to train the trainers?" I asked a Nepali director who had done both.

"The trainers grasp the concepts more easily and they understand the English words for the diseases," he replied, "but they approach the *dhāmi-jhānkri* negatively in the beginning. They say that what the *dhāmis* do is superstition. They say that they don't believe in ghosts. They always say that they don't believe in those things. But everyone believes a little." Educational parables have been designed for changing the outlook of trainers, just as they have for the *dhāmis*. "We ask them whether they would walk around in a big palace with lots of empty rooms in the daytime, and of course they all say they would. Then we ask them if they had to walk in those rooms at night, without a torchlight, whether they would. And none of them would, not a single one. Because even people like us, we're afraid to be alone in the dark because of ghosts. We get them to admit this. As soon as one admits it then all the others start talking. They say '*bhut* [ghosts, spirits] aren't in the science books.' We say 'the science books don't say anything about *bhut*. They don't say whether they exist or not.'"

Though these sorts of discussions about belief and science are common

enough in a modernizing Nepal, they are usually excluded from the sanc-
tioned circle of official development delivery. Often the people who work
for NGOs in rural areas are themselves from villages, albeit from families
that could manage to send their children to school. There is less social
distance between them and their clients. Nonetheless, their identity is in
part grounded in being an educated person among the uneducated. For
most, going to school as a child meant they became involved in a parallel
universe of cosmopolitan knowledge and information, at odds with the
world that surrounded them at home. Learning to maneuver between
these two universes and finding a way to establish a position for themselves
between them is part of their experience of development. As development
delivery workers, they are normally asked to place themselves firmly on
one side. But they are as interested as the people in villages such as Chandithan in finding rationales for integration and logics of connection.
These training programs for shamans open up possibilities for adjusting
their own understanding of the relationship between development and
the village. Some reject this form of engagement, thereby becoming
"problems" for the program planners, while others embrace it enthusiastically.

Asked to tone down the knowing position of development for the sake
of respectful dialogue, they are still told they are there to change villagers'
behavior in certain predetermined ways. The awkward position in which
this leaves the trainers is evident in the words of one of them quoted in
an SCF report:

> It was really difficult to see how motivated the *dhāmi-jhānkris* were on the
> first day, or even on the second. I could not tell whether any of them would
> be able to change their customs and beliefs. I worked without grumbling at
> them and eventually I got them to trust and believe me. I did not interrupt
> them in talking and expressing their views. I was friendly and found myself
> supporting some of their ideas which were good. So in the end the *dhāmi-
> jhānkri* did not hide their mysteries from me (Dhakal et al. 1986: 71–72).

The same trainer's remarks reveal to us the *dhāmis'* perceptions of the
process:

> Later some of them told me that they were just doing *dhāmi-jhānkri* work
> without really believing in it. Because the community trusts them they are
> asked to perform sacrifices, and rituals, and cure patients. If the patient gets
> better, by whatever means, they get the credit—not in material goods, but
> in trust and respect. And they said now, after the training, they really felt
> for the first time that they know what to do to help in a case like diarrhoea,
> or a severely malnourished child. So they will get more trust if their treat-
> ment is successful . . . So now they will come to the conclusion that worship-

ping the god "Nepale" or doing tantra-mantra is not the only way of treating patients (71–72).

The *dhāmi-jhānkris* apparently told their trainer that they were not actually like the shamans the training program presumed existed. They claimed not to really believe in the explanations about spirits and witches that other villagers offer for their cures. Humbly, they accepted the program's view that they are trusted by other villagers, but they were at pains to correct the image of themselves as the guardians of traditional beliefs. They accepted one set of premises about TMPs—that they are influential community members who can, if taught how, do things to improve people's health—while at the same time they challenged the way these assumptions about TMPs placed them firmly on the side of village culture. What these *dhāmis* did was to displace the role of believer in spirits onto other villagers. By denying their own identification with those notions, they aligned themselves with the trainers.

The shamans who showed up for a training had already been engaged in a protracted *local* dialogue about the relation between shamanic rituals and the health post's type of medicine. Shamans, like other villagers, reflect on where they fit in a developing Nepal. However central their shamanic knowledge is to their identity (see Maskarinec 1995), they are subjected to the same social pressures that link increased economic opportunity and status to being a "developed" kind of person. The comments reported by the SCF trainer suggest that (at least some) *dhāmi-jhānkris* use training programs to position themselves as "modern." By doing so, they would be refashioning what a *dhāmi-jhānkri* is. The *dhami-jhānkris'* response to the training helps explain why efforts to make use of traditional healers within biomedically based health services transform these healers' role more fundamentally than the idea of "enhancing existing practices" would suggest. It is not just that these healers are subtly pressured to accept what is correct by biomedical standards, or that their actual ritual role is discredited or overlooked all together. Nor is it that the clientele for shamanic expertise is diminishing—far from it. These programs are embedded in a wider cultural politics in which being a person who stands for "tradition" is the weaker position in a widening power differential. As *dhāmis*, they are in a particularly difficult position, for their role makes them icons of those things most associated with the backwardness of the village. Their knowledge may even be ridiculed by the more *bikāsi* of their fellow villagers. And like every other villager, they are interested in a wide range of medical possibilities. Thus it is possible for the *dhāmis* invited to trainings to find in them a congenial site for working out their own problematic position.[22]

Program planners have stories about villagers who seem model students and then, disappointingly, "still" do some of the wrong things. While planners tend to search for reasons why the message gets skewed or why people persist in some behaviors despite being told it is bad for health, many of their complaints suggest that villagers and planners see the main purpose of trainings in a different light.

"The problem," said a Canadian health worker, "is that as soon as you train these people, they're perceived as government employees." She continued, "everyone talks about democracy these days, and what democracy means is that now the government will pay for everything. That's what people think, and that's what their past experience with projects has been—when a project comes in it pays for everything. That's the attitude held by the project people—'we're the great benefactors'—and that attitude has completely eroded any sense of community responsibility." There is more to this than worries about sustainability, top-down development, and inculcated dependency. When trainees begin to view themselves as part of government service, they challenge the division of development labor.

Training programs typically pay a DA, or Daily Allowance, to trainees to compensate the loss of their labor at home. It is also common for certificates to be handed out in a formal ceremony at the end of a training. But some planners made a point of telling me that they were against these practices. One told me of a shaman who marched into the Chief District Officer's office with his certificate from a training demanding the job he thought was now owed to him. Others say, "We're paying for cooperation. It's not right." Ending the practice is not so easy, however. "They complain, 'Government officials get DA, why shouldn't we?' "

Clearly, there are differing perceptions of what the end result of these trainings should be, as difficulties surrounding the payment of TBAs highlight. "Villagers think that the government is paying the TBA now so they don't have to," an American advisor complained. When a new program for training CHVs (Community Health Volunteers) incorporated payment of a monthly stipend into the scheme, TBAs in the Terai were up in arms. This advisor told me that when she arrived for a site visit she was met with outraged TBAs: "Why do CHVs get paid and not us?" When one woman announced that she would refuse to work, this advisor said she responded, "If you refuse to work then you're not a TBA and you have to give your kit box to me." I said to her, "You said you were doing this for *dharma* [religious charity], for your community." She said that of course she was doing it for *dharma*. I told her if she was doing it for *dharma* she didn't need to be paid.

Who is a worker, who is a volunteer? Who can strike and demand pay for their expertise and who is merely obliged to provide humanitarian service? For the organizations that plan and promote the training of "indigenous medical practitioners," the objective is to use work that is already being done as an extension of a health delivery system. For Nepali villagers under increasing economic pressure, training is associated with a chance to move into some form of government service. When TBAs see themselves as health workers, they, like the *dhāmi-jhānkris* in the previous example, take their training a step farther than the planners' model of working with traditional practices allows.

CONCLUSIONS

What do these examples tell us about the implementation of development ideas? Rather obviously, they show that when key participants reject the way sides are drawn up in a program, planners have "problems," and when participants find that their placement in a program's structure serves a purpose for them, programs seem to run smoothly. More obliquely, these examples invite us to think about a dimension of development that receives little sustained consideration in the face of the overwhelmingly purposive rhetoric of development objectives, targets, and measures.

Development activities are social activities; they bring certain modes of engagement into being. The development discourse that dominates in Nepal is one based on a continual reiteration of linked differences: the dichotomy between the developed and the backward; the modern and the local; scientific knowledge and cultural belief. These terms are now inescapably part of how Nepalis know themselves, as individuals and as a nation. As a result, they form part of any development program whether or not the planners of a particular program accept them or use them.

I have described these training programs as a site where development models of village culture and villager's models of development not only intersect, but interpenetrate. This way of seeing implementation stands in contrast to that of planners. Though in development rhetoric, development plans act on a stable field of indigenous understandings and practices, an ethnographic approach shows development programs to be acting on villagers who are already assuming and seeking certain kinds of relationships to development. And while planners equate development with the objectives their programs are designed to achieve, villagers see development as a kind of social space to which programs give them access. The local context in which any development program unfolds already includes ideas about and experiences of development as part of that context. This is why we need to understand development ideas as part of a recursive process, in which the representations implicit in every new model recombine with signifiers already in circulation.[23]

By now it should be clear that a simple judgment about the worth of training programs for TMPs will not be forthcoming. It is not known whether training programs actually lead a significant number of the designated practitioners to alter what they do, or whether indigenous practitioners really do make better extensions of a health service delivery system than workers hired specifically to do that job. Because training programs in Nepal vary in their approach, take place on a small scale, and occur simultaneously with other activities based on different models, it is difficult to assess their impact.

What we *do* know quite a lot about is how various actors regard these programs, what they think these programs do, and why they see them as good or bad. We also know something about the kinds of social interactions these programs facilitate and the kinds they preclude. I have shown that training programs do a series of things. They serve as one among many modalities through which villagers become familiar with a nonlocal set of health-related knowledge. They create a forum some villagers can use to make themselves into more "developed" kinds of people and which some health workers can use to mediate contradictions in their position as development deliverers. They institutionalize the terms through which village practices are linked to development objectives.

The question to ask about a development project that aims to work with "local culture" is not simply how accurate its information about "cultural beliefs and practices" is, but how its structure will enter into the fluid set of possibilities that exist locally. When health services available to villagers mark and reinforce social distance—as do health posts that regularly chide people for having attempted any other kind of therapy, or training sessions that lecture villagers on "correct" information—the mode of engagement reinforces the perception of the distance and difference between the village and development. Though this message does not prevent villagers from seeking out cosmopolitan medicine, it does imbue the act of going to the health post with a particular social meaning. When programs offer opportunities for villagers to be let into development spaces—as when shamans are encouraged to compare themselves to health post staff—they build on a process of pluralistic integration that has already been taking place in many villages for some time. Villagers, and many Nepali development workers as well, have an interest (in both senses of the word) in finding theories of compatibility and styles of synthesis through which they can realistically engage with a world of development. Training programs that present villagers with a theory of the connection between cosmopolitan medicine and local healing knowledge offer to villagers an officially endorsed version of something villagers themselves have been building all along.[24] Both types of programs mesh with visions of the village-development relation already held by villagers. Both "work," but they work differently.

This observation, in turn, suggests something about how development ideas become powerful. The common image—that distinctively "western" development ideas are imposed on nonwestern locals—is too simplistic. Attempts to explain the hegemonic tendencies of development through a dualistic domination/resistance framework assume too much about the coherence and the stability of both development practices and the societies toward which they are directed. Social scientists critical of development mirror the thinking of development planners when they treat local perspectives as if these consist only of "culture" or "indigenous knowledge" and not of ideas about development. They likewise make development into something more homogenous than it really is when they assume that its technical solutions and social messages always work in perfect tandem.

Anthropology, with its attention to context, easily generates a critique of the generic assumptions about traditional societies that lie behind most development efforts. But could this particularistic mode of inquiry be useful for understanding the *globalizing* force of development? Development, as a modern project, seeks to modernize others through its system of universalizing categories and standardized practices. An ethnographic account of development needs to ask how these universalizing procedures operate in specific contexts. Far from being assumed, the hegemony of the development framework and indeed its changing face needs to be traced. How does something called development continue to cohere as a type of social project? We need to inquire into how it is that certain efforts are recognizable as "development" (Escobar 1995) while also remaining attentive to the frayed edges and scattered effects of these efforts.

The organized effort we call development works in and through a tension between the universalizing thrust of development knowledge and the quirks of local implementation. At the same time that diverse streams of knowledge and practice are drawn together under the umbrella of development, the development idea fragments into different, localized meanings which spill over into realms not strictly defined as development. Rather than assuming we already know how the mobile, internationalized frameworks of development are inserted into national and local contexts, we need to trace the actual practices—including the representational practices—through which certain linkages are forged, reinforced, expanded, or subverted.

One way to do this is by tracing multiple and often divergent levels of communication. First, it is important to consider why and how some development ideas become compelling categories in the common sense social knowledge, as well as the political discourse, of people in a particular place (for instance, Woost 1993; Pigg 1992). In many Nepali villages this occurs not as a wholesale appropriation of the new and foreign terms of development but through semantic slippages that allow the distinction between tradition and development, for instance, to overlap with locally significant social distinctions organized around caste, class, and gender. Development ideas become hegemonic to the degree that they fuse with other ideas, grounded in other social processes, be they those of a nationalist politics or those of local idioms of difference, community, and change.

Second, any given development initiative is a complex bundle of ideas and techniques that are often transmitted unevenly. In health development, for instance, efforts made in the name of preventing or curing disease come trailing more diffuse, and often unrecognized, assumptions about the person, the body, morality, science, and truth. We need to pay more attention to how the elements in these clusters diverge or converge in specific contexts. Although people may decline to boil their drinking water or rely on the health post for the treatment of their diarrhea, they might nonetheless start to participate in a discourse that frames those very actions as distinctively "developed."[25]

Last, there is the question of the mechanisms by which ideas are or are not transmitted into the international lingua franca of development institutions. Whose terms travel through these discursive networks and whose do not? What are the effects of asymmetries in networks of communication? In an earlier examination of these same training programs for Traditional Medical Practitioners, I looked in detail at the way information about "local beliefs and practices" was translated into terms acceptable for development planning (Pigg 1995a). In the twin processes of gathering information on rural people's attitudes and practices and organizing this knowledge in the form of generalizations useful for planning, some aspects of local life are readily packaged in the language of development while others remain inarticulable within the terms of planning. The language of development works systematically to mediate the circulation of diverse discourses about—for example—the body, illness, and personal welfare. The effect is that development frameworks appear as naturally transcendent, logically generalizable, and universally practical systems in contrast to what is depicted as the limited, parochial, and particular quality of "local" understandings.

Translation, as Asad (1986) has noted, occurs within relations of power that make some languages stronger than others. The insights of Nepali shamans, or families caring for pregnant women and infants, or health extension workers can barely be heard, let alone have an effect on development language. Planners believe they must stabilize assumptions for decision-making.[26] To them, nonwestern modes of medical knowledge, as an entire epistemological and moral system, appear too uncertain, fuzzy, chaotic, or implausible to be useful for planning—even though these ideas are the solid ground of common sense for villagers as *they* make decisions. Development tends to confront cultural difference as the unthinkable. It becomes repackaged as discrete "beliefs" unmoored from the context of everyday life.[27]

The reification, decontextualization, and pathologization of "culture" that so often occurs in development discourse sets out objectifying terms of social difference within which villagers go about finding subject positions. These efforts at self-fashioning (which, as we've seen, can be a boon or a thorn in the side for development planners) occur within the logic of a powerful discursive system. Villagers are *made* marginal by a development discourse that turns them into "targets," discusses their lives in terms of isolable and decontextualized "problems," and positions itself as an authoritative system that mediates numerous "local" situations. In other words, to have one's views designated as "local" within development discussions is already to be marginalized—for whatever is "local" is by definition not "development."

It remains an open question whether the tacit tug-of-war in Nepali society over what it means to be developed can alter the marginalizing effects of development's terms for framing cultural difference. In the meantime, we might still ask whether villagers must accept this marginalized position in order to make cosmopolitan medicine their own.

NOTES

1. These programs are not a major component of the national health system. I focus on them here because in them widespread development assumptions about "local culture" are most visible.

2. Research in 1992 was made possible by a President's Research Grant from Simon Fraser University. The 1986–1988 research was supported by a Fulbright-Hays Fellowship for Doctoral Research Abroad and a Doctoral Fellowship from the South Asia Program of the Social Science Research Council and the American Council of Learned Societies.

3. See Maglacas and Simons (1986); Pillsbury (1979); WHO (1975, 1992).

4. For discussions of the fate of PHC policies, see Justice (1986, 1987); Pillsbury (1982); Stone (1986, 1992).

5. Concerns over professional competition and licensing led to disputes over the legitimacy of indigenous medical knowledge, feeding a climate of hostility and polarization (see Jeffery 1982; Leslie 1976). The first major attempt to train indigenous midwives in India, in 1902, emerged under very different political conditions: their work posed no threat to the interests of other practitioners, and the indigenous character of the skills of these poor, low-caste women was not seen as worth defending (Jeffery 1982: 1837). Sargent and Rawlins (1992) show the present-day effects of the history of British policy toward midwives in Jamaica.

6. For example, Packard and Epstein (1991) argue that this occurred when

anthropologists were incorporated into the biomedically defined research agendas in the epidemiological research on AIDS in Africa.

7. Training programs for TBAs are conducted by the Assistant Nurse Midwives (ANM) posted to an area. TBAs receive ten days of instruction (with a four-day refresher course later that year) covering basic physiology, hygiene and safe birth, nutrition, and family planning. TBAs are taught how they should deal with normal births; they are instructed to refer complicated cases to the ANM. At the end of the instruction, they are given a kit of supplies.

8. The idea of working with shamans was first proposed by the Nepal Contraceptive Retail Service (CRS), who enlisted them as retailers of family planning devices. Other programs, run by various NGOs, have trained shamans to make appropriate referrals to health posts or to motivate them to educate people about Oral Rehydration Therapy. Programs for training *dhāmi-jhānkris* are more varied than TBA programs in content, design, objectives, and approach.

9. None of these understandings are quite what planners have in mind when they conceptualize their work as contributing to "development." Hence the frequent complaints about Nepali villagers who exhibit the wrong kind of attitude toward development. Villagers see their relationship to development in terms somewhat different from those development planners have for seeing villagers. See Stone (1989).

10. These issues are dealt with in Pigg (1995b) and in a longer work in progress.

11. The term "doctor" [*dāktar*] is often used to refer to anyone who gives injections or hands out pharmaceuticals.

12. Foster (1978), Justice (1986), and Stone (1989) have all pointed out that development institutions perpetuate cultural assumptions of their own in their bureaucratic structures and goals.

13. This process is described in more detail in Pigg (1995a).

14. Hence the broad generalizations one often finds. An exception is the UNICEF urban poverty program in Nepal. The background studies for these projects describe the conditions in the limited area of specific neighborhoods, rather than relying on broad inferences based on extrapolation from thin sociocultural research in other locales.

15. Foremost among these expectations is the idea that TBAs will be involved in antenatal and postnatal care. Training sessions include information about antenatal health and nutrition as well as about postnatal care and contraception, even though planners know that both antenatal and postnatal care resides with the family, not a non-family specialist. The question of antenatal care is another focus for debate on the viability of TBA training programs.

16. There are reasons for shifting frames from the placation of spirits to the "killing" of "kira." Some villagers in Bhojpur spoke of obligations to spirits as a burden they would be glad to rid themselves of. They equated spirits to stray dogs—"the more you feed them, the more they keep coming back"—and some people suggested that medicine could enable people to turn their back on these creatures and be free of them once and for all.

17. This conviction leads them to view as a failure responses that indicate that

the trained *dhāmis* "still believe" something. Moreover, the early enthusiasm for finding out what spirits the *dhāmis* dealt with, how they identified different conditions, and what kinds of remedies they undertook diminished once the SCF staff learned what local practices were. The amount of time spent eliciting *dhāmis* understandings, eventually shrank as the amount of time spent on health instruction increased.

18. Compare to Jackson (1995b). In a "shaman school" organized in the Amazon for the purpose of cultural preservation rather than promoting Primary Health Care, similar misapprehensions about the shaman's role and the traditional mode of transmitting esoteric knowledge created contradictions on which the program foundered.

19. Jeffery and Jeffery (1993), criticizing the failure of programs for traditional midwives to consider the social and economic contexts in which women give birth, have pointed out that in north India neither the birth attendant nor the woman giving birth has the power to decide how childbirth will be handled. There, midwives perform a menial, perfunctory service. In the case of shamans in Nepal, ethnographic evidence suggests that people take an active role in deciding whose advice to follow (Stone 1986) and that divinations, rather than being regarded as authoritative pronouncements, become the starting point for a process of community interpretation (Sagant 1987).

20. That the comparison is considered plausible, however, does not mean that it is without tensions and contradictions, due in part to the differences between the two practices that anthropologists have described. Jackson 1995b illustrates this situation in her discussion of a school for indigenous shamans in Colombia.

21. Further research into the trained shamans' perceptions of these programs is needed, however.

22. Jordan (1993), writing on training programs for Mayan midwives, noted over a decade ago that what training programs are most successful in doing is producing midwives who are able to sound and act modern. Midwives applied very little of what they were taught in their practice because knowledge was presented to them in an abstract way divorced from its application in the sorts of situations they actually encounter. Jordan concluded that the midwives nonetheless learn something of value to them—they become more adept at negotiating the institutions of the town and forestalling the criticisms of hospital workers.

23. When development experts propose new models out of their criticisms of old ones, they fail to see that the now discredited models continue to circulate in the social world that has been created by development activities. This is why merely proposing "alternative" development models that contest the terms of previous models does not in itself "correct" past mistakes.

24. For two accounts of the informal practices of medical integration, see Burghart (1984) and Reissland and Burghart (1989).

25. See Burghart 1996 for an insightful discussion of the "conditions for listening" in communication of health information.

26. This point was raised by Emery Roe in the workshop as a challenge to the tendency many of us showed to deconstruct and/or contextualize development knowledge.

27. See Burghart 1993 for an example that unravels the equally decontextualized notion of "indigenous knowledge."

REFERENCES

Abu-Lughod, Lila. 1992. "Writing Against Culture". In *Recapturing Anthropology: Working in the Present*, edited by Richard Fox, 137–62. Santa Fe, N.Mex.: School of American Research Press.

Appadurai, Arjun. 1988. "Putting Hierarchy in Its Place". *Cultural Anthropology* 3: 36–49.

Asad, Talal. 1986. "The Concept of Cultural Translation in British Social Anthropology". In *Writing Culture: The Poetics and Politics of Ethnography*, edited by James Clifford and George Marcus, 141–64. Berkeley: University of California Press.

Black, Jan Knippers. 1991. *Development in Theory and Practice: Bridging the Gap.* Boulder, Colo.: Westview Press.

Burghart, Richard. 1984. "The Tisiyahi Klinik: A Nepalese Medical Centre in an Intracultural Field of Relations". *Social Science and Medicine* 18: 589–98.

———. 1993. "His Lordship at the Cobblers' Well". In *An Anthropological Critique of Development: The Growth of Ignorance*, edited by Mark Hobart, 79–99. London and New York: Routledge.

———. 1996. "The Purity of Water at Hospital and at Home as a Problem of Intercultural Understanding". *Medical Anthropology Quarterly* 10: 63–74.

Dhakal, Ramji, Susie Graham-Jones and Gerald Lockett. 1986. *Traditional Healers and Primary Health Care in Nepal.* Kathmandu, Nepal: Save the Children Fund (UK).

Escobar, Arturo. 1995. *Encountering Development: The Making and Unmaking of the Third World.* Princeton: Princeton University Press.

Fabian Johannes. 1983. *Time and the Other: How Anthropology Makes Its Object.* New York: Columbia University Press.

Foster, George. 1978. "Medical Anthropology and International Health Planning". In *Health and the Human Condition: Perspectives on Medical Anthropology*, edited by Michael H. Logan and Edward E. Hunt, 301–321. North Scituate, R.I.: Duxbury Press.

Gordon, Deborah R. 1988. "Tenacious Assumptions in Western Medicine". In *Biomedicine Examined*, edited by Margaret Lock and Deborah Gordon, 19–56. Dordecht: Kluwer Academic Publishers.

Gupta, Akhil, and James Ferguson. 1992. "Beyond 'Culture': Space, Identity, and the Politics of Difference". *Cultural Anthropology* 7: 6–23.

Jackson, Jean E. 1995a. "Culture, Genuine and Spurious: The Politics of Indianness in the Vaupés, Colombia". *American Ethnologist* 22: 3–27.

———. 1995b. "Preserving Indian Culture: Shaman Schools and Ethno-Education in the Vaupés, Colombia". *Cultural Anthropology* 10: 302–329.

Jeffery, Roger. 1982. "Policies towards Indigenous Healers in Independent India". *Social Science and Medicine* 16: 1835–41.

Jeffery, Roger, and Patricia Jeffery. 1993. "Traditional Birth Attendants in India: The Social Organization of Childbearing". In *Knowledge, Power, and Practice: The*

Anthropology of Medicine and Everyday Life, edited by Shirley Lindenbaum and Margaret Lock, 3–31. Berkeley: University of California Press.

Jordan, Brigitte. 1993. *Birth in Four Cultures: A Cross-Cultural Investigation of Childbirth in Yucatan, Holland, Sweden, and the United States*. Fourth Edition. Revised and expanded by Robbie Davis-Floyd. Prospect Heights: Waveland Press.

Justice, Judith. 1986. *Policies, Plans, and People: Foreign Aid and Health Development*. Berkeley: University of California Press.

———. 1987. "The Bureaucratic Context of International Health: A Social Scientist's View". *Social Science and Medicine* 25: 1301–1306.

Leslie, Charles. 1976. "The Ambiguities of Medical Revivalism". In *Asian Medical Systems*, edited by Charles Leslie, 356–67. Berkeley: University of California Press.

Levitt, Marta. 1987. *A Systematic Study of Birth and Traditional Birth Attendants in Nepal*. John Snow Incorporated/Nepal. October 1987.

Maglacas, A. M., and J. Simons, eds. 1986. *The Potential of the Traditional Birth Attendant*. Geneva: World Health Organization.

Maskarinec, Gregory. 1995. *The Rulings of the Night: An Ethnography of Nepalese Shaman Oral Texts*. Madison: University of Wisconsin Press.

Miller, Caspar J. 1979. *Faith Healers in the Himalayas*. Kathmandu: Ratna Pustak.

Ministry of Health, His Majesty's Government of Nepal. 1990. *Suḍeni tālim tathā kārya sanchālan pustikā (Midwife Training and Supervision Manual)*. Kathmandu: Nepal Ministry of Health.

Oswald, I. H. 1983. "Research Note: Are Traditional Healers the Solution to the Failures of Primary Health Care in Rural Nepal?". *Social Science and Medicine* 17: 255–57.

Packard, Randall M., and Paul Epstein. 1991. "Epidemiologists, Social Scientists, and the Structure of Medical Research on AIDS in Africa". *Social Science and Medicine* 33: 771–94.

Parker, Barbara. 1988. "Ritual Coordination of Medical Pluralism in Highland Nepal: Implications for Policy". *Social Science and Medicine* 27: 919–25.

Peters, Larry. 1979. "Shamanism and Medicine in Developing Nepal". *Contributions to Nepalese Studies* 6: 27–43.

Pigg, Stacy Leigh. 1992. "Inventing Social Categories through Place: Social Representations and Development in Nepal". *Comparative Studies in Society and History* 34: 491–513.

———. 1995a. "Acronyms and Effacement: Traditional Medical Practitioners (TMP) in International Health Development". *Social Science and Medicine* 41: 47–68.

———. 1995b. "The Social Symbolism of Healing in Nepal". *Ethnology* 34: 17–36.

Pillsbury, Barbara L. K. 1979. *Reaching the Rural Poor: Indigenous Health Practitioners Are There Already*. Washington, D.C.: A.I.D. Program Evaluation, Discussion Paper No. One. The Studies Division, Office of Evaluation, Bureau for Program and Policy Coordination, United States Agency for International Development.

———. 1982. "Policy and Evaluation Perspectives on Traditional Health Practitioners in National Health Care Systems". *Social Science and Medicine* 16: 1825–34.

Polgar, Stephen. 1962. "Health and Human Behavior: Areas of Common Interests to Social and Medical Sciences". *Current Anthropology* 3:159–205.

Reissland, Nadja, and Richard Burghart. 1989. "Active Patients: The Integration of Modern and Traditional Obstetrics Practices in Nepal". *Social Science and Medicine* 29: 43–52.

Sagant, Phillippe. 1987. "La cure du chamane et l'interpretation des laics". *L'Ethnographie* 83, no. 100–101: 247–73.

Sargent, Carolyn, and Joan Rawlins. 1992. "Transformations in Maternity Services in Jamaica". *Social Science and Medicine* 35: 1225–32.

Shrestha, Nanda. 1993. "Enchanted by the Mantra of Bikas: A Self-Reflective Perspective on Nepalese Elites and Development". *South Asia Bulletin* 13, no. 1/2: 5–22.

Shrestha, Ramesh, with Mark Lediard. 1980. *Faith Healers: A Force for Change.* Kathmandu: Educational Enterprises, Ltd.

Skinner, Debra, and Dorothy C. Holland. 1996. "Schools and the Cultural Production of the Educated Person in a Nepalese Hill Community". In *The Cultural Production of the Educated Person: Critical Ethnographies of Schooling and Local Practice,* edited by Bradley A. Levinson, Douglas E. Foley, and Dorothy C. Holland. Buffalo, N.Y.: SUNY Press.

Stone, Linda. 1986. "Primary Health Care for Whom? Village Perspectives from Nepal". *Social Science and Medicine* 22: 293–302.

———. 1989. "Cultural Crossroads of Community Participation in Development: A Case from Nepal". *Human Organization* 48: 206–213.

———. 1992. "Cultural Influences in Community Participation in Health". *Social Science and Medicine* 34: 409–418.

Vaughan, Megan. 1991. *Curing Their Ills: Colonial Power and African Illness.* Stanford, Calif.: Stanford University Press.

Verderese, Maria de Lourdes, and Lily M. Turnbull. 1975. *The Traditional Birth Attendant in Maternal and Child Health and Family Planning: A Guide to Her Training and Utilization.* Geneva: World Health Organization.

Woost, Michael. 1993. "Nationalizing the Local Past in Sri Lanka: Histories of Nation and Development in a Sinhalese Village". *American Ethnologist* 20: 502–521.

World Health Organization. 1975. *Traditional Birth Attendants: A Field Guide to Their Training, Evaluation, and Articulation with Health Services.* Geneva: World Health Organization.

———. 1978. *Primary Health Care: Report of the International Conference on Primary Health Care, Alma-Ata, USSR, 6–12 September 1978.* Jointly sponsored by the World Health Organization and the United Nations Children's Fund. Geneva: World Health Organization.

———. 1992. *Traditional Birth Attendants: A Joint WHO/ UNFPA / UNICEF Statement.* Geneva: World Health Organization.

TEN

Senegalese Development

From Mass Mobilization to Technocratic Elitism

Mamadou Diouf

Translated by Molly Roth and Frederick Cooper

Reflections on the crisis of African societies increasingly evolve into interrogations of African knowledges and knowledges about Africa—the knowledges that lay behind the plans set into motion in the 1960s as colonies acceded to independence. The notion that seemed to envelop every ambition, practice, and discourse was unquestionably that of *development*. Development entailed simultaneously imagination, knowledge, and progress toward the realization of the nationalist dream. The term was synonymous with modernization, cultural reconquest and renewal, economic progress, and the achievement of social equity; development implied the construction of nation and citizen as much as the reconstruction of the economy. To many at the time, it was well worth the sacrifice of democracy, the legitimation of authoritarianism, and a monocentric orientation of decision making, mobilization, and organization.

Moments of the same temporality, development, citizenship, and nationality are today the sites of the multiform crises that are shaking African societies. From this perspective, analyses of the notorious failure of African development policies and the impotence of African states point toward the failure of the mechanisms, procedures, and modalities through which development knowledges were implemented. The failure of development, by some accounts, is the new Curse of Ham—an often bitter, sometimes derisory, reflection on a failure, coming from inside as well as outside the African continent.[1] Others have sought a more complete analysis of how African's destiny came to be what it is through approaches styling themselves as "from the bottom up" or seeking a "true historicity" of African societies (Bayart, Mbembe, and Toulabor 1992; Chabal 1986; Sall 1993).

Explanation of the failure of development strategies nonetheless falls short of a minute study of the knowledges and discourses that informed and legitimated the developmentalist implementation. The analysis presented here attempts to fill this absence. It is offered at the same time as a manifesto of an intellectual history that puts the debates and controversies over governance back into the *longue durée* of the continuously renewed and reorganized invention of Africa and African societies. Over the period discussed here—a time of pain, misery, and poverty[2]—the indigenous as well as the exogenous knowledges convened to mobilize populations for the purposes of "development" have been torn apart to the point where the fetish concept of the 1960s has lost any resonance other than the ideological and the "humorous." To attenuate this reversal, new meanings are derived from the concept through the addition of qualifiers—"sustainable, indigenous" development—or, more simply, the terms "adjustment," "recovery," or "stabilization" are substituted for it.

The paradigm of development and national construction as an answer to dependency on foreign markets has given way to the current climate in which open markets growth through exports becomes the central ideological tenet of a national and international development apparatus. I would like to offer an account of this trajectory, focused on the Senegalese situation. In assembling this account of the logics behind social and economic policies, it has been important to identify the modes of acquisition of knowledges and the ways in which they have been put to the test.

From the start, postcolonial countries claimed two rights: recognition of political parity (control over the formal processes of sovereignty, the most decisive of which was the right to nationalize economic sectors) and positive economic discrimination through the institution of a system of economic advantages. These claims—what Samir Amin (1993: 152) characterizes as "radical nationalism" and "catching up"—were consistent with what development economists at the time considered the "failure of markets" and the need for "an active role for governments" (Bates 1991: 262).

An economic script qualified as liberal or neoliberal unfolds from the more recent paradigm. The joint authors of this new breviary for the underdeveloped countries are the World Bank and the International Monetary Fund.[3] The new orthodoxy insists on the strong autonomy of the economic vis-à-vis the political. As Olivier Vallée (1992: 10) rightly observes in regard to governance, master stroke of the new political economy, "it nevertheless establishes private conditionality as the role of the economy and as a limit to the political." It bestows a privileged decision-making role (conditionality) upon international financial organizations. What had until now been state functions are transferred to private enterprises. The basic tenets of the new orthodoxy are: the growth of nations is strongly dependent on their degree of openness to the outside world; global supply depends on the optimal allocation of scarce resources; such an optimum is achieved in a competitive marketplace whose rhythm is imposed by the fluctuations of the world market; development is more rapid where the motives of actors are compatible. These appraisals illustrate "the conviction that the world market will naturally arbitrate in favor of the South's cheaper labor, primary materials, and immense markets."

In discussing the role of governments in the economic performance of developing countries, Robert Bates (1991: 262) puts the accent on the central place accorded to the market in the new economic approaches when he writes:

> The new political economy assumes the existence of perfectly competitive markets and builds its analysis upon the market distortions introduced by governments. These distortions are used to measure the power of private interests and political forces.

Obviously it is not only economic policy and its epistemological and political bases that are being faulted, but more certainly still the institutions and the modalities of training and research devoted to development, whether one is speaking of economics, sociology, or geography.

To follow the traces of this trajectory with reference to the concrete history of Senegal is to focus, therefore, on the constitution of a discourse that instituted a problematic whose paramount function was to develop Senegal. This development was counterpoised in a deliberate manner to colonial exploitation and its alienating project; its object was the production of a new society whose members were mobilized, if not to catch up with the developed nations then at least to bring about economic progress.[4]

The object of this study is not to follow in minute detail the outcomes of the policies implemented by the Senegalese state, but to understand the modes of production of development discourses and their relations with economic, social, and cultural policies. In this pursuit, it is essential to delineate the actors, the stakes, and the mechanisms in order to truly discern the imagination at work in the developmentalist problematic of the Senegalese elite. This study addresses, then, the script (discourse, symbols)—its genesis and its regime of truth—that informed the practices directed at development. In effect, I am concerned with identifying the manner in which this knowledge was constituted, reproduced, legitimated, and transformed over the course of the four decades in question.

THE CONTEXT

Senegalese development discourse, in its variations and its contradictions, has deep roots in a historic tradition whose repertoire and grammar are francophone (but not exclusively) and a temporality whose chronological parameters are the Bandung Afro-Asiatic nations conference of 1955 and the oil price shocks in 1975 and their economic and financial consequences. There are certainly some divergences in significance assigned to facts and events, but the authors who focus on development questions are relatively agreed on the temporal frame: the aftermath of the war. The system that derived from the end of World War II, according to Amin, rested on three pillars: Fordism in the capitalist West, Sovietism in the Eastern Bloc countries, and developmentalism in the countries of the Third World. Each region possessed its own certainties. In the first, Keynesianism; in the second, the myth of catching up to the West through the socialism of the Soviet State; and, in the third, the myth of catching up to the West through interdependence (Amin 1993: 9).[5]

The philosophy that emerged following the Bandung conference and persisted through 1975 is defined as the new developmentalism that was supported by independence, modernization, and industrialization. Amin (1993: 23) thus observes that:

> The emergence of the nations of Asia and Africa, produced by the victory of national liberation, constituted one of the major traits of the epoch. The national liberation movements, as well as the establishment of a dominant world system, posed the issue of development. A new literature increasingly crystallized into a couple or more "theories," if not an ideology of development.

The Bandung ideology was perfected during the conference of Afro-Asiatic peoples in 1958. C. Coquery-Vidrovitch et al. (1988: 11–13, 22) consider that development is at the same time an historical process and an ideological project whose approaches were globalized after Bandung. The principal source of inspiration for the model was of western origin. This universal model rested on a tripartite assemblage: industrialization; urban, scientific, and technological modernity; and the procedures of state centralization. They observe that:

> From the chief of the village to the school, the trade union or the party, there are numerous media through which the developmentalist state:
>
> - attempts to take a total control of civil society,
> - subordinates the old prefectorialized centers of social decision making (native authorities) to the state,
> - diffuses discourses, images, and symbols laden with authority and developmentalist modernity—from which derives the importance of linguistic questions and communication procedures in mobilization practices.

There is agreement between these authors and Amin on the founding act, the date of birth, and the compound structure of the developmentalist model adopted by Europe's old colonies, but the historic perspective of the former makes their investigation the more pertinent. It calls for reflection on the modes of accommodation within other societies to a

> concept so typically western, for so long installed in the history of this part of the world. . . . What did they make of it, when it was imposed on them in its "developmentalist form," that is, in the voluntarist guise of an externally imposed recipe for catching up with the West? (Coquery-Vidrovitch et al. 1988: 33).

This universal form is achieved through the intermediation of a technological culture which Herbert Marcuse (1964) identified not long ago as leading to the abolition of public and private life, social needs and individual needs, and instituting very efficient new forms of social control and cohesion.

The Catholic Church reacted to this situation by giving shape to a developmentalist doctrine and an epistemological tradition whose influence in Senegal was hegemonic in the period immediately following independence. Father Louis-Joseph Lebret, who represented the Vatican in important development conferences of the 1960s and became an influential figure in Senegal's development initiative, insisted on the idea that development "is the dynamic harmonization of old values and new values, of native values and imported values" (cited in de Solages 1992: 26–27).

If Bandung was the point of departure, the first manifestations of a Third World–interest block and discussions on development and underdevelopment were given institutional form with the creation of specialized organizations and centers such as the United Nations (beginning in 1945), the International Institute of Research and Education—Training in Development, the Institute for Research and Application of Development Methods (1957), and the Institute of Applied Economic Science (ISEA, 1944); the Institute for the Study of Economic and Social Development at the University of Paris, with its *Third World Review*, and the Cooperative College (1959) at the École Pratique des Hautes Études, with the publication *Community and Cooperative Life: International Archives of the Sociology of Cooperation*; and Christian groups like the Catholic Committee against Hunger and for Development (1965) and the Pontifical Commission on Justice and Peace (1967).

The establishment of this network of institutions with diverse sources of inspiration, strong Christian religious connotations, and a concern with ethical questions of underdevelopment and hunger led to the institution of a difference between growth and development, in which the human factors were primary,[6] and favored the production of a development literature with its own methods, procedures of sanction and legitimation, and paradigms. The development literature of the Bandung period[7] is abundant and pluralistic, concerning itself with themes as varied as the treatments they undergo. We find in its midst authors whom it is difficult today to imagine as former participants in this activity. This literature assisted, in the Senegalese case, in disrupting and reordering ethnological and colonial knowledges about the territory, the land, the family, the individual, the community/collectivity, the group, the ethnic group, and so on. In these investigations, we witness an attempt to return to native sources, the constitution of a new "library", that of the postcolony, against a colonial "library" (Mudimbe 1989).

THE GREAT BEGINNING: KNOWLEDGES AND INSTITUTIONS IN THE SENEGALESE TRAJECTORY

Senegalese nationalists indeed saw their mission on the eve of independence as a great beginning. To recommence history, definitively seal off the colonial sequence, erase the memory that it engendered in the community, its space, and its political and economic logics, these were the calls to order of the bearers of Senegalese modernity.

In their will to adopt a coherent and systematic procedure, the Senegalese elites fixed on a program legitimated by objectives, an ideology, and knowledge. Léopold S. Senghor, in an article entitled "The Facts of the Problem," defined the reversal of perspective needed to unmake "the colonial version of capitalism." The dominant country, he insisted, had kept the dominated an "agricultural nation: in practice, an underdeveloped country. Because there is no development without industrialization." If the Senegalese leader here took up the classic theme of industrialization, the objectives and the ideology of which his party is the bearer are those of "socialism, it is more than a use of the most efficient techniques, (it is) the meaning of *community* that restores its Africanness" (Senghor 1963: 14, 17).

THE KNOWLEDGES AND THE IMAGINARY OF DEVELOPMENT

To development knowledges and imagination in Senegal are attached two names: Council President Mamadou Dia, second in command under Senghor from 1957 to 1962, and Dominican priest Louis-Joseph Lebret—and, influencing both, the father of the theory of the "new development" path (*nouveau développement*), François Perroux (1981). Even though Dia was thrown out of power in 1962 by Senghor, the direction that he had helped to chart remained in force, at least at the level of discourse and ideological references. The reorganization of knowledge and imagination did not begin until 1975 or become effective before programs for "recovery" in 1979 and "structural adjustment" in 1981.

In *Memoirs of a Third World Militant,* Dia (1985: 114–41) very clearly poses the problematic that guided Senegalese policy in a chapter with the revealing title: "My Three Crimes: Socialism, Nationalism and Islamic Reform." This triptych expresses the three domains of action that were critical to the policy of the Senegalese ruling class:

Socialism refers to a planned social and economic intervention whose essential tool is the ability to nationalize and to direct economic activities from the center. As Dia says,

> Many regarded this undertaking with skepticism. Some were ironic, saying: "A Long Term Development Plan! Who is willing to wait five years to get things running?" . . . Without specific mention of political opponents, all the capitalists of the Senegalese Chamber of Commerce, the intellectuals who are against the idea of a development plan, and the entire private sector dug in their heels, saying "What is this? Is this government going to impose regulations on private firms?" (Dia 1985: 115).

Nationalism was continuous with the choice of a socialism that expressed itself in the Senghorian project to reconstruct the African communities disorganized by colonization and assimilation. This reconstitution was accomplished by breaking with the colonial administrative organization and reforming institutions, in order to link planning to receptive structures.

> This administrative reorganization was designed to facilitate the achievement of the development plan, that is to say, a certain decentralization of powers. . . . as a way to allow a certain transfer of power from the summit to the base. It is for this reason that, at the level of each administrative region, there will be a regional assembly, elected through universal suffrage, with powers, a budget, and a local regional executive which will include the governor and two assistants, one assistant for administrative questions and another for development questions (Dia 1985: 115–16).

Islamic Reform, the final "crime" of Mamadou Dia and his supporters, did not solely make allusion to religious questions. In fact, it posited the necessity of constructing an integral state, capable of reaching the masses directly and without intermediation. The ambition pursued was that of mobilizing the masses, especially the peasants, for the dominant party and the mass movements affiliated with it, and thereby definitively superseding the political entrepreneurs of the colonial period, particularly the leaders of the religious brotherhoods and the defenders of traditional legitimacy. In this undertaking, the cooperative, rural education, and the technical structures of assistance had to serve as levers for social, technical, and political transformation. Dia details very precisely the political aims of his manifestly religious reform program: to transform the legacy of the colonial hierarchy of subordination and thus strike a blow against political intermediaries, the marabouts in particular. On this point, he is quite explicit:

> the touchstone of my policy, my objective, [is] the end of the trade economy (*économie de traite*) ... In these conditions, the entire agricultural economy was socialized, not in the statist sense, but in the sense of self-management. I had just taken a certain number of measures that were of course directed at the capitalist sector but also at the local economic feudalisms constituted by certain maraboutic groups (Dia 1985: 12).

The elements of President Dia's policy, sketched above, were in keeping with the direction of the *Economics and Humanism* movement led by the Dominicans. As Dia (1985) notes, the new government of Senegal decided to appeal to the Dominican priest in the wake of the adoption of a development strategy by the National Council of the Union Progressiste Sénégalaise (UPS) at Rufisque on April 10, 1958, and the establishment of the Study Committees charged with defining Senegal's first development policy. Lebret and his colleagues furnished the Senegalese ruling class with a method: to study the complexities of the reality to be mastered, elaborate a doctrine and create the collective forces intent on putting it into application. Father Lebret wrote,

> In 1958, at the request of the president for a long-term plan and timeline, our research uncovered a civilization irreducible to those previously encountered. During the time that the young Senegalese state sought to structure itself to facilitate harmonized integral development, we were very closely associated with its efforts to understand Senegalese realities and to organize the services necessary for the country's development (Lebret 1956: 12).[8]

This approach was based on the absolute necessity of conducting general studies as preliminaries to the elaboration of a long-term development plan. The conception of development that informs the approach of Father Lebret was borrowed, at least in its formulation, by Raymond Barre who conceived it as

> the process of transforming economic, social, political, and mental structures, which cannot be accomplished in a short time. It assumes that, in the developing economy, *the desire for development will be carried by a courageous political and social elite that assigns itself, as an operating principle, the task of constituting productive capital* (Barre 1958: 81, emphasis added).

The role devolving upon a "political and social elite" in the development project made the Senegalese enterprise a process whose unfolding was a function of the enlightenment of the educated, who attributed to themselves a pedagogic and messianic role. It also established the importance accorded to knowledge, inquiry, and long term perspective studies, as modes of rupture with and/or renewal of the knowledges considered to be colonial.

Beyond the instruments and the modalities of inquiry, which we will analyze in the section on implementation, the analytical tools privileged by the *Centre Économie et Humanisme* team were planning and land use planning (*aménagement du territoire*).[9] Land use planning was the cornerstone of political intervention. It was at the same time the frame for the mobilization of popular energies and support for the work of planning. It was the essential instrument of a new economic cartography and human geography that departed from the colonial logic of exploitation—it aimed at nothing less than the creation of a new rhythm and new needs. It created, in some ways, a new territoriality—that, precisely, of development. Father Lebret defined land use planning as the "crucial operation," attributing to it the objective optimization of the use of resources and development of the space and the units it comprised: "The land use planning is about adaptation to economic and social functions resulting from its relief, its hydrology, its soil, its energy potential, and that which history has already made of it" (Lebret 1956: 44, 46).

Land use planning presents itself here as a form of intervention which did not simply aid the division into regions, into a cartography of economic potentialities and human resources. It had to take root in culture, material culture, and lifestyle. More than any other modality of intervention designed for development, conversion and its procedures embodied the extraordinary nationalist pretension of refounding history—to erase, according to Senghor's poetic expression, the "banania laugh"[10] and, in this way, to connect the process of producing itself to the precolonial memory of Senegambian societies. Fashioned in the interstices of this project infused with a religious morality were a discourse and an imagination distinct to the Senegalese ruling class.

As for planning, it became confused with territorial conversion as the procedure that embraced the totality of development. The most important methodological influence on the conception of planning held by Father Lebret's group derived from the work of Gilles Gaston Granger (1955: 353), who pointed out that,

> To plan is to intervene on the scale of an entire economy to rework both the structure and the function. While therapeutic forms of intervention remain essentially treatments of symptoms, planning seeks to penetrate economic reality from one end to the other and, more precisely, to construct the economy according to available resources.

It is through planning that the *Économie et Humanisme* team rediscovered the notion of "development economics" that it defined in radical opposition to "political economy," considered as a discipline. Development economics integrated all domains of the social sciences. Considered as a system, "development economics supposes a symbiosis between sociological structure and political and social institutions" (Lebret 1956: 47).

The policies of land use and economic planning rested nevertheless on a detailed collection of information of both micro- and macroanalytic design. Macroanalysis was concerned with gathering data on the base at different levels by direct observation and field research, while microanalysis was concerned with the situations, the needs, and the motivations capable of indicating the possibility of a favorable outcome. In the first case,

> The studies of *rather typical family budgets* (in kind, in value), determining the purchases and goods acquired by preference, their nature and price, and, eventually, savings, allow one to obtain an approximation of *commercial networks* and to clarify the macro-analysis (Lebret 1956: 88).

And, in the second case,

> Sociological analysis must extract the *values* of traditional society, the *processes of evolution* of populations, the *resistances* to development, psychosociological motives capable of lending dynamism to development (88–89).

Numerous organizations were established in order to complete the studies: the Compagnie d'Etudes Industrielles et d'Aménagement de Territoire (CINAM, Company for Industrial Studies and Territorial Conversion), the Société d'Etudes et de Réalisations Economiques et Sociales (SERESA, Association for Economic and Social Study and Implementation), and two other companies, one for the study of the potential for rice cultivation in the Haute Casamance and the other devoted to possibilities for the economic exploitation of the Senegal River. Supervision of the sociological study was entrusted to J.-L. Boutillier and that of the biological investigation to Dr. Anne Laurentin, in collaboration with the Office de Recherche sur l'Alimentation et la Nutrition Africaine (ORANA, Office of Research on African Diet and Nutrition). It was in the design of the biological studies that the attempt to overturn colonial ethnological knowledge is most clearly affirmed:

> The state of the population's health can also be assessed by more objective methods. For example, the study undertaken in Senegal has instituted a method of observing and recording anthropometric and biological data that can be carried out by a team of doctors, anthropometrists, nurses and secretaries, studying a fraction of the population (Lebret 1956: 137).

The knowledges put at the disposal of the Senegalese ruling class at the dawn of independence were consistent with the forms of popular mobilization that it had adopted. Nevertheless, its ideology would tend to oscillate between approaches that privileged technical experts and those that assigned a leading role to the population. The true test of the knowledges would have to unfold, according to Senegalese Commissar of Planning Cheikh Hamadou Kane, in three phases:

> First a heuristic phase of inventory designed to circumscribe *the problematic* of Senegalese development; second, a phase of material edification centered on planning; and, finally, third, a systematic effort to prolong material construction through an ideological projection (Kane 1963: 108).

To put in place this vast program, numerous committees and worker's groups were created in addition to institutions of study and research.[11] The reconstruction of the economy, the society, was also a recomposition of the geography produced by colonization. In this sense, it was a will to totalization and homogenization, whose totalitarian and clientelist tendencies, inscribed in the design of the project, collided head-on with the extraordinary diversity and plurality of African societies. It thus opened the way for resistances, circumventions, and/or diversions by the populations confronted with development projects.

DEVELOPMENT PUT TO THE TEST: A NEW GEOGRAPHY

The new geography designed by the Senegalese political elite sought initially to identify the poles capable of sustaining a coherent development project, integrating human and ethnic factors, lifestyles, and natural resources. The first Senegalese Planning Commissioner expressed this concern, at the same time that he insisted on the importance, in the choice of the "Main Guidelines" of a rational interpretation of the needs of individuals, of a definition of the requirements of a modern state, and a detailed inventory of the needs of the country (Kane 1963: 11).

The gap, in practice, between the first two objectives, the pedagogical role that the ruling class assigned itself, and the reinterpretation of African "traditions" through the grid of sociological modernity, made the populations, in spite of the rhetoric, more "directed" than "directing" (*agis* vs. *actants*). From this perspective, the voluntarist act of development, as it is defined by Barre, achieved more in the production of development leaders than in an understanding of the population's development needs and potentials.

The individual needs perspective was central, in the procedure adopted. In the first place, because the definition of these was self-fulfilling, and in the second place, because priorities had to be assigned "without any doubt, to the satisfaction of collective needs over those of individual needs." The logic at work here had as its objectives a resurgence and a new "social structure." They were to be completed by the "use of a common language" and "the sharing of a common culture by the different ethnic groups and the incorporation of the modern world inventions to civilization" (Kane 1963: 110, 111). The material support for this sociological construction was precisely the production of a new territoriality, breaking from the colonial economy and mode of exploitation:

> [Senegal's] government has been structured in function of development and the project of general political and administrative reorganization into homogenous zones, including both large and small regions, should be inspired by the same principle (Lebret 1956: 249n1).

A new development-oriented cartography outlined itself. It attempted to break totally with the colonial geography whose centers were the groundnut-growing basin (zones of agricultural production), the four communes (zones of export), and the import/distribution of manufactured goods. This polarity left large peripheral regions (Eastern Senegal, the valley of the Senegal River) fallow except as the sources of seasonal labor migrations.

The new cartography identified four zones of attraction of varying intensity around St. Louis, Dakar, Kaolack, and Ziguinchor. In the interior of each zone, there was competition between areas of more modest attraction, configured as secondary poles. Two zones were not mapped, Eastern Senegal, where the polarization was indistinct, and the region surrounding the city of Thiès, whose pattern was confounded by the strong territorial influence of Dakar. This reading of Senegalese space was translated into a "representation [which] to be meaningful had to be established on a base map representing the population density, the location and size of the villages of the zone, as well as the means of communication between the poles and the zone" (Lebret 1956: 61).

The result was the creation of the seven administrative regions of Senegal within the schema of the municipality, the cercle, the region, and the nation. This administrative geography produced two notable features: the production of the territory drew its inspiration from the spirit of the nation that was in the course of becoming a reality. It did not take into account the external polarizations; the socioeconomic networks constructed in the course of the colonial episode were radically called into question. It indicated, in effect, that: "The typical composition . . . is that which corresponds not to the current situation, but to a norm that it seems at once possible and desirable to realize, with a maximum delay of 20 years."[12]

The unequal productivity of the zones was the most obvious element of the economic situation. It conditioned political intervention. The typology isolated two spaces—privileged zones and virgin zones—as a means of determining which zones to put into production and the criteria to employ: soil quality, means of communication, industrial potential due to primary materials, energy obtained on site, and, above all, the possibilities of adapting labor to technical functions. In this manner,

> we establish the prosperous zones that can be rationally organized and absorb the population surplus from less favored zones. We thus create conditions of urban life that facilitate the training of a technical and cultural elite as well as an increase in savings. In the second phase, it will become possible to extend effective exploitation to the zones that find themselves in worse condition.[13]

In operating the distinction between "prosperous zones," "poor zones," and "true development zones," the recomposition of geographical space effected a triple distinction among poles: the capital of the region, the capital of the ordinary cercle (which are neither of the region nor of the economic sector) and the major ports, which nevertheless had no administrative role.[14] There were thirty-seven cercles, constituting the basic administrative units. Their radius was approximately thirty kilometers and their population 100,000 inhabitants on average. The creation of these entities had as its objective the identification of sites for the establishment of the administrative, educational, social, sanitation, athletic, and cultural facilities. This orientation was the only one capable, in the spirit of the ruling class, of concentrating, "the investment in the 'strategic areas', from which growth will progressively diffuse throughout the entire economy and favor the appearance of mutually reinforcing complementary activities" (Barre 1958: 69).

The geographic and territorial reordering, in conformity with the developmentalist imagination, was accompanied by putting new life into administrative, economic, and political structures. Within this frame as well, stress was placed on information: the education of children and adults, both formal and informal. In effect, to return to C. H. Kane (1963: 118), "The concern of our planning is double: to guarantee precise communication, complete and rapid, on the one hand, and to ensure the involvement of the rural masses with the development of the country, on the other."

The essential sectors for the planning policy were infrastructure, rural production, the fishing industry, the training of farmers, pastoralists, and fishers; the control of adults; and the education of the young (Kane 1963: 114). The totalizing project directed the transformation of human resources in the most vigorous possible manner. As far as education was concerned, each village of at least 150 inhabitants was to have a rural school of three grades with a double program: one in the dry season (5 months) devoted to the acquisition of general knowledge and one, in the rainy season (four months), to agricultural courses and field work. Only the most gifted students would be oriented toward secondary education (in the regional centers) and higher education (in the national capital).[15]

Natives of a region were given priority in the training and posting of schoolteachers. The teacher had to be from the region in which he taught because the task that was assigned to him was above all that of rural leader. The functional character of the contents of the school curriculum and the continuing education of adults created the cultural requirement to train female schoolteachers and managers for the work of women's groups and women's education programs to train female teachers and women leaders.[16] The ensemble of these educational activities was known under the generic name of "animation." It was a distinctive mark of Senegalese socialism.

The second pole of intervention was the cooperative, which was simultaneously to be the site of educational activities, the liberation of the peasantry, and the realization of development. The cooperative was the basic mechanism for the socialization of peasants. It was to be a structure of production, marketing, and diversification of rural production. Nevertheless, the primary purpose of the cooperative was the business of political liberation: "I aimed in this way at the creation of a regional political power built up from the base, because it was the peasants who would become the masters of the game" (Dia 1985: 116).

To turn the peasants toward the acquisition of a technical competence that is the condition of entry into modernity, numerous structures were put in place. They are presented as follows by Dia (1985: 116, emphasis added):

> the Regional Development Committee [CER, Comité Régional de Développement], which was to elaborate regional development plans and which represented an effort to integrate the different technical services . . . , with also a sort of center for technical assistance in the form of CRAD, that is to say, the Regional Center for Development Assistance, which replaced the old SMDR (Mutual Societies for Rural Development). The latter were until that time in the hands of politicians. *I was resolved to displace these by loosening their grasp. It was a hard fight as the politicians took advantage of them for their own profit.*

It is paradoxical that while continuing to make reference to industrialization as the basis for development, the Senegalese ruling class devoted its energies to the peasants and to the rural world. Education of the rural peasantry was the leitmotiv of the Senegalese ruling class. The Rural Education Centers were present at the regional level to supply their assistance to the cooperatives. According to the former president of the Senegalese Council:

> Assuredly, one of the essential originalities of this policy was the launching of Rural Education, most probably the connecting link missing from all co-

operative policies to date, which do not put instruments of training at the service of the peasantry (Dia 1985: 116).

The determination of the Senegalese ruling class to control the population and to mobilize it for the tasks of economic and social development was translated concretely by the establishment of the single party from 1966 to 1974. The logic of "encadrement" went hand in hand with the association of traditional intermediaries (marabouts, traditional chiefs) and political entrepreneurs with state mechanisms of political and economic power.

Three instruments, enjoying diverse fortunes, were used in the course of this sequence: total control of economic and financial activity through the creation of public and parapublic enterprises—the entrepreneurial state; cooperatives of agricultural production which excluded women, the young, and the non-peanut growing zones; and the predominance of membership in the party or its affiliates (youth movement, women's movement, trade unions), as a qualification for a role in the state apparatus, structures of production or commercialization, often to the detriment of competence for the selection of civil servants and businessmen to be financed by the public development bank. The direction of the initiative was still from top down; the state attributed to itself a pedagogical role, it directed and the population enacted. No initiative was left to the latter.

Even if one has to admit that the totalizing enterprise was never fully realized in the terms of its basic schema, it continued to be pursued after the fall of its principal author, Mamadou Dia, in 1962. We will not dwell overly on the reasons for this failure. It should nevertheless be noted that the project was not carried out by those at whom it was directed. More precisely, the political entrepreneurs were able to successfully resist the Diaist enterprise. The marabouts[17] developed a certain capacity to turn the new structures to their advantage, they gained a direct foothold, for the first time, in the modern sectors (the cooperatives and the CERS). The traders who controlled the most important economic network, the groundnut network, were the principal victims of this policy. If the Lebano-Syrians and the old colonial commercial houses were able to resist and to redeploy in other sectors, the indigenous traders disappeared from the economic scene and then from the political scene.[18] The creation of the Senegalese Development Bank (BSD) and a Bureau for European Marketing of groundnuts, definitively sealed off the trading economy from the traders. The other adversaries of this policy, to the extent that they are listed in *Mémoires*, were certain segments of the party in power (UPS) who initiated the process of ousting Mamadou Dia by registering a motion of censure in the National Assembly and the Dakar Chamber of Commerce where metropolitan interests were represented: "It was said that I provoked divestment, by my policy . . . that Capital was afraid. Of course, Capital was afraid. . . . When one takes measures of this nature, capital is discouraged" (Dia 1985: 120–21).[19]

THE RESULTS

The project of totalization and systematic control of the procedures of socialization is at the origin of the great reforms of the independent Senegalese state: the Law of National Domain (1964), the Family Code (1972), and the reform of local and territorial administration (1974). Each was designed to lessen the gap between the administration and the administered, to better supervise the population with an eye to harmonizing social practices and the rules of economic exploitation of natural resources, and, above all, to create national cohesion by mobilizing the whole of Senegalese society for the achievement of the project of African socialism.

This ideal led to the establishment of a policy of price controls on one side and a stabilization of prices to agricultural producers on the other. As stated in a diagnostic of the condition of the Senegalese economy, "For more than twenty years, the system of price controls has remained the crown jewel of the policy of income redistribution and solidarity between the urban and the rural populations organized by the state."[20] To ensure the success of its enterprise, the Senegalese state attributed to itself the role of entrepreneur, industrialist, merchant, farmer, and transporter. The control of the economy by the state was completed in 1969 with the establishment of the National Office of Agricultural Marketing and Development (ONCAD) to control the totality of the groundnut economy. Previously, in 1968, the Society for Development and Popularization of Agriculture (SODEVA) was created to take charge of the supervision of the peasantry and the dissemination of agricultural information. The structures of control rested on a vast system of cooperatives—of which 80 percent were in place in 1963—that had as their essential mission to furnish inputs and manage credit in the groundnut-producing basin.

These reforms were premised on the Law of National Domain of 1964, which allowed the state to intervene in property ownership, from which the colonial administration had been almost entirely absent. It instituted three regimes, a private realm which represented 2 percent of the surface of the national territory, a state realm (3 percent), and a national domain (95 percent). The Law of National Domain aimed

(i) to control the attempt to introduce private property ownership, (ii) to improve traditional systems of land management, often based on feudal relations, (iii) to create uniformity in the principles of land tenure beyond regional differences.[21]

State direction of the economy was completed through the creation, in 1973, of the Office of Price Control and Stabilization (CPSP) charged with the control of prices for principal commodities, import and export, and the establishment in 1974 of the National Senegalese Oil Marketing Company (SONACOS), following the repurchase of the groundnut-oil facilities from the French firm Lesieur. The move toward state control was reinforced by the 1974 to 1977 period during which, thanks to the high prices for phosphates and groundnuts, the Senegalese state had financial resources at its disposal,

> at the height of its ambitions in the social sector. Faced with accumulating budgetary excesses, the Government raised the lowest salaries by 82 percent and the highest salaries by 3 percent in 1974; the price to the groundnut producer (was raised) 30 percent in 1974 and 38 percent in 1975. In tandem, the parapublic sector continued to expand with total administrative expenditures growing 78 percent between 1974 and 1977.[22]

The explosion of groundnut and phosphate prices, between 1973 and 1977, aided consumption above all, from the maintenance of a bold policy of recruitment and remuneration, to financial transfers from the public treasury to public enterprises, and above all to state initiative in the capitalization of enterprises. Table 10.1 shows the evolution of the public sector over the course of this period.

The extension of the parapublic sector was accompanied by a program promoting Senegalese businessmen, to whom the state generously awarded import licenses, administrative contracts and extensive access to credit, facilitated by rapid advances in internal credit beginning in 1975 and the relaxation of private loans from developed to developing countries, for the purpose of recycling petrodollars.[23]

A rapid review of the economic and social development plans corroborates the reading of an economy that failed to reflect the scarcity of resources, but that, through excess, artificially created a feeling of ease. The first plan (1961/1962 and 1964/1965) put a priority on the development or the creation of enterprises in the commercial sector; the second (1965/1966) and the third (1971/1972), even if they marked a pause in financial investment, accelerated the expenditures on social equipment and transport and telecommunications infrastructure. Resources continued to be oriented toward agricultural production; the creation of new organs of control continued; and, in the wake of the adoption of a strategy of import-substitution, local industry benefited from reinforced protection. In this way, economic activities were submitted to administrative control without exposure to market forces.

TABLE 10.1   Number of Establishments in
Public Sector

Branch	1962	1972	1977
Agriculture	4	8	9
Industry	4	9	17
Commerce/Services	10	26	43
Financial Institutions	2	5	6
Administration	1	2	8
Total	21	50	83

SOURCE: Commission de Vérification et de Contrôle de Comptes des Établissements Publiques, Dakar, August 1983.
NOTE: The number of jobs in the public sector went from 37,000 in 1973 to 70,300 in 1983.

The consequence was the emergence of a logic of retreat in the non-public spheres on the parts of the principal actors of social life with, as a corollary, the development of an attitude of total irresponsibility on the parts of those associated with power. In fact, political protection that guaranteed impunity generalized bad management, clientelism, corruption, and the total absence of sanctions, positive or negative.

However, alongside this absence of involvement by the population in the structures and institutions of control (youth groups, women's groups, trade unions, and so on), we witness a proliferation of informal and community-based activities and a resurgence of networks of kinship, age classes, youth groups, women from the same neighborhood, reinventing economic, social and cultural structures to contain the totalizing thrust of political and administrative power.

This duality explains to a very large extent the ambiguity of the Senegalese situation, between the failure of formal institutions and activities and the vitality of informal activities, traditional or other. The enormous potential of these activities, attitudes and behaviors, breaking with statist logics, attained its veritable apogee with the crisis of the 1980s and 1990s.

The large-scale changes that manifested themselves in the course of these years were at the center of the nefarious effects of the crisis. No sector was spared. The great successes of the 1960s and 1970s in the domains of health and education were called into question by the adoption of structural adjustment policies. The debate between the partisans of relaxation of labor market legislation and those of trade unions and social policies posed the problem of the end of the era of the providential state.

LE RETOURNEMENT DU MONDE
[THE WORLD TURNED UPSIDE DOWN][24]

To the next period corresponds a transformation in the modalities of management of the Senegalese economy and the arrival of a new social category in the inner sanctum of power. This new segment was designated under the sign of technocracy—it was opposed to the nationalist politicians of the independence period (Diop and Diouf 1990). The arrival of technocracy did not correspond precisely with the political and economic crisis that rocked Senegal, but followed on the political crisis of 1968–1971 that resulted in the reform of the administrative system and attempts to loosen centralization by devolution. Two steps illustrate the vagaries of the reform: the creation of the post of Prime Minister and the cooptation of a new generation of graduates of the university and the old colonial administrative academies into the ruling class (Fatton 1986).

The new knowledges that were put in place, well before the adoption of the idioms of the World Bank and the International Monetary Fund, were produced by the principal forces behind the *Club Nation et Développement*. They privileged expertise to the detriment of mass movements and popular mobilization. They considered that competence must gain the lead over political clientelism at any cost.[25]

Nevertheless, the best illustration of the reversal was the emergence of a new political repertoire for the analysis of the economic and financial crisis and the remedies proposed. Two expressions capture the ambiance of the period: "the disengagement of the state" and "Minimal State, more efficient State" (*Moins d'Etat, Mieux d'Etat*).

THE CAUSES OF THE CRISIS

It is difficult to follow the thread of the readings of the crisis produced by the ruling class and the Senegalese administration. In effect, they were continuously evolving. The identified causes of the crisis continued to be enumerated, whether by local experts or international ones. The base references are those of the World Bank, the International Monetary Fund, and the agencies of aid and cooperation. These readings have a clearly expressed objective: resolving the question of how to reconstruct African economies. The questioning and the responses were defined by the neoliberal context that proclaimed the primacy of technical competence to the neglect of political competence.

The neoliberal discourse that places the accent on a system of conflicting interests subordinates social existence to the logic of the market. It affirms, in an imperious manner, the dichotomy economic sphere/noneconomic sphere, thus reorganizing social space, economic policies, and political functions. It deconstructs the logic of social totalization that was at the heart of the nationalist vision of development. This, of course, is not a discourse about development but about its conditions of possibility. It is a discourse about growth. The urgent necessity to act against external constraints, which had been the basis for the construction of a viable economy, is called into question. This orientation becomes the cause of the poor performance of African economies. Neither autonomous national growth vis-à-vis the world market nor a delinking that puts an end to international exploitation produces growth and/or economic vitality.

The inversion of the discourse at the end of the 1970s was accomplished step by step. To the symbolic value that was attached to the eviction of foreign capital and nationalization was opposed the indispensable requirement to create favorable conditions for foreign investment, preferably private. The attempts at delinking as an economic preference (as in the Lomé Accords) would have had as their sole consequence the marginalization of Africa and/or its exclusion from the world market due to non-competitiveness. In effect, the only way out of the crisis lay in export-led growth. To the centrality of politics and the motive force of the state was now opposed the surreptitious undermining of certain attributes of political sovereignty, provoked by the claim of an autonomous economic sphere. The consequence was a dissolution of the political that accentuated the marginality of the representative assemblies and the centralization of decision-making processes, restricting them to the presidency and the Ministry of Economy and Finance (Diop and Diouf 1990: 148–83).

This perspective led to the emergence of an administrative personnel who more and more escaped the hierarchical system and whose legitimacy was, rather, a function of international organizations. On these latter was conferred the power to elucidate the causes of the economic and financial crisis—a power without common measure with that of the elected assemblies.

The conclusion of the experts, inside and outside Senegal, was that the cause of the crisis was the overly central role of the state and its protectionist policies, and its consequences were stagnation of per capita GNP (which grew an annual average of .6 percent from 1960 to 1992), weak economic growth, compensated by public assistance and commercial loans. Mamadou Dia's attempt to reform the colonies' economic model had failed. Senegal was still caught in specialization in groundnut production and import substitution limited to light industry. The crisis in the groundnut economy in 1967–1968, despite the rise in world prices in the 1970s, and the limits of the strategy of import substitution, led to ineffective investment and little growth. Local savings and financial investment capacity declined, and Senegal became even more dependent on foreign finance. Foreign capital—capital transfers above all—posed a major constraint on the possibilities for expanding local finance.

This new knowledge put on the marketplace of ideas a powerful conclusion: public savings, the rate of investment, and the material base of the Senegalese economy remained weak while Senegalese dependence on foreign aid had become structural. Political management of the economy—through the logics of clientelism and patronage, excessive Africanization of managerial staff, "Senegalization" of the economy through the extension of the public and parapublic sectors and the policy promoting Senegalese businessmen—had brought about Senegal's macroeconomic destruction.[26]

THE NEW ECONOMIC POLICY

It was the recognition of an unprecedented crisis that drove the Senegalese authorities to put in place a program of economic reforms whose two objectives were: to reestablish financial equilibrium and to ensure the conditions for healthy and sustainable growth. This measure was not to compromise the bases for development (quality of human resources, training, and infrastructure). Planning was henceforth abolished as an instrument of economic policy. Certainly, since the 1970s it had not been more than an empty shell which functioned as a rhetorical reference. Management of the economy, beginning with projects financed by foreign funds, constituted from then on the backbone of investment and offered possibilities for diversions of public funds and support of a clientele.

The ferocious critique that the technocrats produced, in league with the international organizations, had a very rapid translation, initially in terms of the evaluation of prior policies but also in terms of proposals for new policies. In legitimating itself through the production of a discourse, technocracy delegitimated, in the same blow, recourse to the masses. Technocracy attributed to itself an expertise (diagnostic and remedial) that rested on a total mastery of the vocabulary and techniques (statistics, modeling, tables, graphs) of international organizations.

The narrative that was at the heart of the regime of truth of the nationalist episode blurred; the mathematico-statistical style erected itself in the matrix of discourse with, of course, the ultimate consequence of a thrifty rationality of words and a greed for graphics. Dryness and the hard reality of numbers were substituted for the lyric flights of the nationalist economic utopia.

The new Senegalese economic policy was put to the test with the adoption of three economic and financial programs: a stabilization program (1979), an economic and financial recovery plan (PREF 1980), and a program of medium-term and long-term economic and financial adjustment (PAML 1985–1992).

The stabilization program was elaborated and put into practice under the presidency of Senghor. It was a response to the conditionalities of the multilateral donors in the face of imbalances due to an imprudent policy of indebtedness—a rise in the prices of wheat, gas, and rice (1972–1974), in order to obtain

> concessionary resources and to face up to the degradation of the economic situation born of the exceptional amplitude of the imbalances: the deficit and the current balance represent 16 percent of the GNP in 1979 and 1980, as against approximately 8 percent in the past; the deepening of the budgetary deficit leads to a massive indebtedness of the public and parapublic sectors to the banking system; the expansion of credit to rates averaging 25 percent a year between 1973 and 1979 feeds the pressures on prices and the balance of payments.[27]

In fact the borrowing capacity of Senegal deteriorated at the same time that the prices of groundnuts and phosphates began a rapid decline on the world market. The stabilization program was designed to rein in and then to halt the worsening of the external position and public finances. In certain respects, it prepared the way for economic and financial adjustment. The privileged domains of intervention for the policy of stabilization were: a reform of budgetary policy with the diminution of the number of embassies and an initial attempt to control the payroll; an investment policy that set productive priorities; restrictions in access to credit through limitation of the money supply, and

> the institution of a solidarity tax to finance development operations and social assistance in the rural world. This tax, applied to salaries in the public and private sectors was in fact a response to peasants' dissatisfaction (*malaise paysan*) and to rural protest, relayed by the marabouts, over a policy of free-market prices that entailed a rise in the cost of basic necessities (Diop and Diouf 1990: 167).

The stabilization program did not achieve the objectives set at the time of its adoption. Government experts attributed its failure to external constraints.[28] If the first element was one of the standard referents of the Senegalese regime's explanatory mechanism—economic difficulties and necessary sacrifices—the second, in contrast, was a new term, disguising one of the forms of criticism to which technocracy submitted the politicians of the regime. This critique became more and more overt with the growing ascendancy of the technocrats at the center of power.

Following the stabilization program, a plan of economic and financial recovery was adopted in 1980, to address the persistent degradation of public finances which were an indicator of the economy's vulnerability to external shocks. The government confirmed its intention to apply a laissez-faire policy with regard to prices. Salaries and the prices of basic necessities were readjusted, moreover, and in 1985–1986 rice and petroleum prices were increased to collect additional public revenue.[29] And it was precisely over the course of this period that Senegal submitted its economic and financial performance to criteria established by the IMF.

The innovations of the PREF were principally a total transformation of planning procedures by the adoption of a long-term perspective (with the horizon of a generation) and a reorganization of the public and parapublic sectors. According to government experts, encouraging results were obtained thanks to the PREF:

> The budgetary deficit (obligations) has been solidly declining since 1983/ 1984; the deficit of the current account has also routinely been tied to GNP between 1983 and 1986; after the poor harvest of 1983/1984, the real growth of per capita GNP continued to be significant for three years: inflation fell noticeably; the sums allocated to back-payments grew from year to year; a stabilization plan followed by a reduction of the public payroll was decided.[30]

This policy, whose style and terms of reference corresponded to the new modes of economic expression, definitively broke free from a development discourse founded on the primacy of politics and popular mobilization. It incontestably affirmed the appropriation of economic policy by the technocrats and passage from the register of the conjuncture to that of the structure as an explanation for the underdevelopment of the Senegalese economy. From this point on, there was a shift from development as a political vocation to growth as, initially, the task of reestablishing macro-economic equilibrium—and with it, the government of African economic affairs by donors. This sequence began in Senegal with the adoption of the medium-term and long-term program of economic and financial adjustment.

Analysis of this program reveals the interesting fact that it actually prolonged the decade-long policy of rigorous management of demand by the Senegalese government. In contrast to the image of an about-face promoted by the international financial institutions, the Senegalese state undertook to stimulate supply in order to contain the social dimensions of adjustment. The state attempted to reform the institutions of administrative control and adopted the New Agricultural Policy (NPA) and the New Industrial Policy (NPI). The accent was henceforth put on private initiative, the accountability of economic actors, and the institution of incentives for production and export. Government experts insisted on the following elements in their assessment of the program:

> The pursuit of a prudent monetary policy and reform of the banking sector;

launching of fiscal and customs reforms to harmonize legal and regulatory statutes in force in the realms targeted by the PAML and to reinforce administrative structures; actions to reduce, indeed to suppress, the distortions that hamper transactions in the markets in different commodities, services, and factors of production; and pursuit of the process of privatization and disengagement of the state.[31]

These experts assert that there was "backsliding" (*dérapages*), part of the strong resistance of the political class in power in the face of the attempt to destabilize its prebendal political system. The gap between the socialist discourse of the regime and its liberal economic practice illustrates, in a derisory and comical manner, the end of the enterprise of development. One vocabulary chases out the other. A new technology and a new, exclusively economic, knowledge substitute themselves for the nationalist dream of economic development and social equality, discarding the notion of social effectiveness in the name of economic efficiency.

CONCLUSION

The trajectory of Senegalese development discourses and practices was uneven. Over time, knowledge and imagination have been invested in political struggles within the regime and between the regime and its opposition. It is nevertheless a trajectory in two moments because the defeat of Mamadou Dia and the presidential power of Senghor, after 1962, did not in the slightest threaten the prospective enterprise of social and economic totalization. The reasons for Senghor's abdication of the initial developmentalist schema reside not in the tightly knit mesh of Senegalese society, but in the transfer of the centers of political and social decision making to the sites of a new power. Traditional and/or colonial political entrepreneurs were able to invest in and subvert the new social and political logics. In contrast to the violence that attended certain developmentalist undertakings, the victorious resistance of the political configuration derived from the colonial system is one of the principal lessons of postcolonial Senegalese history.

The society was not able to make concrete the reordering premised on a break with the past, and the popular classes were not mobilized to take charge of a project of which they were, according to the principal promoters, the beneficiaries. The latter, on the contrary, very early took refuge in the spaces of other identities, reaffirming the primacy of religious and ethnic affiliations. The pedagogic project of the ruling class was transmuted into a self-reflexive discourse, into a mythology serving the petite bourgeoisie. It tried to reinforce this developmentalist discourse through recourse to the outside, before throwing itself body and soul into the technocratic enterprise, appropriating neoliberal discourse—with its statistics and graphs—and the symbolic apparatus of the "good governance" campaign.

The remaking of the Senegalese economy and the reform of government, underway since the adoption of the stabilization program, have not even begun to achieve the expected results. Nevertheless, they have contributed to the dismantling of the bases of the ideological legitimacy of the ruling class descended from the nationalist period. The new technocracy, by containing its critique within the economic domain, contents itself with repeating the rhetoric and emptying it of content, above all in its popular and ethnic dimension. The ability of the new policies to solve the structural problems of the Senegalese economy remains unclear nearly two decades into the period of reform, and the efforts of the technocrats paradoxically reproduce the basic characteristic of the era of nationalism and development: a capacity to realize their goals through language—and only through language.

NOTES

1. See, for example, the "Afro-pessimist" school as represented in the issue entitled "La Malédiction" [The Curse] of *Cahiers d'Etudes Africaines* (1991); Ka (1993), Manguelle (1990), Kabou (1991); or the reassessment by leaders of France's foreign policy "establishment" regarding their relationship to African development in Michailof (1993). African states have been called "prebendal" (Joseph 1987), "mercenary" (Sandbrook 1993), "predatory" (Fatton 1992), "patrimonial" (Médard 1991), and "masticating" (Bayart 1995). But such descriptions may substitute for analysis of the renewed invention of political Africa (see also Mudimbe 1989; Appiah 1992). See also the assessment of development knowledge—in effect in the archiving of outdated paradigms—in Robineau (1993), Choquet, Dollfus, LeRoy and Vernières (1993), and Davidson (1992).

2. See the *Poverty Profiles* of the World Bank and the literature on the strategies of "Poverty Alleviation" and the ferocious critique of Hancock (1989).

3. This new orthodoxy, described as "private reason" by Vallée (1992), has the 1989 World Bank Report *Sub-Saharan Africa: From Crisis to Sustainable Growth* as its founding reference.

4. The construction of a new society and the "catching up with the West," which are two aspects of the nationalist ideology, are in Amin's view (1993: 7) antinomial, because for him the alternative in 1960 was delinking (to break away from the Western model and create a new society and economy) or adopting the Western model and remaining underdeveloped.

5. On questions of the definition and historiography of the concept, see also Coquery-Vidrovitch, Hemery, and Piel (1988), and de Solages (1992).

6. Here I am thinking of Dominican Father Louis-Joseph Lebret, founder of the Centre Économie et Humanisme (1942), as well as of the Catholic-run conferences, Semaines Sociales, of which the thirty-fifth, in 1945, was devoted to "People Overseas and Western Civilization," and of François Perroux, founder of ISEA,

which published the *Cahiers de l'ISEA*. These two Frenchmen were close to the heart of Senegalese methods and practices (see below). Mamadou Dia, President of the Senegalese Council (1958–1962), writes on the subject: "I began to undertake theoretical economic studies in reading many of the works at the Senate Library which I frequented regularly. I came across the publications of 'Économie et Humanisme' where I discovered texts by Deprat, Lebret, Perroux; that led me to the center directed by Perroux where I made his acquaintance" (1985: 65).

7. Of this literature, I only cite the authors who particularly influenced the Senegalese nationalist elite: Perroux's writing in *Cahiers de l'ISEA* (1955–1957); Lebret (1942, 1956); Dia (1953); Hoselitz (1952); Barre (1958); Galbraith (1952); Myrdal (1957); and Touré (1959). It should be underlined that Touré's paper is the only contribution to the conference where it was presented dealing with economic issues and its author was the minister of planning and cooperation and minister of economy and finance and, both before and after his ministerial appointments, director of the Africa Department of the International Monetary Fund. He is the architect of Senegal's adjustment policy.

8. The previous experiences of the *Économie et Humanisme* team had been with the French fishing industry and the coastal population (in 1938), housing and urbanism in the cities of Lyon, St. Étienne, Marseille, and Nantes (in 1945), and urbanism in a Brazilian city (in 1958).

9. It is important to note that planning and land use planning were a response to "underdevelopment" as it is defined by Moussa (1961: Appendix 1, 456) and in Sauvy's ten tests of underdevelopment (1951: 604; 1952: 241).

10. The reference is to a notorious advertisement of 1915, showing a grinning African soldier eating a canned food preparation.

11. Notably, the Committee of Economic Studies, another for social problems, and workers' groups from different sectors: General Studies, Rural Economy, Industry and Basic Equipment, Commerce and Exchange, Accounting and Financial Circuits. These different efforts gave birth to two documents that informed Senegalese policy during the period from 1960 to 1975: The *Rapport sur les Perspectives*, Government of Senegal, National Printing House, June 1960, and *Étude Générale sur le Développement du Sénégal*, Government of Senegal, 16 Vols.

12. Excerpt from the "Programme d'Aménagement des Pôles," *Rapport Sénégal*, II, 5, pp. 20–25.

13. Ibid., 20.

14. Ibid., 20–21.

15. Ibid., II, 3, pp. 22–23.

16. Ibid.

17. On this question of the relations with the Muslim leaders and the clientelist system of borrowing financial resource and equipment without paying back the loans, Dia (1985: 121) is very informative. He insists that his opposition to such colonial and clientelist mechanisms explain somehow the collapse of his regime. The appearance of communal fields, for the profit of the collectives and to the detriment of "the marabouts' fields," provoked the hostility of the religious brotherhoods.

18. Dia (1985: 121) notes: "The policy of setting up cooperatives was a blow

not only to economic interests of indigenous traders, but also to the marabouts who are also traders."

19. Dia (1985: 121–22) recounts his encounters with Charles Henri Gallenca, who was president of the Chamber of Commerce for more than a decade: "I remember discussing Senegalese Socialism with the president of the Dakar Chamber of Commerce, Gallenca. He said that he was for socialism only if it takes care of unprofitable economic sectors and that we transfer these to the private capitalist sector to the extent that they become profitable through the effects of the Development Plan."

20. Ministry of Economy and Finance, Dakar, "Diagnostic de l'économie Sénégalaise," 1993, Mimeograph.

21. Ibid.

22. Ministry of Economy and Finance, December 1992, "Groupe Options de Politique Économique," p. 7, photocopy.

23. Ibid.

24. This title is borrowed from Badie and Smouts (1992).

25. On the discourse of the technocrats, see *Le Soleil* December 19–20, 1979; R. Fatton, Paper for the 28th Annual Conference of the African Studies Association, New Orleans, Louisiana, November 23–26, 1985; and Diop and Diouf (1992).

26. The construction of this reading can be followed through the literature of the international organizations and that produced by the Senegalese technocracy in its efforts to legitimate its power. See World Bank, *Senegal, an Economy under Adjustment* Dakar, World Bank 1987, mimeograph; "Rapport 6454 SE," République Française, Ministère des Relations Extérieures, Coopération et Développement, *Evaluation. Déséquilibres structurels et Programme d'ajustement Structurel au Sénégal,* Paris, March 1985, 3 vols.; République du Sénégal, *Le Plan d'Ajustement Structurel au Sénégal,* Dakar, February 1987, 2 vols.; Confédération Nationale des Travailleurs du Sénégal (CNTS), "La Classe Ouvrière face aux défis du FMI et de la Banque Mondiale: Déclaration de la CNTS," Dakar, September 25, 1989.

27. "Groupe Options de Politique Économique," 8.

28. Ibid.

29. Ibid.

30. Ibid., 9.

31. Ibid.

REFERENCES

Amin, Samir. 1993. *Itinéraire intellectuel.* Paris: L'Harmattan.

Appiah, Anthony Kwame. 1992. *In My Father's House: Africa in the Philosophy of Culture.* New York: Oxford University Press.

Badie, Bertrand, and Marie Claude Smouts. 1992. *Le Retournment du monde: Sociologie de la scène internationale.* Paris: Presses de la Fondation des Sciences Politiques.

Barre, Raymond. 1958. "Le développement économique. Analyse et politique". *Cahiers de l'INSEAA,* series F, no. 11.

Bates, Robert. 1991. "A Critique by Political Scientists". In *Politics and Policy Making in Developing Countries: Perspectives on the New Political Economy*, edited by G. M. Meier, 261–76. San Francisco: ICS Press.

Bayart, Jean-François. 1995. *The State in Africa. The Politics of the Belly*. London: Longman (English translation of *L'Etat en Afrique: La Politique du ventre*, 1989).

Bayart, Jean-François, Achille Mbembe, and C. Toulabor. 1992. *La Politique par la bas en Afrique Noire*. Paris: Karthala

Cahiers d'Études Africaines. 1991. Special issue, *La Malédiction* 31, no. 1–2.

Cahiers de l'ISEA [Institut des Sciences Economiques Appliquées]. 1955–1957.

Chabal, Patrick, ed. 1986. *Political Domination in Africa*. Cambridge: Cambridge University Press.

Choquet, C., O. Dollfus, E. Le Roy, and M. Vernières, eds. 1993. *État des savoirs sur le développement: Trois décennies de sciences sociales en langue française*. Paris: Karthala.

Coquery-Vidrovitch, Catherine, Daniel Hemery, and Jean Piel, eds. 1988. *Pour une histoire de développement: états, sociétés, développement*. Paris: L'Harmattan.

Davidson, Basil. 1992. *The Black Man's Burden: Africa and the Curse of the Nation-State*. London: Currey.

de Solages, O. 1992. *Réussites et déconvenues du développement dans le Tiers Monde*, Paris: L'Harmattan.

Dia, Mamadou. 1953. *Réflexions sur l'économie de l'Afrique Noire*. Paris: Présence Africaine.

———. 1985. *Mémoirs d'un militant du Tiers Monde: Si mémoire ne ment*. Paris: Publisud.

Diop, Momar Coumba, and Mamadou Diouf. 1990. *Le Sénégal sous Abdou Diouf*. Paris: Karthala.

Fatton, Robert. 1986. *The Making of a Liberal Democracy: The Senegalese Passive Revolution, 1975–1985*. Boulder, Colo.: Lynne Rienner Publishers.

———. 1992. *Predatory Rule: State and Civil Society in Africa*. Boulder, Colo.: Lynne Rienner Publishers.

Galbraith, John Kenneth. 1952. *American Capitalism: The Concept of Countervailing Power*. Boston: Houghton-Mifflin.

Granger, Gilles Gaston. 1955. *Méthodologie économique*. Paris: PUF.

Hancock, Graham. 1989. *Lords of Poverty: The Power, Prestige, and Corruption of the International Aid Business*. New York: Atlantic Monthly Press.

Hoselitz, Bertrand F. 1952. *The Progress of Underdeveloped Areas*. Chicago: University of Chicago Press.

Joseph, Richard. 1987. *Democracy and Prebendal Politics in Nigeria*. Cambridge: Cambridge University Press.

Ka, Mana. 1993. *L'Afrique va-t-elle mourir? Essai d'éthique politique*. Paris: Karthala.

Kabou, Axelle. 1991. *Et si l'Afrique refusait le développement?* Paris: L'Harmattan.

Kane, Cheikh Hamadou. 1963. In *Développement et socialisme: Colloque sur les politiques de développement et les diverses voies Africaines vers le socialisme (Dakar, December 3–8, 1962)*. Paris: Présence Africaine.

Lebret, Louis-Joseph. 1942. *Principes et perspectives d'une économie humaine*. Paris: Éditions Ouvrières, Économie et Humanisme.

———. 1956. *Dynamique concrète du développement*, Paris: Éditions Ouvrières, Économie et Humanisme.

Manguelle, Etounga. 1990. *L'Afrique a-t-elle besoin d'un programme d'adjustement culturel?* Paris: Éditions Nouvelles du Sud.

Marcuse, Herbert. 1964. *One Dimensional Man: Studies in the Ideology of Advanced Industrial Society.* Boston: Beacon.

Médard, Jean-François, ed. 1991. *Etats d'Afrique Noire: Formation, mecanismes et crise.* Paris: Karthala.

Michailof, Serge, ed. 1993. *La France et l'Afrique: Vade-mecum pour un nouveau voyage.* Paris: Karthala.

Moussa, Pierre. 1961. *Les Nations prolétaires.* Paris: PUF.

Mudimbe, V. Y. 1988. *The Invention of Africa: Gnosis, Philosophy, and the Order of Knowledge.* Bloomington: Indiana University Press.

Myrdal, Gunnar. 1957. *Economic Theory and Underdeveloped Regions.* London: Duckworth.

Perroux, François. 1960. *Programmation régionale de théorie économique.* Paris: PUF.

———. 1981. *Pour une Philosophie du Nouveau Développement.* Paris: PUF.

Robineau, Claude, ed. 1993. *Les Terrains du développement: Approches pluridisciplinaires des économies du sud.* Paris: Orstom Éditions.

Sall, Babacar. 1993. *De la modernité paysanne en Afrique Noire.* Paris: L'Harmattan.

Sandbrook, Richard. 1993. *The Politics of African Economic Recovery.* Cambridge: Cambridge University Press.

Sauvy, Alfred. 1951. "Introduction à l'étude des pays sous-developpés". *Population* 6, no. 4: 601–608.

———. 1952. *Théorie générale de la population.* Paris: PUF.

Senghor, Léopold Sédar. 1963. "Address to Colloquium". In *Développement et socialisme: Colloque sur les politiques de développement et les diverses voies Africaines vers le socialisme (Dakar December 3–8, 1962).* Paris: Présence Africaine.

Touré, Mamoudou. 1959. "Address to Congress". In *2ème Congrès des Écrivains et Artistes Noirs*, Rome.

Vallée, Olivier. 1992. *Les Entrepreneurs africains (rente, secteur privé et gouvernance).* Paris: Syros Alternatives.

ELEVEN

Agrarian Populism in the Development of a Modern Nation (India)

Akhil Gupta

This paper attempts to delineate the distinctive character of the relationship between modernity and development in postcolonial India. It does so by analyzing the development of agriculture as a critical link in the forging of a modern nation. Global discourses of development and international food regimes play a critical role in shaping the evolution of national policies and agricultural practices at the local level. One of the most critical ways in which discourses of development has affected the everyday lives of villagers in North India are through populist politics, policies, and programs. Populism has not only been the medium in which the discourses and practices of development are conveyed to villagers but has also provided one of the critical axes along which oppositional groups have organized support for their actions. The failure of development forms the rallying cry for oppositional groups to coalesce. Accordingly, I attend both to governmental and oppositional populisms, and their changing relationship over time. If postcolonial modernity is defined by the centrality of development, then populism, especially agrarian populism, is its most important feature.[1]

As Cooper and Packard point out in their introduction to this volume, discussions of development discourse as a "modern" apparatus of surveillance and control tend to pay far too little attention to the contested nature of "development." At the same time that "development" has been employed as a powerful tool of domination in the postcolonial era, and as the most important "reason of state" in the Third World, it has also been appropriated and reshaped by subaltern groups. The reconfiguration of development discourse, and its re-employment in movements against the national state and international agencies, is not necessarily tied to a progressive politics or to actions that benefit poor people. This essay attempts to show both how development discourse contained in populist programs is redeployed by peasant groups, and how peasant mobilization contains within it a series of exclusions and repressions. One of my purposes, therefore, in presenting this case, is to urge caution in the employment of a celebratory tone in the description of these "new social movements."

THE PLACE OF AGRICULTURE IN A MODERN NATION

To speak of "modernity" is less to invoke an empirical referent than a self-representation of the West. In this self-representation, consciously built on a difference with another (the Orient, the rest), the West emerges as the model, the prototype, and the measure of social progress (Hall 1992: 313). As Hall points out, the "West" is a historical, not a geographical, construct (277). In speaking of "the West," I am referring to the effects of hegemonic representations of the western self rather than its subjugated traditions. I do not therefore use the term simply to refer to a geographical space but to a particular historical conjugation of place, power, and knowledge. The modern, the celebration of western progress, civilization, rationality, and development, came to be instituted as a global phenomenon through colonialism, and through multiple and diverse modes of governance and domination in the postcolonial world (313). After the formal demise of colonialism, one of the chief mechanisms by which this self-representation has been promulgated has been through the discursive formation known as development (Ferguson 1990; Escobar 1984). Development is a discourse that rehearses, in a virtually unchanged form, the chief premises of the self-representation of modernity: the belief in teleological narratives; the idea that progress occurs along a single path; the conviction that western, industrial countries have already arrived at the telos (although it would be more accurate to say that they were always-already there); and, finally, the notion that it is nation-states, configured according to a particular logic of territorial exclusion and certain concepts of sovereignty, that constitute the basis of analysis and action. Development, in other words, is Orientalism transformed into a science for action in the contemporary world.

This self-representation of modernity, as promulgated by the models, doctrines, policies, programs, institutions, and discourses of development, is an inescapable feature of everyday life in contemporary North India, as in many other parts of the world. To live in the village that I have called Alipur is to confront, in many different contexts, shapes, and forms, the self-representation of modernity through the discourses, institutions, and practices of development. When I speak of alternative forms of modernity, I refer in this minimal way to an experience of being, in which the self-representation of modernity is a pervasive and omnipresent fact.[2] At the same time, as will be amply clear in what follows, it does not mean that people in rural India lead, or aspire to lead, western lives.

What, then, does it mean to say that there are other ways of being modern? To the extent that teleological views of history, a belief in progress, a conviction of one's own backwardness compared to the West, and a naturalization of the spatial imperatives of the nation-state, operate to configure the self-understandings of postcolonial subjects, they are indeed profoundly within the space and spell of the modern. However, it is also clear that the state of being modern is not a homogeneous experience, not just across the world, but within the political and geographical space of the nation-state. So what is it that accounts for the difference of "the modern" in India? Clearly, one of the differences lies in that the properties of the modern adumbrated above underspecify its contents. Employing a teleological narrative of history, for example, says almost nothing of its contents. This was evident in the deep conflicts between colonial and nationalist interpretations of the past, both of which were committed to teleological narratives.[3]

There is, however, another factor which is to my mind far more critical. The difference of Indian modernity lies in that difference itself is a constitutive moment that structures the experience of modernity. In other words, what makes the experience of modernity different in India is that, within it, the self-representation of modernity is never absent. It is found not as an "absent presence," in the way that the Rest is to conceptions of European identity, but as an active presence, as present-to-itself. For this reason, the attempt to precisely locate "India" in the narratives of modernity—premodern, antimodern, just plain modern, or postmodern—is doomed to failure if it refuses to recognize its own complicity with the self-representation of modernity.

In emphasizing that discussions and contestations of modernity are a regular feature of everyday life even in Indian villages, I want to underline that this is not merely an esoteric domain of intellectual production and debate, arising largely from the concerns of scholars in the western academy. Questions of modernity have been the focal point of intense debates amongst Indian intellectuals in a wide range of subjects, from secularism, science and technology, medicine, national security, the environment, and education (see in particular the work of Nandy 1984, 1987, 1992; Kothari 1990; Alvares 1992; Das 1990; Apffel Marglin and Marglin 1990; Shiva 1988, 1991, 1993; Visvanathan 1988). Although the work of these scholars does not constitute a homogeneous body of literature with a singular point of view, it demonstrates the convergences and continuities between the nationalist regimes of postcolonial India and colonial rule. Nandy's writings in particular focus on the internalization of colonial rule, from the self to major social institutions. The nation-state itself, a modern form of social organization and identity formation concerned mainly with development, scientific rationality, secularism, and national security, is seen as a major impediment to alternative forms of organization and identity-construction being offered by democratic and popular forces in civil society (Nandy 1992).

However, contestations of modernity are not just to be found in the discourse of urban intellectuals. Critiques of "development" have been articulated by a wide range of social groups from an impressive array of structural and geographical locations. Not all of these groups occupy the positions ascribed to them by urban intellectuals, and many critics of development effectively employ developmentalist discourse in their political struggles. Critics of development face the dilemma that they occupy a space of opposition created by modernity's representation of itself: they can claim an antimodern or unmodern location precisely because the discourse of modernity "recognizes" that such positions exist. In fact, one could add that the effectiveness of modernist discourse depends on its alleged superiority to that which is outside it, and which it variously labels as "premodern" or "antimodern." I do not intend by this to deny the importance of articulating alternatives to development. To the contrary, it is to argue that the search for alternatives can only begin by rigorously acknowledging the impossibility of transcendence. Modernity's representation of itself is a social fact in the villages of North India, not merely an analytical choice available to the scholar.[4] That most social science continues to employ modernity's self-representation as well is a separate, if related, question.

The particular form in which self-representations of modernity are deployed most frequently in the Third World is through development discourse. The symptoms of underdevelopment are clearly revealed through its agricultural sector. If a high proportion of the Domestic Product is dependent on agriculture, and if a large proportion of its labor force is employed on farms, then the nation-state is pronounced to be afflicted with the malady of underdevelopment. For this reason, the development of agriculture is an index of the health of the nation. The normalized narratives of development constructed from the stylized facts of a few nation-states reveal that agricultural surpluses, extracted by taxation and savings, form the basis on which industrial expansion takes place. Food self-sufficiency, as we shall see, becomes a crucial geopolitical issue. For all these reasons, the agricultural sector is absolutely central to the development of a modern nation-state.

In the rest of this paper, I argue that one cannot understand the project of developing the agricultural sector in India without seeing how populism shapes its ideological climate, institutional structures, and the daily practices of different rural subjects. Development practices are crucially shaped by particular appropriations of populist policies and the struggles that ensue from that. Understandings of development are largely dependent on the standardized use of certain kinds of aggregate statistics: national income, employment, trade, output, population, and so on. Although no doubt valuable for particular purposes, such statistics do not reveal what the experience of everyday life means for people in a particular development regime.

POPULISM AND AGRARIAN POLITICS

In this paper, I will concentrate on the oppositional populism of Bharatiya Kisan Union (BKU), an organization headed by well-to-do owner-cultivator groups in North India. I will situate the concrete and specific analysis of the Kisan Union by making the following broad observation. In the study of Indian agriculture, the analysis of parties, interest group politics, and the intent of government policies and their implementation are topics that have already been well covered. Therefore, I focus on an extended analysis of discourses, ideologies, and actions, not merely on what was done, but what it meant, not just to the leaders but to the people who were the objects and subjects of their discourse. How did pronouncements and policies find their way into the everyday lives of village people? What did these discourses and programs mean to them? How were they interpreted?

It is for this reason that I have concentrated on the phenomenon of populism in what is to follow. Populism is the form in which discourses of development, and hence of modernity, infiltrate the crevices of daily life in rural north India. While many analysts have pointed to the phenomenon, few have analyzed it in any detail. How do we understand populism theoretically? Why was it successful? Especially important in what follows are the questions: What kinds of resistance did populism enable? What were its silences, exclusions, and erasures?

Most scholars of Indian politics agree that the 1971 national elections signified a change in the style and content of political mobilization in a direction often termed "populist." Populism may have signified a change in the style and content of political mobilization, but what did such a change imply for the development of the nation-state? Its significance lay in that it represented a quantum leap in the dissemination of discourses of development. This resulted not only from better use of the mass media but by finding new audiences who were receptive to populist messages. Populist politics altered both the content of development and the degree to which development discourses entered the everyday life of the rural poor.

Before going further, it might be worthwhile to briefly explicate what I mean by populism. Theories of populism usually imply that "the masses" are manipulated by charismatic leaders, that populist coalitions typically consist of vertical multiclass alliances, that redistributive policies and programs are central, and that populist rhetoric aims not at linking lower classes to a unified ruling class through democratic processes, but at creating an antagonistic ideological field in which "the people" are pitted against historically privileged social groups (De la Torre 1992: 386; Laclau 1977).

At the risk of oversimplification, the explanation of populism that emerged from modernization theory could be characterized thus: populism was a response to the raising of political expectations beyond the capacities of the economic system to deliver on those promises. Populism, therefore, was characteristic of transitional societies in which modern communication systems had prematurely raised people's expectations and disrupted the synchronicity of political and economic development (Germani 1978; Di Tella 1965).

The other most influential explanation of populism, advanced by Ernesto Laclau (1977), is that populism is not connected to a particular stage of development. Rather, it arises due to the political failure of the dominant coalition to incorporate "the people" in an order of difference, to neutralize class antagonisms through coalition building, as the Congress did successfully in India before 1969, and the PRI did in Mexico until fairly recently. In Laclau's view, populist blocs incorporate the subaltern as an antithetical or oppositional force. Populism is a Manichaean discourse that divides society into two antagonistic camps: the people versus the oligarchy, the authentic, good, moral, just, true, and responsible versus the inauthentic, foreign, evil, unjust, immoral, false, and irresponsible. There is no room for compromise in this discourse as it is founded on the principle of exclusion.

These were precisely the ingredients of Indira Gandhi's victory in the elections of 1971, built on the populist platform of "removing poverty," but also enabled by acting decisively against privilege: nationalizing banks and insurance companies, abolishing payments to former kings, and implementing a series of rural welfare policies. Such policies included the founding of the Small Farmer Development Agency (SFDA), the Marginal Farmers and Agricultural Laborers (MFAL) Agency, a Crash Scheme for Rural Employment (CSRE), and the institution of a Drought-Prone Areas Programme (DPAP). Although none of these programs required large allocations of resources, or reached significant segments of the rural population, their cumulative political impact was considerable. Whereas previous efforts at poverty alleviation were for the most part limited to investments that aimed to achieve redistribution through growth, the

programs introduced by Indira Gandhi decoupled the two objectives
(Frankel 1978: 491). Recipients benefited in the short run rather than
having to wait for payoffs from productive investments to trickle in; at the
same time, the political importance of these programs greatly exceeded
their actual reach because they raised the expectations of potential beneficiaries.[5]

But the question about Indira Gandhi's surprising electoral victory that
has never been asked, and therefore not answered, is: Why did this message succeed? How was it received? Instead of dwelling on these questions,
I will, in this paper, concentrate on a question that goes one step beyond
reception: How was populism reworked and redeployed by those who were
the objects of this discourse?

In the decade after Indira Gandhi first introduced *Garibi Hatao* (Re-
move Poverty), the most important social movements in India were led by
well-to-do farmers, articulating the interests of the countryside against
the cities. Whereas Indira Gandhi's populism mounted an attack on the
failure of national development to reach the poor, the farmers' movement
would target the failure of development to reach the countryside more
broadly, and farmers, represented as a unitary category, in particular. This
was manifest in various farmers' movements that identified the chief contradiction as that between "Bharat" and "India," the country and the city.
Populism, thus, was not just a project of the ruling regime, but was also
deployed by oppositional groups to construct alternatives to the ruling
coalition.

The first organized political party to represent itself exclusively as a
party of peasants (*kisans*) was the Bharatiya Kranti Dal (hereafter BKD)
founded by Choudhary Charan Singh in 1967. In the elections of 1969,
the BKD emerged within just two years as the largest opposition party in
the Uttar Pradesh legislature, with more than a fifth of the popular vote.
Its support was particularly strong in the western part of the state, where
it polled over one-third of the votes.

Shortly after Charan Singh passed away in 1987, several people, including his son, Ajit Singh, staked their claim to the party that he had
helped found and raise to such prominence. The resurgence of peasant
politics, however, came with the founding of the Bharatiya Kisan Union
(BKU), a nonparty organization led by Mahendra Singh Tikait, a rural *jat*
leader from the prosperous cane and wheat growing district of Muzaffarnagar in western Uttar Pradesh.[6] All of these organizations relied heavily
on the stratum of owner-cultivators with substantial holdings for their core
support.

Of the various features of Charan Singh's "peasant" discourse, the one
most emphasized by successor movements pointed to the dual nature of
the country's development, articulated as the division between Bharat and

"India." Taking a cue from dual economy models, the intent was to contrast the vernacular name denoting the ordinary, the rural, the little tradition, the "real" country of small peasants and agricultural laborers to
the western, urban, industrial, internationally oriented modern nation-
state. This division was intended to highlight the "urban bias" of development policies that resulted in a widening gap between urban dwellers
who work for the state and industrial sectors, and rural folk who work in
the agricultural sector. This duality between Bharat and "India," as we
shall see, managed to coalesce a variety of dissatisfactions experienced by
different classes and segments of the rural population into a unitary
framework. In its ability to map different grievances into a singular an-
tithesis, it functioned as a powerful oppositional populism. It was oppositional in that its chief target was the government, which was accused of
failing to deliver on its developmental promises. Peasant populism insisted
that the interests of "India" systematically undermined the well-being of
Bharat.

The peasant movements' use of the notion of "urban bias" within a
dual economy uncannily echoes the scholarly position of academics such
as Michael Lipton (1968, 1977, 1982). Unlike more narrowly focused
analyses of "urban bias" that point to "getting prices right," the critique
advanced by the farmers' movement draws on a broad range of grievances
very similar to those adumbrated by Lipton. This is not entirely surprising
when one considers that farmers' leaders, such as Sharad Joshi of the
Shetkari Sanghatana in Maharashtra, have worked in international agencies and employ the language of international development with great
facility. Charan Singh was himself an "organic" intellectual of the middle
peasantry and combined a life in active politics with writing a series of
books forcefully articulating the positions of what became the dominant
segments of the farmers movement (Brass 1993; Byres 1988). The intellectual justification for the positions adopted by the farmers' movement
has not only been articulated by leaders within the movement, but also
by crucial intermediaries working in economic institutes, regional colleges, and universities, and journalists writing for the English-language
and vernacular press. There are thus multiple avenues for the flow of
development discourse from popular movements to scholarly circles.

Implicit in the division between Bharat and "India" was a more wide-
ranging critique of the model of a modern nation being pursued by successive postcolonial regimes.[7] The envious disdain for India shown by the
proponents of Bharat often included an explicit critique of the lifestyles
of the denationalized, decultured, urban elite who sought to mimic the
West. The implication, by extension, was that a plan for national development built on the mimicry of the West was guaranteed to fail, since it
would adversely affect the rural population. The agrarian populism es-

poused by peasant groups, therefore, attempted a far-reaching critique of development models, one that quite consciously sought to build a modern nation that was not a pale imitation of "the West."

The next section takes a closer look at peasant populism and its relation to the actions of the Kisan Union at the ground level. Before doing that, however, it may be useful to ask where the Kisan Union drew its support and what kinds of concrete programs and activities it undertook. The core group of the Kisan Union was constituted of that strata of the peasantry that owned more than 2.5 acres of land. This group was the chief beneficiary of the green revolution, the high-yielding varieties of hybrid wheat that had rapidly increased output in western Uttar Pradesh since the late 1960s. The green revolution depended on steadily increasing support prices for wheat, and heavy subsidies for inputs such as fertilizer, electricity, and irrigation water. This combination of output and input subsidies resulted in a fairly substantial group of surplus-producing peasants, whose new-found wealth financed the activities of the Kisan Union. The Kisan Union's agitations and demands centered on maintaining fertilizer, electricity, and water subsidies; keeping support prices high; and eliminating corruption at lower levels of the state. They pursued these objectives by resorting to mass protests such as demonstrations, sit-ins, and passive resistance (*dharnas* and *gherao*), blocking streets, the forcible removal of equipment such as electric transformers, the "capture" and "imprisonment" of corrupt officials in village homes, and the collective refusal to pay electric dues or pay back loans. It is important to keep the class basis and strategies of the Kisan Union in mind while reading the analysis that follows because one can then accurately position the ideology and discourse of peasant populism in a field of social relations and class power. My sources for the discussion in the rest of this paper are interviews with the residents of the village in western Uttar Pradesh where I did fieldwork, and reports in vernacular newspapers in the area.

Bharat Versus "India"

The contrast between Bharat and "India" finds one powerful axis in the critique of "urban bias," in pitting the countryside against the city. One of the chief resentments harbored by peasants focused on the better infrastructure available in cities. For example, in a meeting called by the Kisan Union in the town of Danpur in Bulandshahr district, the chair of the district unit, Gangaprasad, blamed the government for the poor quality of educational services available to village children in schools. He said, "Our village children should receive exactly the same education as that available to the children of ministers and industrialists in Delhi. We cannot tolerate this stepdaughterly treatment."[8]

Grievances also centered on the insufficient and erratic supply of electricity and the government's perceived enthusiasm for debt collection. Gangaprasad went on to say, "We want to tell the government that the villages should be supplied electricity twenty-four hours a day, just as Delhi is." He highlighted the inequalities in the government's loan collection policies: "Rich and famous people owe the government millions of rupees but we have never seen them go to jail for it. But if the farmer owes a little bit, he is promptly hauled off to jail."[9] This statement has to be understood in the context of the Kisan Union's long-standing demand that the farmers' debts should be "forgiven" or written off, a position also adopted by almost all other farmers' organizations.[10] Since a disproportionate amount of loans were made to those farmers who had some land as collateral, the class implications of these agitations are clear.

Another major argument that fed into the "urban bias" thesis was that the terms of trade were set against agriculture. In fact, a central demand of the farmers' organizations was that agricultural prices be restored to pre–green revolution levels, using 1967 as the basis of comparison. This tied into the perception that the discrepancy between those working in the industrial and government sectors and agriculture had actually widened.

However, it was not just in critiques of "urban bias" that the dualistic view, and identification with Bharat, as against "India," found expression. Apart from communicating a range of grievances, it also created a particular kind of subject position, one whose moral bearings were quite different from those found in "India." This was the virtue of those who were poor, politically helpless, exploited, but who, on gaining power, refused to exploit it. The implicit contrast was with the high-handedness, arrogance, and corruption of the powerful, both government officials (a favorite target) and the urban bourgeoisie.[11] Poverty, and the lack of political power, was a constant theme in the discourse of Tikait, the leader of the Kisan Union. When asked of the role that the Kisan Union would play in the elections in 1989, he typically replied:

> what can the farmer do to change electoral fortunes? Look at them [pointing to his followers]—they are so poor, they can only listen when we speak, no more. We have no power.[12]

It was as if the poverty of the farmers, iconicized by their soiled clothes ("look at them—they are so poor"), was also what rendered them mute—unable to represent their interests or desires ("they can only listen"). Their appearance, therefore, represented both their poverty and their lack of political voice. But then there is a subtle transference from the poverty which rendered the peasantry mute to its leader ("they can only listen when we speak . . . We have no power"). By a series of transpositions, the iconicized poverty of the peasants becomes a generalized signifier of peasant powerlessness.

The rhetorical employment of sartorial signifiers was absolutely crucial to everyday life in Alipur. The enterprising son of the wealthiest household in the village deliberately wore torn clothes as he went about his work. When, in the course of conversations with others, he was accused of being "greedy," he loudly pointed out that if he was indeed as wealthy as they claimed, why did he continue to wear the kind of clothes that no self-respecting person who could afford better would want to? Those village men who had obtained jobs in the city signified their status by wearing a trouser and shirt rather than the *pajama-kurta* or *dhoti* worn in the village. Clothes made the man a villager or a city slicker. What a person wore signified not merely how wealthy he was but where he belonged. Clothes thus possessed great representational efficacy. Those who lived in the village and continued to think of themselves as farmers therefore went to great trouble not to stand out in the way they dressed. Therefore, when Tikait pointed to his followers, saying "Look at them," he was pointing to a highly charged signifier.[13]

The poverty and helplessness of the "farmer" were connected with the effort to recuperate "his" self-respect (*swaabhimaan*).[14] In another incident between Kisan Union activists and the police over the kidnapping of a young Muslim girl, Naiyma, the police had reportedly pushed three tractors belonging to peasant activists into a canal near the town of Bhopa in Muzaffarnagar District. When Tikait reached the scene, he proceeded to lay camp by the side of the canal where thousands of farmers joined him in a protest for the "recovery of Naiyma." Pointing to the submerged tractors periodically burping oil to the surface, Tikait announced dramatically, "See, there lies the self-respect of the kisan—immersed in that canal."[15] Taking up the cause of an unknown Muslim woman may have had the strategic intent of consolidating the Kisan Union's position as an organization of farmers that crossed religious lines. But it was also related to dominant discourses about male honor being tied to the successful control of female sexuality. It was widely rumored that Naiyma's abductor was the relative of a powerful minister in the Uttar Pradesh cabinet. Hence, the Kisan Union was protesting the inability of male peasants to protect their women against representatives of the state.

Naiyma became the means to mobilize people, but her misfortune was displaced by the sunken tractors, which were obviously more potent symbols of the self-respect of (male) peasants.[16] Tikait demanded that the chief minister of Uttar Pradesh or the prime minister "come and see what their minions had done to the peasant's self-respect (swaabhimaan)."[17] Tikait repeatedly emphasized the powerlessness of the peasantry and their suffering at the hands of urban rulers for centuries. He told the gathered farmers that the city-based government (*sarkaar*) would never provide real justice for the farmer. After the body of the abducted Naiyma was found, Tikait vowed that the struggle for the farmer's self-respect would continue.[18]

Although they had stopped the administration from doing what it pleased, Tikait emphasized that the Kisan Union did not wish to be arrogant about its own strength. He thus underlined one big difference between the collective strength of peasants and the bureaucratic power of the state. Once again, the demonstrable difference between Bharat and "India" was made apparent.

Urban commentators noted how themes of poverty and helplessness, and the perception of injured pride, lent a "moral" character to the evocation of Bharat struggling against an all-powerful "India."[19] The emphasis on the poverty and helplessness of the peasant, and the mistreatment of Bharat at the hands of "India," formed the ground on which the Kisan Union appealed for peasant unity. One commentator, Chandan Mitra, wrote in *The Times of India* that Tikait's success depended on his ability to invoke and reinscribe a "rural" moral code. Drawing from the Kisan Union's rhetoric and from modernization theory to invert Marx, Mitra concluded:

> A modernizing state can ignore this kind of rural backlash only at its own peril. But before it devises a strategy to combat the resurgent peasant, it needs to understand the peasant mind, dispassionately, but not without empathy. Analysts of "India" have so far tried to change "Bharat." The point, right now, is to interpret it.[20]

The analytical force of such statements depends on their reliance on "the peasantry" as a singular category: "the resurgent peasant," "the peasant mind," "a rural moral code," "rural backlash," and so on. This is indeed exactly what the Kisan Union attempts to do in its depiction of Bharat.

The Failure of "Development"

"Development" has served as the cornerstone of the legitimation efforts of the postindependence Indian state. The success of Indira Gandhi's populism lay precisely in its attack on the failure of the previous regime's "development" efforts to go far enough, and to influence the lives of those in whose name they were being launched, namely, the poor. Much of the Kisan Union's rhetoric, which was aimed at protecting the interests of peasants and consolidating them into a unitary force, translated into attacks on the state for its failure to properly implement development policies. A large proportion of the Kisan Union's local level organizing was around issues of corruption, and the failure of the government to implement rural development programs. However, members of the Kisan Union sometimes articulated a broader critique of those development strategies that put industry first, and that kept agriculture backward. Although both critiques built on the modernist premises of the discourse of development, they had different implications for how those premises became lived realities. To speak of alternative modernities, therefore, is not just to tag nonwestern modernities, but to indicate that it is a contested field of possibilities whose shape and form is inherently unpredictable. This helps us qualify the theoretical discussion which often posits modernity in the singular, as if it were a unitary phenomenon.

That the appeal of the Kisan Union owed to its stand against corruption and government mismanagement was evident in my conversations with peasants in Alipur. Although no one from Alipur actively participated in Kisan Union rallies, there were many who were extremely sympathetic to it. For example, Ranbir, a relatively prosperous jat farmer, told me that he supported the Kisan Union because of its ability to fight corruption:

> If I go to officials of the Electricity Board, they won't listen to me. They will ask me to give them Rs. 100 or even Rs. 200 to get my work done. Even after I pay them, they won't do the work. With the Union, why will I go alone? We will all go in strength, forty or fifty of us, then the electricity officials will automatically do our work.

He recounted how electricity officials had come to a neighboring village and attempted to cut off some connections soon after a Kisan Union rally had encouraged farmers not to pay their electric dues and land taxes. Someone got wind of the officials' actions and informed Kisan Union activists. They rushed to the spot where the connections had been cut with a large group, caught the officials, forced them to reconnect the lines, took them back to the village, and locked them up as an additional measure!

However, corruption, conceptualized as a failure of the government's ability to implement its policies, was not the only source of the Kisan Union's dissatisfaction with "development." Explicit criticisms of the model of development adopted by successive regimes in independent India questioned the utility of concentrating on industrialization. The following critique appeared in a local vernacular newspaper:

> The question remains why the condition of the peasant remains what it is despite thirty-eight years of planning in which the progress of agriculture and the development of villages has been so much the focus of discussion. Have the benefits of development been unable to reach them? What happened to those resources that were spent in the name of agriculture and farmers? . . . it is evident that the concern for agriculture has been a sham whereas the truth is that from every viewpoint the farmer has been discrim-

inated against and agriculture has been deliberately kept backward compared to industry and other sectors. There is no need to deny that the price of grain was deliberately kept low right from the beginning so that the urban population and industrial workers could be protected from the burden of expensive food. The results have been predictable: the price of other goods has risen sharply compared to agricultural products. This has meant that farmers' incomes have risen more slowly than other sectors. Their dissatisfaction is therefore entirely understandable.[21]

"Despite thirty-eight years of planning"—here is a sentence whose parallels are encountered with numbing regularity in conversation and reportage. If one needed an example of how thoroughly teleological and developmentalist discourses are imbricated in everyday life, one need not look beyond such formulations. The expectation of change inherent in such teleological narratives in fact enables the author to formulate his well-articulated critique of the model of development that has been followed in India since independence. The question is not one of implementing existing policies better but of changing course completely because the entire model of development discriminates against the agricultural sector. This critique found tangible expression in the demand that the support price of wheat, the chief cash crop in the area, be raised, and subsidies for fertilizer, water, and electricity be increased.

The Kisan Union's employment of that very discourse of "development" that was used as a legitimizing strategy by the postcolonial state demonstrates the instability of hegemonic ideologies. The ability to rearticulate "development" into an oppositional discourse, one that challenged the coherence and stability of the ruling bloc, relied on a successful inversion of its claims. There was no reason why the same discontent that had so successfully been nurtured into electoral success by Indira Gandhi could not be rearticulated into an oppositional ideology. The Kisan Union did this not only by claiming that the project of development had failed by its own standards, but also by a thoroughgoing critique of the industry-centered model of development itself. It is for this reason that, despite analysts having repeatedly emphasized its "kulak" nature, the Kisan Union was so successful in constructing a genuinely multiclass alliance. If, as Gramsci has argued, the success of a hegemonic bloc depends on the mastery of a whole series of positions simultaneously on different fronts, then the Kisan Union did in fact manage to cohere a remarkably disparate set of concerns and subject positions through an oppositional, populist discourse.

Divisions Within Bharat—A Split Subject?

Although the Kisan Union was remarkably successful in forging a multiclass, multicaste alliance that simultaneously managed to cross the religious divide between Hindus and Muslims, there were other fault lines in rural society that it was unable to paper over. In fact, the very source of the Kisan Union's strength—its rootedness in the concerns, ideologies, and idioms of the owner-cultivators of western Uttar Pradesh—was also its chief limitation. The Kisan Union proved unable to work constructively with (potentially competing) farmers' movements in other states. Moreover, the Kisan Union did not attempt to forge a strategy that encompassed all sections of rural society. I will now concentrate on some of these divisions, attempting to demonstrate why the Kisan Union succeeded or failed to overcome the fractures that run through the rural areas of western Uttar Pradesh. Coming to terms with the nature of these splits within Bharat may help us understand whether the Kisan Union's critiques of development were aimed at bridging these fissures or at consolidating the dominance of a particular group. Despite its universalizing claims, development had very different consequences for different groups within rural areas. Therefore, which vision of development prevailed was not inconsequential. The politics of caste, class, and gender circumscribed and refracted the ability of the Kisan Union to construct a hegemonic bloc.

Perhaps the most remarkable aspect of the Kisan Union's activities was its ability to straddle the divide between Muslims and Hindus.[22] It did so not by denying religious differences but by aggressively emphasizing their solidarity and joint interests. For example, Kisan Union meetings brought together key leaders of the BKU such as Swami Omvesh, the district president of the Bijnor unit, who favored the saffron garb of Hindu holy men, and Ghulam Mohammed, the district president of the Muzaffarnagar unit, who was a Muslim. A *maulana* was invariably present on the dais at public meetings. The slogan consistently employed at Kisan Union rallies daringly combined the religious slogans of Muslims and Hindus. From the dais, someone would shout "Allah-O-Akbar," to which the gathered crowd would respond with "Har Har Mahadev." This slogan was used in all public meetings and in the BKU monthly meeting (*panchayat*) in Sisauli. Instead of attempting to deny the importance of religion or proclaim its irrelevance for its purposes, the Kisan Union stressed that only by being a good Hindu or a good Muslim could one also be a good human being.[23]

Apart from ensuring that Muslims occupied leadership positions within the organization, the Kisan Union also played an active role in mediating disputes between groups. Sometimes these disputes spilled over into interclass conflict. The tension between owner-cultivators and laborers coincided, to a large extent, with the conflict between the backward cultivating castes and *harijans*. The difficulty of containing it could be discerned from the defensive tone adopted by Kisan Union leaders and sympathizers when faced with this question. When asked whether the

Kisan Union also represented landless laborers, Tikait attempted to side-step the question by saying:

> There is no *mazdoor* (laborer) as such. We are all laborers. Some are big laborers, some are small. . . . Who is the rich farmer? There is no rich farmer. This house we're sitting in belongs to a farmer who is considered the third richest in this village of 20,000 people. And yet he doesn't even have 18 acres of land—the ceiling.[24]

Tikait thus denied that there were structural antagonisms among the rural population by pointing to their common need to expend family labor in farming activities, to work with their own hands.

I put the same questions to Ranbir when he was telling me about all the wonderful things that the Kisan Union had done. First, Ranbir disagreed that the Kisan Union was pitting agriculturists against nonagriculturists. "Everyone is a farmer these days," he said, "even the merchant (*baniya*) who owns 100 *bighas* (approximately sixteen acres) is a farmer." When land consolidation took place, some land was taken away from each plot and later distributed to the landless, mostly lower-caste, population. "So now even they are farmers. Everyone, therefore, is eligible to join the Kisan Union." If the Kisan Union does not help all farmers, he inquired, how will it forge ahead? But my skepticism was not dimmed. I asked, "Does it benefit small farmers as much as big ones?" Ranbir replied:

> There is no difference between small and large farmers. The small farmer uses water for irrigation; so does the large one. The small farmer puts chemical fertilizer on his fields; so does the bigger farmer. The small farmer has to plow his field; so does the large farmer. The only difference is that the small farmer has a small income and the large farmer a large one. Even if the small farmer does not sell his output, he is still a peasant (kisan).

Ranbir's point was that all classes of peasants had a common interest in policies like input subsidies. If irrigation water was cheap, chemical fertilizer inexpensive and plentiful, and tractors to plow fields readily available, then it benefited all farmers. However, unlike Tikait, Ranbir did not pretend that the Kisan Union supported landless laborers as well. Ranbir implied that the Kisan Union didn't need to look out for wage laborers because they already had the government in their corner. Given the Kisan Union's fervent antigovernmentalism, this was in itself a revealing statement. Ranbir at least acknowledged that laborers needed help to better their condition. Other supporters of the Kisan Union denied even that.

However, it was not just differences between richer and poorer segments of the peasantry that were at issue. The Kisan Union encountered great resistance from other sections of the rich peasantry. This was partly because support for the Kisan Union was heavily based among the jats, the better-off segments of the Backward Castes. The rise of the Kisan Union was interpreted as a threat by the established, land-owning, upper castes. Specifically, they saw it, quite correctly, as a means by which the Backward Castes like the jats were asserting their own power in the countryside. One of the reasons why there was not much overt support for the Kisan Union in Alipur was that the *thakurs*, who were once the landlords of the entire village and still the dominant political force, were strongly opposed to it.

The Kisan Union thus followed a two-pronged strategy to deal with the multifarious conflicts that afflicted Bharat. The first was to downplay structural contradictions by denying their salience: thus everyone is a laborer, those who use caste are enemies of the nation, there are no rich farmers, and so on. The other aspect of their strategy was to take up different causes that affected various segments of their supporters. The campaigns against corruption, and the melioration of conflict between Backward and lower castes, and against social ills such as dowry, all fell within this category. Despite these efforts, however, the tensions and conflicts among those the Kisan Union wished to unify always threatened to rend the fabric that held the organization together. Oppositional populism such as that promulgated by the Kisan Union, which deployed a Manichaean discourse of Bharat against "India," itself constructed a certain kind of location to be occupied by its followers. What united those included in Bharat was not a singular subject-position as much as a shared space of opposition. But although Bharat represented a contradictory unity which allowed the articulation of different interests and positions, it was also built on particular exclusions.

The Place of Patriarchy

I have already dealt with those exclusions having to do with landless laborers, lower castes, and the poor. Now I come to the conjugation of discourses of place and patriarchy, self-evidently rooted in the ideology of the upwardly mobile Backward Caste groups that form the backbone of the Kisan Union.

In the summer of 1989, when Rajiv Gandhi was still prime minister, he had instituted a policy to reinvigorate village governance (*panchayati raj*) through new laws and through changes in the manner in which development programs were implemented. Instead of relying on those state bureaucracies that had been set up to implement rural development, he proposed that all the money in a new scheme called the Jawahar Rojgaar Yojana (Jawahar Employment Scheme) be allocated directly to village headman (*pradhan*). In this manner, the money intended for villages would not be siphoned off by corrupt officials. When Tikait was asked for his opinion on Rajiv Gandhi's panchayati raj scheme, he replied:

Only a man whose line of succession is clear, who can reel off his paternal grandfather and great grandfather's name without a slip, can suggest pan-chayati raj. A *panchayat* is run on patriarchal lines, not matriarchal. Rajiv Gandhi has come to power through his mother—even a Harijan whose *gotra* (subcaste or lineage) line is quite clear is better than such a man. . . . What right then does the prime minister have to announce panchayati raj?[25]

In Tikait's formulation, Rajiv Gandhi lacked legitimacy as a leader because he had come to power through his mother. Since it was self-evident that legitimate succession could only be through males, Rajiv Gandhi was worse than an untouchable who had a clear line of patriarchal descent. According to Tikait, any person who did not understand this (self-evident) principle was inherently unqualified to talk about, or institute, panchayati raj. Significantly, Tikait's own power base as the head of the Balian Khap, a panchayat of eighty-four villages in Muzaffarnagar District, was obtained after an intense struggle in which he displaced his own father-in-law.

Tikait elaborated these concerns in a letter to Rajiv Gandhi just before Independence Day, August 15, 1989. Traditionally, the prime minister unfurls the national flag from the Red Fort and addresses the nation on that day. Tikait wrote:

Those who have no lineage (*hot-khot*) have no right to fly the national flag. If Rajiv Gandhi does not announce his lineage by August 15, then he too should not touch the national flag. . . . I do not want to sling mud at anyone. I do not hold any grudge against you [Rajiv Gandhi] but we must have a record of the lineage (*pataa*) of the country's prime minister. Therefore, Rajiv Gandhi should announce which village he comes from, in which state that village is located, and what the names of his father and grandfather are. . . . He who has no lineage should not attempt to besmirch this spiritual nation (rishiyon kay desh ko bigaadnay ki koshish na karay).[26]

What I have loosely translated as lineage also connotes a sense of place or belonging. The lack of rootedness that Rajiv Gandhi exemplified, and that, by extension, afflicted others who lived in India, was revealed by his failure to claim descent in terms of a patriarchal lineage. Place and patriarchy are completely interchangeable: to have one is to have the other. That is why the shift from which village he comes from and in which state that village is located to what the names of his father and grandfather are . . . was completely transparent. To know your village and to know the name of your grandfather is the same thing. There are several reasons why these things came together. Almost all marriages in this part of Uttar Pradesh were exogamous. Most married couples also resided virilocally. The system of inheritance was patriarchal and coparcenary: only the sons received an equal share in a couple's property. Thus, daughters were given dowry, married outside the village, and usually moved to their husband's villages. Sons, by contrast, inherited an equal share of the land along with their brothers, stayed in their father's village, and brought a wife from another place.[27] Therefore, to know your village, and to know the names of your male ancestors, was to be a man whose antecedents and social position was knowable. To not know these things was to be rootless, one not fit even to touch the national flag.[28]

That this was neither an isolated incident nor one of Tikait's idiosyncratic views was clear from statements made by other peasant leaders. Sharad Joshi, addressing the farmers who had gathered to condole the death of the abducted woman, Naiyma, said: "It is deplorable that even today in our country the poor cannot protect the honor of their wives and daughters. To stop the recurrence of these shameful incidents, we have to fight poverty with renewed vigor."[29] Joshi's concern was to rescue the manly virtue that protected the honor of women rather than with the more direct issue of patriarchal violence against women themselves. He linked the failure of the fight against poverty with the failure of poor men to protect their women. Thus, his concern was for poor men rather than about violence against women. Although he was correct in suggesting that poor women were vulnerable to acts of violence by strangers, he did not entertain the thought that domestic or familial violence could be equally devastating for women.

Male descent was part of a larger discourse about the gender specificity of lineage, in which boys inherited the qualities of their fathers, and girls of their mothers. Explaining why he chose to stay apart from, but not oppose Ajit Singh, the son of Charan Singh who had originally founded the BKD, Tikait pointed out that he couldn't possibly oppose Ajit Singh because of his descent, emphasizing the point with a saying:

> A girl's like her mother;
> A son his father.
> If not much,
> At least a touch.[30]

Tikait's concern with Rajiv Gandhi's paternal line was entirely consistent with this view of a gendered genealogy.

Another way in which discourses of gender were completely naturalized was evident in the Kisan Union's relations with subordinate groups. When asked what his organization had done to help Harijans, Tikait responded with a telling analogy:

> Show me one instance in this village of any Harijan being harassed and the aggressor going unpunished. We are compassionate towards Harijans. As far as petty quarrels go, even husband and wife are entitled to them. People merely exaggerate discord, because they want to politicize everything.[31]

Here is a transposition that explicitly equates social domination to gender inequalities. There is no doubt who is positioned as the wife in the petty quarrels between supporters of the Kisan Union and Harijans.

What I have attempted to demonstrate in this section is that the very rhetoric that helped consolidate Bharat as a counterhegemonic populism, and that enabled its opposition to India, was built on certain powerful exclusions. Whereas I previously explored the limits of unity in the face of existing tensions, I have focused here on the silences and evasions of peasantist discourse. The completely taken-for-granted, commonsensical, elision of place with patriarchy in the construction of Bharat had serious implications for gender inequalities. These inequalities were, in turn, conjugated with caste and class domination.

More generally, this discussion of populism and agrarian politics demonstrates that populism is not merely an electoral strategy of ruling regimes. It was employed rather forcefully against the governing regime by peasant movements that sought to consolidate a hegemonic bloc by pitting Bharat against "India." The discourse of Bharat vs. "India" shared all the trademarks of populism outlined earlier: exclusion; a Manichaean characterization of the other; the articulation of diverse interests through negation; and a claim to speak in the name of the popular.

CONCLUSION

The larger themes hinted at in this examination of developmental populism are that focusing on the agricultural sector can enable us to map some of the complex interactions between global transformations, governmental ideologies and actions, and the everyday lives of a particular set of rural people. Agriculture occupies a central place in development discourse. Underdevelopment afflicts those nation-states in which a high percentage of the national product comes from agriculture and where a high percentage of the labor force is employed on farms. Therefore, to be out of agriculture, preferably as fast as possible, is a most desirable goal for a modern nation. These desires are inscribed within plans to modernize or develop the agricultural sector by appropriate doses of capital and technology. Agriculture, however, is not just a sector in an input-output table. It is a field of power with its own discourses and regimes of truth. It is in these discursive fields that becoming modern can be articulated, where institutions can be changed, and practices altered. This paper has attempted to trace the changing contours of this discursive field, its ideological struggles, idioms, alliances, interests, and organizations. Although I have concentrated on some people in western Uttar Pradesh whom I got to know particularly well, the objectives of my project are to convey a sense of what the lived experience of modernity feels like more broadly.

What specifically is it about the postcolonial experience that enables us to speak of alternative modernities? Any answer to that question must begin by keeping the relationship between modernity and development in the foreground. One of the dimensions in which the experience of modernity in the Third World is significantly different from in the West is that a sense of underdevelopment, of being behind, of being not like powerful Others, is a constitutive feature of social and political life. I have explored how particular representations of modernity embedded in narratives of development circulate through agrarian populism. Rather than seeing developmentalism as a hegemonic ideology employed by a coalition of ruling classes, I demonstrate its internal fissures and its contentious redeployment in the discourses of antiurban, rich peasant groups. Therefore, one has to be careful in asserting that there is something about development that is inherently legitimating of certain classes and sectors.

Just as the reorganization of national agricultural policy in India in the 1960s prompted a shift in the institution and tactics of peasant politics, global changes in the recent past have, and will continue to, create new transnational alliances of peasant groups and others who are affected by these changes. Populist struggles within the country promise to take a different turn with the imposition of a structural adjustment program, the signing of GATT, the impending arrival of a new kind of plant biotechnology rooted in genetic engineering, and the entry of food-sector multinationals. The terrain on which populist struggles in the agricultural sector were based has irrevocably shifted as a result of the transformations in the world food economy since the early 1970s. A particular strategy of development, in which agricultural subsidies played a central role to ensure national food self-sufficiency, has been undermined, and is being replaced by an export-oriented, market-friendly orientation. And just as populism has been appropriated and turned against ruling regimes, so will contestations of the market-friendly ideologies of multilateral institutions and multinational corporations shape the nature of the emerging world system.

NOTES

1. I am grateful to Purnima Mankekar for detailed comments, Prabhu Mohapatra and Stacy Pigg for discussions about alternative modernities, and to participants at the Workshop on the Dynamics of Production and Transmission of Development Ideas, Ann Arbor, May 13–15, 1994. A fuller exposition of global discourses of development and international food regimes can be found in Gupta (forthcoming).

2. I have borrowed the term "alternative modernities" from Arjun Appadurai

(1991). Rofel (1992) has developed an argument about rethinking modernity for China along similar lines.

3. For the similarities between colonialism and nationalism, see Chatterjee (1986).

4. Stacy Leigh Pigg (1994, this volume) makes a fascinating argument using the case of Nepal, where development discourses seem to be employed in an even more aggressively self-reflexive manner.

5. Frankel's assessment of these schemes puts the emphasis in the right place: "On the whole, the central sector SFDA/MFAL projects could not be distinguished from social welfare programs that temporarily—for the duration of the subsidy scheme—increased the consumption of impoverished participants, but could not create additional opportunities for productive employment to raise their income permanently" (1978: 499).

6. At about the same time, other peasant organizations emerged in different parts of India, of whom the Shetkari Sangathana in Maharashtra, led by Sharad Joshi, and the Karnataka Rajya Ryota Sangha, led by Dr. Nanjundaswamy, have achieved the most prominence subsequently. At a meeting for "unification" of peasant associations from different states in 1989, thirty farmers' organizations from twelve states were present. This bid for peasant unity, however, ended in failure over questions of leadership. A recent review of farmers' movements in different parts of India is to be found in Tom Brass (1994).

7. I do not mean to imply that development policy was unwavering in its focus on industry in the entire postcolonial period. There were obviously shifts in the emphasis placed on industrialization at different periods, with the Shastri inter-regnum (1964–1966) and the Janata party period (1977–1980) representing two of the most important shifts toward agriculture in national policy and planning. However, these shifts, while significant, did not represent fundamental challenges to the model of development as mimicry of the "West."

8. *Aaj,* July 19, 1989.

9. Ibid.

10. For example, Sharad Joshi has led *karjmukti* (liberation from debt) agitations to do the same in Maharashtra.

11. Interestingly enough, the urban poor are completely erased in this discourse. It would be difficult to fit them into the image of "India." It is sometimes hinted that farmers and workers are in the same boat, that somehow they belong together in Bharat but this is rarely explicated. For the most part, this remains a Manichaean discourse whose positive pole is agricultural and rural. Thus, sectoral concerns and constructions of place are fused.

12. *Times of India,* July 31, 1989.

13. The effectiveness of this discourse was clear in that it "made sense" to an urban reporter.

14. The implications of a singular "peasant" identity and its masculine form are explored further below.

15. *Times of India,* Tuesday, August 8, 1989.

16. It should also be pointed out that, given the price of a tractor, and the minimum amount of land necessary to justify purchasing it, only the biggest and

most prosperous farmers can afford one. For instance, only two farmers in Alipur owned tractors.

17. *Times of India,* August 8, 1989.

18. *Bijnor Times,* August 18, 1989.

19. Notions of pride, of course, are deeply gendered. If a man is caught stealing, the village council often prescribes what they consider the worst possible humiliation: being hit on the head with a *chappal,* in public, and on top of that, by a woman.

20. *Times of India,* August 9, 1989.

21. *Bijnor Times,* August 11, 1989, p. 3.

22. The analysis of the Kisan Union presented here is restricted to the period before 1990. Hasan (1994) demonstrates how communal harmony disintegrated after October 1990, and the Kisan Union went into a decline as an organization.

23. *Times of India,* August 9, 1989.

24. Quoted in Rashmee Z. Ahmed, "V.P. Singh Is Honest, But a Dabboo," *Times of India,* July 31, 1989.

25. Ibid.

26. Reported in the *Bijnor Times,* August 12, 1989. Bob Goldman has suggested to me that Tikait might be implying that Rajiv Gandhi's father, an urban Parsi, belonged to that denationalized elite that constituted "India."

27. To speak of compulsory heterosexuality would be to understate the situation. The pressure to produce a male heir, preferably within a year of marriage, weighs heavily on both bride and groom.

28. That this discourse about roots which fuses patriarchy, genealogical descent, and location, is not peculiar to Chaudhary Tikait, but is found, with various inflections, elsewhere, is elaborated in Malkki (1992).

29. See *Bijnor Times,* August 18, 1989.

30. The Hindi version is as follows: Maa pay dhi/Pitaa pay choraa/Bahut nahin/To thodaa—thodaa.

31. Quoted in Rashmee Z. Ahmed, "V.P. Singh Is Honest, But a Dabboo," *Times of India,* Monday, July 31, 1989.

REFERENCES

Alvares, Claude. 1992. *Science, Development and Violence: The Revolt against Modernity.* Delhi: Oxford University Press.

Apffel Marglin, Frédérique, and Stephen A. Marglin, eds. 1990. *Dominating Knowledge: Development, Culture, and Resistance.* Oxford: Clarendon Press.

Appadurai, Arjun. 1991. "Global Ethnoscapes: Notes and Queries for a Transnational Anthropology". In *Recapturing Anthropology: Working in the Present,* edited by Richard G. Fox, 191–210. Santa Fe, N. Mex.: School of American Research Press.

Brass, Paul R. 1993. "Chaudhuri Charan Singh: An Indian Political Life". *Economic and Political Weekly* 28 (25 September): 2087–90.

Brass, Tom, ed. 1994. "New Farmers' Movements in India". Special Issue. *Journal of Peasant Studies* 21, no. 3–4: 1–286.

Byres, Terence J. 1988. "Charan Singh, 1902–87: An Assessment". *Journal of Peasant Studies* 15, no. 2: 139–89.

Chatterjee, Partha. 1986. *Nationalist Thought and the Colonial World: A Derivative Discourse?* London: Zed Books.

Das, Veena, ed. 1990. *Mirrors of Violence: Communities, Riots, and Survivors in South Asia.* Delhi: Oxford University Press.

De La Torre, Carlos. 1992. "The Ambiguous Meanings of Latin American Populisms". *Social Research* 59 (Summer): 385–414.

Di Tella, Torcuato. 1965. "Populism and Reform in Latin America". In *Obstacles to Change in Latin America*, edited by Claudio Véliz, 47–74. London: Oxford University Press.

Escobar, Arturo. 1984. "Discourse and Power in Development: Michel Foucault and the Relevance of His Work to the Third World". *Alternatives* 10: 377–400.

Ferguson, James. 1990. *The Anti-politics Machine: "Development," Depoliticization, and Bureaucratic Power in Lesotho.* Minneapolis: University of Minnesota Press.

Frankel, Francine R. 1978. *India's Political Economy, 1947–1977: The Gradual Revolution.* Princeton, N.J.: Princeton University Press.

Germani, Gino. 1978 [1971]. *Authoritarianism, Fascism, and National Populism.* New Brunswick, N.J.: Transaction Books.

Gupta, Akhil. Forthcoming. *Postcolonial Developments: Agriculture in the Making of Modern India.* Durham, N.C.: Duke University Press.

Hall, Stuart. 1992. "The West and the Rest: Discourse and Power". In *Formations of Modernity*, edited by Stuart Hall and Bram Gieben, 275–320. Oxford: Polity Press.

Hasan, Zoya. 1994. "Shifting Ground: Hindutva Politics and the Farmers' Movement in Uttar Pradesh". *Journal of Peasant Studies* 21, no. 3–4: 165–94.

Kothari, Rajni. 1990. *Rethinking Development: In Search of Humane Alternatives.* Delhi: Aspect Publications.

Laclau, Ernesto. 1977. *Politics and Ideology in Marxist Theory.* London: Verso.

Lipton, Michael. 1968. "Strategy for Agriculture: Urban Bias and Rural Planning". In *The Crisis of Indian Planning: Economic Planning in the Sixties*, edited by Paul Streeten and Michael Lipton, 83–147. London: Oxford University Press.

———. 1977. *Why Poor People Stay Poor: Urban Bias in World Development.* London: Temple Smith.

———. 1982. "Why Poor People Stay Poor". In *Rural Development*, edited by John Harriss, 66–81. London: Hutchinson.

Malkki, Liisa. 1992. "National Geographic: The Rooting of Peoples and the Territorialization of National Identity Among Scholars and Refugees". *Cultural Anthropology* 7, no. 1: 24–44.

Nandy, Ashis. 1984. "Culture, State and the Rediscovery of Indian Politics". *Economic and Political Weekly* 19 (December 8): 2078–83.

———. 1987. "Cultural Frames for Social Transformation: A Credo". *Alternatives* 12: 113–123.

———. 1992. "State". In *The Development Dictionary: A Guide to Knowledge as Power*, edited by Wolfgang Sachs, 264–74. London: Zed Books.

Pigg, Stacy Leigh. 1994. "The Credible and the Credulous: The Questions of 'Villagers Beliefs' in Nepal". Paper Presented to the Agrarian Studies Seminar, Yale University, April 22.

Rofel, Lisa. 1992. "Rethinking Modernity: Space and Factory Discipline in China". *Cultural Anthropology* 7, no. 1: 93–114.

Shiva, Vandana. 1988. *Staying Alive: Women, Ecology and Survival in India.* New Delhi: Kali for Women.

———. 1991. *The Violence of the Green Revolution: Third World Agriculture, Ecology, and Politics.* Penang, Malaysia: Third World Network.

———. 1993. *Monocultures of the Mind: Perspectives on Biodiversity and Biotechnology.* London: Zed Books.

Visvanathan, Shiv. 1988. "On the Annals of the Laboratory State". In *Science, Hegemony and Violence,* edited by Ashis Nandy, 257–88. Delhi: Oxford University Press.

Compositor:	Impressions Book and Journal Services, Inc.
Text:	10/12 Baskerville
Display:	Baskerville
Printer and Binder:	Edwards Brothers, Inc.